The Blood of Guatemala

A book in the series

Latin America Otherwise Languages, Empires, Nations

Series editors:

Walter D. Mignolo, Duke University

Irene Silverblatt, Duke University

Sonia Saldívar-Hull, University of California

at Los Angeles

GREG GRANDIN

The Blood of Guatemala

A HISTORY OF RACE AND NATION

Duke University Press   Durham & London   2000

© 2000 Duke University Press

All rights reserved

Printed in the United States of America on acid-free paper ∞

Designed by C. H. Westmoreland

Typeset in Monotype Fournier with Marigold display

by Keystone Typesetting, Inc.

Library of Congress Cataloging-in-Publication Data appear

on the last printed page of this book.

ABOUT THE SERIES

Latin America Otherwise: Languages, Empires, Nations is a critical series. It aims to explore the emergence and consequences of concepts used to define "Latin America" while at the same time exploring the broad interplay of political, economic, and cultural practices that have shaped Latin American worlds. Latin America, at the crossroads of competing imperial designs and local responses, has been construed as a geocultural and geopolitical entity since the nineteenth century. This series provides a starting point to redefine Latin America as a configuration of political, linguistic, cultural, and economic intersections that demands a continuous reappraisal of the role of the Americas in history, and of the ongoing process of globalization and the relocation of people and cultures that have characterized Latin America's experience. *Latin America Otherwise: Languages, Empires, Nations* is a forum that confronts established geocultural constructions, that rethinks area studies and disciplinary boundaries, that assesses convictions of the academy and of public policy, and that, correspondingly, demands that the practices through which we produce knowledge and understanding about and from Latin America be subject to rigorous and critical scrutiny.

The Blood of Guatemala tells a two-hundred-year history of K'iche' (Mayan) power, examining its dynamics both within the K'iche' community and in relation to dominant Ladino political structures. In taking up an indigenous point of view, this account challenges traditional assumptions. We see, for example, the power wielded by K'iche' elites, who acted as middlemen between state and community and who left an unheralded inscription on the Guatemalan nation. Their struggle for political legitimacy necessitated the development of a "Mayan" identity, and *The Blood of Guatemala* describes its genesis, redefinition, and broad vision of racial equality.

With its centuries-long sweep, *The Blood of Guatemala* documents defining changes in the political culture of that nation, including the shifting tensions created by competing concepts of race and ethnicity. This book also portrays the limits of the elite cultural vision, which was ultimately obscured by class antagonism within the Mayan community itself when K'iche' elites refused to cede power to indigenous peasant groups mobilizing for land reform. Grandin boldly—and convincingly—argues that these actions helped contribute to the collapse of Guatemala's brief democracy of the early 1950s.

TO THE MEMORY

OF MY FATHER, EDWARD

But then the blood

was hidden behind the roots,

it was washed and denied.

—PABLO NERUDA,

Canto General

Despite the opinion of some North American anthropologists who have all the vices of electronic computers and none of the virtues, Indians participate in every aspect of the country's economy: They participate as victims, but they participate. They buy and sell a good part of the scarce goods they consume and produce, exploited by middlemen who charge too much and pay too little; they are workers on the plantation and soldiers in the mountains, and spend their lives working and fighting. Indigenous society does not exist in a vacuum, outside of the larger context: Indians form part of the social and economic order, where . . . they are the most exploited of the exploited. The indigenous bourgeoisie of Quetzaltenango . . . is the exception that highlights the situation in which the descendants of the Maya live. The key to their liberation is the key to the liberation of the nation: Will they discover an identity that unites them with other Guatemalans in the struggle against the oligarchy and imperialism? Will they ever struggle, shoulder to shoulder, with other peasants and workers against their oppressors?

—EDUARDO GALEANO, *País ocupado*

Contents

List of Illustrations

Acknowledgments

Acknowledgments perform an essential Marxist task: they situate the production of an individual work in a long chain of influence, love (the early Marx), and encouragement. I've worked over this section many more times than I have any other part of the book, so I'll just stop here, apologize to anybody I may have missed, and start at the beginning.

While at Brooklyn College, I had the good fortune to be first taught the connection between politics and history by Renate Bridenthal, Paul St. Clair, Steve London, Hoby Spalding, Teo Ruíz, Nancy Romer, Bart Meyers, Nick Papayanis, Jonathan Abraham, Leah Rosenberg, Stuart Schaar, and David Blancuzzi. This work began there, through their teaching and friendship.

In Brooklyn and New Haven, Guatemala City and Quetzaltenango, a great many people made this work and my life richer. More than thanking them for their contributions, I want to take this opportunity to appreciate the friendships of Carlota McAllister, Arturo Taracena, Diane Nelson, Valia Garzón (*y su tío*), Marcie Mersky, Liz Oglesby, who, along with Marcie, Diane, Arturo, and Carlota, helped me understand this work in relation to larger issues of rule and violence in Guatemala, Tani Adams, Matilde González, Charlie Hale, Erwin Rabanales, Frank Goldman, Bob Perillo, John Pauly, José Osorio, Wendi Walsh, Patricia Mathews, Deborah Levenson, Clara Arenas, Rachel Sieder, Daniel Rothenberg, *los de Lo de Bran*, who put up with early morning typing and Frank Sinatra: Fernando Bances, Alison Crosby, María Baquero, Kate Doyle, Richard Wilson, René Reeves, Deb Coltry, Todd Little-Siebold, Krista Little-Siebold, Kieko Matteson, Aníbal López, Barbara Grandin, Kit Grandin, María Montoya, Robert Perkinson, Billy Fitzpatrick, Peter Brown, Rebecca Haggerty, and Michelle Stephens, who certainly has a right to be presumptuous.

In Quezaltenango, I am indebted to a number of people who made research and writing possible. Above all, the faculty and friends of the Proyecto Lingüístico Quetzalteco de Español—especially Federico Velásquez, Sonia Alvarez, Marleny Castillo, Carlos Sánchez, Teresa Serrano, Juan Pablo, Aaron Polack, Rosabla Piazzi, Leslye Rivera, David Mastrodonato, Linda Mastrodonato, Manuela Méndez (the best frijoles and dinner company in all of Guatemala), Alfa Escobar, Irma González—always made returning to Quezaltenango, no matter how long the absence, feel like coming home. I especially want to mention Daniel Wilkinson. Throughout this work, he has been a constant companion, sharing *chismes*, *tristezas*, *alegrías*, and *esperanzas*, and helping to make Edificio Ramírez a great place to live, at least when he bothered to get cinnamon rolls and coffee. Daniel and I took so many *vueltas* around *parque central* discussing the city that this is as much his project as it is mine.

Ana Rosario de Tobar not only facilitated work at the Archivo de Gobernación de Quetzaltenango (AGQ) but made it enjoyable with warm *atol* and wry humor. I also want to thank Rigoberto Quemé, Irma Alicia Velásquez Nimatuj, René Girón, Juan Girón, and the *socios* of the Sociedad El Adelanto, especially Ulises Quijivix and Noé Quijivix, whose interest in this study provided me with a powerful incentive to get it right. I hope that in some small way my interpretation of their history helps them in their work. I am also grateful to Silvia Esperanza Velázquez Xicará, Quetzaltenango's 1955 Reina Indígena, for graciously sharing her memories and photographs. Special appreciation is due Jorge Mario Aguilar Velásquez for sharing Sergio's story and for reminding me that Quetzalteco history did not end in 1954.

As I was finishing my dissertation, on which this book is based, I began work with the Comisión Para el Esclarecimiento Histórico—Guatemala's Truth Commission. Not only did my time there keep this project in perspective, but it also gave me the opportunity to work with many unforgettable people, including Rebecca Cox, Ana González, Alejandro Valencia, Sonia Zambrano, Rocío Mézquita, Veronica Puentes, *y un hombre que lucha todos los días*, Fernando López.

In Guatemala City, the staff of the AGCA, especially Anna Carla Ericastilla, was always incredibly patient and helpful. The work of a research assistant and friend, Ana Bela Castro, was invaluable. I want also to acknowledge Melba Luna for generously helping with the Spanish editing. In Antigua, the staff of Centro de Investigaciones Regionales de Mesoamérica—especially its director, Tani Adams, and its photo archivist, Valia Garzón—provided essential support. Back in Guatemala City, the Museo Gerard granted me kind permission to use a number of its photographs. I also want to thank Arturo Taracena and Jorge González for sharing their research and enthusiasm for Los Altos with me. Chris

Lutz read the work in progress and offered wise advice, suggestions, and encouragement at a number of crucial points.

I want to thank Betty and Rick Adams at the main branch of the Patzisotz History Company in Panajachel for always graciously receiving unannounced pilgrim researchers and their guests.

I am grateful to Radhika Wijetunge and the staff of the Yale map collection, who patiently helped with maps. In the nick of time, Jeffrey R. Ambroziak and Russell A. Ambroziak of Ambroziak Third Dimension Technologies did a heroic job of rescuing what seemed a doomed map project. The digital conversion and visualization that produced the regional map of the area around Quetzaltenango are all their doing. Thanks. And I also want to acknowledge Carlos Eugenio Rojas Loarca for reproducing Quetzaltenango's city map.

I owe my greatest intellectual debt to my principal advisers, Emilia Viotti da Costa and Gil Joseph. Every good thing about this work is a result of their observations, criticisms, and support. Emilia especially always pushed me to reach beyond clichés, facile observations, and easy critiques of past work. It has been an honor and a privilege to work with her. But more than this, both Gil and Emilia went well beyond their academic obligations to form for their students a network of creative support and encouragement. It would be impossible to mention this support without also mentioning Jack "Sangre" Wilson and Patricia Pessar, who, along with Emilia and Gil, graciously shared their homes and comments on countless occasions. In Gil's toast to Emilia during her retirement *homenaje*, he said if there was anything he wanted to emulate in Emilia as an adviser, it was her ability not only to be an intellectual mentor but also a friend and confidant. He has more than done so. John Demos likewise contributed to this work with his interest, support, and observations.

Perhaps my most important lessons on how power operates in daily life came from my experience working with Yale's Federation of Union Employees—Locals 34 and 35, and our own teaching assistants' union, Graduate Employees and Students Organization (GESO). Not only does being part of an effort to build a common community provide an escape from the isolation and self-importance that afflicts many of those engaged in academic work, but it also offers what I think is an important model for scholars concerned about the political relevance and integrity of their work. If the actions of the Yale administration, and many of the faculty, never ceased to shame and anger, the commitment, courage, and goodwill of fellow union members never ceased to amaze and inspire.

Many people read and commented on this work as it progressed. Aside from the attention of my advisers, I greatly appreciate the interest given to this work by Diane Nelson, Charlie Hale, Carol Smith, Jeff Gould, Todd Little-Siebold, Richard Adams, Jorge Aguilar, Irma Velásquez, Deborah Levenson, Chris Lutz, Marcie Mersky, John Watanabe, George Lovell, Arturo Taracena, Daniel Wilkinson, Corey Robin, Di Paton, John Tutino, and Lowell Gudmundson. While gratefully acknowledging all of these readers for their suggestions, I want to mention two of these friends in particular. For some reason (perhaps it was our shared experience at Yale as graduate students trying to organize a union), Di, Corey, and I have chosen to write about repression. It's been a privilege to be able to share my work with them, and, despite our chosen themes, they continue to be sources of hope, inspiration, and commitment. I also want to thank Valerie Millholland, for being the kind of editor graduate students dream of.

I would also like to recognize the funding institutions that made this work possible: The Social Science Research Council, the Mellon Foundation, Yale's Center for International Area Studies, the Agrarian Studies Program at Yale, the Foundation for the Advancement of Mesoamerican Studies, and the Fulbright Program for Latin America and the Caribbean.

Finally, I owe particular thanks to a group of friends I either made or learned to value anew in 1995–96. As I was getting ready to write up my research, my father suddenly died. The love these people gave me taught me that family is more than blood. Gordon Lafer, Di Paton, Bob Wheeler, Daniel Wilkinson, Corey Robin, and Dave Sanders—what can I say except thanks? This work is dedicated to the memory of my father, because in his own way it was he who first taught me the consequences of history.

The Blood of Guatemala

1. Guatemala, Western Highlands.

Introduction:
Searching for the Living among the Dead

The memory of the living gives life to the dead.

—*Inscription above the entrance to Quetzaltenango's general cemetery, 1894*

A Walk in the Cemetery

It is easy to imagine the city of Quetzaltenango's sprawling general cemetery as a metaphor for Guatemalan society. Shaded by bowers of pepper trees, elaborate mausoleums of prominent Ladino families line the main path at the front of the graveyard.[1] Gated enclaves segregate and protect the graves of wealthy European immigrants—Italian manufacturers and German planters and merchants who helped build Guatemala's coffee economy. At the end of the walk, stairs abruptly rise to a plateau where the poor are buried under crowded dirt mounds. Amid patches of wildflowers, simple crosses and headstones bear mostly Indian surnames. It seems as if even in death, Quetzaltecos could not escape an unjust and racially divided existence.

If one were to venture off the main path, however, and examine the lowland graves more closely, a more complicated picture of the city emerges. Mixed among the Ladino vaults, numerous mausoleums of Maya-K'iche's testify to the existence of a large urban indigenous middle class comprised of artisans, builders, farmers, merchants, and political elites. These Indians, their importance in regional and national politics, and how they managed to avoid the fate of similar indigenous communities are the subject of this work.

Just down the path from the pantheon of former Guatemalan president Manuel Estrada Cabrera, stands the tomb of Agatón Boj, who died in 1915. Boj, in his day a skilled mason and one of the largest employers in the city, built Estrada's tomb—replete with an ornate frieze and fluted columns—in 1907. A few rows away, Santiago Coyoy's modest grave understates his importance. In the late nineteenth century Coyoy was a key leader of his

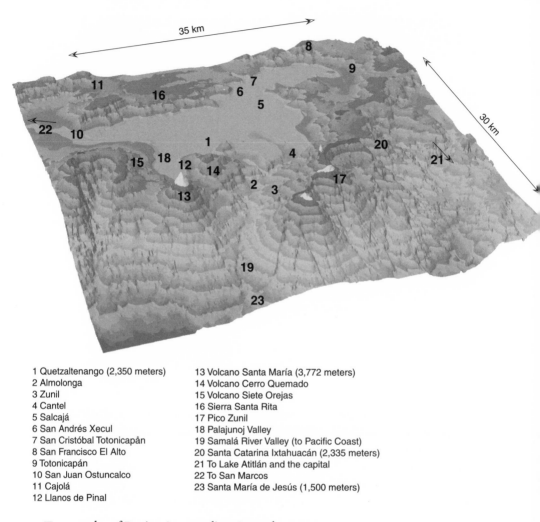

35 km

30 km

1 Quetzaltenango (2,350 meters)
2 Almolonga
3 Zunil
4 Cantel
5 Salcajá
6 San Andrés Xecul
7 San Cristóbal Totonicapán
8 San Francisco El Alto
9 Totonicapán
10 San Juan Ostuncalco
11 Cajolá
12 Llanos de Pinal

13 Volcano Santa María (3,772 meters)
14 Volcano Cerro Quemado
15 Volcano Siete Orejas
16 Sierra Santa Rita
17 Pico Zunil
18 Palajunoj Valley
19 Samalá River Valley (to Pacific Coast)
20 Santa Catarina Ixtahuacán (2,335 meters)
21 To Lake Atitlán and the capital
22 To San Marcos
23 Santa María de Jesús (1,500 meters)

2. Topography of Region Surrounding Quetzaltenango.
Courtesy of Ambroziak Third Dimension Technologies, Inc.

community; now only a hoe, sickle, shaft of wheat, and ear of corn carved
over his name bespeak his position as one of the city's wealthiest late-
nineteenth-century K'iche' landowners and farmers. Below him rests his
wife, Micaela Pisquiy de Coyoy. Her burial plaque hints at the indispensable, yet often unacknowledged, role women's labor played in underwrit-
ing the economic activity of their husbands: market scales and measuring
weights dangle over a basket overflowing with chilies and bread. Her

1. Agatón Boj (left). 2. Santiago Coyoy (right).
Courtesy of Sociedad El Adelanto.

3. Tomb of Micaela Pisquiy de Coyoy. *Photograph by Daniel Wilkinson.*

carved portrait also suggests the importance women had in maintaining ethnic identity, which, as we shall see, was crucial to the functioning of men's political and economic power: While in life Santiago donned Western-styled lapeled jackets and buttoned shirts, Micaela's sepulchral bust presents her in an intricately woven K'iche' tunic and hair wrap.

The cemetery reveals the city in other ways. The neoclassical tombs of notable liberal Ladino families, embellished with compasses, sextants, sphinxes, and glyphs, capture the confounding mix of European rationalism and mysticism that infused nineteenth-century Latin American liberalism. The crypts of various burial societies speak to the importance guilds and mutual aid associations continue to play in urban life. Memorials recalling historical events and liberal martyrs attest to the city's importance in national politics. That many of these tombs were built by skilled male K'iche' masons highlights the complex intersection of ethnicity, gender, class, and national identity in Quetzalteco history. And the many European and Mayan surnames not common to the city testify to Quetzaltenango's openness and cosmopolitanism.

Although Quetzaltenango did not experience the same levels of political repression that the Guatemalan military inflicted on other communities throughout the 1960s, 1970s, and 1980s, local activists were nonetheless selectively killed or disappeared. The large number of tombs of young men and women who died during these decades (both K'iche' and Ladino) provide glimpses of the hopes that motivated their lives and the forces that caused their deaths: "He struggled for a just and noble society"; "she gave her life for a new Guatemala." Similar epitaphs occasionally convey feelings left unexpressed in public life, belying the tranquillity that often seems to characterize the city's ethnic relations: On the tomb of Thelma Beatriz Quixtán Argueta, the city's K'iche' beauty queen who died at the start of her reign in 1970, are inscribed the words: "We have been beaten and humiliated, but the race was never defeated."

The cemetery also captures the evolving relationship between indigenous culture and state formation. Throughout periodic epidemics during the 1820s and 1830s, for example, indigenous communities vehemently resisted the efforts of liberal reformers to transfer burial grounds outside town limits. In Quetzaltenango, as we shall see, Indians repeatedly obstructed attempts to move their graveyard. Yet by the 1890s, Quetzalteco K'iche's had begun burying their dead in a public cemetery outside the city, in tombs embellished with Western symbols: broken columns evince human mortality, sculptured angels point toward hoped-for redemption, and carved tombstones recall a person's life and work. How and why this turnabout occurred is one of the questions I hope to answer.

Purpose and Argument

This study examines the transformation of the city of Quetzaltenango's K'iche' community over the course of two centuries. Starting with the Bourbon Reforms of the mid-eighteenth century and ending with Guatemala's doomed land reform in 1954, this work will focus primarily, but not exclusively, on the actions and ideologies of patriarchs and political leaders within this community.

The astute ways in which K'iche' elders reconfigured communal relations and meanings so as to retain their social and cultural authority had a profound effect on the formation of the Guatemalan state and nation. I hope therefore to transcend the often narrow boundaries of community studies to link power and culture in two ways. First, I will examine how K'iche' elites brokered the regional formation of imperial and republican governments. Not only did they stand as intermediaries between the local Indian and non-Indian populations, but they also strategically played off national and local tensions to further their interests.

Changing political and economic circumstances led to shifting alliances and strategies. In the eighteenth and early nineteenth century, K'iche' *principales* (elders, community leaders) and local Creoles (specifically, American-born Spaniards but here Hispanic elites in general) developed a contentious yet mutually dependent relationship. In the face of political and economic changes that quickly transformed their Indian pueblo into a commercial, multiethnic city, principales came to rely on Creole elites for help to maintain their cultural authority, reinforce their political power, and gain access to capital. Creoles needed principales to help them administer the city and divide the plebeian population along caste lines, thus limiting the possibility of a multiethnic popular alliance. Following independence in 1821, as liberalism wore away at the ideological foundation of their caste authority, K'iche' elites allied with José Rafael Carrera's conservative regime in order to maintain their privileges and power. In the latter nineteenth century, the appeals of principales to the national government curtailed the long-standing separatist tendencies of highland

Ladinos and contributed to the centralization of power. Finally, in the 1950s, some K'iche' elites joined with local Ladinos in opposition to a national government that was encouraging popular organizing, and thus helped to end Guatemala's decade of democracy.

Second, the work examines how K'iche' elites subjectively experienced, and tried to control, larger processes of state formation and capital accumulation—processes to which Guatemalan historiography often assigns "objective status" and places outside the purview of the "ethnographic gaze."[2] A central argument of this book is that the cultural anxiety brought about by Guatemala's nineteenth-century transition to coffee capitalism forced Mayan patriarchs to develop an alternative understanding of ethnicity and nationalism.[3] As Guatemala evolved into an agro-exporting nation, communal customs of labor reciprocity transformed into class relations. In order to continue justifying their ability to mobilize indigenous labor, including female household labor, K'iche' elites needed to redefine the nature of their community. They developed a conception of ethnicity intimately linked to the progress of *la nación*. Unlike Ladinos, who viewed nationalism and indigenous ethnicity as mutually exclusive—the progress of the nation depended on the suppression of the Indian—K'iche' principales viewed these concepts as mutually dependent—one could not go forward without the other. For K'iche' elites, regeneration of the Indian would lead to civil and political equality, which, they argued, was the basis of a democracy. By linking the progress of the nation to cultural renewal, such regeneration justified the principales' position of caste authority to the local and national Ladino state; conversely, by connecting ethnic advancement to the progress of the nation, it legitimized to common Indians and women the continued political power of K'iche' patriarchs.

As with Ladino nationalism, K'iche' nationalism had to resolve contradictions: contradictions between the Ladinos and Indians; men and women; the wealthy and poor. To do so, K'iche' patriarchs developed a highly self-conscious ethnic identity promoted through an adherence to blood strictures, a search for common provenance, and the maintenance of cultural markers.[4] They used new technologies, such as photography, and the establishment of new public rituals, such as a Mayan beauty pageant, to link the traditional to the modern.[5] Women, with the children they bore and the clothes they wore, became subjected to increased patriarchal pressure as the bearers of cultural authenticity. This alternative national vision, however, could not take hold in a country rent by class and ethnic divisions. My study ends in 1954, when, prior to a coup that ended Guatemala's decade of democracy, the K'iche' community divided along class lines: Mayan elite founded an anticommunist committee and violently opposed land claims made by indigenous peasants under an agrarian reform law.

Violence and Nationalism

This is a book about nationalism, race, class, and gender. It is specifically about Guatemala, but its story is similar to that of scores of countries whose efforts to build a national culture ran headlong into the realities of economic dependency, ethnic division, and class struggle. Guatemalans today live with the consequences of that clash—a society dealing with the aftermath of nearly four decades of state terror and one of the most unequal distributions of wealth in the hemisphere.

Guatemalan history in the second half of the twentieth century is marked by momentous intervals of hope and mobilization, followed by fierce periods of reaction and repression. In 1944, following a thirteen-year dictatorship, middle-class revolutionaries took over the state and initiated a series of unprecedented social and political reforms that radically challenged the power of Guatemala's landed oligarchy. In 1954, however, an alliance between the United States' Central Intelligence Agency and sectors of the country's elite beat back this challenge, ending Guatemala's democratic opening. From this date forward, the Guatemalan state met nearly all demands for social reform with ever increasing violence and terror, which in turn drove broad sectors of Guatemalan society to oppose the government: from 1960 to 1996, armed insurgencies challenged the legitimacy of the state and the oligarchy; in the 1970s, trade unionists, Mayan activists, peasants, students, and social and Christian democrats came together to push for reform. No other country in Central America witnessed the level of political mobilization that took place in Guatemala during this period. According to the 1999 report of the United Nations-administered Truth Commission (officially known as the Historical Clarification Commission), the state responded to both the insurgency and civil movement with unthinkable repression, climaxing in 1981–82 in a yearlong bloodbath in which the army committed over four hundred massacres, laid waste to hundreds of Mayan communities, and tortured, murdered, and disappeared over one hundred thousand Guatemalans.[6]

Historians are nearly unanimous in their judgment that the Guatemalan liberal state, founded in 1871, was bereft of popular support and legitimacy.[7] Analysts often use this absence of legitimacy to explain the intense state repression of the last forty years.[8] The Truth Commission, for example, concluded that the origins of the political violence can be traced to an unjust social system founded on racism, economic exploitation, and political exclusion:

> Due to its exclusionary nature, the State was incapable of achieving social consensus around a national project able to unite the whole population. Concomitantly, it abandoned its role as mediator between divergent social and economic interests, thus creating a gulf which made direct confrontation between them more likely. . . . Faced with movements proposing economic, political, social or cultural change, the State increasingly resorted to violence and terror in order to maintain social control. Political violence was thus a direct expression of structural violence.[9]

It is certainly true that the Guatemalan state, compared with most other Latin American nations, was much less successful in creating a national identity and establishing political legitimacy. A brutal model of capitalist development combined with profound ethnic divisions to prevent the evolution of an inclusive national project. Nevertheless, this study starts with the premise that the "failure" of Guatemalan nationalism needs to be explained, rather than presented as explanatory.

It is a common conceit among many scholars that nationalism is a social phenomenon that needs to be measured against the relative success of a handful of countries in constituting their populations as "citizens" by integrating them into a cohesive economic, political, and cultural project.[10] Eric Hobsbawm, in his arguments against liberal theorists who posit common ethnicity or language as the origin of nations, has forcefully presented a class-based analysis of nationalism.[11] For Hobsbawm, nationalism is intimately linked to the organization of industrial capitalism and the formation of economic elites. While this perspective has reintroduced the concept of social struggle in analyses of national formation, it also has de-emphasized the ethnic content of elite nationalism. In so doing, Western biases are confirmed: nationalism is presented as universal; ethnicity is understood as particular.[12] In developing countries that have been unable to build or maintain a cohesive economic or political structure, emerging social movements attempting to construct or challenge national identities are often dismissed as "tribal" or "ethnic."[13]

In this work, I try to separate the emergence of two competing ethno-nationalisms—K'iche' and Ladino—from the social processes of state and economic formation. Thus, the inability of Ladinos to project their national vision as universal is presented not as failed nationalism but as *a* failed nationalism.[14] In so doing, just as I do not reject K'iche' nationalism as "ethnic," I also do not dismiss the ideology of Ladino reformers and revolutionaries as racist.

As this work will show, for both K'iche' and Ladino elites, national identity mattered. In Quetzaltenango, the formation and maintenance of K'iche' ethnicity was inextricably linked to the formation of regional and national consciousness. And many of the questions regarding race, culture, gender, and nationalism raised by today's pan-Mayan movement—in which Quetzalteco K'iche's are key players—have their origins in nineteenth-century efforts by Ladinos to create a homogeneous national identity. Rather than its being viewed, as it often is, as an entirely new occurrence emerging from the ruins of a failed Ladino national project, this work suggests that the pan-Mayan movement's origins and development need to be understood within the social processes of state formation—the very processes that spawned the project the movement now seeks to displace.[15]

The book's title, therefore, has a double meaning. It refers first to the contestation that took place throughout Guatemala as to what constituted national identity. Paradoxically in the late nineteenth century, as Ladinos increasingly stressed the cultural content of "race," urban Quetzalteco K'iche' artisans and merchants—Hispanicized in dress, occupation, language, and living conditions—insisted on defining race by blood. But this contestation over national identity failed to be resolved in a country rent by class and ethnic divisions, and herein lies the title's second meaning. In 1954, the most serious effort by Ladino leaders to create an integrated nation collapsed under the combined weight of political division, class struggle, and foreign intervention. For the next four decades Guatemalan blood flowed as the most repressive state in the hemisphere slaughtered two hundred thousand of its citizens.

Culture and Power

Writing a history of power these days is a difficult task. Power, we are told, permeates all relations; multiple and shifting subjectivities, both within individuals and throughout societies, make it impossible to establish a standard on which to rank these relations, much less to take a stand and say here is where power resides and here is where it should be confronted. Across disciplines and regions, this complexity has confused academic writing and paralyzed political commitment.[16] In Guatemala, this scholarly agnosticism, combined with the repercussions of a failed socialist revolution, unimaginably high levels of state repression, and the emergence of the pan-Mayan movement, has created a climate of intellectual doubt and uncertainty; the surety with which academics supported the guerrilla movement during the 1970s and 1980s has given way to self-criticism and intellectual revisionism.[17] While this rethinking is a healthy corrective to the traditional arrogance of first-world intellectuals, much of it draws on deeply ingrained tendencies of Guatemalan historical and anthropological writing to situate the Maya outside of historical processes.

Two questions have dominated Guatemalan academic interest. The first, chiefly a historical problem, concerns the ways in which liberals after 1871 were able to establish political control and lay the foundation for what became Guatemala's modern agro-exporting nation state. The second question, largely an ethnographic consideration, addresses the ways Indians have managed to resist, at least to a qualitative degree, strong pressures of cultural assimilation while still maintaining to this day a recognizable community structure. Despite the fact that Guatemala, with its unique historical and cultural legacy, provides an auspicious opportunity for multidisciplinary work, history and anthropology have shared an uneasy relationship. Historians for the most part offer generic and facile summaries of cultural change, and anthropologists give no more than cursory nods to larger, national-level social and political processes. Neither historians nor anthropologists have as yet produced a thickly described study of historical and ethnic transformation.

The central question of nineteenth-century Guatemalan history turns on two successive attempts by liberals to create a cohesive state with political and military, if not cultural, hegemony. In the years following independence from Spain in 1821, enlightenment liberals limited the institutional power of the Catholic Church and abolished the corporate protection of indigenous communities.[18] Elite factionalism and a massive popular rebellion, however, soon smashed the liberal dream. Beginning in 1839, the conservative Rafael Carrera ruled Guatemala and dominated Central American politics for twenty-six years.[19] In 1871 liberals once again took power; and the state, led by the coffee planter Justo Rufino Barrios from 1873 to 1885, passed legislation that made indigenous land, labor, and revenue available to the rapacious needs of the new coffee economy and a burgeoning bureaucracy.[20] While the deleterious effects on indigenous *municipios* of the reforms decreed by the first liberal regime pale in comparison with those enacted by the "coffee state," no sustained popular resistance ensued after 1871.[21] Why?

Guatemalan historiography is still in its infancy, and the responses to this question fairly reflect the academic literature's nascent development. Preliminary answers have focused on the state's increased technical and financial ability to repress Indian dissent.[22] Recently, mostly because of the meticulous work of David McCreery, historians have begun to pursue more sophisticated inquiries. The process of land expropriation and labor exploitation now seems less abrupt than historians had previously assumed, and continuities between the conservative and liberal regimes are being stressed.[23]

Despite this increasingly subtle interpretation of Guatemalan state consolidation, however, some sharp edges still remain. In Guatemala, where exploitation *generally* runs along ethnic lines, literature tends to code Indians as victims and Ladinos as villains. Thus, historians still hesitate to examine the complex relations that bind the Maya to their communities as well as to Ladino society. McCreery wrote in 1994 that Indian "relations with the elites and the state have been almost entirely those of reaction and avoidance."[24] Indigenous culture, then, remains analytically juxtaposed to and distinct from class and state power.

This dichotomy is reflected in historians' account of cultural survival. In Guatemala, as in many areas of Latin America, the persistence of Indian ethnicity is most often explained away by theories examining the "articulation of modes of production," that is, how dependent capitalism not only allows but needs other relations of production to function.[25] In Guatemala this reason is often used to account for the persistence of Mayan communities. Unable to support a full-time labor force, coffee production relied on Indian communities and their noncapitalist relations of production to supply the subsistence needs of seasonal workers. Indian communities, in effect, subsidized Guatemala's transition to coffee cultivation. This conceptualization is very useful in understanding why seemingly subordinate modes of production—along with their cultural correlates—not only linger on but at times thrive. However, it does little to explain how individuals both simultaneously reproduce and understand alternative consciousness—be it Indian ethnicity or popular nationalism—and how that reproduction and understanding inscribe local, regional, and national relations of power and dominance.

These theories often adhere to a top-down analysis of cultural transformation: the ability to articulate a nationalist discourse is assigned solely to the dominant social class (read the bourgeoisie). Subordinate classes are capable only of conceptualizing fragmentary or parochial identities. Hence as articulation takes place, nationalism or liberalism, the universalizing discourses of the dominant, trumps ethnicity, the localizing identity of the dominated. Weak, dependent capitalist development produces a fragile, defensive nationalism that is constantly challenged by local discourses, centered on ethnicity or some other manifestation of regionalism.

Guatemalan ethnography, on the other hand, has been very sensitive to the processes by which social actors reproduce and interpret their cultural world.[26] And as anthropology became more historically and globally minded, Guatemalanists increasingly studied the links between power and culture.[27] But as in history, a sharp divide continues to exist between the two concepts, with "communal authority" examined as something apart from "state power."[28] Common questions are concerned with how global processes such as colonialism, capitalism, increased commodification, or the creation of a centralized state had an impact on the social structure of indigenous communities. Yet with few exceptions, there is no exploration of the ways in which culture infused ongoing state formation.[29]

This work argues that only through an examination of the long-term historical role popular classes played in the transformations that swept Guatemala before and after independence, can we develop a deeper understanding of the political turmoil of the last forty years. Neither dependency theory, which understands the state and foreign capital to be omnipotent, nor the current academic fashion to situate subalterns outside of larger hegemonic processes, is useful in explaining the tenacity and endurance of *both* popular culture and the state.[30] This is true even in a country such as Guatemala, which resorted to extreme levels of violence and terror to maintain order. What is needed, I believe, is a methodology that bridges the two positions. Drawing on the work of cultural theorists, such an approach is being created in similar regions of Latin America, such as Mexico, Nicaragua, and the Andean countries.[31] This study is an attempt to apply this methodology to Guatemalan history.

What I have found most useful in this approach is the emphasis on struggle in the creation of social meaning. Florencia Mallon's work on popular nationalism in Peru and Mexico, for example, has been extremely helpful in my understanding of the alternative national vision of the K'iche' elites. In challenging theories that view nationalism as a "positivist, unilinear" process of historical development that "assigns no creative role to nonbourgeois classes," Mallon has suggested a more fluid, dynamic model.[32] In studying the development of nationalist consciousness among Peruvian and Mexican peasants, she raises two questions that are pertinent to the study of Guatemala: To what degree can nationalism vary according to class? And to what extent do certain forms of nationalist consciousness develop in conflict with and contradiction to the process of national unification? It is the latter question in particular that provides us with a useful analytic distinction in studying ethnicity's link to the development of nationalism. By separating feelings and expressions of nationalist consciousness from the process of national unification, we can examine how the transformation and expansion of ethnic identity in Guatemala came into conflict with the national project of Ladino elites. Where my work differs from Mallon's is in our characterization of local discourses of the nation. What she describes as "popular nationalism," I identify as the nationalism of regional brokers, in important ways no less elitist then its Ladino counterpart.[33]

Likewise, my use of the concept of hegemony draws on the work of such writers as William Roseberry and Jeffrey Gould. Rather than a set of common beliefs that binds subalterns to elite projects, hegemony is understood as a "common material and meaningful framework for living through, talking about, and acting on a social order characterized by domination."[34] This view rejects *both* a totalizing Geertzian or Foucaultian view of ideology *and* a conspiracy theory of hegemony, through which elites consciously manipulate symbols, rituals, and language to gain the consent of the governed.[35] Roseberry in particular insists on restoring the political meaning of hegemony first suggested by Gramsci.[36] In examining the material relations and social alliances that produce a ruling class, we can understand how a set of ideas of how society should be organized becomes dominant.

Three points are crucial in understanding hegemony's relationship to rule and historical change. First, although hegemony here operates within a "common framework," not all in society have the ability to project their ideas as the dominant vision for social organization. Through the material processes of state formation and capital accumulation, certain classes and subgroups within those classes gain differential access to political and economic resources—such as, legal backing, military force, control of means of production, communication, and education—which in turn allows them to project their vision as the dominant vision. Second, in order to be truly effective, hegemony needs to create a "common social and moral project that includes popular as well as elite notions of political culture," so that those in power are "able to rule through a combination of coercion and consent."[37] This common project could include religious symbols and rituals, local and regional histories, language, as well as ideologies that cut across class divisions and unite individuals in gendered or ethnic alliances. Finally, elites themselves are bound by this project, and it is here where struggle and change occur. Dominated groups can use the language associated with their rulers to make demands.

Beyond Florencia Mallon's academic work on popular groups in Mexico and Peru, the nationalist rhetoric of the Zapatistas in southern Mexico is a striking example of this phenomenon.[38] And in Nicaragua, Jeffrey Gould has charted how peasants' creative interpretation of liberalism, hacienda paternalism, and Somocista populism "exacerbated divisions in the agro-export elite, and thereby pushed the regime to rely exclusively on its only remaining base of support, the National Guard."[39]

The importance of this approach is that it not only makes room for the histories of popular actors, but it also depends on them for an integral analysis of how power functions and change occurs. Along with other highland communities, Quetzalteco K'iche' political participation contributed to the failure of the first postindependent liberal regime (1821–38), the defeat of a highland separatist movement (1838–40), the endurance of Rafael Carrera's long conservative rule (1840–65), the establishment of the liberal coffee state (1871), and both the triumph *and* defeat of Guatemala's democratic revolution (1944–54). This work attempts to understand these events in light of the political consciousness that informed ethnic relations.

In Quetzaltenango, at least since the Cortes de Cádiz (the Spanish parliament formed during the Napoleonic crisis) at the beginning of the nineteenth century, indigenous political leaders had to contend with liberalism—an ideology that threatened their caste power. From this contention emerged by the end of the nineteenth century an alternative nationalism that drew heavily upon Ladino elite notions of progress, race, and nationalism. This K'iche' nationalism failed to take root. The harsh realities of Guatemala's model of development and the limits of dependent capitalism overpowered this alternative vision of the nation. By the 1950s, the K'iche' community had split along class lines; caste struggle—the incessant fighting over city resources between Indian and Ladino elites—gave way to class struggle as urban K'iche' elites initiated a campaign of intimidation and repression against rural indigenous campesinos organizing under the aegis of Guatemala's vaunted agrarian reform. The ensuing political instability contributed to the local collapse of Jacobo Arbenz's government and helped usher in the four decades of state terror that followed.

This work starts with the assumption that indigenous culture as it is understood today has been formed within the very same historical processes—colonialism, capitalism, and state formation—that have produced a variety of outcomes, including Ladino identity, resistance, repression, racism, ethnic revival, nationalism, and political illegitimacy. In the studies cited above, popular classes are portrayed neither as autonomous nor powerless in the face of economic and political transformation; they are not the heroic redeemers of history, the silent victims of colonialism and capitalism, nor the autonomous bearers of precapitalist and pre-state traditions.

In Guatemala today, however, it is difficult to take this approach. A number of factors have combined to reproduce the view that popular classes, in particular the Maya, have a history and a culture apart from the forces that have produced the Guatemalan state.[40] Even though caste affiliation was formed and strengthened as a result of colonialism, capitalism, and state formation, the ongoing salience of indigenous identity has contributed to the belief that Mayan culture exists outside of national life. Unlike what took place in many areas of Mexico, Guatemala's peripheral colonial and early republican economy did not break down indigenous ethnicity into a more homogeneous rural identity.[41] With the introduction of coffee cultivation in the mid-nineteenth century, the creation of Guatemala's agrarian proletariat took place along clearly defined ethnic lines. The development of a republican racism in the nineteenth century further deepened caste divisions. Guatemala's political trajectory usually entailed alliances between conservatives and indigenous communities.[42] When liberals took control of the state and its ideological apparatus in 1871, Indian political participation was either denied or portrayed as reactionary and ahistorical.[43]

Recent events have reinforced this bias. Indians participated on a mass scale in the revolutionary upheaval of the 1970s and 1980s.[44] Organizations comprised of Indians continue to give life to what remains of an oppositional movement. Nevertheless, there are strong pressures at work to deny this participation. The failure of the revolution combined with the inability of the rebel groups to protect their indigenous base against horrific levels of military repression led many of their early supporters to rethink and to distance themselves from their initial political commitment. Further, the rhetoric of Guatemalan resistance reinforced the denial of indigenous participation. After 1983, when in retrospect the rebels lost all chance of gaining state power, the struggle became no longer understood as a fight for revolutionary change but rather as a rearguard defense against wholesale slaughter. The formulation of indigenous rights, reinforced by a worldwide interest in the plight of native peoples, came to be an effective weapon in forestalling army violence. In many communities, the argument "Not the guerrillas, not the army" kept the military at bay to various degrees.

Framing the violence in this fashion, however, has transformed the memory of the repression. Until 1981, the majority of victims of state violence were Ladinos—students, peasants, union organizers, politicians, and revolutionaries. Not until the military launched its scorched earth campaign in 1981 were Indians targeted as Indians. Throughout this repression, the state never stopped killing Ladinos. Nevertheless, rather then being remembered as directed against a multiethnic popular movement, the terror at times is described as the "third Mayan Holocaust."[45]

The intent of this work is not to dismiss this point of view but rather to understand how and why it was produced.[46] I argue that scholars and activists need to be particularly careful about understanding history, conflict, and violence in simple, dichotomous terms.[47] In the particular case investigated here, it means examining contradictions *within* a community and alliances *between* Indians and Ladinos so as to understand how the

Maya from one important region actively engaged and understood the transition to coffee capitalism and liberal state formation. This is particularly urgent for the conflict that has transpired in Guatemala over the last four decades. It serves as little purpose to understand twentieth-century Indians as being caught between two armies as it would to understand nineteenth-century Quetzaltecos as mere victims of an omnipotent state, even if that is how they themselves remember events. In Quetzaltenango at least, K'iche' engagement with the state and Ladinos went well beyond "reaction and avoidance." Indian history did not end with the conquest. If a popular, inclusive identity is to be constructed in the wake of the war, then the role Mayan Indians played in the unfolding of Guatemalan history has to be recovered.

Book Structure

The narrative of this book is driven by the dialectic between reciprocity and repression. By reciprocity I mean the ideological contests between elites and commoners, men and women, K'iche's, Creoles, and Ladinos that forged both elite obligation and subaltern deference. At key points in this history, reciprocal bonds were strained and, at times, broken, and elites—Creole, Ladino, K'iche'—had to call on the repressive power of the state to restore order. The working out of the dialectic of reciprocity and repression produced new configurations of communal and municipal authority, new expressions of ethnic and national identity, and new forms of state power.

The first two chapters examine how commoners, women, principales, and royal officials constructed a complex political and economic community based on expectations of subsistence, gender rights and obligations, deference to authority, caste protections, commerce, and colonial power. Chapter 3 focuses on Ladino political elites as they manifested their racial fears in reaction to the 1837 cholera epidemic; chapter 4 then turns to K'iche' principales as they took advantage of the political opening offered by Carrera's rebellion to reestablish their communal authority. Chapter 5 examines the ways in which wealthy and common K'iche's negotiated the privatization of communal land and intensification of wage labor that took place in the nineteenth century. Chapter 6 focuses almost exclusively on K'iche' principales, as they developed a highly ideological ethnic identity in response to the economic and political changes discussed in previous chapters. And chapter 7 describes how gender and class relations informed this nascent nationalism and urban development.

A central purpose of this work is to explore how Guatemala's coffee economy produced a contradictory effect. K'iche' elites developed a more self-conscious ethnic identity to deal with the political, cultural, and economic changes brought about by coffee capitalism; at the same time, confronted with growing class stratification and weakening communal authority, these elites increasingly relied on the ideological and repressive function of the Ladino state to maintain their power and privilege. Ethnic identity deepened while state power increased. Chapter 8 examines the crisis produced by this contradiction: vestiges of caste struggle gave way to class struggle as urban K'iche's confronted indigenous peasants from the city's rural hinterlands trying to make good on the promise of land reform and national redemption.

The conclusion is an attempt to apply the arguments laid out in the book to a broader discussion of Guatemala's recent bloody history. This work shares the Truth Commission's judgment, highlighted in the paragraph cited earlier, that the failure of the Guatemalan state to mediate between competing social groups contributed to an important "structural" cause of recent political violence. While taking many forms, one manifestation of the state's failure to mediate social conflicts was the changing relationship between indigenous communities and the state. Following 1954, rapid economic growth, a violent breakdown of a governing consensus among Ladino elites, foreign intervention, and escalating state repression combined to undercut the ability of indigenous elites to fulfill their role as brokers between local, regional, and national interests. In ways not dissimiliar to the rebellion that brought Rafael Carrera to power in 1840, Indians, according to the Truth Commission, joined other "citizens from broad sectors of society . . . in [a] growing social mobilisation and political opposition to the continuity of the country's established order."[48]

While state violence usually furthered Ladino authority, at times unique alliances produced unexpected outcomes. Following independence in 1821, liberals attempted to build what they imagined was a modern nation formed by five Central American states.[49] Incessant insurrections by conservative elites, however, gave way in 1837 to a popular rebellion of peasants and Indians reacting against unaccustomed state intervention, taxation, and land expropriation.[50] The uprising started in eastern Guatemala and was headed by an illiterate Mestizo swineherd named José Rafael Carrera. Guatemala City quickly fell under siege. Meanwhile in the western highlands, in February 1838, Ladino patricians took advantage of the capital's troubles to secede from Guatemala and establish the sixth state of the Central American federation—the Estado de los Altos—with the city of Quetzaltenango as its capital. As Carrera battled his liberal foe, the Salvadoran Francisco Morazán, Altenses (highlanders) attempted to erect a state that held little legitimacy with the highlands' majority indigenous population.[51] By the final months of 1838, Indians were appealing to Carrera for help in withstanding the demands of the new nation. When in April 1839 Carrera rode victoriously into Guatemala City at the head of a ragtag Indian and Ladino peasant army, the days remaining to the Estado de los Altos were numbered.

The time period covered by this study begins in the Spanish colony, but the story opens with a crimson scene in Quetzaltenango's plaza—on the last day of the Estado de los Altos.

Prelude:
A World Put Right, 31 March 1840

It is not clear why the anonymous Indian messenger lingered in Quetzal-tenango rather than traveled on to Guatemala City to deliver the letter. Written by Roberto Molina, Quetzaltenango's Ladino *alcalde* (mayor), to his brother Marcelo, the message declared again the establishment of Central America's sixth state, El Estado de los Altos. Perhaps the mes-senger's delay was a political act, based on his opposition to the highland nation of which Quetzaltenango was the capital, or maybe it was a more mundane calculation, based on the dangers of traveling the highways of Guatemala during a time of violence and revolution.[1]

Nor do we know what compelled Molina to entrust the delivery of the letter to an Indian. The false rumors of Morazán's victory over the "bandit" Carrera must have turned the world right side up for the city's notables, if only for a brief moment. For decades, Quetzalteco Ladinos dreamed of creating a republic free from the control of Guatemala City. In 1838, Altenses had joyously celebrated their long-sought independence with Te Deums, parades, fireworks, and bullfights.[2] But Los Altos patri-cians had watched nervously as Guatemala City fell in 1839 to Carrera's peasant army.[3] Their worst fears were realized as the highland Mayan population increasingly invoked Carrera's name. Rebellions broke out in a number of indigenous communities over increased taxation, land expro-priation, and trade restrictions. In January 1840, Carrera invaded the highland republic. With widespread indigenous support, he easily de-feated Los Altos's defending army. As the invaders marched toward the city, Indian communities received them with processions, carrying crosses and banging makeshift kettledrums, through streets covered with flowers, "as if they were representatives of Jesus Christ himself."[4] Indige-nous leaders from one coastal town presented the severed head of an Altense officer to Carrera's troops. When Carrera entered the city's plaza, Indians from surrounding regions arrived bearing presents and swearing allegiance. Carrera convened a new municipal council, declared the highlands once again to be part of Guatemala, and then rushed back to Guatemala City, where he definitively beat Morazán's forces.

It is easy to understand why Altenses, with their world now gone awry and hearing false reports that Morazán had recaptured Guatemala City, would hastily again declare their independence. Maybe it was a sense of euphoric relief that led Molina—notwithstanding the region's ethnic tensions—to unthinkingly dispatch an indigenous courier. Or maybe it was simple arrogance in denying, despite compelling evidence to the contrary, that Indians were political actors.

Hearing of the Altenses' *pronunciamiento* (revolt), Carrera furiously headed back to the highlands. Municipal officials, fearing the consequences, sent a delegation comprised of Father Urbano Ugarte, the city's priest, Balentín Cayax, the K'iche' alcalde, Juan Lavanigna, a Genoese merchant and Carrera sympathizer, and Gerónimo Pais, the highland *corregidor* appointed by Carrera, to meet and placate the general. As he approached the delegation on a mountain ridge overlooking the city, Carrera flew into a rage. Yelling that the priest was Morazán's brother, he ordered his men to shoot him on the spot. Cayax threw himself in front of Ugarte, pleading, "Do not kill my priest." Furious, Carrera drew his sword and slashed twice at Cayax's shoulder. He arrested the priest and the merchant and proceeded into the city, where he found a few municipal authorities, including Molina, nervously awaiting him. It was then that the Indian messenger handed Molina's dispatch to Carrera.

Before his secretary could finish reading the letter, the illiterate Carrera again pulled his sword and attacked Molina. As the military band played the *degüello* (dirge), troops plundered the city and arrested anyone associated with the Estado de los Altos. The next day, Molina and seventeen of his fellow municipal officers were taken one by one to the plaza and shot. As execution followed execution, Carrera sat in a window overlooking the plaza playing his guitar while the Genoese Lavanigna, at Carrera's insistence, danced with a servant woman. Soldiers piled the bodies of the executed in the center of the plaza and mutilated them with bayonets. The remaining prisoners were then taken from their cells and marched in a circle around the mound of mangled corpses. The corregidor, himself threatened with death by Carrera for losing control of the situation, warned the prisoners that "were it not for the great humanity of General Carrera, they too would be on that pile. And if they were ever to bother the population again, he would return and not even the smallest child would escape." He then ordered them to shout "*vivas*" to their tormentor before they were finally released.[5]

With a victorious Carrera consolidating his power in Guatemala City, it was now the highland Maya's turn to believe that their world was put right side up. From the Bourbon Reforms of the eighteenth century, through the political turmoil of the independence period, to the establishment of the Estado de los Altos, Mayan communities of Guatemala's western highlands had experienced a gradual but persistent curtailment of their political power, loss of cultural autonomy, and increased levels of economic exploitation in the form of taxation and land expropriation. While reaction and resistance to these changes took many forms, by the last months of the Estado de los Altos, a number of highland and coastal Indian villages moved into open rebellion.

Carrera immediately made good on a number of promises. He reestablished many of the communal corporate protections that had been slowly eroded by liberal reforms—in effect approximating a postcolonial *república de indios*. He ordered the municipality of Quetzaltenango to suspend the collection of the hated *contribución directa* (head tax) and "in no way continue bothering the pueblos of this department."[6] In July 1840, K'iche's from Zunil refused to pay transport tax on cotton that they were bringing from the coast, threatening to beat the tollhouse collector with sticks and claiming that "Carrera told us we can pay what we want."[7] Immediately following the defeat of Los Altos, Indians from Cantel filed a suit in a national court to have land returned to them that they felt had been unjustly expropriated, while in San Sebastián, Indians simply retook *ejidal* (common or corporate) land recently appropriated by Ladinos.[8] In fact, Maya throughout the highlands and the coast responded so enthusiastically to the fall of Los Altos that Carrera had to move quickly to avoid a caste war, dispatching troops to communities where Indians were threatening to "do away with all Ladinos."[9]

Principales acted not only to restore a balance between Indian and Ladino worlds but within indigenous communities as well. Laws were reestablished that placed the administration of Indian affairs once more in the hands of principales who were accountable only to the departmental corregidor. Authorities pressed for the restoration of traditional methods of disciplining and punishing that had been abolished by liberal reforms. Within weeks of Carrera's victory, whipping posts were reinstalled in village plazas. In March 1840, in Santo Tomás Chichicastenango, the first public floggings since the liberals outlawed the practice were held. In front of an all-Indian crowd, village principales sat silently as the *alguacil* (sheriff) whipped one prisoner after another. Each lashing continued until the alcalde ordered it stopped. Among those disciplined was a married couple—chained together with bars so they could not touch each other— who had offended the moral sensibility of the community by living apart.[10]

In the city of Quetzaltenango, the world to be restored was a complex one, and it is unclear how much support Quetzalteco K'iche's actually gave to Carrera at the beginning of his insurrection. City principales did receive him upon his first entrance, but compared with the violence and rebellion that occurred in villages such as San Sebastián Retalhuleu or Santa Catarina Ixtahuacán, the quiescence of the indigenous population of Quetzaltenango is notable. Of course, considering Carrera's violent attack on Balentín Cayax, it seems as if the general was not feeling particularly beholden to Quetzalteco Indians. None of the reports of disturbances in the city prior to Carrera's arrival mention the participation of Indians. Nor were there any notices following Carrera's victory of Indians acting in the ecstatic manner that they did in other communities, where drunken revelries and retributions against Ladinos became commonplace. One account notes that following Carrera's second departure, the city was in such a state of shock from the executions that the streets were silent for days, save for the appearance of "a few women and Indians."[11]

While Quetzalteco K'iche's were not exempt from the pressures that drove Indian communities throughout Guatemala to rebel, they were often in a stronger position to mediate the effects of such pressures. Economic, political, and ethnic relations between the city's Ladinos and Indians were more reciprocal, dependent, and complex. Perhaps this accounts for the Indians' ambivalent reaction to the Carrera revolt. And perhaps it also partly explains why Molina entrusted his letter to an Indian.

This is not to say that Quetzalteco K'iche's felt they had no world to put right. For decades before independence, K'iche' principales had struggled against restrictions placed on their political power and autonomy. In 1806, for example, the Crown granted local Creole notables the right to form their own city government parallel to the indigenous municipality. Following independence in 1821, city Ladinos dissolved the K'iche' *cabildo* (town council) and required indigenous officers to sit in as observers on the weekly sessions of the city's now single *ayuntamiento* (city council). K'iche' alcaldes and *regidores* (council members) attended council meetings until Carrera's first appearance.[12] Yet following the executions, principales not only refused to attend the Ladino municipal sessions but reestablished their own separate cabildo "in the form and manner that by custom our ancestors practiced."[13] Ladino authorities repeatedly insisted that the Indians reincorporate themselves into their municipal body; they claimed that Carrera had affirmed that the city has "only one corporation."[14] This demand continued throughout the 1840s, with the Ladinos repeatedly summoning the indigenous authorities to their sessions.[15]

K'iche's, refusing these attempts at reincorporation, asserted that they were answerable only to the corregidor and that the two municipal bodies should remain separate, "as they have been for close to three hundred years."[16] Not until 1895, twenty-four years after liberals managed to take—and this time hold—state power, were Quetzalteco Ladinos able to abolish the K'iche' cabildo, and then only after having made considerable political concessions.

At the heart of this clash of competing *municipalidades* existed a struggle for control of resources. Under an autonomous indigenous cabildo, the community's resources—money, land, and labor—remained corporately protected and controlled by indigenous elites, subject to the mediation of national authorities. Ejidal land, community funds, and Indian labor were part of the *común* (indigenous corporate community), and following the fall of Los Altos, that común would continue to be administered by K'iche's, at least for a time.

Chapter 1
The Greatest Indian City in the World:
Caste, Gender, and Politics, 1750 – 1821

Quetzaltenango . . . is the greatest Indian city in the world. . . .
[It] is rich with her own atmosphere, a city of thousands of Indians
living in brick and adobe houses, dressing, most of them, in the clothes
of the modern world, and yet its streets have grown here from the goat-
tracks of a prehistoric Indian village. — WALLACE THOMPSON,
The Rainbow Countries of Central America, 1926

Quetzalteco Indians in general are applied to agriculture . . . and
it is very rare to find those who do not have forty or more cuerdas
planted with wheat, corn or potatoes. Many who live in the town are
inclined toward the commerce of pigs, woolen goods and other products
which they transport to Guatemala and as far as the province of
Sonsonate, San Salvador, San Miguel and Esquipulas. They have enough
land, sheep, horses and oxen and a sufficient number of mares. Like all
of their kind, they are inclined to drink, but not so much that they
neglect their work and trade. As a result they respect authority . . . and
are becoming Ladinos. It is the opposite case with Ladinos, only a tenth
of whom apply themselves to agriculture and commerce with honor and
Christian thoughts. The rest of them lie, drink, gamble, and deceive. It is
shameful to see their children without clothes, confused, poor, and sick.
—*Royal assessment, 1817*

Between the later half of the seventeenth century and the Bourbon Reforms of the eighteenth, a segment of Quetzaltenango's K'iche' population constituted itself as a landholding class. The ability of K'iche' elites to secure property rights—which in turn allowed them to thrive as farmers, merchants, traders, and artisans—reinforced their cultural and political authority within the larger colonial framework. This interplay between class and caste power allowed Quetzalteco K'iche's to effectively respond to and at times best various threats to their economic and political well-being.

The emergence of a regional Creole elite, the commodification of land and labor, and the end of Spanish colonialism devastated many similar Mayan communities. In Quetzaltenango, however, the uneven spread of agrarian capitalism and the slow, torturous making of a nation-state was accompanied by the creation of new forms of indigenous power and survival.[1] This chapter will examine the colonial political economy that allowed for indigenous resiliency. It will explore how K'iche' elite men used their overlapping roles as political leaders and family patriarchs to successfully participate in an expanding regional market. Contrary to royal predictions, rather than bringing about a loss of caste identification, this participation explains how, well into the twentieth century, Quetzaltenango remained, at least in the prose of one excitable traveler, "the greatest Indian city in the world."

Land and the Long Seventeenth Century

The first decades (1524–41) of Spanish rule in Guatemala were years of plunder and confusion.[2] Xelaju, or for that matter the nearby K'iche' capital of Utatlán, was no Tenochtitlán. The subjugation of western Guatemala took place early enough in the Spanish conquest so that the promises of riches to be found elsewhere were not unreasonable. Memories of Mexico and dreams of El Dorado led the conquistadors to treat the first pillaged settlements as little more than bivouacs and their inhabitants as forced conscripts. Pedro de Alvarado himself led expeditions of Spanish and Indian soldiers and slaves through what is now El Salvador into the Andes. Native uprisings, Spanish rivalries, and rumors of easy wealth the next region over created a volatile climate, and Alvarado's impulsive, vicious, and autocratic rule provided little incentive for colonial settlement.

Following Alvarado's death in 1541, the Crown, anxious to move from a conquest to a colonial society, dispatched a corps of royal bureaucrats to the highlands and confiscated many of the *encomiendas* (grants of tribute-paying Indians) handed out by Alvarado and his rivals.[3] After decades of pillage, warfare, forced migration, and demographic collapse, Indians were forcibly resettled in *congregaciones* (concentrated populations).[4] Administrative districts were carved out and a semblance of colonial order was imposed. Yet with little mineral wealth and a shrinking labor force and tribute population, Guatemala, particularly its Western Highlands and Pacific coastal lands, would remain politically and economically marginal.[5]

In the town of Quetzaltenango, K'iche' *principales* took advantage of a weak state and prolonged economic contraction to standardize their land claims within the Spanish legal system. Of all the town's recorded land transactions prior to 1687, 53 of the 65 *caballerías* (in Quetzaltenango, 111 acres) were claimed by Spaniards.[6] Yet following 1687, of the 139 caballerías taken, 88 were claimed by K'iche's. All told, Spaniards took 104 and K'iche's claimed 100 caballerías.

Under Spanish colonial law each Indian *congregación* was to receive and hold in common title one league (roughly equal to thirty-nine caballerías) of ejidal land, usually comprising pasture, agricultural and woodland.[7] In Quetzaltenango, within what was commonly called the town's *ejidos* existed a complex mix of private and corporate land tenure and use.[8]

The town sits in the southwest corner of an extended highland plain ringed by volcanoes and mountains. Its borders comprise the majority of the valley's arable land; its southern limits reach up into the eastern folds of the volcanoes Santa María and Cerro Quemado, which separate the valley from the Pacific piedmont and lowlands. The majority of Quetzaltenango's indigenous peasant population farmed *milpas* (small subsistence corn, bean, and squash parcels) of ten to forty *cuerdas* (sixteen cuerdas equals one acre), while relying on the rocky, mountainous forest land—*bosque*—for their wood, water, and pasture needs.[9] Many of these small plots were within what could be considered the ejido proper—land within the municipal limits held and administered corporately by the indigenous cabildo. In Quetzaltenango, the cabildo did not charge rent for these lands. After several generations, peasants often came to regard their milpas as their property—to be sold, mortgaged, and passed on to heirs.[10] A sector of the K'iche' population owned farms or ranches of up to five hundred cuerdas, which they planted with corn, wheat, and beans and on

4. Plaza of Quetzaltenango, 1875. *Photograph by Eadweard Muybridge, courtesy of the Boston Athenaeum.*

which they kept pigs, sheep, goats, and cattle.[11] And a smaller number of Indians claimed large tracts of land ranging from one to up to ten caballerías in size. At times these K'iche' landlords would not cultivate their holdings themselves but would rent it to either Spaniards or other Indians.[12]

The securing of property rights provided a select group of K'iche's with protection from both a capricious regional economy and a rapacious aspiring Creole class. Landholding K'iche's were able to engage with an expanding market on fairly good terms: continued subsistence production not only underwrote their commercial activity, but it also provided Indians a refuge when the economy contracted, as it did in the decades before and after independence. Further, population growth in the nineteenth century began to limit access to the town's commons. On the one hand, more and more Indians were using the town's ejidos, and, on the other, Ladino land encroachment was reducing the total amount of land available for use. Absolute subsistence rights came under threat. K'iche's who held title to their land, however, were less vulnerable to these threats than were poorer *macehuales* (commoners) who relied on the commons for wood, pasture, and milpa.

Commerce and the Emergence of the City

By the turn of the nineteenth century, the city of Quetzaltenango had been transformed from a colonial administrative backwater (the town had often been omitted from sixteenth- and seventeenth-century maps) into a thriving regional commercial, political, and military center with a rapidly growing nonindigenous population. By 1797, the Crown, recognizing the city's importance, established a post office, gunpowder, saltpeter, and tobacco agencies, a consulate, and the offices of sales tax collector and land judge.[13] By the onset of the Napoleonic Wars, three militia companies were established that comprised nearly eight hundred men and consisted of Spanish officers and Mestizo troops.[14]

An expanding regional market created by the indigo boom and Bourbon economic reforms led Altenses to invest in the cultivation of wheat and the manufacture of textiles.[15] Demand for highland products further increased when a 1773 earthquake destroyed Santiago (the colonial capital of Guatemala and today known as Antigua) and disrupted the economy of Guatemala's central valley. By the end of the eighteenth century, Quetzalteco wheat and textiles reached the northwestern provinces of southern Mexico, north into the mountain towns of the Cuchumatanes and the Verapaces, south to the coastal plains of the Pacific, and east to the capital, El Salvador, and Honduras.[16] The majority of goods were sent to Nueva Guatemala (the new capital), where they were either shipped to Nicaragua and Costa Rica or sold for retail in the stores and markets of the city. Other shipments went to smaller provincial centers such as Retalhuleu, Esquipulas, and Sololá, where they would then be divided into smaller wholesale lots for sale in Indian communities. Trade often increased in the month prior to a village fiesta—Mazatán in November, Esquipulas in December, Chiantla in January, and so on.[17] Spanish, Mexican, German, and Italian merchants (recall the Genoese who went out to placate Carrera) set up businesses in the city. By the beginning of the nineteenth century, there existed in the city over one hundred stores selling local and imported goods, including luxury items such as Iberian wine, clothes, and furniture.[18]

On another less celebrated level, regional trade took place through extensive indigenous routes connecting village plazas.[19] This commerce

5. Plaza of Quetzaltenango, 1875. *Photograph by Eadweard Muybridge, courtesy of the Boston Athenaeum.*

centered around weekly or twice-weekly village market days and, like the larger wholesale trade, took advantage of the Catholic liturgical calendar to trade during fairs and fiestas. At the beginning of the nineteenth century, visitors to the city gushed at what was described as the most bustling plaza second to Guatemala City, stocked with a variety of goods reflecting the ecological diversity of western Guatemala.[20] From the Pacific lowlands, Indians brought fish, citrus, cacao, salt, cotton, cattle, *panela* (residue produced from the milling of cane), and sugar. Corn, which on the coast had two annual growing cycles, supplemented the highlands' single harvest. K'iche's from the town of Zunil, which straddled the coast and the highlands, traded cotton, sugar products, and citrus in exchange for wheat and livestock. Communities populating the Quetzaltenango and Totonicapán valleys traded pigs, poultry, wheat, corn, vegetables, beans, and fruits. Northwest of the valley, Mam communities raised livestock and traded corn and limestone (used in the making of cornmeal for tortillas and tamales, as well as in construction). Cantel, with its large reserves of pine and fertile soil traded wood for fuel, furniture, and construction. Mames from the mountain towns of the Cuchumantanes supplemented the region's own wool supply.

Regional Relations of Production

Due to Los Altos's peripheral economy and its consequent weak regional state apparatus, labor relations by the end of the eighteenth century in and immediately around the town of Quetzaltenango were not coercive.[21] While forced labor drafts in the form of the infamous *repartimiento* were periodically levied following the decline of cacao and the Bourbon Reforms, they never became the primary mode of labor relations in the communities surrounding Quetzaltenango.[22] In addition, royal financial exactions in the city were not particularly burdensome. K'iche's did have to support parish priests, maintain the church and convent, and pay liturgical fees and occasional emergency taxes, but they were exempted from the tithe and the *alcabala* (royal sales tax). And while there was a tax charged on goods sold in the plaza, it was irregularly and ineffectually enforced.[23] As to the tribute, by 1766 Quetzaltecos were paying annually one and a half pesos, in addition to a quantity of corn, wheat, and poultry.[24] By 1796, however, the payment in kind had been eliminated and Indians now paid only the one and a half pesos.[25]

What resulted, at least to a degree, was the formation of *relatively* noncoercive agricultural and artisanal relations of production. Elite Creoles and Spaniards never gained monopoly control of the textile and agricultural trade, either in terms of supply of raw material, production, transport, or markets. At least until the early twentieth century, local K'iche' families dominated the city's wool supply (supplemented by traders from Huehuetenango and the Sija-San Marcos valley), herding large flocks of sheep on private and city property.[26] The extension of subsistence and commercial cultivation did not cut into the amount of private and common land available for pasture until the beginning of the twentieth century. Furthermore, although no extensive documentary evidence exists, judging from the number of complaints by indigenous traders over the establishment of toll taxes at the beginning of the nineteenth century, the supply of cotton from the coast was likewise controlled by Indians.

Throughout the late colonial period, as the regional textile industry developed, some wealthy Hispanic (and K'iche') entrepreneurs provided

credit or material—wool or cotton, dyes, and machinery—to indigenous
and Hispanic families in exchange for a share of the finished products.
These merchants would then ship their goods in large wholesale lots to
the capital and other provincial centers. This "putting out" system, however, never managed to gain control over the city's artisan sector. By 1797
there existed in Quetzaltenango thirty wool and cotton textile workshops employing 190 masters and apprentices and producing over 107,520
yards of fabric a year, as well as a large number of unregistered K'iche'
workshops.[27] According to inventories in K'iche' wills, textile-producing
households often maintained access to the array of resources—land,
sheep, machinery, labor, and dyes—needed for textile production.[28]

Neither could Creoles establish a monopoly over cargo labor. At the
turn of the eighteenth century, wholesale wheat and textile exporters were
having difficulty conscripting mule drivers to carry their freight. In 1804,
for instance, the *Audiencia* (royal government based in Nueva de Guatemala) granted the Spaniard Juan Antonio López, perhaps the wealthiest
farmer and merchant in Quetzaltenango, permission to conscript two
hundred mules and drivers to ship his wheat harvest to the capital.
K'iche's from nearby towns (the K'iche' pueblos to the east of the city
controlled the transport industry) refused the request, arguing to the
Audiencia that the two and half to three pesos they would receive for the
six-day trip was not worth their time. The royal prefect complained that it
was nearly impossible to get Indians to fulfill labor obligations because of
the money they were making hiring themselves out to individuals willing
to pay more than the Crown-sanctioned four reals a day.[29] The Audiencia
reversed its previous decision, and López was forced to negotiate pri-
vately with the teamsters.

Generally, the social relations governing the city's textile industry
structured commercial agricultural production as well. Spaniards and
Creoles profited from wheat in three ways. First, they cultivated the crop
on their large estates, using a mix of wages and debt to procure labor.
While evidence is sketchy, it appears unlikely that Quetzalteco peasants
were forced, through pressure on their subsistence capacity, into peonage. Even as population density climbed and commercial cultivation expanded, the majority of the K'iche' population still had access to subsistence production. Rather, debt relations seem to parallel those described
by John Tutino for the Bajío region of central Mexico.[30] Estates had to
offer high wages, food, and secure conditions in order to create and

maintain a labor force. Debt functioned more as incentive than coercion. Quetzalteco workers could therefore "insult" (as the corregidor once put it) planters by demanding relatively high wages.[31]

Second, Creoles and Spaniards rented out sections of their estates for a take of the harvest. The specifics of these arrangements are not documented, but it appears that by the first decades of the independence period, a number of families lived on and cultivated Hispanic estates.[32] Finally, merchants would finance indigenous production, lending large sums of money against a portion of the harvest. Records indicate that wealthy K'iche's borrowed large sums from Creoles in advance of their corn harvests.[33] Yet as in the textile industry, Hispanic commercial agriculture never came to monopolize indigenous production, since a large number of K'iche's continued to cultivate and trade wheat and corn into the twentieth century.

A number of factors combined to prevent Spaniards and Creoles from consolidating a monopoly over the textile and wheat trade. Compared with the situation in other areas of New Spain, Spaniards and Creoles entered the game rather late in the colonial period.[34] By this point, Indians in and around Quetzaltenango had already secured their property holdings and access to markets. An independent land base allowed Indians to retain control over key aspects of the production process and provided them with a strategic advantage in relation to their would-be competitors. This not only allowed for cheaper production costs but satisfied household subsistence needs during hard times. But even the standard colonial response to indigenous control over productive resources—the putting out system—could not take hold. Access to indigenous markets and community credit provided an important escape route from the potential entrapment of Spanish and Creole loans.

Also, because they entered the textile trade relatively late, Spaniards and Creoles could not consolidate their position in an industry that, starting in the late eighteenth century, was constantly in crisis.[35] Political unrest, British contraband, liberalization of mercantile restrictions, and tax breaks that benefited the Spanish textiles industry all undercut highland commerce. Furthermore, despite a regional celebration of nonindigenous textiles ("superior to those of Cuzco and Quito!"), highland production was in fact mediocre.[36] Royal officials were constantly trying to improve the grade of highland textiles so as to compete against cheaper and higher-quality imports. In contrast, neither economic fluctuation nor European imports greatly diminished peasant demand for locally-produced textiles, thus providing household producers a degree of stability throughout the late colonial period.

Community Relations of Production

Communal sources of credit likewise allowed K'iche's to maintain a sig-nificant degree of control over production. Capital needed to fund subsis-tence and commercial production was obtained in the form of money, land, or resources in three ways.[37]

First, through private lending, poorer Indians would borrow money either for their more modest commercial and subsistence enterprises or to cover their communal obligations of tribute and church and cofradía support, paying back their debt in labor or coin. In a cash-scarce colonial society such as Guatemala, much of the small debt recorded in wills was debt in kind, valued in pesos. Food, goods, and services were bartered and advanced, with their estimated values in pesos recorded in testaments or collateral inventories.[38]

Second, money from the *caja de comunidad* (community treasury) funded indigenous production. In Quetzaltenango, funds were raised from the sale of agricultural products grown on municipal land, a local tax, a fee on water wells, and the rent on sixteen stores in the plaza.[39] Although the corregidor was responsible for auditing these funds, evi-dence suggests that the indigenous gobernador had considerable latitude as to how this money was used.[40] In 1710, Joseph Gómez Tih, the K'iche' gobernador, lent 260 pesos to another Indian, Baltazar Cachachulac. Ca-chachulac was to give one-half of his earnings gained from this loan (invested in an unspecified enterprise) to defray the costs of maintaining the cemetery.[41] In 1804, María Salomé Quijivix and her son, Manuel, needing access to cash owing to the recent death of her husband, Gober-nador Anizeto López, borrowed from the caja 1,000 pesos "to plant corn and wheat."[42] And in 1810, Manuel Jocol received 400 pesos from the caja "to support his family and his [religious] obligations."[43] In addition to these large loans, smaller advances occasionally were made from the caja to poorer Indians and Ladinos, either for immediate subsistence needs or to finance a commercial harvest or other business venture.[44]

Finally, *cofradías*—confraternities modeled on Iberian burial and mutual aid societies that venerated and cared for a titular saint—were another important source of credit. In 1770, there existed twenty-one K'iche' and eight Ladino cofradías.[45] In contrast to the nearly moribund Ladino confraternities (many of which by 1848 had not held elections for decades and were nearly bankrupt), K'iche' cofradías were economically and politically vibrant. In 1810, the combined capital held by the Quetzaltenango indigenous cofradías totaled 11,857 pesos.[46] Cofradías funded their activities—burials for members, charity for the poor, masses for souls, wax and incense for altars, and food, music, and drink for their yearly fiesta— through membership fees, obligatory contributions, interest on money lent, rent on lands, and bequests.[47]

Women and men donated money and property to cofradías in the stated belief that by honoring saints with processions, fiestas, and masses, they were placing themselves under the divine protection of heavenly beings. Individuals would often post a given amount of capital for loan, the interest of which would go to the assigned cofradía. Chantries comprised another common form of cofradía income.[48] Either to fund pious works or to say masses for their souls, individuals would bequeath to the church or cofradías the value of a lien taken out on a piece of property.[49] Renters or purchasers of the land usually then paid 5 percent annually of the value of the lien to the assigned cofradía. After fulfilling stipulated obligations, cofradías could lend out their surplus capital, usually for a two-year period at 6 percent interest.

Cofradía property therefore not only provided credit to producers but also allowed cultivators access to affordable land. In 1803, for example, Domingo Fuentes and Victoria Vela purchased 320 cuerdas of land from the estate of Blas Vela. Although assessed at 170 pesos, the land contained a lien of 120 pesos to support a cofradía, the couple paid only 50 pesos and promised to pay to the fellowship 5 percent of the chantry.[50]

Subsistence was guaranteed not only by access to the vast tracts of municipal land and the absence of extended colonial labor requirements but also by the regulation of communal resources by indigenous and royal officials. Indian principales protected woodlands from deforestation and pastures from overgrazing, oversaw a communal planting, and regulated when the town's harvest was to begin. Starting in the mid-eighteenth century, the Crown decreed that every *pueblo de indios* was to plant and harvest a *siembra de comunidad* (community planting), which would either be used to pay tribute or to provide subsistence during periods of famine.[51] Following a bad wheat harvest in the spring of 1810, for example, the corregidor ordered that communal grain be distributed, that corn be planted on the coast as soon as possible, and that highland cultivation of wheat and corn be increased by a third "in order to provide for future emergencies."[52] Also in 1810, both Creole and K'iche' elites worked together to calm a panic brought about by the combined effects of an early frost, the previous year's poor harvest, and fear of theft. Poor *milperos* (subsistence corn farmers) had been harvesting their corn before it was ripe, and women demanded the distribution of wheat.[53] The Spanish cabildo distributed 2,668 pounds of wheat to city bakers and sent a commission to surrounding regions to buy more.[54] As royal power receded during the first decades of the nineteenth century, Creole municipal authorities took the place of royal officials in working with indigenous elites to provide relief during times of scarcity and crisis.[55]

Indigenous commercial production was carried out by a complex mix of wage labor, debt obligation, and patriarchal control over family and communal labor. At the highest levels of wholesale textile trade, wealthy K'iche's either lent out money, machinery, or goods to indigenous households in exchange for manufactured textiles or took manufactured goods on consignment, selling the products on behalf of the producers in Guatemala City. In the year before his death in 1804, the K'iche' *gobernador* Anizeto López shipped a staggering 10,500 pounds of textiles to Guatemala City.[56] The terms governing the production or shipment of these goods is not known, but this does suggest that as gobernador, López exercised a good deal of control over the K'iche' textile production. That other K'iche's likewise shipped large orders of textiles suggests however that this authority was not absolute.[57] Whatever the case, artisan families retained, well into the nineteenth century, significant control over textile production. Many of these family operations had evolved by the second half of the nineteenth century into workshops that relied on the labor of apprentices and wage laborers.[58]

Mirroring the Spanish institution of apprenticeship, tutorship and adoption were important practices in the K'iche' population. In 1760, twenty-two indigenous orphans were placed in K'iche' families.[59] Numerous references in indigenous wills and testaments suggest that adoption not only served to mitigate high mortality rates but fulfilled labor needs as well. These adopted children fit well into an artisanal and agricultural productive system that relied primarily on family labor. In 1831, for instance, Mateo Pac inherited his adopted father's textile workshop.[60] And in 1840, María Ygnacia Coyoy recognized as heir her adopted son Juan, who after her husband abandoned her, lived with her "until this day, providing me with important services . . . and working without abandoning me for even a single moment."[61]

Domestic work likewise occupied a significant part of the city's labor force. In 1813, 323 servants worked in Quetzaltenango's 2,015 households: 210 servants worked in the 127 Spanish families, and 109 served in the 734 Mestizo and Ladino households.[62] And while the 1813 census lists only 4 servants working in the city's 1,154 K'iche' families, this is not an accurate representation of domestic labor in indigenous households, for the patronage relations described in the preceding paragraph most likely included household work, especially among the wealthier K'iche'.

Of the 323 servants, 130 were K'iche' and the majority—193—were listed as Mestizo. Of the total, 229 were women and 94 were men. The majority of the women were Mestizas or Ladinas (141 were Mestiza or Ladina; 88 were K'iche'). Of the 229 women, 197 were single, 12 were widowed, and 9 were married (status was not listed for 11 individuals). Of the 94 men, 80 were single, 6 were widowed, and 7 were married (status was not listed for 1).

Note the intersection of caste and patriarchy in the formation of labor relations. Single individuals, particularly single women, with limited access to family labor and patriarchal ties, and hence subsistence production, found themselves entering into relations of servitude at a higher rate than did married individuals. That non-Indians comprised a majority of the servant labor force suggests that the social safety net was drawn a little tighter among the K'iche's than among Ladinos or Mestizos. K'iche' orphans, for example, were placed in K'iche' families.[63] As Indian identity broke down, so too did the patriarchal bonds weaken that characterized indigenous communities (recall the description of Ladinos in this chapter's second epigraph). A ladinoized K'iche' could make fewer claims on filial obligations and hence chose or was forced to rely on wage or indebted servitude to survive.

In agriculture, debt helped secure labor. But as with Creole and Spanish planters, this debt was not coercive. Anizeto López died in 1804 with his field workers collectively owing him "great quantities" of money.[64] This practice was standardized to the degree that he employed an overseer to keep accounts of debts, yet there seems to have been no attempt to collect them either before or after his demise.[65] By the early nineteenth century, records indicate that a number of landholding K'iche's allowed other Indians to reside on their property. In exchange, residents either worked their landlords' fields or provided them with a portion of their own yield.[66] Dispossession, increases in paternal obligations, deaths of family members, and loss of communal rights undoubtedly forced many into a greater reliance on debt in order to survive, but there is no indication that by the late colonial period peonage was as coercive or important an institution as it would later become in the coffee economy.

Women

Quetzalteco women were highly visible and active in the public sphere and participated in nearly every facet of production and trade. Through trade and credit, women created a world of countervailing power that mitigated the vicissitudes of patriarchy. Women farmed, herded, wove, traded, owned land, livestock, tools, and businesses, lent money, and litigated property. Market women fought each other with knives over customers and came together to protest new municipal taxes on plaza stalls.[67] By the turn of the nineteenth century, as many as four hundred women, both from Quetzaltenango and the surrounding pueblos, traveled to Quetzaltenango's market every Sunday.[68] Aside from selling agricultural products, Quetzaltecas made and sold soap, lard, pine pitch, incense, candles, tortillas and bread, and other common handicrafts and foodstuffs; others, often the wives of principales, traded high-quality textile products, such as the famed Quetzaltenango *huipil* (indigenous female tunic), honey, meat, and poultry. The money or goods earned from this trade provided them with a modicum of independence and, in the absence of a male head of household, survival.

Lacking the political ability to mobilize community resources to the degree that men could, women relied on money and credit to obtain control over productive forces. While wealthy Spanish and Creole women could simply afford to pay for labor and goods, most other women needed to borrow to participate in the local economy. Since women did not have access to the large-scale loans available to men, they depended on the credit circulated among them through relatives, friends, and patrons. Between 1801 and 1804, women borrowed 1,830 pesos of the total recorded 21,667 pesos lent out in the city.[69] Women also advanced a significant 2,982 pesos of the total amount of credit extended. If we subtract the large transactions of 1,000 pesos or more conducted by men, however, women actually lent a majority of the credit. Further, women tended to donate generously to cofradías, thus contributing to the funds available for credit.[70] This was perhaps attributable to the fact that women, lacking the resources available to men, relied more on cofradías as providers of social security.

Yet women bought and sold, lent and borrowed within a social structure that granted them only limited *political* power over their activity. The social relations of labor, land, and capital so far described took place within a larger context of patriarchal caste power in which men—principales, royal officials, Creole elites, parish priests—controlled the economy through a set of communal, legal, and political norms and sanctions.[71]

Men controlled production, trade, and property at a number of crucial junctures. While women had access to small-scale credit, men could draw on their political connections to obtain significant amounts of capital. Gobernador Anizeto López was able to borrow money to finance his various capital-intensive enterprises and to establish patronage relations with other Indians, thus increasing his power; women did not have access to this kind of credit. Further, men could expect to receive loans from the community treasury. In contrast, when the widow of Anizeto López, María Salomé Quijivix, requested a loan of one thousand pesos from the caja in 1804, her son was required to sign the promissory note. Likewise, indigenous municipal officers could use their political position to draft communal labor for their private enterprises.[72] And while women energetically participated in local trade, men controlled the long-distance and lucrative commercial networks.[73]

At the household level as well, women were dependent on men for access to productive resources. The household was represented in the común by the oldest male member, and it was through him that women gained access to communal land, pasture, wood, and water. Further, according to colonial law married women needed permission from their husbands to engage in transactions involving property, even if the woman had acquired the property through her own labor or prior to marriage. In the absence of a husband, women had to ask authorization of the corregidor when they conducted transactions. In 1803, for example, Rosa

López had to receive permission from the corregidor to sell land left to her by her deceased husband.[74] In 1876, principales from Cantel accompanied María Francisca Hernández of Cantel to attest that she was a widow and approve the sale of her bequeathed land to her grandson, Juan Yac.[75] In addition to this, men had the privilege of controlling household income, often either lending women's earnings to other men or pledging women's property as collateral when borrowing.[76]

More than just producing gender inequality, these relations are key to understanding the city's economic transformation.[77] As described above, much of the city's credit—requisite to both the relative independence of K'iche' producers and the nascent formation of capitalist relations—passed through networks formed by women. Furthermore, because most women were deprived of the political power exercised by men to mobilize family or communal labor, they were often forced to sell houses or land left to them by fathers and husbands.[78] As with credit, these transactions hastened the commodification of community property. In 1801, for example, Micaela Salazar sold the house left to her by her deceased husband Nicolás Coyoy.[79] And in 1803, Rosa López, the aforementioned K'iche' widow, sold the 194 cuerdas on the outskirts of the city left to her by her husband, so she could "buy a small house in town to live, because she does not want to live alone in the fields and be exposed to danger."[80]

The balance between survival and ruin, especially precarious for single women, could easily be tipped by acts of nature. In 1773, Jacinta Nimatuj, widow of Lorenzo Cortés, lost the house left to her by her father when a plague killed sixteen tenants.[81] Left with no income from the residents and forty pesos in debt she owed to the Spaniard Antonia Barreto y Pompa, Nimatuj had no choice but to turn over the property.

The contradiction between women's dynamic economic activity and their inability to mobilize labor—at least to the degree that men could—is underscored in María Ygnacia Coyoy's 1840 will. Abandoned seven years earlier by her husband, who did not leave her "even one real," Coyoy was forced to sell her house "in order that she could feed herself."[82] She managed to make a living supplying limestone to construction projects through the labor of her adopted son Juan. In gratitude, Juan alone was to be her heir: "Not my husband" she stressed, "nor anybody else can dispute the property I have, since it was acquired by my work alone, as declared by a competent judge. My husband has no rights whatsoever to my goods." But even this asserted independence from her husband could not lead Coyoy to forsake her perceived obligations. In her will she stipulated that if there was ever notice that her husband was sick or suffered from some other misfortune, Juan was to go find him, bring him back to Quetzaltenango and "treat him as if he were his father."

Men

Some Quetzalteco K'iche' men were able to participate in the highest reaches of regional and city commerce. That they were able to do so was based on their ability to combine "Hispanic strategies of accumulation" with patriarchal caste power.[83] This combination afforded them a number of competitive advantages: as patriarchs, control over women's and children's labor subsidized their commercial activity, and access to subsistence production provided them refuge during hard times; as principales, they could apply communal resources to their private enterprises; and as political elites, they used their connections with Creole society to gain access to credit and markets not available to most commoners or women.

As political elites of an ethnically subordinate population, principales used their access to credit and capital to fund their economic activity. The 1801 merchandise inventory of Desidero Cayax, a K'iche' principal and merchant, included four barrels of Spanish wine, sixty-eight grosses of rope, twenty-four shoes made from Moroccan leather, six blankets, seventeen hats, and forty-six pounds of dye. Cayax owned a house worth three hundred pesos, fifty cuerdas of land, two horses, and a mule.[84] He supplemented his commercial enterprise with agricultural and textile production. This level of economic activity required a degree of investment that was usually only available from Spaniard or Creole creditors. For example, Cayax funded his 1801 corn harvest by contracting to provide five thousand ears (from a ten-thousand yield) to a Spaniard prior to the harvest. That same year Cayax capitalized his commercial activity by borrowing 400 pesos from two Spanish women, bringing his total debt to 665 pesos.[85] However, the gender subsidy that underwrote this activity became manifest with Cayax's death in 1803. Poverty-stricken, his widow, Teresa Mejía, was forced to sell their house to pay back his debts. Valued in 1801 at 300 pesos, the house was sold by Mejía to another K'iche' for 160 pesos.[86]

The most stunning example of indigenous enterprise, however, is the previously mentioned Anizeto López. López lived on the city's most prestigious street—a neighbor to some of Quetzaltenango's most powerful Creole residents—and served as K'iche' gobernador (highest community office held by an Indian) from 1786 to his death in 1804. His economic activity was diversified—he made money as a farmer and textile trader, and, it seems, as a land speculator, buying and selling property for a profit in the last years of his life. López's social connections and authority as gobernador allowed him access to commerce, land, and credit beyond the reach of most K'iche's.

At the time of his death, López owned property totaling over three hundred acres, as well as a number of city lots and houses.[87] The gendered nature of property transfer described above is to be seen in López's purchase in 1800 of a farm from the widow of don Diego Simón.[88] In 1803 he bought a house that contained a lien of 600 pesos to pay for masses for the soul of Sebastián Tzunún.[89] Perhaps drawing on his political ties with the city priest, López received a reduction in the chantry due the church, and he quickly resold the property to a Creole for 1,600 pesos.[90] Furthermore, López was apparently willing to use force to acquire land. In the closing years of his life and tenure, other K'iche's repeatedly charged López with abusing his political power to accumulate more property.[91] And in 1813, nine years after his death, his son, Manuel, was prevented from claiming five caballerías of his father's property. The royal fiscal ruled that the land was not purchased from Ladinos, as Manuel claimed, but from Indians intimidated into selling to López by "force and fear."[92]

López had access to large amounts of credit and capital to underwrite his ventures. At the time of his death, he controlled the funds of three cofradías, totaling 701 pesos.[93] He probably had some discretion in how this money was used. Further, as gobernador, López used his political and social connections to borrow from the city's most powerful residents. At the time of his death in 1804, López owed over 6,000 pesos to the city's wealthiest Creoles and Spaniards.[94]

López's will gives a limited, but telling, illustration of how debt was used to create patronage ties among the K'iche' population. Aside from the "great quantities" lent to his unnamed and unnumbered field hands mentioned above, López made a number of small loans ranging from 5 to 125 pesos to various individuals, most of whom were K'iche'. His benevolence continued after his death: López stipulated that his estate would assume the religious obligations of a number of impoverished women, such as the widow of Felipe Aguilar Tunai, who owed one cofradía thirteen pounds of wax and 60 pesos. In addition, he donated 900 pesos to the Cofradía Santísimo Sacramento for its fiesta and for an unspecified holy work.

López's demise again illustrates the degree to which K'iche' economic activity was predicated on patriarchal power: following his death, his children and wife had to sell off nearly all of his property to repay his loans.[95]

The consolidation of a community economy—including a political guarantee of substance, access to land, raw materials such as wool and cotton, markets, and credit, and patriarchal control over family resources—allowed indigenous agricultural and artisanal production to articulate with an expanding regional market. Community credit lessened dependence on Hispanic capital and allowed for flexible and secure relations of subsistence and commercial production. Access to land combined with a chronic labor shortage to provide agricultural workers with leverage in their dealings with planters. A growing urban economy absorbed many of those who fell through the filial safety net as either apprentices, servants, or market women. Thus, while evidence remains scarce, it appears that in the last decades of the eighteenth century the highland economy offered stable and at times beneficial material conditions to the city's K'iche' population.

The Not-So-Fragile Politics of Cultural Legitimacy

Across class and ethnic boundaries, Quetzaltecos participated in rituals and daily actions that gave meaning to a society structured around cultural authority, status, deference, and obligation. Despite this collective participation and despite the regulation of resources according to communal norms, there was no simple moral community. Quetzaltenango was a stratified, contested polity in which struggle created meaning. Competing factions, interests, and identities vied with each other to form cultural significance—all of which took place within a larger context of colonial domination and power.[96]

Politics

The indigenous municipal body of the city was simply composed.[97] Two K'iche' alcaldes and four regidores each served a term of one year. In addition to these six, one or two *síndicos*, a treasurer, and a scribe usually also served. Heading the cabildo was an indigenous gobernador, who held the office for an extended period that usually ended with his death. These municipal authorities were responsible for administering the K'iche' population of the city. They collected tribute, conducted censuses, conscripted labor for public and religious projects, and protected the social and moral welfare of the community by regulating resources and production and attempting to compel each member to fulfill his or her religious, familial, and social responsibility.[98]

The selection of all K'iche' officers except the gobernador was made by the larger body of principales, which convened once a year, usually in December. While Spanish documents refer to the yearly convocation as an election, consensus rather than voting was used to choose new officers. To become an alcalde, principales had to have earned the respect of their peers not only through years of service as *cofrades* (members of a cofradía) and regidores but also by their political acumen as defenders of K'iche' interest within colonial society. After the selection, the new cabildo had to be approved by the priest and the corregidor.

The gobernador was chosen by the corregidor. The qualifications needed to hold this office were similar to those required to become an alcalde. The position usually capped a long career of religious and municipal service to the community. Under Hapsburg rule, moral rectitude and the ability to ensure that Indians fulfilled their religious obligations were important qualifications, at least rhetorically, for governorship. Bourbon corregidors, however, chose principales whom they felt, to put it simply, they could work with.[99] Three criteria filled this requirement: Spanish proficiency, sobriety, and "ability to reason." In 1780, for example, when the corregidor nominated Manuel Silverio as gobernador, he noted that Silverio spoke Spanish along with his "mother tongue," did not drink, and, as a result, was "very rational."[100] Silverio's nomination was facilitated by his recent marriage to the widow of the former gobernador. Again, gender dependency underwrote caste power, this time in the political sphere.

By the late colonial period, social relations in Quetzaltenango experienced what Rodolfo Pastor has identified in his study of the Mixteca region of Mexico as "macehualization," the process by which the rigid political division within the indigenous común broke down. Caciques (indigenous nobility) lost political power and became absorbed in larger bodies of principales; divisions within the community drove principales to ally themselves with macehuales, who, in turn, took advantage of this new flexibility to advance themselves politically and economically.[101] In Quetzaltenango, by the beginning of the eighteenth century, principales and macehuales had become the two politically salient social groups in the K'iche' community.[102] By this time, the classification "cacique" had ceased to exist in the city. Principal status was hereditary (male children of principales were considered principales and female children usually married into elite families), but new channels opened up that allowed macehuales to gain access to political power. Commoners who provided service to the Crown could improve their social position. Nicolás Quijivix, for instance, after helping to "pacify" the famous Cancuk Maya rebellion in Chiapas (1708–13) became a principal.[103] Perhaps owing to the marginal importance of the repartimiento in and around the city, royal officials were not particularly careful about maintaining a sharp divide between commoners and principales.[104] Further, as the colonial process wore on, commoners increasingly took advantage of divisions among indigenous elites to advance their positions, as we shall see in following chapters.

Culture

In nearly every aspect of daily life, cultural authority was displayed and enacted, ironically and precariously, by an adhesion to Spanish norms and practices. Religious rituals were especially pregnant with ideological content. At the beginning of every year, the selection of the new indigenous cabildo was solemnized with a mass and a Te Deum. K'iche' elites sat in the front of the church, in order to differentiate "principales from macehuales."[105] Principales demonstrated their social status by funding and serving the city's most prestigious and wealthy cofradías, whose processions they would lead, dressed in regal ceremonial dress, through the streets. The altars of the most elite cofradías surrounded the central nave of the cathedral, while poorer confraternities kept their icons and shrines either in one of the four barrio churches or in private homes.

After a person's death, ritualized distinction continued through memorial rites and practices. Cofradías served as burial societies, and wealthy confraternities, augmented by money left by their departed cofrades, hosted elaborate funerals that reinforced the social importance of the deceased.[106] Likewise, one's final resting place was governed by social

6. Cofradía del Niño Salvador del Mundo, c. 1900. *Photograph by Tomás Zanotti, courtesy of Museo Girard.*

status. Until the beginning of the nineteenth century principales were usually entombed in the church proper whereas macehuales were buried in the churchyard.[107] Even care of the soul was ranked by status. Principales bequeathed longer-lasting chantries for annual masses than did macehuales.[108]

Clothing played an important part in the construction of Quetzalteco identity.[109] By the middle of the nineteenth century, the quality and intricate design of principal women's huipiles, shawls, and pleated dresses increasingly set them apart from poorer Quetzaltecas. Male principales wore Spanish-style cotton trousers, lapelled jackets and shoes, gradually giving up the daily use of accessories that symbolized indigenous culture (for example, waist belts and head scarves). In contrast, commoners dressed in coarse cotton or wool trousers and simple shirts or ponchos, and they wore sandals or went barefoot. For ceremonial occasions men attired themselves in European-style velvet or cloth blue cloaks, sashes, and wide-brimmed felt hats while women donned special tunics, hair wraps, and veils. A few of the wealthier K'iche' men sported waist swords and rode horses. Many K'iche's affected the Spanish use of "don" and "doña," while some, such as Francisco Xavier Cojulún y Aguilar, adopted the Hispanic practice of multiple and / or hyphenated surnames.

Wealthy K'iche's tended to live in the urban center: they owned houses in one of the four barrios while maintaining farms in the city's hinterlands. The closer one lived to the plaza, among the Creoles, the more prestigious was one's position. Increasingly throughout the late eighteenth and nineteenth centuries, the homes of principales matched those of Spaniards in size and luxury.[110] Anizeto López, for instance, lived in a large walled house, with a patio, multiple rooms, and a separate kitchen, which he purchased from a Spaniard. Tiles replaced the straw thatch and dirt floors of indigenous residences. Starting in the nineteenth century, Indians in the town's center made numerous requests to the municipality to be supplied with their own water wells, and then, later in the century, they petitioned to have water piped directly to their houses.[111] The wills and inventories of principales show that they slept in beds and used other European-style furniture such as tables, dressers, desks, and chests. Poorer macehuales—shepherds and milpa farmers—lived in the city's rural confines, in one-room wood or adobe-thatched houses. Those who did live in the city proper either owned or rented a small house, or they rented a room in a larger residential complex. Creole descriptions of Indians' living conditions often lamented their unhealthy habit of sleeping on the dirt floor, on straw *petates* (mats), and breathing in the smoke from their wood stoves.[112]

Mastery, or at least its approximation, of the Spanish language was a crucial component of the cultural authority of principales. Spanish proficiency, however, entailed not just the ability to speak and perhaps read and write the language of the dominant caste but also knowledge of how to deploy that language effectively. In Quetzaltenango, K'iche' principales—"well versed in Castellano," according to the corregidor in 1683—learned early in the colonial process how to use the Spanish legal and rhetorical tradition in their numerous petitions, contracts, and wills.[113]

Language was part of a cycle of legitimization and power by which interaction with colonial society increased the proficiency of principales. This yielded greater success in their economic and political dealings with Spaniards and Creoles, which in turn reinforced their linguistic and political knowledge. Those excluded from significant interaction—macehuales and women—became caught up in a converse cycle of political dependency and economic disempowerment. Their relative lack of engagement with the dominant group perpetuated not only a linguistic analphabetism but also a political illiteracy that deepened their isolation and dependency on patriarchs. Spanish proficiency among a select group of patriarchs permitted access to political and economic power, and legitimated that power through gender and class dependency in the cultural realm.

K'iche commoners and women were attuned to this cycle and participated in rituals of deference and dependency to press their interests. In 1815, for example, following the arrest of their macehual husbands for participation in a plaza riot, unnamed women wrote a petition to the corregidor defending their husbands.[114] Contrasted with the assured letters of principales—usually written in crisp handwriting by an indigenous scribe and replete with signatures bearing ornate Spanish-style paraphs—the letters of the anonymous women were simple and tentative, reflecting their aforementioned unfamiliarity with Spanish procedure. The letters were not dated or signed, and the women's names were not even listed by a scribe. Nevertheless, the petition contained a clear analytical discussion of the facts leading up to the protest as evidence as to why their husbands were innocent. Upon receiving no response, the women wrote two more, increasingly desperate appeals: "We have been left alone to tend to our crops and houses, our animals and work, selling what we can in order to be able to eat and maintain our husbands in prison. We have no one to defend us or take care of us. We beg you with all submissiveness to take up our cause anew . . . in order that our husbands might leave prison and you might treat us with piety and compassion as our protector."[115]

Not only do the women represent themselves as having no one to care for them, but they paint a picture of a subverted natural order—with them now providing for their jailed husbands—in order to elicit patriarchal charity. The absence of a scribe and the silence of the K'iche' cabildo suggest that the women were indeed alone in their efforts to free their husbands (principales denied participating in the riot and blamed the disturbance on commoners). Without other recourse, the anonymous women quickly abandoned their reasoned attempts to defend their husbands and engaged in an expected performance of gendered submissiveness.

In another petition composed eighty years later (this one supported by K'iche' authorities and written by a scribe), 257 K'iche' women protested new municipal taxes on market stalls: "All of our husbands are in the militia. When necessary, they will go to war without any complaints, secure in the knowledge that their wives will be able to support themselves and their children by working in the market. But if the new municipal tax forces us out of the market, we will have to do a thousand things merely in order to survive."[116]

Both these petitions, as well as the aforementioned will of María Ygnacia Coyoy, reveal the degree to which communal relations were structured by gender ideology and control. Women, therefore, were forced to reconcile assumptions of female helplessness with their in fact indispensable role in community and family reproduction so as to press their interests.

Legitimacy

Public manifestations of social prominence, as well as everyday forms of unrecorded deference by which K'iche' women and commoners acknowledged the authority and rank of principales, were part of how Quetzaltecos organized their world. Principales exercised that authority, as we saw earlier, not just as patriarchs—controlling resources for individual, family, and communal production—but as public officers: alcaldes, gobernadores, and judges.

As municipal officers, K'iche' principales had the responsibility to provide workers for the numerous public projects required by a fast-growing city. These projects included maintenance of the church and other public buildings, the yearly repair of roads, bridges, and drains during the dry season, and construction of the city aqueduct. As the city grew, the K'iche' alcaldes enlisted a corps of municipal *auxiliares* (volunteers)— forest sentries (*guardabosques*), night patrollers, and auxiliary alcaldes from rural *cantones*—to help protect communal land, keep order, and administer the city's rural areas. These positions were voluntary in the sense that they entailed no salary but obligatory in that all male heads of households were expected to serve.[117]

Indigenous authorities were also responsible for auditing communal funds and raising revenue. Aside from controlling the cabildo treasury, the gobernador kept a written account of the revenue of all the city's indigenous cofradías. Likewise, he and the alcaldes were responsible for collecting and paying the tribute as well as other local or imperial taxes. In turn, control of these funds reinforced the communal authority of principales, since money from the treasury and (following independence) cofradías was used during times of famine and disease to insure survival and administer relief.

Even as labor repartimientos diminished in importance, indigenous alcaldes retained the power to conscript haulers for private needs.[118] Nineteenth-century travel literature often vividly describes the tired and dusty European travelers who, landing in some remote pueblo, seek out the alcalde to announce their arrival and secure a mule and a few indigenous *cargadores* (haulers) for the next leg of their trip, for which they were to pay the legal rate.[119] In 1840, for example, John Stephens recounts how the Indians he hired through the alcalde were placed in jail by the indigenous authorities (incidentally, only a few weeks after Carrera's arrival in Quetzaltenango), thereby ensuring they would be available for the next day's trip.[120]

As part of their responsibilities as municipal officers, K'iche' alcaldes served as judges and had the power to adjudicate community matters.[121] K'iche' judges penalized drunks and workers who fled from labor obligations, arbitrated minor personal conflicts, and refereed family and communal disputes according to patriarchal norms. Their authority allowed them to jail rapists, adulterers, and men and women who abandoned their family. After independence, the alcaldes executed their power through the network of auxiliares. Patrols from the four barrios or the rural cantones were responsible for reporting any instance of impropriety or disorder; guardabosques were expected to defend the town's communal land. Auxiliares were responsible for insuring that those summoned in their jurisdiction appeared in the indigenous *juzgado* (court).

The extent of their authority is illustrated in a case from 1870, when the gobernador and alcaldes jailed Saturnino Pisquiy.[122] Pisquiy protested to the corregidor that he had been arbitrarily kept in jail by the "alcaldes of my class" for nearly a month, "with chains on my feet" and under the constant threat of being whipped, because he was financially unable to take on any more cofradía *cargos* (positions, or obligations).[123] He had already served in four of the city's fraternities, spending over 800 pesos and owing another 150. The corregidor sided with the K'iche' principales, ruling that Pisquiy had been placed in jail not for refusing to serve on cofradías but for unwillingness to serve as an alcalde auxiliar. Whatever the truth in this case, it illustrates that indigenous authorities had considerable latitude in dispensing justice as they saw fit, with the expectation that their rulings would be upheld if appealed. Whether it be for cofradía or municipal service, communal obligation was subject to judicial enforcement backed by threat of arbitrary incarceration.

The ability of the principales to mobilize resources and exercise authority was double-sided. It rested not only on an economic, political, and cultural adhesion to Spanish society but was also predicated on the maintenance of relations of obligation and deference. Principales, particularly municipal officers, had to walk a fine line between the Spanish world, which granted them political power, and the K'iche' world, which allowed them to exercise it.[124] Obedience to and respect for K'iche' authorities were conditioned on the fulfillment of certain expectations. These expectations—provision and support during times of crisis, defense of the común's interest (which often included struggles not only with Spaniards and Ladinos but also with surrounding indigenous communities), and administration of power in a just and accepted way—became increasingly difficult to fulfill as the eighteenth century wore on.[125]

The complex nature of this authority and power are illustrated by an example from 1783, when the K'iche' gobernador, Manuel Silverio, tried to conscript labor to construct a parish house and repair the church building.[126] The work stalled as Silverio ran into opposition. Other Indians complained that Silverio worked too closely with the corregidor and did not represent their interests, "for being a Ladino," that is, for not being a full-blooded K'iche'.[127] They not only objected to the requests for labor but chafed at the temperance campaign that Silverio, with the backing of the corregidor, had been waging. A street fight took place between Silverio and two principales, Juan Estacuy and Yldefonso Estrada, in which the two dismissed the gobernador's labor demands as a "joke" and threatened that "with little concern they would cut off four heads," apparently Silverio's and the corregidor's being two of them.[128] When Silverio tried to have the two principales arrested, they scoffed, claimed that he lacked the authority to do so, and continued on to the square. Upon arriving at the center of the plaza, a scuffle broke out, soldiers were summoned, and Estacuy and Estrada were arrested.

This anecdote would appear to be a clear example of the fragility of power based on cultural legitimization. Ridiculed and dismissed as a Ladino, Silverio lost credibility with his peers and had to rely on royal soldiers to enforce his authority. Indeed, in the interrogation of the principales that followed, the corregidor focused his questions on why the principales laughed at their gobernador and refused to let themselves be arrested. But the meaning of the conflict is more complex than this. The recent migration into the pueblo had opened the community up to greater commercial exploitation. Silverio was indeed allied with the corregidor, but it was chiefly an alliance formed to counter the power of a recently arrived cohort of Spaniards. These Spaniards in turn joined with another group of K'iche's—Estacuy and Estrada among them—who were opposed to Silverio. The resulting tensions would explode in 1786.

Despite the enthusiasm with which many K'iche's pursued economic self-interest and despite the commodification of indigenous staples and resources, a number of factors created a slow, uneven transformation to a class society. Throughout most of the nineteenth century, subsistence rights, although increasingly restricted, mitigated the effects of the market and permitted Indians to engage with the larger colonial economy on their own terms, allowing them to withdraw from or supplement market relations. Further, a heavy reliance on credit coupled with gender inequality often led to the rapid dissolution of a lifetime of acquired capital and property. Likewise, pressure from macehuales to remain loyal to the común, as we will see in the next chapter, could limit efforts of principales to accumulate private wealth. Principales were susceptible to these pressures from below because of their need to maintain cultural legitimacy—a crucial prerequisite for their successful participation in the regional economy.

As long as a "bedrock of subsistence rights" existed, production could remain centered around cultural patterns of communal and patriarchal relations, themselves predicated on and situated within a larger caste system that formed the political heart of Spanish colonialism.[129] Tensions and conflicts (both among K'iche's and between Spaniards and K'iche's), which inevitably resulted from the commodification of social relations, could erupt without any dramatic changes in those cultural patterns. And as long as access to subsistence production allayed these tensions, principales could devote their energy to defending their political power, which they had to do with ever increasing frequency as royal power waned.

Highland society was changing rapidly. Spain was growing weaker and local Creoles stronger. The rising Creole class had political aspirations, and the Crown was not the only obstacle in its way.

Chapter 2
Defending the Pueblo: Popular Protests and Elite Politics, 1786–1826

We do not have anyone to defend the pueblo, so we are going to have to defend it ourselves. —*Macehual appraisal*, 1786

They say that we have betrayed the pueblo. —*Principal defense*, 1813

During the last half century of Spanish rule, K'iche' elites witnessed a slow but continuous erosion of their political power. While caste autonomy was more the ideal than the norm, it was the very ideal of ethnic sovereignty and cultural division that allowed K'iche' principales their economic and political power. In the last decades of the colonial period, this ideal was threatened in three ways. First, as the city grew, both from immigration and a rise in population, mestizaje created new social groups that proportionally decreased the number of people principales had under their political control. Second, as Creoles consolidated their position as a regional elite, they challenged principales for control of the city's economic resources. Creoles literally built their city around the K'iche' común, isolating the principales and limiting their political power. Finally, ideological and legal changes brought about by imperial tensions during the last decades of Spanish rule abolished the corporate protection afforded indigenous subjects. Following the Cortes de Cádiz (the Spanish liberal parliament established in 1809) and independence, Indians became citizens with supposedly the same rights and freedoms as Creoles.

This chapter will examine how K'iche' commoners and elites responded to these changes, and in so doing "defended their pueblo." A central argument running throughout this study is that as a changing, increasingly commodified, economy disrupted communal relations, K'iche' elites came to rely to an ever increasing extent on the state to maintain their caste power and privilege. This produced an apparently contradictory effect: ethnic identity deepened while state power increased. This chapter explores the colonial roots of this dynamic. As their communal authority weakened, principales came to depend on alliances with nonindigenous elites to an ever greater extent. These alliances went well beyond the simple need for force to keep order, although this, too, certainly was important. These elite pacts were predicated on the continuance of ethnic division. Principales used the language of community, increasingly backed up by imperial and then national power, not only to maintain their caste privilege in relation to commoners but also in their struggles against opposing factions of K'iche' elites.[1] For their part, macehuales themselves allied with the city's non-K'iche' plebeian population and used communal ideologies—the source of principales's authority—to press their interests.[2] This is how community identity thrived while communal relations fractured.

Defending the Pueblo I: The Riot of 1786

Demographic Change

By the late colonial period, Quetzaltenango had ceased resembling anything approximating a closed-corporate Indian-peasant community. Its rise as a regional commercial hub attracted Europeans, Creoles, Mestizos, and other Indians. Fugitives and exiles from Guatemala's central valley found their way to Los Altos, and traders and artisans from Genoa and France as well as other Latin American countries set up shop. Following the 1773 earthquake, many moved to the highland city rather than participate in the difficult construction of a new capital.[3] Between 1689 and 1770, the city's non-Indian population increased over 1,000 percent (see Table 1). Indians likewise migrated to Quetzaltenango to take advantage of increased economic activities and, possibly, to avoid or satisfy tribute, demanded in coin since 1747, to the Bourbon state. In 1755, out of a total of 675 indigenous families, 223 included spouses not born in the city.[4] This immigration supplemented a slow rise in population that followed the demographic collapse brought about by the conquest. In 1689, Quetzaltenango's population was 2,650. By 1830, it had nearly tripled, to 7,632.

The percentage of the city's population considered K'iche' decreased at a rate greater than can be explained by intermarriage. (The 1737 census listed 27 "mixed" marriages.)[5] In a growing frontier town removed from the efficient enforcement of colonial power, non-Indians from the

Table 1 Population of the City of Quetzaltenango, by
Ethnicity (1689–1840)

Year	Spanish/Ladino	K'iche'	Total
1689	150	2,500	2,650
1770	1,539	2,589	4,128
1813	4,143	4,174	8,317
1817	NA	4,485	NA
1830	4,241	3,391	7,632
1840	3,298	4,149	7,442

Source: See Grandin, "Blood," Appendix 11, for a discussion of
the sources of these counts.

lower classes often found themselves free from political and economic
demands.[6] K'iche' authorities exercised much greater control of their
portion of the city's population than did their Spanish counterparts. Indians who wished to be considered Ladino so as to avoid tribute and labor
obligations undoubtedly took advantage of the confusion brought about
by high rates of indigenous and nonindigenous immigration and intermarriage. Of the 4,143 non-Indians in 1813, 3,310 were considered acculturated Indians. Pedro Ysqueregua, for example, in 1765 presented to the
indigenous alcaldes a legal document signed by the city scribe declaring
that he was—"far from being a *tributario*"—a Ladino.[7] Joseph Saquiel,
again in 1765, argued that his wife, Antonia Coyoy, was a Mestiza, perhaps hoping their children would be exempt from caste obligations.[8]
Further, the growing number of K'iche' servants employed in nonindigenous households undoubtedly led to shifting cultural identity. Likewise many Indians, both men and women, emigrated from Quetzaltenango, either in search of work or a spouse, or in an effort to avoid tribute
payment. In 1765, 212 Quetzalteco K'iche's lived outside the town's
jurisdiction.[9]

The economic, political, and social changes brought about by this
demographic shift led to a rise of popular anxiety, a breakdown of communal leadership, and a realignment of class relations. Even prior to the
riot, principales must have realized the threat that these demographic
changes posed to their power. Not only was the number of non-Indians
increasing but a large percentage of those who were Indian were not from

Quetzaltenango, and hence not as closely obligated to the political authority of principales. Indian tributaries from other pueblos, for example, were only required to pay one-half of the tribute to which Quetzalteco K'iche's were subject.[10]

To the Plaza

The central plaza was the heart of the city. Within it, Quetzaltecos conducted their daily trade and held their weekly market surrounded by buildings in which elites, both Spanish and K'iche', exercised religious, political, and judicial authority. On the plaza stood the parish church, Espíritu Santo, its burial grounds, and its cloisters; the home and office of the corregidor and other bureaucrats; the royal court, barracks, and jail; the K'iche' cabildo; retail stores; and, after 1806, the Creole ayuntamiento. On its surrounding streets, wealthy Creoles and K'iche's maintained large homes that were both rewards and displays of their wealth and power.

To move closer to the plaza was a political act, as when Gobernador Anizeto López purchased his house on San Nicolás Street, thereby becoming neighbor to the city's most illustrious residents.[11] To move closer to the plaza could also provoke ethnic resentment, such as occurred in 1778 when Domingo Gutiérrez Marroquín, a recently arrived Spaniard and militia captain, purchased a house just east of the plaza from the heirs of principal Manuel García Ixcot.[12] On finding masons extending the building's foundation four yards into the street, K'iche' authorities vociferously objected to this expansion, "as if the street belonged to him." It was around the plaza that orphaned or widowed women, such as Rosa López, set up market stalls or became domestic servants in the wealthy central residences; it was where both military parades and religious processions marched; it was in the plaza that Indians ritualized the conquest in masked dances; it was where criminals were whipped and, occasionally, executed, political pronouncements were read, and riots broke out. And it was in the central plaza that a crowd of more than 1,500 men and women, K'iche's, Mestizos, and Spaniards gathered in the early morning of 19 April 1786 to present a petition to the corregidor, Fernando Corona.

The immediate cause of the protest was to demand the expulsion from the city of three recently arrived Spaniards—Joseph Rodríguez, Domingo Gutiérrez Marroquín (the same who thought he owned the street), and

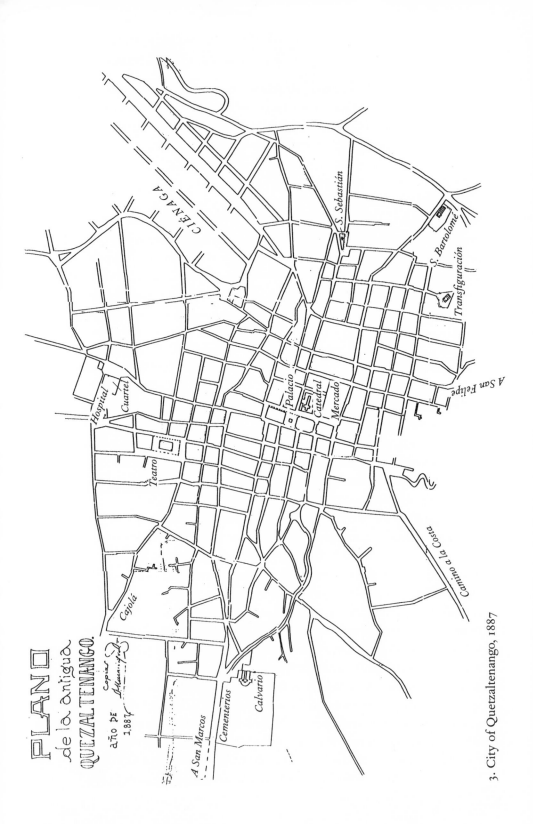

3. City of Quetzaltenango, 1887

Pedro Maceyras—who had recently purchased the right to administer the royal liquor monopoly. After the corregidor begged them to understand that he lacked the authority to issue such an order, the crowd rioted.

In the late 1770s, the Crown attempted to regulate *aguardiente* (bootleg distilled cane liquor) by auctioning production and distribution monopolies—*asientos*—to the highest bidder. In March 1785, the Audiencia granted a five-year contract to Joseph Rodríguez, who then went into business with Gutiérrez Marroquín and Maceyras. With the exclusive right to distill and sell liquor came also the responsibility (and will) to suppress clandestine production, which the three partners did with a vengeance.[13] Rodríguez himself led patrols that broke into the houses of suspected bootleggers, "in the name of the king."[14] "Flying squads" stopped women on the streets and searched their baskets.[15] Any signs of distillation or sale—stills, large pots, furnaces, bottles—were grounds for further persecution. Individuals were sent to jail and property was confiscated. Paulino Silverio, Manuel's brother, for example, was arrested for bootlegging, and his house, livestock, furniture, corn, and wheat were seized.

City alcohol production cut across ethnic, class, and gender lines, and resentment toward the *asentistas* (monopolists) quickly became widespread.[16] Many were affected by the crackdown on bootleg production: poorer K'iche's and Ladinos who produced aguardiente in their homes;[17] women who sold the liquor from their doorways or the market (of the seventeen recorded arrests during Rodríguez's tenure, nine were of women); Spaniards and Indians who milled panela (sugar loaves made from the blackish residue of refined cane); Indian men who carried the loaves into the city, either from the coast or the cane-growing lowlands of the Verapaces; and wealthy Spaniards—such as the corregidor Fernando Corona—now cut out of the profitable liquor trade.

Rodríguez's house and store were the first sacked. After relieving his guards of their weapons, the crowd broke the windows and doors and robbed merchandise, aguardiente, and money. A Mestizo silversmith rolled a barrel of Rodríguez's liquor into the plaza and smashed it open, yelling that this was what he was going to do to all three asentistas.[18] Seven liquor warehouses, a number of taverns, and the houses and stores of the other two monopolists were looted. Liquor was spilled out into the street; plates and bottles were shattered; and money and goods were robbed. A large number of the rioters then broke off from the crowd and walked two leagues to Maceyras's hacienda and distillery, looting it as well. After the initial round of plunder, a crowd conducted a search of the warehouses, looking for "barrels of the King's liquor."[19] Along the way, the group came upon the royal tax collector and his guard and said that soon they were going to "do away with all *alcabaleros* (tax collectors)." Lacking military support, Corona acceded to the petition and ordered the expulsion of the three.[20]

The next day, two Indians were found beaten to death in the woods near Maceyras's hacienda. The bodies were brought back to the city and laid on the church patio, and more than one thousand K'iche' men and women began to assemble. Leaders of the crowd insisted that the victims had been killed by employees of Maceyras and that if the corregidor would not punish those responsible, they would "relieve the corregidor of his scepter in order to teach him how to administer justice."[21] They also threatened to riot again, this time "against all."[22] The corregidor sent a detachment of militia to arrest the hacienda workers (none were found) and released the bodies to the crowd for burial. Another near riot occurred later in the day when a K'iche' started beating on a drum in the church plaza, summoning a crowd of "*indios y indias.*" After a half hour of milling in the plaza, the crowd dispersed. The following day, another group of Indians showed up at the corregidor's office, demanding the confiscation of Maceyras's property to compensate the widows of the two murdered Indians. Later, militia reinforcements arrived from Huehuetenango and order was restored.

The King's Liquor

In the years preceding the riot, tensions in the town had deepened to the point that factions of principales battled each other in the streets and in the courts.[23] Rodríguez, Gutiérrez, and Maceyras were recent arrivals to the city. Gutiérrez, for example, arrived from Santiago just after the 1773 earthquake.[24] With access to capital and political connections, they were among the most powerful and ambitious of the eighteenth-century newcomers to the city and represented for many Quetzaltecos the worst effects of this migration. They, along with a number of others, were accused of speculation in wheat and corn, driving up the prices of other necessities, forcing Indians to sell property, diverting town water for their cattle, and taking over pasture and woodland.[25]

When the Audiencia first ordered the establishment of the asiento in

1784, Corona stalled, possibly because of his own interest in the aguardiente trade. He begged for clarification: he inquired whether the asiento policy, which according to the royal regulations was only to be established in Spanish communities, was perhaps not applicable in Quetzaltenango, which was legally still a pueblo de indios.[26] Once the monopoly was established, Corona complained of the increase in drunkenness and accused the asentistas of intentionally promoting dependency by plying poor Indians with liquor and credit.[27] He closed down one tavern after finding two Indians passed out on the floor.[28] Gutiérrez in turn accused Corona of resenting him as a business competitor and of encouraging the K'iche' gobernador Manuel Silverio to file charges against him.[29] In 1781, Silverio complained to the Audiencia that Gutiérrez was a "smuggler of various products" and that he tricked Indians into selling him land.[30] He asked that Gutiérrez be expelled from town.

The asentistas likewise cultivated indigenous support. Rodríguez turned over goods confiscated from bootleggers to Indians who served as witnesses when he presented his accusations.[31] Corona, Silverio, and others charged Gutiérrez and Rodríguez with provoking a group of eighteen principales—including Juan Estacuy and Yldefonso Estrada, who two years earlier picked a street fight with Silverio (see chap. 1)—to file a suit against the cabildo in 1785.[32] The suit charged that the gobernador was fomenting opposition to the asiento, and that he conspired with Corona to enrich himself by making unfair labor demands. The opposing principales went on to demand that he be removed from his office because he was not fully indigenous. After consulting birth records, the judge ruled that Silverio was indeed a Mestizo and removed him from office.

Flushed with victory, this same group of principales, in December 1785, elected Estacuy as first alcalde.[33] Corona refused to recognize the results and convened another vote, which elected a cabildo headed by Francisco Cojulún, Silverio's associate and former scribe. The principales who elected Estacuy immediately declared that they would not obey the new cabildo.[34] Because of the split común, the matter was sent to a royal judge, who ruled in favor of Corona and Cojulún.

Cleansing the Town

On the first day at least, the riot was not a homogeneous "*motín de indios*" (Indian riot) but rather an orchestrated protest comprised of men and women, Indians, Ladinos, Mestizos, and even a few Spaniards. As one witness described it, there were "a million souls of both sexes and all classes demanding in a single voice that the three leave town."[35] Following the riot, of thirty-four prisoners arrested whose ethnicity was noted, fifteen were listed as Mestizos, ten as Spaniards, three as castizas, three as Ladinos, and two as Indians.[36] The majority of the prisoners represented the nonindigenous artisanal sector of the city. Of the occupations listed, there were seven manufacturers of course wool cloth, five weavers, two tailors, two farmers, one baker, one silversmith, one painter, one trader, one rancher, one swineherd, and one tanner. At least three were bootleggers, including one who claimed he made aguardiente only to support his blind mother and one whose house and other property had been confiscated by Rodríguez.[37]

What was most frightening to the authorities, however, was the large number of milicianos who took part in planning and carrying out the riot.[38] Twenty-eight of those arrested were soldiers in the militia, including two sergeants and three corporals. Florencio Cancinos, a captain of a militia unit, was found guilty of being the "chief leader of the riot" and sentenced to death. His body was to be decapitated and his head, along with the offending petition, hung from a pike in the plaza. Eleven of the twelve accused "second heads" of the riot were militia soldiers, who were likewise sentenced to death.[39] Except for the officers, all the soldiers were identified as Mestizos or Ladinos, and all were occupied in the kind of small crafts and trades mentioned above. The importance of militias in maintaining colonial order rested in more than their ability to repress dissent. Military rank, even that of a simple militia volunteer—with its privileges, exemptions, and status—served to divide the lower classes along caste lines.[40] That so many Ladino members of the militia were willing to ally themselves with Indians undoubtedly unnerved Spanish authorities and explains the harsh sentences.

If read carefully, the lengthy defense of the militia captain, Cancinos, who had been charged with organizing the protest, provides evidence of how commoners responded to the opening up of Quetzaltenango's economy and population.[41] Cancinos admitted to being the leader of the protest. He claimed that on 16 February he was out rounding up a few stray heads of his cattle when he came upon a large crowd of Indians on the outskirts of town. When he asked what the meeting was about, the macehuales apparently responded with a long disquisition on changes in the political and cultural economy of the town since the influx of *forasteros* (migrants). Cancinos included their complaints in his defense. Of course, Cancinos's account has to be approached with some skepticism. Whatever the Indians did or did not say was filtered through the imperatives of Cancinos's defense, his prejudices, months of memory, and the rhetorical demands of narration. Yet given the specificity of complaints listed in his petition and their agreement with both the events surrounding the riot and the charges levied by other individuals, Cancinos's retelling of macehual anger rings true. The leaders of the meeting reportedly began:

> You well know, señor, that our pueblo was rich and all was well. The plaza was always well supplied. Wheat cost six reales a *fanega*, fifty or sixty ears of corn for half a real, ten or twelve eggs for half a real, good bread, good meat, all was cheap, a load of wood cost one real. But now . . . everything is in ruins. All is lost when you see during harvest time six ears of corn being sold for half a real, wheat for four pesos . . . a pound of beef, which is not always available, for half a peso, three eggs for half a real, a load of wood for three to four reales.

According to Cancinos, the macehuales blamed "those who come from outside of town" for hoarding, speculation, and driving up prices. "Yes there is corn, but I am not going to sell it to you," the newcomers tell them. They continued, "All is lost and very poor in town. And why? Because of . . . Gutiérrez, Maceyras, La Francesa [Gutiérrez's wife] . . . El Capuchino [Rodríguez's nickname] . . . José Carballo [the tax collector threatened during the riot] and many other forasteros. They have taken our land, our houses, our money."

The monopolists had set up their taverns "as if this were Guatemala City." The macehuales charged the asentistas with adding the bark from "who knows what tree and maguey" to the liquor and observed that many Indians had died from the cheap and lethal quality of aguardiente that was being sold.

With no prohibition against drinking as in the past, the macehuales went on, it was easy to take advantage of Indians. Gutiérrez would entice them with liquor: " 'Here is a nice drink. How much do you want? You are a good man.' La Francesa was worse: 'Come here my friend. Look what good aguardiente. Is it true that you have lands? Is it true that you want to sell them? Sell them to me. Take this drink.' That is how they took our money and land."

The macehuales, again, according to Cancinos, claimed that through intimidation and deception the asentistas had taken much of the town's commons. Maceyras's hacienda, which would soon be looted, used to belong to the común, "where we poor maintained ourselves, where we earned money to pay the tribute." Through threats and force, Maceyras purchased it from a previous cabildo for a mere twenty-five pesos. They charged Gutiérrez with doing the same with another tract of woodland, and with acquiring the house he tried to expand off the plaza through deception, by paying the heirs of Manuel García Ixcot ten pesos in cash and thirty in liquor.

Through it all, the macehuales lamented, their principales had failed to defend the community's interest. Past cabildos had been duped out of large amounts of land, and soon, "what has happened with the town's mesón (hotel for travelers) will happen" with their remaining forest land. Rodríguez and Maceyeras plied the alcaldes with drinks, and when the principales "opened their eyes, the mesón belonged to Maceyras." They accused the asentistas of raising up six or seven "half principales" to challenge Silverio's authority. These "traitors" were given free food, liquor, money, and gifts such as capes and silk tobacco purses. The Indians singled out Anizeto López, who later would be installed as gobernador, as having particularly noxious dealings with the asentistas.

Cancinos went on to relate a number of other lesser injustices. No water was reaching the town's fountains because Gutiérrez was diverting it for his cattle; Carballo, the tax collector, was trying to collect taxes from plaza traders before they sold their goods rather than after, as was the custom; he was also confiscating merchandise and jailing those who refused to comply; and, finally, the asentistas were paying their field-workers one and a half reales a day, rather than the previous prevailing daily wage of two reales.

Now that the asentistas had managed to remove the gobernador from office, the crowd threatened, "Los pobres macehuales do not have anyone to defend the pueblo . . . and we are going to have to defend it ourselves." Cancinos wrote that the leaders of the gathering revealed to him their plan to kill every newcomer to the city on the night of Sábado de Gloria (Easter Sunday eve): "We will go from house to house of the forasteros, whether they are Indians or not, break down the doors and kill them . . . only natives will remain, and those that escape will run to their own pueblos in order that the pueblo is cleansed (*para que quede el pueblo limpio*).'' Cancinos claimed that he talked the leaders out of the massacre by evoking the holiness of Easter and that he came up with the alternative of demanding the expulsion of the three asentistas. This is how he became the reluctant organizer of the protest.

Our Leaders Are Good for Nothing

Notwithstanding Cancinos's claims of having forestalled a massacre, the petition when read against other evidence indicates that the riot indeed was driven more by macehual anger than by principal leadership. According to most accounts, while the principales allied with Corona did help organize the original demonstration, once the petition was delivered to the corregidor, the leaders of the protest lost control of the crowd. Popular anger erupted in a multiethnic riot that, according to Cancinos's defense, shocked those who organized the protest. In the days following the riot, the cabildo asked for legal certification that "not one principal" participated in the protest, and he blamed the disturbance on Ladinos and macehuales.[42] In fact, the cabildo went on, it was the principales who, after the death of the two Indians, calmed the crowd down and prevented further violence. The corregidor confirmed their claims, noting that he did not see one blue cape—the kind usually worn by principales—during the riot.[43]

In the wake of a failure of communal leadership, macehuales took matters into their own hands. The riot was directed not only at those of the ruling caste but at their own leaders as well—leaders who had ceased to be "good for anything (*no servan para nada*)."[44] Commoners expected defense and justice from their leaders. These expectations not only permeated Cancinos's account of macehual criticisms of their alcaldes but were reflected in their actions during the riot. After finding the bodies of the two dead K'iche's, a gathering crowd (which testimony indicates was all indigenous) demanded retribution. If they did not receive it, they would take the corregidor's scepter and teach him themselves how to administer justice.

Little historical research has been conducted on the processes of economic and social differentiation within Mayan communities in Guatemala, or on how this differentiation manifested itself in political conflict. But drawing on work done for similar communities in the Andes and Mexico, we can theorize, through the aperture of the riot, the underlying political relations that formed community identity.[45]

Principales had greater access to resources in that they could adopt Spanish modes of production and commerce, while at the same time continuing to control communal resources as patriarchs and municipal officials. Further, they could enter into alliances with Spaniards to strengthen their position in relation to both macehuales and other principales. Anizeto López managed to parley economic dealings with the asentistas into political power. And we have seen how through his tenure as gobernador, he thrived in the Hispanic world while continuing to mobilize communal land, labor, and capital.[46] The kind of wealth and political power that K'iche's such as López amassed inevitably led to destructive political conflict, and the competing factions that emerged from these conflicts all sought to draw on extracommunal political resources to speak in the name of the community. When Estacuy and others, for instance, appealed to the Audiencia to have Silverio removed as gobernador, they did so in "the name of the principales and the pueblo."[47] Their effort to speak in the name of the community also entailed an attempt to define who was part of the community. Thus they managed to prove that Silverio, who throughout his life had been K'iche' enough to hold other political and religious positions, become gobernador (with no recorded protest), and marry his predecessor's wife, was in fact a Mestizo and suddenly not eligible for political office.

Macehuales, faced with both loss of land from which they derived subsistence and tributary production, and with drifting and ineffectual leaders, would pressure elites to maintain their allegiance to the community in order to limit the worst effects of internal differentiation. This pressure undoubtedly occurred at everyday, undetectable levels. In 1786, it exploded into violence and riot. Macehuales, too, would seek to define the community on their terms, as a place where subsistence was guaranteed, where goods were exchanged for their expected value, free of speculation, hoarding, and other abuses by outsiders. When their leaders could not guarantee such a community or, worse, participated in its undoing, they assumed the right to defend the pueblo themselves. Having less political resources to draw on than did principales, macehuales allied with other sectors of the town's popular classes to protect their interests.

For the elites, the very position of privilege that allowed them to mobilize resources in both the Hispanic and the K'iche' worlds also caught them in a "double bind."[48] To avoid social ostracism and loss of communal power, they had to respond to popular pressure and limit, to a degree, their attempts at private gain and Hispanic acculturation. Accepting a silk tobacco purse was one thing; working with Spaniards to despoil the community of land was quite another. Thus, the construction of communal identity, power, and expectations was a precariously negotiated endeavor, with competing groups drawing on differential resources to have their vision of the community understood as the dominant vision.

The riot of 1786 marked a watershed in city relations.[49] New political and commercial opportunities deepened divisions among principales and limited their ability to respond effectively to macehual demands. As a result, K'iche' elites intensified their reliance on Spanish authority as they struggled to hold on to their power and privilege in relation to other principales, would-be principales, and an anxious and angry urban population.[50] As we have seen in the events leading up to the riot, both K'iche' and Spanish elites relied on each other to prop up their own positions in their internecine struggles and to maintain control over an increasingly contentious plebeian population, comprised of both Indians and Ladinos.

A frank admission of this mutual reliance comes from 1802. Anizeto López had served as gobernador for sixteen years, and, as mentioned earlier, in the later years of his rule he was increasingly beset by charges from other principales and macehuales that he had misused his power to acquire large amounts of land.[51] The corregidor brought the gobernador's detractors to trial for "insubordination" and "lack of respect," and he stressed López's value in maintaining public order. He reminded the judge that López had been made gobernador in 1786 "not only for personal merit, but for his help in calming the riot. In the century that just ended alone, this city has witnessed four riots."[52] The judge sentenced Isidro Ixcot, identified as the leader of López's accusers, to jail for fifteen days and prohibited him from holding municipal offices for four years.

Ironically, this class alliance was predicated on the deepening of ethnic divisions. Both to maintain their political prerogatives and mobilize communal resources, K'iche' elites needed caste divisions to be maintained; Spaniards, and later Ladinos, needed principales to help administer the city and maintain order. Thus, as we shall see in following chapters, even during periods when their corporate protections were legally dissolved, K'iche' elites managed to retain their caste power. The maintenance of these ethnic divisions not only facilitated governance but culturally divided the popular classes and thwarted the development of multiethnic alliances, such as the kind that fueled the 1786 uprising.

Defending the Pueblo II: Cortes and Costumbre

For K'iche' principales, alliances with Creole and Spanish elites may have been enough, at least throughout the eighteenth century, to withstand the challenges to their authority posed by a growing population and a changing economy. Nevertheless, more ominous threats loomed as the nineteenth century approached. On the one hand, receding royal authority offered K'iche's less protection from the pretensions of the Creole elite; on the other, the Crown increasingly demanded more and more revenue as it desperately clung to power. Meanwhile, Creoles took advantage of the prolonged imperial crisis to wrest control of the town's resources, building their political and economic administration around the K'iche' cabildo. Finally, new ideologies redefining the relationship between the governed and their governors legally removed the corporate protection of principales and strengthened the rhetorical position of the Creoles in the struggle for political control of the city. City officials could now tap into K'iche' funds and regulate a wide range of social activities in the name of public health and welfare.

Los Altos in the Twilight of Empire

The growing commercial importance of the highlands was accompanied by the emergence of a network of local elites, both Creole and Spaniard, centered in the city of Quetzaltenango.[53] Making their living as traders, merchants, farmers, speculators, military officers, and bureaucrats, they developed by the end of the eighteenth century a defined regional identity that was increasingly at odds with imperial and *capitalino* interests. These elites built up alliances through family and commercial connections that extended throughout the major nonindigenous settlements of the highlands—Huehuetenango and the Sija-San Marcos valley—down into the piedmont and coastal plain.

As a rising class, these elites took advantage of the crisis brought about by the onset of the Napoleonic Wars to demand representation in the political affairs of the city, the province, and the Audiencia. They increasingly found themselves in opposition not only to the corregidor—the most immediate representative of imperial interests—but to capitalino merchants and politicians, who controlled trade and credit. Quetzalteco notables resented the politically powerful merchants of Guatemala City, who, as monopolists and smugglers, profited from both the application and avoidance of mercantile restrictions.[54] They resented the merchants' control of large-scale credit, and they especially resented the manner in which the capital merchants dismissed their political aspirations.

At the beginning of the crisis, Altense demands were relatively modest.[55] Aside from political representation in the newly formed Cortes de Cádiz and replacement of the office of the corregidor with local governing juntas, Quetzaltecos wanted remedies for the severe economic depression that had afflicted the region since the beginning of the century. Chronic warfare, natural disasters, foreign competition, and illegal smuggling nearly destroyed the indigo economy. Regional demand for highland products plummeted. According to local observers, Los Altos experienced a rise in banditry and violence; vagabonds roamed the towns and countryside; and people in large numbers migrated elsewhere in search of work, thus leading to a decline in population.[56] In their various recommendations and petitions to the Cortes, Altenses repeatedly asked for a more vigilant policy against trade in contraband British cotton goods and freedom to trade highland products throughout Spain's American possessions.

Despite their growing restlessness, Altenses never publicly wavered in their professed allegiance to Spain. Peru in 1780, France in 1789, Haiti in 1804, Mexico in 1810, and, closer to home, a number of local indigenous riots and rebellions had forced highland patricians into what they hoped would be a long and healthy alliance with royal authority and Spanish tradition.[57] The anxiety of the Altenses was palpable, both in their actions and in their writings, as they lived in a remote highland town through an extended period of political crisis during which legitimacy was challenged on every front; rebellions and rumors of rebellions were commonplace; and speculation and hearsay circulated faster than official news, among a population the Creoles perceived to be an impediment to their political and economic ambitions.[58]

Altenses were particularly edgy at the thought of indigenous sedition.[59] Following the independence movements that briefly flared up in León, Granada, and San Salvador in 1811, the newly formed Spanish ayuntamiento asked the Audiencia if a full military battalion could be stationed in the city and passed a number of emergency resolutions to prevent the "encouragement of bad desires in Indians due to their unhappiness with the tribute."[60] The municipality decreed that all visitors to the city would be questioned, traders coming from San Salvador would be counseled to keep quiet regarding events they might have witnessed, and restrictions would be placed on the use of aguardiente.[61] The president and captain general of the Audiencia, José de Bustamante y Guerra, counseled Altenses to proceed with the collection of tribute, but with "circumspection."[62] When Oaxaca fell to Mexican rebels in 1813, city officials hastily sent conscripts to aid the counteroffensive.[63]

Indeed, Altenses clearly believed that the highland's majority indigenous population, along with the corregidor and Guatemala City merchants, were a major obstacle to their dreams of political autonomy and economic prosperity. Nowhere was this obstacle more formidable than in their own city. Until 1806, Quetzaltenango was legally a pueblo de indios. As such, the town's common resources—land, taxes, and labor—were controlled by K'iche's.[64] As they strengthened their position, city notables literally set out to build a political apparatus around the core of the K'iche' común. After years of petitions and struggles between Quetzalteco Creoles and local imperial agents, the Audiencia, on 3 January 1806, approved the installation of Quetzaltenango's first Spanish ayuntamiento.[65]

The most pressing concern of the new Spanish municipal officials was how to raise revenue for their administration. Until 1806, the only regular funds available for city projects were the fees, taxes, and rents assessed through the caja de comunidad, which, as we have seen, was controlled by the K'iche' authorities, the corregidor, and the priest.[66] The Spanish ayuntamiento received permission to establish a *caja de ladinos* (funded by a half-peso tax on all non-Indians) which would exist parallel to the indigenous treasury.[67]

To supplement this new treasury, the ayuntamiento repeatedly requested the imposition of new taxes on a host of goods and services that reflected the growth of the city as an important commercial and urban center—levies on all wheat, cacao, cotton, sugar, fish, meat, and livestock brought to market; on market stalls that sold locally produced cotton clothes; on the houses of Ladinos and Spaniards; on city bakeries; on the more than a hundred stores selling Spanish imports and locally made products; on every "trunk, bail, box, and load" of goods from Europe; on the right to play music until a "reasonable hour" of the night; and finally, on the use of artificial lighting.[68] Most of these requests for new taxes were denied, and Creoles grew increasingly frustrated by the royal reticence.[69]

Quetzaltecos used the opportunities they had to present their grievances to Spain to expound on their Indian problem. Debates concerning the best way to assimilate Indians into Hispanic society had long been part of the Bourbon Reform project, and during the decades leading to independence they had grown increasingly urgent.

In 1810, Quetzaltecos were asked by the Guatemalan ayuntamiento to prepare a petition of concerns for the region's representative to the Cortes. In addition to the requisite political and economic demands, the municipality called for a campaign that would incorporate Indians into the Hispanic culture, thus prefiguring later nineteenth-century assimilation views.[70]

In 1811, the corregidor, Miguel Carrillo de Albornoz—who, unlike his predecessor, had a good working relationship with Altense elites—unsuccessfully petitioned the Audiencia to restore the labor repartimiento.[71] Writing to the president, the corregidor claimed that reinstitution of the levy would make the town prosperous again and would provide affordable labor by ending the "outrageous" wages demanded by Indians. A revival of the repartimiento and an end to corporate political status, while perhaps philosophically contradictory, jibed well with the political and economic vision of Altense elites. Breaking the political autonomy of the Indian elite meant, for the Altenses, gaining control over indigenous resources, including labor. This contradiction in fact foreshadowed the reinstitution under the second liberal regime of the forced labor drafts, retooled to fit the needs of coffee *finqueros*.

Citizens and Indians

When Ferdinand VII showed signs of breaking his alliance with revolutionary France in its fight against England in 1808, Napoleon invaded Spain, captured the wavering king, and installed his brother as Spanish monarch. Before leaving Spain, Ferdinand called for the convocation of an assembly of notables to raise money and an army to fight the French. The following year, the famed Cortes de Cádiz convened and its delegates—from every province in the empire—immediately set about drafting a constitution. Dominated by liberals, the Cortes passed sweeping legislation intended to reform colonial governance.[72] In 1811, the Cortes abolished indigenous tribute. In 1812, the constitution decreed that Indians were citizens. And in 1813, labor drafts of any sort were outlawed. Further, the dissolution of corporate protection and the establishment of constitutional ayuntamientos radically transformed local government. In indigenous towns with only one municipal structure, non-Indians were now eligible to vote and hold political office. In towns such as Quetzaltenango, with a dual municipal system, it was expected that the indigenous cabildo would be abolished and Indians would participate in local government as citizens, with rights equal to those of Creoles.[73]

In an empire as far-flung and diverse as Spain's, legislation from the Cortes was subject to creative regional interpretation. In Guatemala, for example, the abolition of tribute was delayed nearly a year. Some communities insisted on continuing to pay the tribute rather than be subject to the sales tax and tithe citizens were obligated to pay.[74] In Quetzaltenango, the Creoles were not able to abolish the indigenous cabildo during the first constitutional period. Nonetheless, despite the inability to execute many of the reforms, it would be wrong to underestimate their importance. Throughout the nineteenth century, the ideological shift that transformed subjects into citizens, and Indians into equals, would continue to radically transform the terms under which Quetzalteco K'iche's engaged with Hispanic society.

Taxes and Death: The 1815 Plaza Riot

Taxes

In 1813, upon the promulgation of the decree substituting for the tribute a tax code where all "citizens" would pay equally, the priest and principales wrote the corregidor warning that macehuales had come to them to protest the "lifting of one tax only to apply another."[75] The principales wrote that commoners were complaining that

> We [principales] have betrayed the pueblo (*diciendo que vendemos el pueblo*), because as leaders we should represent them. Because antiquity makes their customs unchangeable and because of the diverse opinions in this tense pueblo, reason cannot be established with one stroke (*un golpe*). In order to maintain control, and in order to quiet the commotion . . . we had no other recourse than to promise to the people that we would petition to your authority to suspend the execution of the august decree, until the sovereign Cortes, with our representation, can reconsider the matter and rule again as is just. The principales of the pueblo say that they cannot obey the new

order . . . in order to avoid problems and consequences. As such we reiterate our blind obedience and loyalty in fulfilling our important obligation to the pueblo.[76]

Even if macehuales did not make these complaints, the fact that principales would use their political obligations as justifications for their actions highlights the assumed importance of reciprocity in establishing and maintaining cultural legitimacy.

Despite claims that they were speaking on behalf of the "pueblo," it seems that it was the priest and principales and not the commoners who wanted to maintain the "custom" of the tribute. As I have argued, the maintenance of ethnic division was fundamental to the political and economic power of principales, and the tribute was a tangible marker dividing the city population along caste lines. Quetzalteco principales proved particularly vigilant in collecting the tribute and, later, republican taxes.

Events two years later support this interpretation. On 17 April 1815, after years of anxiety and dread on the part of Creoles, Quetzalteco K'iche's rioted.[77] As would occur in the Atanasio Tzul uprising in Totonicapán five years later, rumors of the abolition of the tribute ignited tensions. In their defense, jailed rioters claimed that they had simply gathered in the plaza to hear the latest proclamation issued by King Ferdinand, which, according to the defendants, would once again free them from tribute obligations (following the 1813 principal petition, tribute was not abolished in Quetzaltenango). The riot started when a K'iche' climbed on a table with a document in his hand and started gesturing angrily at the casa real. The ayuntamiento's first alcalde, substituting for the corregidor, panicked and ordered armed troops to fire. Witnesses report that six hundred Indians took part in the initial protest. After order was restored the first day, one hundred armed men were dispatched around the street entrances to the plaza to keep Indians out. For nine days following the initial riot, after a failed effort to retake the plaza, groups of K'iche's roamed the barrios surrounding the square, creating disorder.

As in the Totonicapán rebellion five years later, rumor and heavy-handed attempts to enforce colonial authority ignited long-running tensions and anger.[78] As in Totonicapán, the arrival of mysterious "papers" from Guatemala legitimized the rumors and became the focal point of crowd excitement.[79] Read against the 1813 principal demand for the restoration of tribute, the incident suggests that opposition to tribute came from commoners, not from principales. The anonymous prisoners were collectively referred to as macehuales, and the cabildo, as discussed in chapter 1, did not come to their defense.[80]

Principales may not have been eager to see the abolition of tribute, an important source of their political power and, at times, personal enrichment.[81] This interpretation is supported both by David McCreery's study of the Totonicapán rebellion five years later and Terry Rugeley's work on the Yucatán Maya during the independence period. McCreery identifies the tensions between commoners and principales, which emerged during the uprising, as likely stemming from class struggles. In one instance, macehuales had principales who continued to collect tribute whipped until they fell unconscious.[82] In the Yucatán, Mayan peasants quickly took advantage of the Cortes abolition of tribute to not only withhold paying a range of religious and imperial taxes but to act in a way that suggested they "believed that all social obligations to the dominant classes were at an end."[83] In some communities, Mayan peasants called for the dissolution of the indigenous república—the Yucatec equivalent of the K'iche' cabildo.

Death

The 1815 riot, however, was sparked by more than macehual desire to be free of tribute. Disease, pestilence, and catastrophe were a customary part of colonial life.[84] Since the conquest, smallpox, typhus, plague, whooping cough, measles, and unidentified fevers and *pestes* had decimated the highlands with a ferocity that only tenacious population growth could counter. Natural disasters, crop failures, and famines exacerbated the effects of disease, giving life, especially rural highland life, an unpredictable, precarious quality.[85] What was not common was the meddling of a state in nearly every aspect of community life—as would increasingly occur in the years preceding independence.

By the turn of the nineteenth century the same intellectual trends that had transformed Indian subjects into citizens now began to change the role of government in relation to its population.[86] The Spanish government, increasingly influenced by liberal reformers, began to emphasize prevention and cure, rather than comfort and Christian resignation, in its attitude toward what was increasingly being referred to as "public health."[87] The quarantine of towns, regions, and people, the enforcement

of hygienic regulations, and vaccination programs had become commonplace responses to epidemics.

In 1803, following the development of a smallpox vaccine made from
cowpox pus, the Spanish Crown launched its famous medical mission to
its American and Asian colonies. Led by Dr. Francisco Xavier de Balmis,
the mission was intended to inform local doctors of the new vaccination
and inoculate the population; by 1807, thousands of Indians had been vaccinated.[88] Bureaucratic ineptitude, indigenous resistance, and an erratic
supply of the vaccine, however, all led to continuing outbreaks of smallpox throughout the early nineteenth century.[89]

Cirilio Flores, a doctor and prominent Quetzalteco Creole, helped
administer the campaign in the western highlands and, after its conclusion, continued to be in charge of the state's health initiatives in the
region. A recent graduate of the medical school of Guatemala's Universidad de San Carlos, Flores was an archetypal liberal. Not only did he
vigorously implement medical reforms, but he also attempted to regulate
a wide range of social behavior. He urged the city government to take a
greater role in supervising the butchering of livestock, both in the city's
slaughterhouse and in private residences. During outbreaks of diseases he
led house inspections to check on hygienic standards. And in 1815, he
compelled the ayuntamiento to control cockfighting.[90]

Smallpox reappeared toward the end of 1814, and a royal commission
headed by Flores was contracted to administer the vaccine.[91] Five-eighths
of the cost of the vaccination campaign—for salaries, production and
transportation of the vaccine, food and other items to care for the sick—
was drawn from community cajas, and the balance was covered by taxes
on Spaniards.[92]

The corregidor was given mixed reports as to how indigenous communities received the vaccinators. Indian authorities from San Bartolomé
Sipacapa praised the doctor assigned to their district.[93] Residents from
Quetzaltenango and surrounding towns, however, were less enthusiastic
about Flores's comportment. Resisting Flores's efforts to administer the
vaccine, Indians and Ladinos hid their children and insulted the vaccinators. In nearby San Juan Ostuncalco, Flores encountered more passive
resistance; he claimed that the campaign took longer to complete than
it should have because the indigenous authorities did not assist in its
administration.[94]

Smallpox continued to spread, reaching Quetzaltenango by the end of March 1815. Flores ordered the doctors to return to the infected towns and revaccinate the population. In the parish of Quetzaltenango, Flores himself revaccinated 3,726 individuals.[95] In a number of towns, Indians abandoned their homes and fled to the mountains to escape both the epidemic and the doctors.[96] In Comitancillo, town leaders insisted that they were getting sick and dying from the vaccination itself: they claimed they were contracting both cowpox and smallpox.[97] The priest from Tejutla reported increasing anger over armed house inspections (presumably to check for cleanliness) and the quarantine of the town, which cut off commerce. Fearful of a riot "we wouldn't be able to resist," the priest ordered the suspension of the inspections and the vaccination. Flores defended the vaccination and insisted that it continue.[98] Confronting increased popular anxiety, the president of the Audiencia ordered the ayuntamiento to post sixty armed men around the plaza during Easter week, to maintain public order.[99]

These unaccustomed interventions into the daily life of the population generated hostility and, during a particularly tense moment, sparked resistance. In the days following the April riot, groups of Indians attacked Flores's quarantine house and, after a missed first attempt, freed the hospitalized smallpox victims, who then fled the town. A week after order was restored in Quetzaltenango, another riot broke out in the Mam towns northwest of the city. On 1 May authorities claimed that over four thousand Indians from San Martín, Concepción, and San Juan Ostuncalco had gathered in the latter's plaza to demand the removal of Ostuncalco's alcalde, who was vigorously persecuting Indians engaged in "idolatry" (possibly on the rise as a response to smallpox) and administering the vaccination campaign.[100]

Murder in the Cathedral

The rules of governance had changed. On the one hand, concepts of public hygiene and health provided Creoles and then Ladinos with new incentives to regulate a range of social behavior previously ignored by the Crown. For the rural and urban plebeian population, violations of houses and bodies increasingly brought the state into the most intimate and corporal realms of social life. On the other hand, Ladinos began to mobilize indigenous labor to build a city worthy of their political aspirations. To pay for this new vision of government, Ladinos increasingly tapped into communal, church, and cofradía treasuries. Throughout, the financial dictates of chronic warfare—both imperial and republican—likewise drained indigenous coffers.

In April 1826, smallpox once more struck Los Altos. By May, the disease had reached epidemic proportions and had arrived in the city.[101] Flores, now the vice president of Guatemala, once again personally took charge of the vaccination campaign. Believing that vapors given off by decomposing corpses contributed to the spread of the epidemic, he prohibited burials in the cathedral and began plans for the construction of a new public cemetery.[102] He also insisted that construction on a new waterworks project proceed. Living up to his overbearing reputation, Flores demanded that revenue from the church and cofradías fund these projects.[103] The city priest and K'iche' principales resisted Flores's requisitions.[104] To make matters worse, the epidemic occurred during a period of civil war, when conservatives had taken control of Guatemala City.

In October, Flores, now serving as Guatemala's provisional president, decided to move his besieged government to Quetzaltenango. It was a fateful decision. To fight his conservative foes, Flores imprudently and imperiously conscripted men, confiscated horses and guns, and levied a special war tax on the city's population. On 13 October 1826, a crowd of Indians from the city and surrounding towns gathered in Quetzaltenango's plaza to protest Flores's taxes, conscriptions, and attacks on the clergy. Upon catching sight of the object of their hatred, the crowd chased Flores into the cathedral, where, according to witnesses, hundreds of K'iche's literally ripped him apart as they chanted "death to the tyrant, death to the heretic, death to the thief."[105]

While subsequent observers placed the immediate blame for Flores's death on his conservative and clerical opponents, the anger that drove the crowd (judging both from Flores's record in administering public health in the highlands and in raising ethnic tensions) had been building for some time.[106]

Caste Struggle

Quetzaltenango's calm on the eve of independence in 1821 is noteworthy. Just thirty kilometers away in Totonicapán, between March and August

1820, indigenous rebels offered royal authority its most serious challenge in nearly three centuries of highland rule. Yet there exists no documentary evidence that Quetzaltecos were affected by these events, which perhaps testifies to the stability of the pact worked out between K'iche' and Creole elites. This interpretation is supported by events in the Yucatán, where Mayan peasant resistance did not turn into open rebellion owing in large part to the role of indigenous elites in maintaining order.[107] Nevertheless, the alliance between K'iche' and Hispanic elites, while mutually beneficial, was also mutually contested.

With the reinstitution of the Spanish constitution in January 1820 (an army coup forced Ferdinand to reinstate the charter, which had been abolished since his restoration in 1814), the ayuntamiento actively sought, as it had not in 1812, to disband the K'iche' cabildo. Ladinos demanded that the corregidor "adhere to the exact fulfillment" of the constitution and abolish the position of gobernador.[108] Despite threats by principales to refuse to collect tribute ("We will not permit our ayuntamiento to join with the Ladino ayuntamiento because of the royal tribute; the two scepters have to remain apart"), elections for a single municipal body took place in January 1821.[109] Although a majority of principales refused to participate in the event, two K'iche's were elected to office.

For nearly two decades following independence, until the arrival of Carrera, the single municipality was comprised of three alcaldes, eight regidores, and two syndics. The third alcalde was to be K'iche', as were four of the eight councilmen. It is not known if a separate, dissenting body of principales continued to meet outside of documentary purview. K'iche' officials, collectively referred to as *ciudadanos alcaldes indígenas* in the municipal minutes, were now expected to administer the indigenous population of the city as subordinates within a larger whole. They were to serve on committees and attend municipal sessions together with Ladinos. K'iche' attendance, however, was spotty, and it seems that Ladinos demanded that they be present only during emergencies or for special requests.[110]

Property law enacted by the federal congress in 1825 and then, following the civil war, in 1829, did not radically transform colonial land tenure.[111] It still allowed for church, cofradía, and communal holdings and even provided mechanisms by which communities could increase the size of their ejidos.[112] The intention of the laws, however, was to promote

agriculture—"the primary source of public wealth"—through the auctioning of public land (*baldíos*). Subsequent land law enacted in the 1830s
further encouraged the conversion of public land into private property. In
1832, a land tax of half a peso per caballería replaced the colonial tithe. In
April 1836, the national assembly authorized communities to divest themselves of communally held property and decreed that all baldíos and
ejidos would be converted into private property.[113]

For many historians, these decrees and the abuse they spawned appear
to be the provocation for the popular insurgency that propelled Carrera to
power.[114] Indeed, in Los Altos, Ladinos used the new laws to appropriate
significant extensions of indigenous holdings. In Tecpán and San Martín
Jilotepeque, for example, Ladinos deployed the laws to despoil indigenous lands.[115] Closer to the city, Agustín Guzmán and Totonicapán's *jefe
político* (the liberal equivalent to the corregidor), Macario Rodas, took
advantage of the legislation to win title to large tracts from surrounding
communities.[116]

While the private property of Quetzalteco K'iche's was never threatened to any significant extent, the abolition of the K'iche' cabildo re-
defined the administration of communal property. Were ejidos of former
pueblos de indios to be controlled by indigenous comunes or by municipalities that were now often dominated by Ladinos? While the new land
laws were vague on the issue (perhaps intentionally), an 1829 decree
flatly stated that "all vecinos . . . will enjoy the use, without any distinction, of ejidos . . . free of rent, notwithstanding any prior laws or disposi-
tions that favored a particular class of citizens."[117] This legally removed
any vestiges of caste privilege that might have continued to determine
access to the city's ejido.

Quetzalteco Ladinos used the new laws to press for control of the
community's land. Municipal land comprised 283 caballerías. The 1825
land law required that municipalities survey property within their borders
and file the results with national authorities. Those that held lands "from
time immemorial" without legal title would have the opportunity to
register them, provided that they made the request within six months of
the law's enactment.[118] Unowned land would then be made available for
public auction. Ladinos attempted to use this and subsequent laws to
standardize landholdings, officially reducing the city commons to forty
caballerías and placing it under municipal control. They also hoped to be

able to charge rent on this land. On 21 July 1826, the municipality published a broadsheet ordering all vecinos to present title to their property within fifteen days.[119]

Principales flatly refused to cooperate. For nearly a year they ignored a state surveyor's request to present their titles and maps and refused to attend municipal sessions to clear up the matter.[120] Despite being summoned personally by the first alcalde, the K'iche' alcalde, Tomás Coyoy, and the four indigenous regidores continued to boycott the meetings.[121] The jefe político fined the principales fifty pesos and placed Coyoy in jail for three days.[122] The principales still refused to produce the requested material, claiming that it had been lost. The surveyor protested that without the titles and maps, his work would be "paralyzed."[123] He went on to blame the municipal scribe for not being in possession of the documents. The scribe defended himself by claiming that "the titles have always been guarded in an ark by the principales indígenas."[124] Despite assurances that the survey might, in fact, result in an increase of ejidal land, Coyoy continued to refuse to supply the material.[125]

The Ladinos could not pursue the matter. In the middle of another smallpox epidemic, they needed the indigenous authorities to maintain order. Just a few days after his release from jail, for example, Coyoy was asked to help clear up a street that had become congested and fetid owing to a surfeit of indigenous pig vendors.[126] The horrors of civil war, made manifest with Flores' still fresh blood on the cathedral floor, undoubtedly dampened the zeal of Ladino elites to press the issue.

The 1786 riot transformed the city's ethnic relations. The debate as to whether Quetzaltenango was eligible for the establishment of a liquor asiento reflected the rapid economic and political changes discussed in the opening chapter. An important commercial center with a large nonindigenous population, Quetzaltenango ceased being in any way (except legally) a pueblo de indios. While many principales were able to master Hispanic forms of production and exchange to enrich themselves, they were ill equipped to respond to the political challenges offered by the rapid economic and demographic changes under way. In many ways the riot issued from a crisis of leadership within the indigenous común that resulted in increased reliance by the K'iche' elite on extracommunal alliances to prop up their positions.

For the K'iche' elites, these alliances could not entail a complete conversion to Spanish society, for their economic and political power remained predicated on their ability to control and mobilize communal resources. Cultural legitimacy had to be maintained and communal expectations met. As such, commoners retained a significant degree of leverage over the power of principales. Macehuales, however, were ultimately not successful in closing Quetzalteco society to outsiders. The demographic, political, and economic forces that were opening up the city were too strong to be withstood by the pressures macehuales could bring to bear.

For their part, Spaniards were also caught in a double bind. They came to rely on alliances with indigenous elites not just to maintain their caste power over Indians but to maintain their class power as well. Spaniards confronted increasingly antagonistic demands from the city's Mestizo artisans. The strengthening of ethnic divisions would serve to prevent multiethnic popular solidarity such as that which fueled the riot of 1786. In the years leading to independence, Spaniards and Creoles came to view the power of principales as a necessary obstacle—both standing in their way of control of communal resources and standing between them and the city's poorer classes. As their position strengthened, Creoles would try to break their dependency on the corporate power of the principales, with mixed results.

Riots, plots to kill all foreigners, breakouts from quarantines, forgery of royal decrees, and murder in the city cathedral: these are just a few of the sensational popular responses to the historical transformations discussed in the last two chapters. More difficult to chart and assess, however, is how individuals reacted to more mundane changes within the común—changes between men and women, children and parents, the wealthy and the poor. Throughout the nineteenth century, political and class divisions within the K'iche' community would deepen, especially in the years following the transition to coffee cultivation. But as long as social relations remained only partially commodified and as long as a majority of the city's population had access to at least some subsistence production, these divisions could be contained. Thus, throughout the nineteenth century, the predominant axis of struggle would remain one of caste, as K'iche' elites fought Ladinos to regain lost ground.

Chapter 3
A Pestilent Nationalism:
The 1837 Cholera Epidemic Reconsidered

The crisis consists precisely in the fact that the old is dying and the new cannot be born; in this interregnum a great variety of morbid symptoms appear.—ANTONIO GRAMSCI, *Prison Notebooks, 1971*

They were Indians with yellow, soft swollen faces the color of ripe lemons. With transparent skin and monstrous, bloated bellies. Luis touched them and felt the cysts on their scalps. "What have you given them as a remedy?" ". . . They prefer a witch who robs them of their money." The Indian, deathlike, collapsed on a chair . . . shaking with convulsive trembles—his mouth, his nose, his ears, running threads of blood. Luis thought about the melancholy destiny, the fatal augury of this race. Race? . . . suffocated, twisted, beaten down by his environment . . . the Indian . . . spurned by the very mestizo who exploits his flaws . . . forgetting that this Indian is mixed in his very own blood.—FLAVIO HERRERA, *El tigre,* 1934

Historians and anthropologists have long been stymied by Guatemalan nationalism. It purportedly denies the importance of blood, yet historically has been viciously racist against Mayas.[1] On the one hand, nineteenth- and early-twentieth-century national reformers have promoted the transformation of Indians into Ladinos through a series of cultural, educational, and behavioral changes.[2] On the other, Guatemalan nationalism permits nothing like what is found in Mexico, where there is a rhetorical celebration of the Mestizo as representative of *la raza cósmica*—the genetic and cultural hybrid who supposedly bears the best of both European and American "races." In Guatemala, in contrast, the term

Ladino, which in the years following independence came to represent all non-Indians, refers to an exclusively European identity.

By focusing on the 1837 cholera crisis, this chapter explores the colonial and early republican social relations that produced this contradiction. The reaction of state elites to the coming of the epidemic arose from, and helped confirm in their minds, an emerging tendency to explicitly define Indian identity in class terms. It is this equation of culture and class that accounts for the enduring power of Guatemalan racism, despite a supposed faith in cultural assimilation.

In the spring of 1837, cholera entered Guatemala from Belize, and within a few months it had spread throughout the republic. As the disease approached, state and municipal officials took actions to contain the epidemic, cordoning off infected regions, regulating behavior thought to cause the plague, and quarantining and treating the sick. As earlier with smallpox, indigenous and peasant communities resisted these health and hygienic interventions. But while anger at previous Creole and Ladino efforts to contain smallpox remained isolated and contained, by the end of 1837 large regions of the country's east were in open rebellion, united behind Rafael Carrera. This rebellion would eventually bring about the end of Guatemala's first liberal regime, the downfall of Quetzaltenango's Estado de los Altos, and the dismantling of the Central American federation.

Today historians dismiss the notion, first advanced by nineteenth-century liberals, that Indian participation in Carrera's revolt was an atavistic reaction, spurred on by conservatives and clerics, against state initiatives designed to contain the epidemic. While earlier writers focused on the rumors that circulated throughout rural Guatemala that Ladinos were poisoning water supplies, scholars now point to loss of land and political autonomy as the prime motives for widespread indigenous opposition to the first liberal state.[3] But in their rush to understand the rebellion as a rational response to increased exploitation, they pass over the significance the coming of cholera had both for representing and defining racial and national identities.

Mixed in Their Very Own Blood

One of the most enigmatic results of the formation of Guatemalan national identity was the reduction of a complicated colonial racial schema—one that included Españoles, Mestizos, Indígenas, Castas, and Ladinos—into two salient political categories: Indígenas and Ladinos. Arturo Taracena has argued that the current use of the term *Ladino* to refer to all non-Indians was initially a regional highland phenomenon that emerged during the late colonial and early republican period.[4] An overwhelming indigenous population, a relatively noncoercive market economy, and a desire to set themselves off from their capital rivals led highland Creole and Mestizo elites to promote a national identity that was premised on racial categories but that demanded cultural assimilation. In 1871, when Altense planters took over the state, highland terminology governing ethnic relations became generalized throughout the nation.

The term *Ladino* has a long and complicated etymology in Guatemala. Throughout the sixteenth and seventeenth century, it referred to acculturated Indians, usually in terms of their ability to speak Spanish.[5] By the eighteenth century, as caste divisions broke down after centuries of colonialism, it often came to refer to all those of "mixed race" who could not be considered European or Native American. In Quetzaltenango, both usages were prevalent through the end of colonialism, since Anizeto López, a full K'iche', could be called in 1802 "un indio muy Ladino." It was also a derogatory term, given the fact that Ladino through the eighteenth century was used to describe the poorer, often homeless, sectors of the city's plebeian population.[6] By the eve of the nineteenth century, however, in the region surrounding Quetzaltenango, Ladino came to refer to all who could not be considered Indian.

Of course the collapsing of all non-Indians into the category of Ladino occurred mostly at the level of public discourse, and belief that behavioral change could result in racial transformation could only be pushed so far.[7] Guatemalan society continues to be made up of multiple racial, ethnic, and class identities. Ideologies of blood that mark these identities remain powerful, despite the emphasis given to culture.[8] Nevertheless, in the century after independence, the term *race*, at least in public discourse and particularly in the highlands, became understood in cultural rather than biological terms, with all those not engaged in an identifiable indigenous lifestyle referred to as Ladinos.[9]

The emphasis on assimilation makes sense considering the social and political relations that governed the city and its surrounding regions. The economy of the highland region surrounding Quetzaltenango was not based—until later in the nineteenth century with the coming of coffee—

on massive state mobilization of labor such as that which took place in some parts of the Andes and Mexico. Relatively noncoercive market relations of production allowed for a somewhat blurred line separating the two ethnic groups, since there was no driving interest on the part of the state and local elites to enforce a strict racial divide.[10] Rather than understanding Indians as a caste to be maintained and mobilized for its labor, the region's ruling class—Spaniards, Creoles, and eventually Ladinos—came to view indigenous culture as an obstacle to be eliminated through assimilation.

Further, many of the highland elite were Mestizos, who saw in freedom from Spain an opportunity to dismantle the rigid racial hierarchy that had refused them a political voice.[11] Promoting assimilation and acculturation as forebears of civilization and progress allowed these emerging Ladino elites, both in Quetzaltenango and throughout the new nation, to challenge the racial hierarchy imposed on them by Spaniards and Creoles. This inchoate nationalism based on assimilation was repeatedly manifested in the political writings of Altense Ladinos.[12]

A Defining Disease

The 1837 epidemic was the first major crisis in which Guatemala's new political elites had to deal directly with the population, without the mediation of the Crown or the church, or the distraction of civil war. During this period of intense political uncertainty, as liberals pursued their factional efforts to build an independent, legitimate nation, elite attitudes and responses to the epidemic emerged from the racial and political logic of colonialism.[13]

In Quetzaltenango, municipal officials regarded cholera, as did state agents in other areas of the world, as a disease of the poor.[14] Quetzaltecos, however, threw ethnicity into the mix, casting cholera as a disease of the indigenous poor.[15]

For Altenses, cholera became a defining disease in three important ways. The collapsing of class into ethnicity and equating the result with the disease provided fragmented and politically weak Ladinos with an opportunity to culturally consolidate their identity and legitimacy. If economic, political, regional, and ethnic differences would not let Ladinos define who they were, then Indians and, by equation, cholera helped them to define who they were not. Second, the failure of the national state to respond to their repeated requests for financial aid to fight the epidemic deepened the Ladinos' alienation from Guatemala City. As they had under colonialism, Altenses continued to resent being caught between the interests of the national government and the highland's indigenous population, and their experience with the epidemic strengthened their resolve to break from Guatemala. Finally, by casting themselves as saviors of "unfortunate indigents," they created for themselves the chance to imagine that their vision of the nation was universal. These universalizing assumptions, in turn, provided Ladinos with new ideological justification with which to mobilize city resources and regulate social behavior.

The Disease Approaches

Unlike what had happened with past epidemics, Quetzaltecos had ample warning of, and plenty of false alarms about, cholera's approach. In 1817 a seemingly new strain of cholera emerged from Lower Bengal to afflict nearly the whole of India.[16] As cholera spread westward, the disease's association with colonialism, race, and poverty, its sudden and dramatic symptoms, rapid death, and unknown cause worked to generate an exceptional amount of fear, debate, and preparation in Western Europe and the Americas.[17] By 1832 cholera was in London, Paris, Quebec, Montreal, New York, and Chicago. In 1835 it was in Mexico and Belize. Bulletins and instructions issued first by Guatemala's newly formed Academia de Estudios's medical school and then by the emergency *junta de sanidad* kept city officials and regional elites informed of the approach of the disease.[18] In 1834, the municipalidad stockpiled medical supplies to fight cholera, and, in 1835, the national government sent troops to close the border between Los Altos and Mexico after receiving reports of an outbreak in Chiapas.[19]

Guatemalans likewise kept abreast of the international controversy regarding the cause of the disease. Was cholera transmitted by individuals—that is, was it contagious—or was it caused by the environment, by unsanitary living conditions? The debate was most advanced among Parisian medical professionals, and each side had persuasive evidence to muster in support of its positions.[20] Contagionists pointed to a long history of successful quarantines, recent advances in vaccination, and a strong correlation between transmission of the disease and troop movements and trade routes.

Notwithstanding these arguments, the anticontagionist position steadily gained ground. In city after city, cholera brought the hitherto isolated and ignored poverty of the urban underworld into view of nineteenth-century reformers. Suddenly, disease was not something that came from without but emerged from within the body politic.[21] Every aspect of the underclass's living habits—the clothes they wore, the liquor they drank, the food they ate and eliminated, the manner in which they disposed of their garbage, the way they buried their dead—was subject to debate, condemnation, and reform. The "strong correlation . . . found among filth, poverty, disease, and death convinced [medical professionals] of the dangers that lie in putrid miasmas, the poisonous air that arose from repulsive matter such as stagnant water, cesspools, rotting garbage, decaying animal carcasses, and rotting corpses."[22] Further, the fact that cholera appeared in disparate areas of a given city and, unlike smallpox, could be repeatedly contracted seemed to undermine the contagionists' argument.[23]

Because both sides made correct assumptions regarding the disease (cholera is transmitted by a waterborne bacterium and sanitary reform does prevent its spread), the debate often became one of confused semantics, serving more than anything else to express bourgeois anxieties regarding disease, poverty, and social disorder.[24] Prophylactic initiatives—quarantines, cordons sanitaires, and hygienic reforms—were actually informed by both positions.[25]

As in other Latin American nations, Guatemala's medical establishment was very influenced by French medical opinion, and Guatemalan doctors followed the debate regarding the nature of cholera closely.[26] One member of the national emergency health committee established during the epidemic, José Luna Arbizú, received his medical training in Paris at the height of the French cholera epidemic.[27] In 1833, the academia issued an opinion, quoting at great length two French doctors who stood on opposing sides.[28] The report related Alexandre Moreau de Jonnès's contagionist argument that cholera was transmitted through trade and troop movements and took particular notice of Moreau's critique of religious gatherings and pilgrimages. It cited a number of Indian examples, such as an 1825 religious pilgrimage: after cholera attacked "multitudes de indios," thousands died, the corpses infested the water supply, and the fleeing survivors spread the disease throughout the region. For Guatemalan doctors, the local relevance of this correlation between religious rituals, "indios" and disease must have been particularly poignant. The report then gave a number of anticontagionist arguments. After relating, with a trace of postcolonial insecurity, that even the "powerful nations" do not know the causes of cholera and cannot stop its spread, the report closed with a number of suggestions drawn from both positions: cut off communication with infected areas; establish quarantine houses; prohibit public meetings, both civil and religious, "in order to avoid the bad consequences such meetings can cause during moments of crisis"; ensure that only healthy food is sold in the market; create reserved areas for the sale of fish, meat, fruit; separate prisoners; and supply the poor with healthy food, because, as one municipal official put it, that "class eats whatever it finds, even if it is rotten."[29]

On the eve of cholera's outbreak, a degree of bourgeois conceit tempered a growing sense of dread. Indeed, as late as early spring 1837, medical professionals felt that because of its "very pure" air, "steady temperature," "clean streets," and dispersed population, Guatemala would be spared the epidemic.[30] In circulars and reports, the academia stressed that the best way to elude the plague was to avoid all excess: doctors counseled a regular diet of bland food and exercise but not to the point of exhaustion. Activity that would bring about an extreme mood change— fear, sadness, and anger—as well as "venereal pleasures" were to be avoided.[31] Victorian self-control was thought to be the best prophylactic. One doctor prescribed "innocent distractions, summer walks, gentle conversations" as healthy diversions from the fear of cholera's approach.[32] Notably, doctors considered foods associated with indigenous culture as harmful: chilies, spicy foods, and homemade liquor—*chicha, pulque* (fermented liquors), and aguardiente—predisposed the body to cholera; wine, however, in moderation was "healthy."[33] That it had attacked first in Belize likewise contributed to the contradictory opinion that cholera both invaded from without and emerged from within unhealthy lifestyles; indeed early reports from the coastal department of Izabal insisted that only "Africans" were dying of the disease.[34]

The first case in Guatemala was reported on 8 March, and a cordon sanitaire was set up in the east to protect the capital.[35] The government ordered eastern towns to clean their streets and establish health committees.[36] By early April, cholera had reached El Salvador and was believed by city officials to have been spread by thousands of pilgrims (*romeristas*) gathered during Easter to worship the Black Christ at Esquipulas.[37] The Federal Congress, based in San Salvador, suspended its sessions.[38] Guatemala's national assembly closed on 11 April.[39] As the city's population ignored or resisted efforts to contain the disease's spread, doctors and political leaders grew desperate and felt besieged.

Many of the early initiatives were drawn from previous experiences in fighting known epidemics such as measles and smallpox, as well as the firsthand experience that Luna Arbizú had had with cholera in Paris.[40] Dr. Luna had interned in the famous Parisian public hospital Hôtel Dieu, the target of popular anger during the French epidemic.[41] The anticontagionist position, which had come to dominate the French medical profession, undoubtedly influenced his understanding of the disease. The municipality and the junta de sanidad ordered houses to be cleaned and trees to be pruned, urged that local sanitary and charity committees be established, and prohibited liquor production and sale.[42] The municipality barred fruit from entering the city, because it was believed to irritate the stomach and thus predispose the body to the epidemic.[43] Warnings of the disease's imminent approach appeared in the *Boletín de Noticias de Cólera Morbo*, which began publication on 4 April. To combat the indifference of the city's population, the municipality granted police special powers to inspect houses and enforce sanitary standards.[44] Police were to search markets and confiscate and destroy any fruit they found.[45]

Cholera struck Guatemala City at the end of April and within a month 640 cases and 204 deaths were reported.[46] City officers panicked in the face of the population's intransigence. Not only were people refusing to live up to the new sanitary requirements but the sick were not seeking medical help. Soon city and health officials no longer acted as if it were an invading disease that needed to be prevented; it was now the population that had to be subdued. The municipality ordered block captains, under penalty of fine and imprisonment, to report sanitary violations and hang white flags on the houses of the infected.[47] Authorities called for a house-by-house search to find those afflicted and to administer a cure.[48] The police paid "spies" one peso for each illegal sale of liquor they reported.[49] The municipality increased penalties up to imprisonment for violations of emergency ordinances and automatically doubled sentences for any crime committed during the epidemic.[50] People caught intoxicated were to be sentenced to public work for five days under police supervision.[51] The ringing of church bells and religious gatherings were prohibited.[52] The municipality, to avoid speculation, confiscated and took charge of distributing wheat.[53] Houses of the sick and individuals entering the city, along with their clothing and goods, were subject to lime, salt, and vinegar fumigation. Even materials that the lower classes used in their daily lives were suspect: the municipality prohibited the use of sackcloth and ordered tanneries, whose organic waste was thought to spread the disease, to move their production outside of town.[54]

In April, reports started arriving of disturbances in the countryside.[55] Speculation and shortages were causing unrest, and people were refusing to help form cordons.[56] Alcaldes and departmental governors complained that they could not stop the sale of liquor or prohibit religious gatherings, because of "a lack of proper authority."[57] By the beginning of May, rumors were circulating that cholera was caused by poisoned water or that the medicine itself was tainted.[58] In San Martín Jilotepeque, dogs and pigs dug up hastily buried corpses; in the city, popular accusations spread that people were being buried alive, thereby forcing authorities to rescind a previous order to inter bodies as fast as possible.[59] It was as if Guatemala, like Paris five years earlier, had lost the ability "to absorb its dead."[60]

Although cholera did not reach the city of Quetzaltenango until June, Altenses were kept informed of national events through publications such as the *Boletín de Cólera Morbo*, *El Editor*, and *Boletín Extraordinario*.[61] These and other similar publications of the new postindependence press emerged from the enlightened belief that legitimate government could only be based on an informed public, educated by the proper authorities. Such publications also offered the government a venue through which to demonstrate to the literate that it was effectively managing the crisis, thus hopefully establishing an appearance of order and authority.

Yet rather than conveying a sense of dispassionate scientific management, such a description as the following of a cholera victim in a nearby town, published in the *Boletín* on the eve of cholera's debut in Guatemala City, must have produced apprehension and dread in those who read it:

The face is pallid and disfigured; the eyes are glassy and sunken; the mouth dry. The face is always covered with an ash-like yellow crust.

The respiration is accelerated as if short-winded; the voice is feeble. The pulse . . . is undetectable. [The victim] is very anxious; and he finds himself flat on his back with very little power to move. The skin is cold, particularly at the tip of the nose, the ears, the hands and especially the feet; the whole body is covered with an oily sweat.[62]

The *Boletín* went on to report that an autopsy following death revealed empty entrails and a shrunken, bloodless heart.

The ideological shift that converted the disease into an internal political pathogen was captured in the description of another victim in the same issue. After drinking himself into a stupor with chicha the day before, the victim contracted cholera. As he vomited, "the *chicha* turned into bloody matter."[63] That chicha is a homemade fermented drink closely associated with Indians could not have been lost on the literate public.

Quetzalteco Ladinos between Two Fires

It was a short step from the paternal benevolence practiced by the Quetzaltenango municipality during times of famine to the more interventionist posture aimed at administering public health. Citing its "primordial obligation . . . to care for the health" of the population, on 13 April 1837 the municipality placed under contract, for 1,500 pesos, an English doctor who supposedly had had success treating cholera in Mexico. He was to remain in the city for four months, and if cholera arrived, he was to "visit the houses of the poor . . . providing medicine and treatment" free of charge.[64] From the onset of the cholera days, municipal records inevitably and repeatedly referred to the disease's victims and potential victims as *indigentes*.[65] Considering that, indeed, the vast majority of those afflicted in the highlands were indígenas, this choice of cognate was more than fortuitous.[66] On at least one occasion, the city scribe used the word *indigente* when it was clear municipal officials were discussing Indians.[67]

Casting the disease as an affliction endemic to the indigenous poor allowed Ladinos the opportunity to consolidate their identity and attempt to project that identity as universal. Equating Indians with cholera emerged from, and helped crystallize, the inchoate nationalist notion of assimilation discussed above. With progress and civilization, Indians would become Ladinos, and Guatemala, or at least Los Altos, would become a prosperous Ladino nation. Within such a vision, notions of class needed to be understood in cultural or ethnic terms. While "Ladino" was to be the universal category that could contain all classes, there was to be no place in the new nation for rich Indians.

Ladinos attempted to establish their political legitimacy by demonstrating that the crisis was under their control. The municipality posted instructions on how best to avoid the disease, set up health and charity committees to distribute medicine and clothes to the afflicted, and dispatched commissions to procure food and other supplies for the needy.[68] Authorities set up a quarantine house and a cordon that prohibited commerce on the routes in from the coast and Guatemala City.[69] A number of decrees were issued prohibiting the consumption of pork, fruit, and alcohol, and regulating the slaughter of meat.[70] The municipality conscripted prisoners to maintain the cordon and to drain fetid ditches and swamps.[71] Perhaps owing to an association of the disease with menstruation, authorities closed the girls' school.[72]

Two obstacles stood in the way of the Ladinos' attempt to construct cultural and political hegemony: a lack of funds and popular hostility. On 3 April, the municipality requested of the central government money to "provide to the poor, who are the majority of the population, clothes, food, medicine and doctors."[73] The municipality was deeply in debt, having borrowed large sums of money to pay for public projects (such as the never-ending aqueduct). There were no funds to fight the disease. During an emergency session on 13 April, municipal officers debated how best to raise the needed revenue. While they legally could appropriate money from cofradías, as per an 1824 law, it was decided that, considering the anger it would provoke, this "remedy would perhaps be worse than the disease itself."[74]

With no money forthcoming from the national government, authorities became increasingly anxious. Since the beginning of Mariano Gálvez's term as national president in 1831, relations between the highland city and the capital had been tense and strained. Gálvez had suspected Quetzaltenango of being a conservative stronghold and had removed the *jefatura política* to San Marcos, thereby antagonizing many Quetzaltecos.[75] The failure of Gálvez to provide financial assistance increased the hostility and alienation between Altenses and capitalinos. Except those received from a few wealthy Ladinos such as Manuel Aparicio, requests for voluntary contributions yielded little.[76] On 8 June, the municipality, despite its earlier hesitation, ordered that money be taken from cofradías.[77] However, the city priest, Ugarte (the same cleric who had been threatened by Carrera three years later), insisted that the brotherhoods' account books were lost and K'iche' cofrades refused to present lists of their assets.[78]

Cholera arrived in the city on 9 June; by the end of July it had killed over 161 people. As the body count rose, municipal authorities grew increasingly frantic and resentful in the face of public "indifference" and hostility.[79] They could not get enough men to maintain the cordon, staff the health and charity committees (which they complained existed "only in name"), or contribute to the emergency fund.[80] Even though the municipality repeatedly increased the penalties for the sale and use of alcohol, incidents of drunkenness increased, at least according to the authorities. The municipality granted police special powers to go from house to house to inspect for cleanliness and force the infected to seek medical treatment; it also decreed that all fruit trees within the city be destroyed; closed the workshops of tanners and potters, whose ovens were thought to be harmful; and restricted the slaughter and sale of meat to three Ladino butchers.[81]

With the arrival of cholera also came notice of unrest throughout the country, including in nearby highland towns. On 5 June the Ladino officials of Sololá asked for permission to maintain a standing military force in order to prevent any indigenous uprising that might occur as a result of cholera.[82] On 25 June, news came of the Mita revolt in the east.[83] Violence was reported in indigenous pueblos in the department of Sololá, and on 9 August Ladinos and Indians in Huehuetenango joined forces to protest the new taxes.[84] Confronting widespread rebellion, the national government abandoned efforts to collect the taxes and suspended a number of judicial and land decrees that had previously provoked unrest.[85] On 26 June, municipalities received the following instructions from the national government: "In towns where there are a considerable number of Ladinos, arm them to avoid whatever trouble the ignorance of the Indians could cause. In completely indigenous towns, if symptoms of discontent are noted and they refuse to receive medicine . . . leave them to their fate . . . arrest the agitators and send them to the capital to be sentenced to public works."[86] The telling use the word *symptom* highlights the Ladinos' conflation of indigenous behavior with disease.

Conflict in the Time of Cholera

It is harder, obviously, to gauge Quetzalteco K'iche's' perceptions of cholera than their Ladino counterparts. Epidemics were regular occurrences in Los Altos.[87] The postindependence generation of K'iche' leaders witnessed outbreaks of *calenturas* (fevers) in 1824 and smallpox in 1826.[88] And many must have been alive during the 1815 epidemic. As cholera broke out and municipal initiatives grew more frantic, the indigenous "indifference" about which Ladinos complained turned into active hostility. Infected K'iche's did not present themselves to the doctor, cofrades refused to contribute money, and Indians protested many of the emergency municipal regulations.[89] While this resistance did not evolve into the full-scale insurrection that was seen in eastern Guatemala behind Carrera, conflict surrounding Ladino attempts to stem cholera does provide an important window onto the city's ethnic relations.

Many of the reforms and decrees cut into the productive and commercial activities of indigenous communities. In Quetzaltenango, the prohibition on liquor and pork sales, the closing of tannery and pottery workshops, the cutting down of fruit trees, and the cordon that broke off trade must have elicited resentment. In mid-July, for example, there is mention that Indians barred from bringing panela into the city were "angry."[90] And restricting the slaughter and sale of meat to three Ladinos must have incensed the city's twenty-five K'iche' butchers.[91]

Not all indigenous resistance, however, can be explained in economic terms. The refusal of many K'iche's to submit to medical treatment needs to be understood in a historical context. In the decades preceding this epidemic, similar municipal initiatives had resulted in violence and death. Likewise, the efficacy, not to mention the salubriousness, of the treatments was by no means assured. One cure advocated by Francisco Quiñones, a doctor working in Quetzaltenango, prescribed four grams of mercury to be taken orally every half-hour; it also recommended that menstruating women be stood in a vat of hot water, salt, and mustard, so that the vapors could bathe their vulvas.[92] Further, the arrogance and racism of Ladino doctors undoubtedly led to brusque and discourteous treatment. In the beginning of August, for example, K'iche's from a rural canton demanded that an abusive doctor be removed.[93]

Mourning rituals were particularly fertile ground for conflict, and throughout Guatemala a number of protests and riots broke out against attempts to regulate burial rites and practices. Since the close of the colonial period, the state had mandated that cemeteries be located outside of towns. The "miasmas" that the decomposing corpses gave off were thought to cause disease, and, after centuries of interment, there was not much room left in churches. After independence, liberals, in their effort to define a national identity, made burial reform a priority. During the first decades of independence, however, it remained a mark of status for many to be buried in the church—either under the floor or, for those able to pay the fees, in crypts. In 1840, a U.S. traveler gave a rather graphic account of one such burial. Because the father was "rich," he could afford to bury his son in the earthen floor of the church. After watching the child being laid in his grave and covered with dirt, the traveler recalled the "brutal and disgusting scene" in which the sexton raised a log and with "all his strength" pounded the dirt "over the head of the child." The father took the mallet and finished pounding, until the child's body had been "crushed to atoms."[94]

As with elite perceptions of cholera's symptoms, such spectacles helped articulate and reduce liberal notions of progress, religious fanaticism, disease, and hygiene to a personal, corporeal realm. The horrific episodes brought to light by cholera and other epidemics—piles of decomposing bodies, corpses disinterred by animals, superstitious rituals that propagated the disease, ungovernable passions fueled by reckless alcohol use and ignorant rumors, unremitting vomiting and diarrhea — represented to Ladinos what they were not, and what Guatemala, if it was to become a modern nation, would have to escape.

In 1834, the national government ruled that, henceforth, all burials were to be performed in new cemeteries built outside of towns.[95] Attempts to implement the new policy resulted in what became known as "cemetery revolts" throughout the indigenous zones of Guatemala. Indians from towns such as San Miguel Totonicapán, Momostenango, Quiché, San Martín Jilotepeque, and San Pedro Chipilapa protested the new policy, either violently refusing to abide by it or appealing to local religious or political authorities for suspension of the decree. It is tempting to view these conflicts as a clash between opposing cultural norms and social visions. One historian has suggested that Indians' resistance to the new cemeteries sprang from a desire to maintain spiritual links to their ancestors, and hence spatial proximity to their earthly remains.[96] Many protests logged by Indians against the 1834 decree, however, while suggestive of divine fears, were eminently mundane in nature. In Momostenango, Indians objected that the new cemetery was a mile away. In Quiché and San Pedro Chipilapa, community leaders complained that animals and birds were eating the bodies. And in San Martín, a principal protested that the ground of the new cemetery was too rocky. Graves could not be dug deep and the winds blowing into town from that direction carried with them diseases, a belief notably similar to the views held by Ladino reformers.

In March 1800, Quetzaltenango opened a graveyard just outside the cathedral.[97] Prior to this, most Quetzaltecos, K'iche's and Ladinos, had been buried in and around the church building. While the majority of burials following 1800 took place in the new cemetery, interments within the church (mostly in the cathedral but occasionally in one of the four barrio chapels) were still relatively common, particularly for wealthy K'iche's, until the late 1820s.[98]

Following a smallpox epidemic in 1826, the city's health committee urged the municipality to establish a cemetery outside of town.[99] By the time of the 1837 cholera epidemic a chapel and adjacent graveyard were functioning about half a kilometer west of the plaza. The new cemetery, however, was not equipped to deal with the large number of bodies produced by cholera. By 18 June, corpses were lying exposed on the ground, "particularly those of the *clase indígena.*"[100] The epidemic lasted for over four months, and the mortality rate was so high that Ugarte, the city priest, stopped recording deaths in the church's burial registers.[101] Convicts were conscripted to dig collective graves near the church of San Bartolomé, east of the plaza.[102] Burial was to take place as soon as possible, and lime was to be poured on the bodies. Fearing that exposure to the corpses would spread the disease, the municipality banned public mourning and prohibited cofradías from singing and carrying the deceased through the streets.[103]

These measures angered city K'iche's, although their reasons were unspecified. The K'iche' population had already incorporated cemetery burial into their mourning practices, and the protest could have been directed at the crude and disrespectful manner in which bodies were being handled, as well as at municipal restrictions on grieving customs. The opening of the new burial ground was delayed by what the municipality described as a "general restlessness, particularly among Indians," provoked by some "troublemakers of their class who do not recognize the good it will bring."[104] Despite this hostility, the graveyard was opened and used for the duration of the epidemic. Fear of further indigenous protest, however, prevented the Ladinos from opening a second collective grave.[105]

As usual, the role of principales in the protest was ambiguous. The indigenous alcalde and regidores attended most municipal sessions throughout the crisis and served on emergency committees. The committee charged with finding a location for the new graveyard was composed of two prominent Ladinos, Manuel Aparicio and Florencio Molino, and two indigenous regidores, as well as a private K'iche' "citizen," José María Paz. Some principales, convened by the K'iche' alcalde, attended the hastily arranged blessing of the new burial ground.[106]

Julio Cambranes states that when highland liberals of Mestizo origin finally gained state power following the 1871 revolution, their views were as racist as those of any Spaniard.[107] He is right. But now it was a more malignant racism based on culture rather than blood.[108]

Casting Indians as impoverished victims and attributing the spread of cholera to their behavior gave Ladinos the opportunity to project their identity and values as universal and to promote assimilation as the cure. The obsession of Guatemalan Ladino reformers with equating squalor and pestilence with indigenous culture bears an uncanny resemblance to a later Latin American social reform movement that historian Nancy Leys Stepan has described as "preventative" or "neo-Lamarckian" eugenics.[109] In the decades before and after the turn of the nineteenth century, Latin American proponents stressed environmental modification (as opposed to U.S. and European advocates who promoted regulation of sexual reproduction) as the way to induce permanent racial improvement.[110] Ladino reaction to the cholera epidemic suggests that this social movement had an important prehistory. An interpretative framework that, as Stepan puts it, "linked a sanitary environment to racial health," allowed Ladinos both to escape the blood strictures imposed by Spanish colonialism and to make sense of Guatemala's abiding ethnic divide.[111] At the same time, it allowed Ladinos, as promoters of social reform, to inscribe themselves as the agents of national regeneration.

Poverty and disease were no longer considered a fated condition of the lower classes. They were the result of circumstance, behavior, and education. This attitude radically changed the relationship between the government and the governed and allowed for the kind of proactive social intervention practiced by Flores and other Guatemalan reformers. With the blood strictures of caste colonialism out of the way, Ladinos came to see Indians as capable of improvement through education, behavior modification, and environmental change. Indigenous identity, like poverty and disease, was now something that could be remedied. However, this ideological shift, which set the terms of Guatemalan nationalism, created the conditions for a more profound, vicious racism. Now, despite all the self-serving talk of Ladinos regarding Indians as being "potentially" the political and intellectual equals of Europeans, it was felt that if Indians did not fulfill that potential, it was their fault. For the Ladinos, the tendency of cholera to attack Indians was confirmation that it was indigenous culture that needed to change. Cholera thus became an internal pathology caused by a diseased populace.

Cholera not only helped Ladinos consolidate their identity in relation to the highland's indigenous population but also in relation to their capitalino rivals. They begged for financial assistance to fight the epidemic: "The supreme governor is father of the people. In these critical circumstances we ask you to extend a beneficent and protective hand and to not let us for lack of resources fall victim to this horrible disease. Oh! Supreme leader! . . . in the name of humanity . . . we ask you to give us the funds we so desperately need."[112] However, not only was money not forthcoming but capital authorities could neither stem the epidemic nor contain Carrera's rebellion. Taking advantage of the disintegration of the Guatemalan government, on 2 February 1838—just months after the end of the epidemic—the Estado de los Altos formally declared itself the sixth state of the Central American federation.[113]

Within less than a century, on the eve of the creation of the Estado de los Altos, Quetzalteco K'iche's went from being an overwhelming majority to a minority of the city's population. Despite chronic political turmoil and economic depression, this demographic trend continued apace throughout the first half of the nineteenth century. Quetzaltenango was quickly becoming a Ladino city—that is, until the coming of Carrera.

Chapter 4
A House with Two Masters:
Carrera and the Restored Republic of Indians

Lord, is this the time when you will restore the kingdom? —ACTS 1:6

Both liberalism and conservatism were born in this climate of violently
oscillating public opinion, and they are tied together, not only because
each would lose its very substance without the presence of its opponent
in the field of theory and ideology, but because both are primarily
concerned with restoration, with restoring either freedom or authority,
or the relationship between both, to its traditional position. It is in this
sense that they form the two sides of the same coin, just as their
progress-or-doom ideologies correspond to the two possible directions
of the historical process as such; if one assumes, as both do, that there is
such a thing as a historical process with a definable direction and a
predictable end, it obviously can land us only in paradise or hell.

—HANNAH ARENDT, *Between Past and Future*, 1961

A week after Carrera's execution of the Ladino municipal officers in 1840,
Quetzaltecos celebrated Christ's execution in the city cathedral.[1] Terrified
by recent events, notable Ladinos steered clear of the church and the
processions. The high-backed chairs reserved for the city patricians remained empty. Except for two travelers and the priest, there were no
"white people" in attendance. Thousands of Indians from the city and the
surrounding towns filled the church. Men sat in the pews, while women,
formally barred from witnessing the agony, knelt on the floor. At the base
of the altar stood a large, silver filigreed cross covered by an arched arbor
of pine and cypress branches. Driven by "wild Indian music" and led by
the K'iche' cabildo, a cortege approached the altar bearing Christ's body.

Clerics lifted the Savior, and Balentín Cayax, the indigenous gobernador wounded by Carrera, dressed in a long black cape and wide-brimmed felt hat, raised a silver hammer and nailed Christ to the cross.

By design or circumstance, K'iche' attempts at political renewal took place around Easter. The outcomes of these popular interventions, like a Guatemalan Catholicism that places more emphasis on the calvary and the crucifixion than on the resurrection, were ambiguous. Considering the role principales played in city politics, it is this ambiguity that is none too subtly evoked in the casting of the gobernador as the executioner of Pilate's death sentence.

Whatever influence the popular protests so far discussed may have had on local politics over the long run, they could not stem the social transformations that had turned the pueblo of Quetzaltenango into the capital of an independent state in 1838. Yet following Carrera's forcible reincorporation of Los Altos into Guatemala just two years later, K'iche' principales immediately set up their separate cabildo, restoring their authority "in the form and manner that by custom our ancestors practiced." But what, exactly, did they restore?

Defining the Nation

Above all else, K'iche' community leaders reclaimed the power to define their position in the new nation. During the chronic political turmoil and confusion during the first two decades of independent rule, competing visions of Guatemalan society emerged to vie for dominance. Chief among these competing visions were the requisite rivalries between conservatives (mainly Guatemala City's merchant and governmental aristocracy) and liberals (made up mostly of middling city and provincial elites). Following a brief two-year annexation to Iturbide's Mexican empire (1821–23), the United Provinces of Central America was declared. The failure of liberals and conservatives to reach a governing consensus, coupled with a weak executive who was indirectly elected by a divided congress, quickly led to civil war (1826–29). Led by Francisco Morazán, liberal forces eventually beat back the conservatives and ruled Central America until 1839.

With Morazán as the federation's president, the state of Guatemala, headed by Mariano Gálvez, became a testing ground for enlightenment policies designed to transform Central America into a modern, prosperous nation.[2] A generation of liberal politicians and intellectuals came of political age. Through proactive social reforms, these new leaders attempted to dismantle what they felt were archaic Spanish institutions, including the corporate protection afforded to the Catholic Church and indigenous communities. Liberals enacted free trade policies and attempted to simplify Guatemala's convoluted system of taxation. They tried to make public and private lands available to the expanding cochineal economy and invited foreign capital and immigrants. The government legalized divorce and civil marriage and removed education from church control. Clerics felt to be hostile to the liberal cause were exiled; religious orders were suppressed, church property confiscated, the tithe abolished, and religious liberty proclaimed. In 1837, the government adopted the infamous Livingston Codes, which were intended to reform the judicial system by abolishing *fueros* (special privileges or immunities granted certain social groups), multiple courts, and corporal punishment, and establishing trial by one's peers.[3] Building on the 1824 federal constitution that declared all inhabitants of the federation equal, "without distinction or race," liberals passed a series of laws that they hoped would further the incorporation of Indians into the new nation.[4] The state congress declared Spanish the national language and the goal to "extinguish aboriginal tongues."[5] The government promoted education and granted scholarships to indigenous children so as to promote assimilation.[6] For the time being, liberals had won the power to define what the new nation was to be—at least rhetorically and legally.

A Republican Republic of Indians

The reaction of Quetzalteco principales to the first liberal state was mixed, and K'iche' authorities practiced selected forms of resistance. In the weeks before Flores's murder in the cathedral in 1826, for example, principales straightforwardly declared that "not they, nor any of their class would contribute" to Flores's emergency levy.[7] In 1824, indigenous regidores refused to participate in a vaccination campaign against smallpox.[8] And principales had refused repeatedly—with mixed results—to obey decrees that would curtail their corporate privileges, whether they were land, tax, or political reforms.

But aside from these conspicuous incidents, principales continued to engage in everyday forms of public administration. The most stunning example of this was their collection of the new head tax, the contribución directa, which was established in the 1825 federal constitution but not assessed until liberals consolidated their power following the civil war. As mentioned earlier, K'iche's, although now citizens, were still expected to govern the indigenous sector of the city, which included collecting revenue assessed under the contribución directa. Between 1833 and 1836, principales managed to collect far greater sums (4,000 pesos) than did their Ladino counterparts (836 pesos), even though by 1830, K'iche's, at least as statistically defined, were a minority of the city's population (see Table 1 in chap. 2).[9]

The explanation for the continuing willingness of the principales to help govern the city may lie in the regional state's increased capacity for repression and coercion. In 1826, three days in jail and a fifty-peso fine may have convinced K'iche' authorities to be more cooperative. But that conflict resulted in a negotiated settlement of sorts, as Ladinos never did get to review ejido titles or charge rent for municipal land. More likely, the explanation is to be found in the continuing relevance of cross-ethnic elite alliances for understanding city politics. José María Paz, for example, who helped collect the contribución directa in 1835 and 1836 and served on the municipality's cemetery commission as a private citizen, went on to become K'iche' gobernador in the 1840s.

As we have seen in preceding chapters, liberalism was the most serious threat to the authority of Quetzalteco principales. K'iche's continued to exercise political power over the indigenous sector of the city, but they were now expected to do so as citizens. Without the state sanction of caste privilege, principales were threatened with a loss of power on two fronts. Ladinos increasingly sought to wrest control of communal resources while commoners had more latitude to escape their control.

Notwithstanding the relative quiescence of the Quetzalteco K'iche' community, the creation of the Estado de Los Altos in 1838 provoked highland pueblos into active resistance to the new state. Indians deployed the centuries-old tactic of appealing to a distant authority, first to Guatemala City then to Carrera, to protect them from the predatory demands of local elites.[10] Communities around Lake Atitlán wrote numerous letters to state officials in Guatemala City, pleading that they wished to remain part of Guatemala so their trade with the capital would not be cut off.[11]

Other communities, such as San Sebastián on the coast, objected to the labor demanded by Altenses to build the roads and bridges needed to transport highland products.[12] Other indigenous pueblos resisted the appropriation of their lands and the assessment of new taxes, and Indian traders protested the increased tariffs charged on goods brought into Quetzaltenango so as to pay for the city's public projects.[13] In August 1839, Quetzaltenango dispatched Ladino troops to Santa Caterina Ixtahuacán to forcibly collect taxes. The subsequent conflict left thirty-nine Indians dead, including two principales.[14]

Carrera put this resistance to good use. Indian communities actively supported his two incursions into Los Altos in the early months of 1840, using their deep knowledge of the mountainous terrain to help him defeat the Altenses' defending army. Throughout his long tenure, Carrera would skillfully take advantage of his repute as a defender of indigenous interests to consolidate his power.[15] The alliance between Carrera and indigenous communities was tenacious enough to resist numerous rebellions and would-be separatist movements, including a brief attempt in 1848 to reestablish the Estado de Los Altos. In return for indigenous communal support, throughout the next two decades the national government restored many of the corporate protections afforded to these communities during the colonial period. Before Los Altos was even reincorporated into Guatemala, the national constitutional assembly issued a series of decrees that reinstated the colonial *leyes de Indias*—the body of Spanish legal protections afforded Indian communities.[16] The new legislation reestablished indigenous municipal and judicial autonomy, as well as the offices of the *protector de indios*, corregidores, indigenous gobernadores, and interpreters. The government committed itself to publishing decrees and laws in indigenous languages and convened a commission of five individuals to process indigenous complaints and concerns. Although liberal taxes were suspended, the government did not carry out a wholesale restoration of community lands lost under the various baldíos decrees. Carrera, however, often personally intervened to grant land to aggrieved Indians.[17]

While more research needs to be conducted to confirm it, it appears that the cultivation of cochineal—Guatemala's main export by the 1820s—created an auspicious political economy as a background for Carrera's willingness to grant communities a significant degree of autonomy.[18] Although it was possible to produce cochineal (a red dye made from insects that feed on nopal cactus) on large plantations using wage labor, cultivation was predominantly carried out by indigenous families, especially in the area around Antigua and Lake Amatitlán, with non-Indian merchants profiting from trade and export.[19] Decentralized production may have combined with a less ambitious and therefore less financially needy state to allow Carrera's alliances with indigenous communities.

Many historians have recognized the importance of these alliances for the centralization of power in Guatemala City, yet few have studied how it played out within indigenous communities.[20] Throughout the highlands, principales took advantage of Carrera's support not only to resist Ladino pretensions but to reassert their authority within their own communities. One of the first demands of principales after Carrera's victory was that whipping posts be reinstalled in town plazas.[21] The new laws reinvested in the principales a considerable amount of power to judge and punish. Most cases of minor violations committed by Indians were to be decided by indigenous alcaldes, who also acted as *jueces de paz* (justices of the peace).[22] More serious infractions were to be adjudicated by first circuit judges, who were to be a given "general training . . . so that the cases against Indians are settled with the fairness stipulated by the *leyes de Indias*."[23] In Quetzaltenango, the corregidor circulated these decrees throughout the city and the department and ordered that "no cases against Indians be heard in municipal courts."[24]

But the restored power of the principales was far from absolute. It now functioned within the parameters of a consolidating nineteenth-century state. While the regime dominated by Carrera and his allies for thirty-one years was certainly conservative and pious, it was not a simple throwback to colonial rule. Government and society continued to experience secularization, as the state promoted private property, industry, and technological improvement, albeit at a much slower pace than liberals had previously attempted.[25] Carrera's state was essentially Burkean in its understanding of social reform and authority. Indeed, in its first decree reestablishing the corporate protection of Indians, the constitutional assembly wrote that laws were needed not only to "protect" Indians and "promote their customs and civilization" but also to give Indians the "means to acquire and increase their small properties and industries."[26] What was established was in effect a republican república de indios.

The law reestablishing the office of indigenous gobernador is a particularly fascinating example of how the new leyes de Indias allowed for an articulation of state and patriarchal interest. It set out the terms and conditions under which principales were expected to exercise their restored authority.[27] As before, the corregidor was to nominate the gobernador. This time, however, no qualifications were given for eligibility to serve. Indeed, there was not even any mention that the gobernador had to be indigenous.[28] Many of the law's articles make specific reference to reciprocal and patriarchal responsibilities and obligations. The gobernador was to tour his pueblo during the first days of the week, putting to work all able-bodied men not otherwise employed. He was also responsible for managing the communal planting and, "in case of hunger, disease or other such crisis," for distributing corn from this planting first to the elderly, then to the widows and invalids, and finally to all other Indians. During normal times, the profit from the planting was to be sold and the money placed in the newly restored communal treasury. In addition to revenues earned from these sales, a three-real community tax, a one-half peso tax on each slaughtered cow, rent on community property, and fines were to go to the caja. The gobernador was to manage these funds, keeping strict records and sharing the keys with the indigenous alcalde and priest. Profits were to be invested in public projects and teachers' salaries.

Given the power, by the new legislation, to arbitrate marriage disputes, gobernadores counseled couples that in "peace and union they should mutually support each other." If the counseling failed, gobernadores could sentence men to work on public hygiene projects and put women to work weaving textiles, the sale of which would supplement the caja. If an indigenous man "seriously" injured his wife, or engaged in other "cruel treatment," the gobernador was to dispatch him to the alcalde so he could defend his actions. The accused could then be passed on to the first circuit judge. Any indigenous man who failed to provide food and clothing for his family would either be docked money or forced to work to pay for his obligations. Further, gobernadores were to ensure that Indians attended religious events and doctrinal talks. They were charged with caring for the destitute elderly and orphans, paying for their upkeep with community funds, and placing children in decent Ladino or indigenous homes. The fact that there were no blood standards specified for occupancy of the position and that indigenous orphans could be placed in Ladino homes reflects the assimilationist assumptions that continued to exist throughout the conservative regime.

In exchange for this authority, gobernadores were expected to help the new state govern. They were to strictly obey the orders of the corregidor, who had the power to remove gobernadores from their position. And most important, they were to carry out many reforms previously attempted by liberals, thus demonstrating the skillfulness with which the conservative regime deployed communal authority to establish and maintain power. Gobernadores were also to collect any taxes assessed and help maintain public order. They were to ensure that indigenous children attended school and that public works projects, particularly those having to do with public health, were carried out. They were required to collaborate with municipal authorities in the construction of aqueducts, fountains, and communal washbasins, and they were to police the cleanliness of public areas and private houses, with the power to fine those deemed in violation of hygienic codes.

The new law attempted to limit abuse, forbidding gobernadores from using their position to conscript labor or revenue for their private enterprises. In 1847, the government ruled that indigenous authorities could not force Indians to serve or financially contribute to cofradías, whose "antieconomic expenses" led to drunkenness, bankruptcy, and the "ruin" of communities.[29] Other laws and decrees restricted the punishment that could be meted out by indigenous authorities. One judicial reform ordered that "if [the gobernadores] use more excessive punishment than is warranted by custom, they are to be held, reprimanded and themselves punished."[30]

Despite these strictures, the position, like its colonial counterpart, was rife with abuse. Gobernadores were to be paid annually 180 pesos from the community caja, thus creating pressure to fine and assess taxes and other fees so as to cover salaries, particularly in poorer communities with limited sources of revenue. The arbitrary power invested in gobernadores to jail, fine, conscript labor, and control funds must have created ripe conditions for corruption. In Quetzaltenango, in 1847, macehuales complained to the national minister of government that their gobernador, José María Paz—the same who served on the cemetery commission during the 1837 cholera epidemic—was abusing his power and forcing them to work on the community planting without pay and without them knowing how the profit from the sale of the harvest was used.[31] Defending Paz, the corregidor stated that the money went to build a new cabildo, repair the jail, and provide for the poor. Further, he argued that since Quetzaltenango had not cultivated a communal planting since 1812, the "young

Indians" were unaccustomed to this obligation and therefore resisted supplying their labor. The corregidor praised Paz. He wrote that it is "not easy to find another Indian" with the ability to maintain public order and harmonious relations between K'iche's and Ladinos, thus highlighting the endurance of the colonial pact between K'iche' and state elites.[32]

A House with Two Masters

Quetzalteco Ladinos stridently objected to the reestablishment of the K'iche' municipality. Over Ladino protests, the corregidor used the new *ley de las municipalidades* to rule in favor of the Indians. For the next fifty-four years, principales would come together in December to choose the two alcaldes and four regidores who would serve in the following year's K'iche' cabildo.[33] Throughout the next two decades, Ladinos would periodically try to have the indigenous municipality abolished. In 1846, for example, the Ladino municipality wrote a lengthy petition to the national government demanding that it suppress the indigenous municipality.[34] With selective historical memory, the Ladinos claimed that there had been only one municipal corporation since 1806. Their petition correctly pointed out that the ley de municipalidades was vague regarding communities that have a large number of Ladinos: "Not in the old laws, nor in the modern ones, nor in the many laws that grant protection and privileges to Indians, can be found one single reference that says that, in populations comprised of both classes, Indians should have their own . . . municipality. What has resulted here is a confusion equal to a house that has two masters."[35] After reviewing the case, the *ministro de gobernación* agreed that the law was vague but ruled on behalf of the K'iche's and ordered the Ladinos to desist from demanding that the Indians attend their sessions.[36]

As before, what was at stake in this struggle was the control of communal resources, as the Ladino petition makes clear: "The Indians say that the city property is theirs, but this municipality invests the rent for the public benefit, without excluding one single inhabitant no matter what his class. We maintain the prisoners, who are in the majority Indians, and we provide medicine and doctors when they are sick. The newly established community treasury is a considerable amount of money and we do not know what they do with it."

In 1847, Ladino authorities requested a loan of one thousand pesos from the K'iche' treasury to buy wheat so as to alleviate the effects of a grain shortage.[37] The gobernador, José María Paz, refused the request, replying that even though they "would like to lend the money," they were not able to. Aside from the money spent paying workers to harvest the community planting, they had to buy material to repair the roof of their processional cloister. Lifting passages almost verbatim from the ley de gobernadores, Paz stated that whatever funds remained had to be reserved in case of disease or another calamity and to pay for a school for indigenous children. A few years earlier in 1845, Ladinos requested that Indians help them construct a new public slaughterhouse.[38] The K'iche' authorities replied that even though they were in favor of the project, they were against the proposed location, which was on what they considered to be their communal lands: "The land belongs to the ejidos of this city, and as such is our property. It is also the only place we have to pasture our animals."[39] In both requests the national government supported the K'iche's' decision.

More than gaining renewed control over city resources, Carrera's victory halted the ladinoization of Quetzaltenango. K'iche's, once again, became a majority of the city's population, which they remain to this day. Part of the explanation for this reversal can be found in the flight of Ladinos. Fearing continued violence, many left for Mexico. But more than this, the restoration of the republic of Indians gave K'iche' authorities much needed reinforcement in the struggle to define ethnicity. During the period of Spanish rule, population counts were often related to tribute obligations and were conducted under the supervision of the corregidor, the priest, and indigenous officials. After independence, Ladinos assumed the responsibility. The city's 1830 census, for example, while continuing to divide the city into two ethnic categories, was conducted by a committee of four Ladino municipal officers.[40] This provides a partial explanation for the rapid demographic reversal discussed earlier, in which Ladinos had become a majority of the city's population by the 1830s. Prejudiced by assimilationist expectations and finally unencumbered by the restrictions of Crown, church, or tribute demands, Ladino counters were more likely to provide a higher tally of the city's non-K'iche' population. Further, common Indians, who hoped to escape taxes and other community obligations, may have taken advantage of Ladino prejudices to pass into a less controlled caste. But following Carrera's triumph, *padrones* were to be conducted separately by caste, with principales in charge of counting

Indians.[41] Facing the threat of continuing intermarriage, migration, and cultural assimilation, principales could now use their reestablished political power to reestablish the K'iche's as a majority of the city's population.

Carrera's victory provided K'iche's respite from the social and ideological processes that produced the long rise and quick fall of the Estado de los Altos. The restoration of their corporate protections gave them time and political space to regroup and reestablish their political authority as practiced by their "ancestors."[42]

K'iche' principales did more, however, than engage in rearguard maneuvering in the face of inexorable historical forces. For the next three decades, political stability allowed for general economic growth throughout the region.[43] After 1840, exports to Latin America and Europe increased and agricultural production expanded.[44] In the 1820s, the indigo economy had a brief revival followed by the intensification of cochineal production.[45] In the 1850s and 1860s, as cochineal exports lost ground to natural and synthetic dyes, coffee trees began to be planted in the nopal groves and eventually expanded onto the volcanic slopes of the Pacific coast. The steady rise of the value of coffee exports throughout the 1860s and 1870s signaled that Guatemala's coffee revolution had begun.

Economic growth, combined with political stability and corporate protection, allowed city Indians to strengthen their economic positions. As we shall see in greater detail in the following chapter, many K'iche's were able to consolidate their control over local commerce and dominate certain trades. The newly affirmed hold K'iche's had on ejidal land allowed them to carry on the practice of combining commercial activity with subsistence production, and the reinvested political authority of patriarchs allowed them to continue to mobilize community resources to participate in the regional market. In addition to consolidating their economic positions, Quetzalteco K'iche's also developed an urban and national identity that, while drawing on the racist premises of Ladino nationalism, rejected the notion that Indians were a disappearing race. By promoting an alternative national vision based on their unique class and political position, K'iche's played a crucial role in the formation of the Ladino state. It is to this nationalization of ethnicity that we now turn.

Chapter 5
Principales to Patrones, Macehuales to Mozos: Land, Labor, and the Commodification of Community

The word *ejido* has been erased from the municipal vocabulary.

— *Quetzaltenango's annual municipal report*, 1883

In 1871 liberal insurgents from the western highlands took state power. Less inspired by an enlightened belief in liberty than by precepts of progress and order, if not necessarily law, these new coffee liberals, led by Justo Rufino Barrios, enacted land and labor reforms intended to promote coffee cultivation and exportation. The state also passed a host of lesser decrees and laws designed to raise revenue and effect social control.[1] In many ways, the liberal revolution represented a final triumph of the old Estado de los Altos—this time extended throughout the country.[2] Following the brief presidency of the Spanish-born Miguel García Granados (1871–73), the next four presidents were from Los Altos. Two of them, Barrios and his successor, Manuel Lisandro Barillas, were coffee planters. Barrios was from the department of San Marcos, and, immediately after the revolution, he returned to consolidate his power as military commander of the highlands before assuming the presidency in 1873. Altenses in exile or politically dormant during the long Carrera period now assumed a prominent place in national politics.[3] If the economic base of highland society had changed over the decades—moving from regional trade to coffee production—many of the players, or at least the families, remained the same.[4]

If the long Carrera period provided the K'iche' community with time to regroup and consolidate, it could not stem the economic and political changes that propelled the liberals to victory. For centuries, self-sufficiency based on household and community production had allowed many K'iche' peasants to participate successfully in a commercial regional market. As we have seen, the communal ideologies that structured this production cut in many directions. Macehuales called on expectations of reciprocity to ensure subsistence and hold elites accountable for their actions; principales used these same ties to mobilize labor and establish their authority; women manipulated patriarchal assumptions to press their economic and political interests; and competing elites spoke in the name of the community to win legitimacy. As long as a "bedrock of subsistence rights" continued to exist, communal divisions could be contained and collective interests defended. In the second half of the nineteenth century, however, a number of factors began to chisel away at this subsistence foundation.

The shift to coffee cultivation and the construction of a militarized state dramatically transformed relations between Guatemala's ruling class and its majority Indian population. More than ever before in the history of the colony or the nation, elites viewed Indians as a labor force to be mobilized.[5] For the next seventy years, through a series of "reforms" and decrees, the state, in effect, legislated primitive capital accumulation, using its political and military power to break the subsistence base of communities and make indigenous land and labor available to the rapacious needs of finqueros. The predatory nature of the coffee state and its effects on indigenous communities have been graphically detailed elsewhere, and, despite attempts by scholars to render a more nuanced interpretation, Guatemala's entrance into the nineteenth-century international coffee market remains one of the most brutal in the hemisphere.

In Quetzaltenango, the land and labor reforms enacted by the restored liberal regime had contradictory effects on social relations within the city. Quetzaltenango's unique economic and political niche shielded many K'iche's from the worst effects of primitive capital accumulation. Because the city was at too high an altitude for coffee growing, would-be finqueros did not covet Quetzalteco land, and Indians were able to hold on to a good part of their property. Likewise, Quetzaltenango was too politically important for the kind of wholesale appropriation of land that took place in other nearby highland towns.[6] Therefore, a sudden loss of subsistence land did not, as it did in many other communities, compel Quetzaltecos to become plantation workers. Further, the *mandamiento*, a forced labor draft enacted between 1877 and 1894, was not applied in Quetzaltenango.

Despite these relative protections, there were nevertheless powerful factors pushing poorer Quetzaltecos into relations of wage or debt labor.

Guatemalans now needed money to pay a series of new taxes and "contributions" to finance the growing state bureaucracy and coffee infrastructure. And while wholesale appropriation of land did not take place, a rising population combined with an increase in land concentration resulted in a diminishing subsistence base. A growing urban economy and expanding agricultural production, however, could absorb much of this growing class of alienated labor. Within the indigenous population, many K'iche's could find jobs either as workers in the growing construction industry, as laborers on highland farms, as artisans, or in many other occupations servicing the city. Many of these wage laborers went to work for other K'iche's, as an emerging indigenous bourgeoisie consolidated its economic base.

Land

Almost immediately upon taking the presidency in 1873, Barrios initiated a series of decrees that made land available to coffee planters.[7] As was the case during the 1820s and 1830s, these laws encouraged privatization by simplifying the procedures for the conversion of community property into individually titled holdings. Contrary to popular belief, however, Barrios and his successors did not abolish communal rights to ejidos, as their contemporaries did in neighboring El Salvador.[8] It was in the interest of coffee elites unable or unwilling to support a full-time labor force that Indians retain access to some subsistence production. The most immediate effect of land reform was in the coffee-producing regions of the southern coast and the Verapaces, where thousands of caballerías of communal and uncultivated land were turned over to coffee. Nevertheless, the new legislation did have a substantial, although contradictory, impact on highland Indian towns. The way these laws played out in specific communities often depended on social relations within the communities. In some pueblos, Indians desirous of land, either for enrichment or subsistence, formed alliances with Ladinos to take advantage of liberal laws and convert municipal land into private plots; in other towns, leaders were able to present a united front and actually increase communal holdings. In Quetzaltenango, these new laws hastened a process that had been long under way; the commodification and privatization of land, which had taken place slowly and unevenly over the last three centuries, was brought to a rapid conclusion. By the turn of the twentieth century, the vast majority of all agricultural land within the municipality had been distributed to individuals, and the word *ejido* was now used strictly to denote municipal forests and unclaimed land considered too rocky or too poor for cultivation. The crucial difference between this period and the first liberal interlude was that now K'iche' authorities willingly participated in the application of the new land laws.[9]

Privatization in Quetzaltenango took place in three ways. First, at various points over the next four decades, individuals were required to title and register their holdings. This not only recognized their claims but facilitated sale and mortgage transactions.[10] Over the course of the following four decades, hundreds of large and small landholders—K'iche's and Ladinos—requested title so they could register their property. In 1874, José María Paz, for example, the former K'iche' governor, registered six caballerías of land just outside Quetzaltenango's municipal boundaries, which he claimed were left to him by his mother in 1851.[11] Paz immediately sold four of the six caballerías to José Aguilar.[12] Second, after 1871, for the first time, the Ladino municipality rented unused land. Following the promulgation of the 1877 decree, which allowed individuals to purchase the rented land for a percentage of its estimated value, this rented property was converted into private holdings.[13]

Finally, the city's agricultural ejido was distributed among the city's poorer classes. The first major concession occurred in an area called Llanos de Pinal, a large plain that spreads out from the northern foothills of the volcano Santa María. From 1877 to 1889, 790 K'iche' male heads of households received parcels of land ranging from four to twenty-five cuerdas.[14] All told, 8,813 cuerdas were distributed. To a large degree, this distribution simply standardized land relations already in existence, as individuals received land they already considered theirs.

Distribution of city land reflected the difficulty the liberal state had in developing a cohesive ideology governing the nation's ethnic relations. Despite his liberal rhetoric, Barrios was eminently practical in matters concerning ethnic politics. In 1876, he denied a Ladino request to participate in the distribution of Llanos de Pinal. Ladinos, he wrote, had received land in a previous distribution. Therefore, "in order to preserve the good harmony of the two classes that compose this city," he ruled that the distribution of Llanos should take place strictly among Indians.[15] Barrios's successor, Barillas, reversed course. In 1887, he ordered that the remaining ejido be distributed evenly among both Ladinos and Indians: "The fusion of the two races into one is what is desired," he opined; to distribute the land solely among Indians would only "exacerbate mutual antipathy between neighbors of the same population."[16] His successor, José María Reina Barrios, switched back once again. In 1892, Reina Barrios, whose government flirted more than any previous one with indigenista rhetoric and policy, ordered that land in Chichiguitán be distributed exclusively among "los indios pobres."[17] Further reflecting his indigenista proclivities, Reina Barrios decreed that the distributed land could not be sold or mortgaged for a period of five years.

Two concurrent trends accompanied the privatization of Quetzaltenango's ejidos: an increase in the amount of land cultivated annually and the concentration of land among fewer and fewer owners. Despite chronic recessions and economic downturns, the steady rise in population and the making of a coffee workforce created new markets for the city's agricultural products. Quetzalteco farmers, both K'iche's and Ladinos, responded by cultivating more wheat (see Table 2). Since this shift happened before any appreciable technological innovation (yields per cuerda of corn and wheat remained constant throughout the late nineteenth century), the increased cultivation of wheat entailed the extension of cultivation into land previously left fallow or reserved for corn.[18] This had the effect of forcing poor milperos to push the municipio's agricultural frontier into the city's woodland, leading to increased conflict between the milperos and the indigenous authorities, who were charged with the job of forest conservation.[19] As the K'iche' alcalde put it in 1879, "The needs of the people are forcing them to use land that in the past was unused (*dejado al olvida*)."[20]

For centuries, K'iche' men planted crops for sale outside of the community, yet an erratic market, communal ideologies, subsistence concerns, and a lack of capital limited the ability of K'iche's to accumulate wealth and fully participate in the regional market. While it would be decades before easier access to credit and technological advances would turn K'iche's into agrarian capitalists, this fin de siècle generation of indigenous farmers may have been the first for whom profit incentives and market factors rather than status, consumption, or subsistence concerns came to dominate production decisions. More than two-thirds of all the farms owned by K'iche's comprising fifty cuerdas or more produced some wheat. Further, Indians began to experiment with other crops and

Table 2 Total Caballerías Cultivated in Wheat, Corn,
Oats, and Alfalfa within Municipal Limits (1840–1900)

Year	Total	Corn	Wheat
1840	48.0	34.0	14.0
1878	68.0	—	—
1882	80.0[a]	53.0	25.0
1900	97.5[a]	61.0	36.5

Source: AHQ, caja 1840, 1878; AGQ, 1882, 1900.
[a] The fact that these figures also include oats and alfalfa
cultivation accounts for the slight difference between them
and the figures in Table 4.

production techniques. In the 1890s, Tomás Pac and Pioquinto Guzmán
chopped down acres of forest to plant potatoes, and by 1910 José María
Citalán supplemented five hundred cuerdas of highland wheat production
with five hundred cuerdas of coastal corn cultivation.[21]

Subsistence farmers not only had to contend with a shrinking land base
because of a growing population and the extension of wheat cultivation,
but they also had to deal with the concentration of land. A comparison of
the years 1894 and 1901 reveals that there was a sharp decrease in the
number of owners of farms of twenty-five cuerdas or more (see Table 3).
But while the total number of owners decreased, the amount of land
forming medium to large farms *increased* (see Table 4). Thus, within a
few years the amount of land left for small subsistence milpas dropped
precariously as the population continued to climb.[22]

As discussed in chapter 1, gendered dependency furthered the concentration and commodification of property. In 1870, for example, the
widow Juana Pac sold fifty cuerdas to Francisco Acabal, and in 1896, Rita
Coyoy de Bautista, a widow at age twenty-eight without "determined
employment," sold the land her husband left her to Bonfacio Nimatuj.[23]
Within the K'iche' común, these transactions often took place within extended families and between generations. In 1875, Lucio, Pedro, Manuela,
and Eulalia Cayax sold the 272 cuerdas they had inherited from their
father to their cousin, Manuel.[24] In 1876, the widow María Francisca
Hernández sold her house and land to her grandson.[25] These sales likewise reflected the generational shift from a predominantly peasant society
to an urban artisanal economy that was taking place in the city. In 1897,

Table 3 Farms of 25 Cuerdas or More within the Municipal Limits, by Size and
Ethnicity (1894 and 1901)

Size (in cuerdas)	Total Number		K'iche'		Ladino	
	1894	1901	1894	1901	1894	1901
25–49	103	36	70	26	33	10
50–99	79	29	45	14	34	15
100–499	83	63	41	29	42	34
500–999	14	9	7	4	7	5
1000+	6	13	1	1	5	12
Total	285	138	164	64	121	76

Source: AGQ, Catastro de Fincas, 1894; AHQ, caja 1894; AGQ, Libros de Matrículas,
1874–77; AGQ, Encuesta de Ministerio de Fomento, 1901.
Note: The number of small farms owned by K'iche's needs to be viewed with some
skepticism. It is probable that this number should be higher. For ethnicity, I simply
used surnames as a criterion. Some Ladinos had K'iche' names, but the chance of
error is greater in the other direction, for many more Indians had Spanish surnames.

for example, Manuel Coyoy, a sixty-year-old farmer, sold his house in the
center of the city to Vicente García, a thirty-six-year old mason.[26]

Table 3 indicates that land ownership tended to be concentrated in
Ladino hands at the expense of the K'iche' population, but these figures
do not tell the whole story. While many small and medium-sized indigenous farmers lost a large portion of their land, some K'iche's actually
managed to increase their holdings significantly. Out of a selection of
eighteen indigenous landowners between the years 1894 and 1901, seventeen of them increased their holdings. Manuel Tucux, managed to increase his land through inheritance, while others, such as Agatón Boj and
Tomás Pac, did so through purchases (see Table 5).

Despite that fact that a significant minority of politically important
K'iche's benefited from the privatization of Quetzaltenango's ejidos, the
question remains: What had changed over seventy years that disposed
K'iche's to go along with the liberal land reform? Although the coffee
regime was much more effective than the first liberal government in
responding to protests, it would be too easy to attribute the sudden
tractability of the principales to the increased repressive power of the
state. It is true that an expanded bureaucracy and a fortified military set
the limits of dissent, but there was still much room to maneuver in defense

Table 4 Caballerías of Land in Production, by Farm Size (1894 and 1901)

Year	Land in Production	Land in Production, Farms More Than 25 cuerdas	Land in Production, Farms Less Than 25 cuerdas
1894	78	35	43
1901	96	49	37

Source: AGQ, Catastro de Fincas, 1894; AHQ, caja 1894; AGQ, Libros de Matrículas, 1874–77; AGQ, Encuesta de Ministerio de Fomento, 1901.

of interests. Rather, the reasons explaining indigenous support for privatization need to be found in changes in the political economy of the K'iche' común.[27]

In the nineteenth century, Quetzaltenango's population began to push at the limits of its subsistence capacity. This produced broad, cross-class support within the indigenous population for privatization. No longer could subsistence rights be guaranteed through the ejido system, which theoretically provided each K'iche' family with enough land to support itself. Although it is often difficult to get at why commoners either acquiesced in or worked for privatization, it seems that poorer Indians now saw ownership, guaranteed by title and registration, as the best means to ensure access to sufficient land. In one case, in 1884, twenty-three K'iche's presented a petition for title to ejidal land they worked as individual households, arguing that with legal protection they would not suffer the same "fate" (*suerte*) as other vecinos who were forced to migrate after losing their corn plots (the petition did not specify how their less-fortunate neighbors lost their holdings).[28]

Liberal rhetoric surrounding privatization likewise allowed commoners justification to appropriate city land set aside for uses other than cultivation. In 1891, a group of ten K'iche' men charged with clearing forest land defended themselves by arguing that land held by "individuals" was "always" more productive than common land.[29] Often, the language of privatization masked nascent class tensions within a community. In nearby Cantel, the efforts of K'iche' commoners to cultivate municipal forest land put them at odds with a group of wealthy Cantelense K'iche's who made their living from harvesting and trading lumber. The leader of the commoners argued to the president that "land under the communal system produces little or nothing. Is it prudent and economical to take

Table 5 Selected Changes in Cuerdas of K'iche'
Landholdings (1894–1901)

Name	1894	1901
Tomás Pac	300	470
José María Pisquiy	200	100
Juan Quemé	50	90
Florencio Tuc	115	410
Juan Coyoy	236	270
Eulogio Sac	50	120
Pablo Boj	214	400
Manuel Tucux	26	1,500
Agatón Boj	60	342
Benito Reyes	140	270
Cruz Sacalxot	300	500
Gabriel Yax	50	150
Fermín Quemé	30	50
Antonio Qaquix	60	70
Tiburcio Cayax	25	100
Esteban Cayax	60	80
José María Citalán[a]	50	1,000
Cirilo Pol	100	60

Source: AGQ, Catastro de Fincas, 1894; AHQ, caja
1894; AGQ, Encuesta de Ministerio de Fomento,
1901; AGQ, and José María Citalán, mayor de edad y
de este vecindario . . . , 1910.
[a] comparison from years 1901 and 1910.

these lots from us so that they can be placed again under the . . . unpro-
ductive system of communal property?"[30]

K'iche' elites, on the other hand, perhaps not as anxious about survival
as macehuales, supported privatization for two reasons. First, as the city's
population grew, it became harder for principales to regulate the distribution of milpa land to guarantee access to sufficient production. By pri-
vatizing the ejidos, they absolved themselves of the political responsibility
of ensuring the survival of commoners. Further, as successful commodity
producers, wealthy K'iche's increasingly saw their relationship to land in
class, rather than caste, terms. The nature of the value of land was

changing. Previously, the ability to provide access to subsistence production was for them, as caste elites, an important factor in garnering communal legitimacy. This legitimacy allowed elites to mobilize household
and communal labor, which, in turn, permitted them to participate in
a commodified regional market. Now, for the principales, the *economic*
value of land began to outweigh its *political* worth.

Labor

In 1877, the state instituted the infamous mandamiento, a forced labor law
designed to meet the needs of coffee planters.[31] Based on the colonial
repartimiento, the new law was in fact a rationalization and expansion of
state labor obligations in effect since the 1830s. Under the revised law,
pueblos were required to supply to coffee plantations work gangs of up to
sixty people for periods of fifteen to thirty days as requested by the
department's jefe político. The mandamiento complemented a growing
reliance on debt labor, as conscripted workers willingly or unwillingly
borrowed large amounts of money they could not pay back.[32] Peonage
offered peasants a method of escaping the labor corvée. Since it was illegal
to draft someone who was already in debt, *mozos* (laborers) could exercise
some control and seek protection by allying themselves with relatively
preferential *patrones* (bosses / landowners).[33] At the same time, a host of
new national and local taxes and "contributions" were assessed to pay for
an expanding state and coffee infrastructure. Individuals more than ever
needed money with which to pay off financial obligations or to commute
labor requirements. The 1873 *contribución de caminos* (road tax), for example, decreed that all able male citizens were obliged either to give three
days' work on public projects or pay twelve reales in a commutation fee.[34]
Further, efforts to avoid military drafts aided in the creation of a labor
force, as *colonos* (resident workers), indebted workers, and those able to
pay the thirty-peso exemption fee were released from service.[35]

These measures to create an agricultural working class varied greatly
according to region. In the area surrounding Quetzaltenango, this diversity was most vivid between the Mam towns northwest of the city of
Quetzaltenango and the K'iche' towns (including the city itself) to the
southeast. The municipal origins of the indebted peons indicates the
differential impact that the corvée had on highland communities. Infor-

mation on 1,302 colonos from the Costa Cuca coffee region just south-west of the city reveals that while 378 were from Mam-speaking towns, only 71 were from the K'iche' towns of Cantel, Zunil, Almolonga, and Quetzaltenango.[36] The majority of the colonos were from the more peripheral departments of San Marcos, Huehuetenango, and Quiché.

For the region immediately surrounding the city, the importance of K'iche' towns as regional suppliers of basic grains and raw materials, plus their proximity to larger urban centers, provided their inhabitants with leverage to resist the mandamiento. The more remote, isolated, and poor Mam towns, in contrast, were hard hit by the labor laws. Alcaldes from the Mam pueblos of Huitán and Cajolá repeatedly protested that they could not give an adequate count of their population, for the majority were working on the coast. They also complained that they had no land on which to plant. An 1884 letter from the alcalde of Huitán to the jefe político provides a brutal portrait of the town's vulnerability. After the mayor protested that he could not comply with an order for twenty workers because all the town's men were already conscripted, Ladino troops arrived "to arrest and tie up the unlucky workers. They hit them as if they were beasts. They committed the worst abuses, robbing corn, poultry, food, and money, raping our wives and daughters, taking advantage of the fact that their husbands and fathers are away working on the railroad. Huitán is extremely miserable, scarce of population, with land . . . that after much work barely produces what is necessary to live . . . there is no industry or commerce."[37]

Economic integration and location may not have been all that spared the K'iche' towns from the worst effects of the mandamiento. The development of a regional market centered around Quetzaltenango, and its satellite pueblos created a significant degree of social stratification within those communities. By the end of the nineteenth century, whether through relations of wage, debt, kin, or clan, residents of these communities worked on local enterprises that made money, and, as we have seen in chapter 1, had done so for some time. In Cantel, for example, authorities repeatedly claimed that all the able men not already working on coastal fincas were "all contracted with the señores agricultores of this pueblo, cultivating corn and wheat."[38] And by 1894, at least forty-three Cantelenses were indebted at more than fifteen pesos each to six landowners, at least four of whom were K'iche' and vecinos of Cantel.[39]

Quetzaltecos did migrate to the coffee regions, but proportionally fewer than did their more impoverished neighbors. Spurred on by a shrinking subsistence land base, along with labor, military, and financial obligations, many of the new "free wage laborers" were able to find work within the city, either in the expanding agricultural sector or in servicing the needs of a growing urban economy. This process not only deepened class relations throughout the city as a whole, but it also recast relations of reciprocity in economic terms. Many K'iche's now went to work for other K'iche's. Wage and debt relations among K'iche's had long been in practice, but during the first decades of the liberal state they became dominant. Yet as can be said of the colonial period, it is doubtful that debt was as coercive a mechanism of labor recruitment for the region's wheat and corn production as it was for the nation's coffee cultivation.[40]

In the city's agricultural sector, the number of indebted peons grew rapidly. In 1894, there were 189 mozos colonos—who, from their surnames, were overwhelmingly K'iche'—on farms within the city's limits.[41] Forty-nine of these mozos were indebted to *fincas* owned by K'iche's. By 1901, this number had grown to 258.[42] Of these, 220 were K'iche' by their surnames: 120 worked on farms owned by K'iche's and 100 on farms owned by Ladinos (no Ladinos worked on a farm owned by a K'iche'). The total number of fincas with more than ten colonos grew from four in 1894 to eight in 1901, which suggests an end to the small-scale patrón-colono system that probably existed prior to the expansion of commercial production. On Crecencio Sáenz's two-caballería finca, for example, the number of mozos increased from fourteen to forty; on Santiago Coyoy's three fincas, the number of mozos went from seven to fourteen, all of them indigenous.[43] And José María Citalán, a prominent K'iche', went from having no colonos on his property in 1894, to having twenty-three in 1910, all but three from Quetzaltenango.[44] Likewise, whole families became trapped in residential debt servitude. In 1901, for example, six indigenous families, made up of seven men and six women, lived on Mariano Luna's two fincas, while four men, three women, and three children lived on Ramón Corredor's five-hundred-cuerda plot.

Thus, rather than resistance to agricultural labor drafts successfully forming within networks of communal autonomy and solidarity, in the K'iche' towns surrounding Quetzaltenango it was actually regional integration and intracommunal stratification that tempered the effects of the mandamiento. Socially homogeneous and isolated towns in the Mam region were hard hit by the labor drafts, while in Cantel and Quetzalte-

Table 6 Occupation and Number of Employed in Quetzaltenango (1894)

Occupation	No. Employed	Occupation	No. Employed
purveyors	118	jewelers	12
lawyers / notaries	23	engineers	11
masons	308	soap makers	44
potters	14	agricultural workers	1,070
woodcutters	6	brick makers	28
barbers	31	laundresses / ironers	189
butchers	47	public school teachers	47
embroiders	6	machinists	4
candle makers	46	marimba players	17
quarrymen	107	doctors	9
woolers	3	dressmakers	20
carpenters	286	millers	9
wheelwrights	9	breadmakers	224
carriage builders	2	cake makers	35
wax chandlers	9	reporters	3
cigarette makers	328	painters	23
coppersmiths	8	firework makers	35
midwives	2	silversmiths	14
traders	275	watchmakers	7
seamstresses	305	priests	2
tanners	30	tailors	261
dentists	2	servants	869
shop assistants	11	hat makers	26
distillers	7	saddle makers	31
public employees	74	tamale makers	88
bookbinder	1	telegraph operators	15
sculptors	3	shopkeepers	17
pharmacists	22	booksellers	11
musicians	47	dyers	6
florists	10	grinders	29
smelters	2	tortilla makers	120
engravers	4	cowherds	36
blacksmiths	59	grocers	65
weavers	380	shoemakers	243

Source: Dirección General de Estadística, Censo general de la república de Guatemala (Guatemala City: Tipografía Nacional, 1894).

nango, potential corvée victims found refuge in the interstices of intra-communal labor relations.

Apart from the agricultural sector, many Quetzaltecos found work in the growing urban economy (see Table 6). Out of an official employed population of 6,205, only 1,070 had their primary occupation listed as being directly related to agricultural production. Nearly half—3,009—worked as artisans. The remainder were employed either in commercial or service activity. The high number of barbers, teachers, florists, book-sellers, cooks, and jewelers reveals an intensification of the division of labor needed to service an urban economy. K'iche's, for example, had managed to dominate bread production. In 1857, eleven Ladino *panaderos* (breadmakers) complained that they could not compete with the city's sixty-one indigenous breadmakers.[45] The Ladinos groused that not only did a majority of the city's poor eat only corn tortillas but that their K'iche' rivals were able to undersell them because they did not have high operating costs. Ladinos claimed that K'iche's, by bypassing the toll-houses and grinding the wheat themselves, evaded transport and milling taxes; moreover, by selling from the plaza and the streets, they avoided paying high rents.

The growth of the city expanded the employment possibilities previously opened to women through trade and small-scale production. Although the numbers are not broken down by gender, a large number of occupations were obviously filled by women, such as servants (869), seamstresses (305), tortilla makers (120), laundresses, and ironers (189). Further, the division of labor created a greater market for indigenous women's traditional clothing, which was now increasingly purchased rather than made at home. This allowed female skilled weavers and traders of high-priced goods to profit from the commodification of urban relations.[46]

Although the term *artisan* covers a range of activities and occupations, it does not convey the complex labor relations that united this sector of the city's workforce. The 1894 census does not differentiate from among these tradesmen between masters, apprentices, laborers, or self-employed people, nor does it reveal the family and kinship relations through which trade knowledge was passed on and tasks divided. The city's craft sector was stratified, not just among artisans of differing skills and opportunities but within families, since masters used household labor to practice their trade.[47] Artisan *talleres* (workshops), owned by K'iche' or Ladino masters, employed up to fifty workers during this period. As the city expanded, select craftsmen were able to take advantage of their trade skill and control over labor to become politically and economically powerful.

Leading this emerging group were the construction tradesmen, particularly stonemasons. Since at least the first half of the nineteenth century,

K'iche' carpenters and masons controlled the city's building trades. In 1839, a Ladino municipal officer lamented the drunkenness that beset masons, who are "almost exclusively Indians."[48] This dominance would continue, and throughout the nineteenth century K'iche's secured relatively high-paying jobs as masons, carpenters, and laborers.[49] In 1853, for example, the Ladino municipality approved Vicente Sum's estimated budget for the construction of a public fountain.[50] The projected cost of the work was 181 pesos, seventy-five of which were for salaries. In 1863, three K'iche' *albañiles* (masons) earned three and a half reales a day on an aqueduct project, and eight K'iche' laborers earned one and a half reales a day on another job that lasted for nearly a year.[51]

In the decades after the second liberal triumph, a public and private building boom transformed the city. Not only did Ladinos build roads, bridges, ports, and railroads to meet their export needs, they turned the city of Quetzaltenango itself into a public showcase for their liberal ideals. The town council began construction on a new municipal palace, built a new departmental penitentiary, opened schools, widened and tree-lined boulevards, laid out public gardens, erected statues to heroes of the Estado de los Altos, and drained swamps. The public works line in the municipal budget grew from 400.00 pesos in 1860 to 11,480.09 in 1894.[52] As Ladinos attempted to build a city worthy of their aspirations, they came to rely even more on K'iche's for their building needs. Hundreds of mozos, masons, carpenters, and quarrymen found long-term employment on public and private projects. Construction on the municipal palace alone, which lasted from 1884 to 1892, regularly employed over eighty K'iche' laborers, who earned from one and a half to six pesos a week.[53] This was a good salary, considering that one cuerda of good corn or wheat land in the early 1890s could be purchased for two to three pesos. Agatón Boj, a prominent principal who started his career as one of the head masons on this project, earned six pesos a week.[54] Within ten years Boj had become the largest contractor in the city.[55]

Work in the construction industry usually entailed a mix of wage work, debt servitude, and family labor. Master masons formed enterprises with their brothers and sons and drew on family and communal ties to build a workforce. In 1894, Félix and Esteban Sum built the city's new Teatro Municipal. The municipality paid the brothers two and a half pesos for every square *vara* (roughly a yard) of the building they completed; from this sum, they were to pay their work crew, composed of twenty-five

K'iche's.[56] Esteban Sum went on to build the bridge over the Río Sibilia, contracting the job for 5,500 pesos. Work lasted for three months and Sum's weekly payroll averaged 125 pesos a week for twenty to twenty-five men, all K'iche's.[57] In 1907, Boj and his son Enrique employed fifty-seven K'iche' full-time workers on their restoration of the facade of the city's municipal theater, which had been destroyed in the 1902 earthquake.[58] Most of these workers were paid weekly salaries, but at least three provided Boj with labor to work off a debt to him.[59]

Community

The dissolution of Quetzaltenango's ejidos and the increasing reliance on wage labor did not entail a disappearance of subsistence production or a complete erosion of household production. Rather, it marked a fundamental shift in how peasant production functioned within the K'iche' community. Prior to the transformations of the nineteenth century, access to land allowed some K'iche's to accumulate a significant amount of wealth and to consolidate that wealth into capital. But formidable checks on the ability of individuals to accumulate capital meant that the predominant function of land remained to guarantee household survival. This survival was predicated on identification with and participation in a larger indigenous peasant collective. As such, the political regulation of land formed the basis of communal relations, binding K'iche's in a nexus of reciprocal entitlements and obligations.

By the late nineteenth century, however, land use had undergone a fundamental change. Rather than guaranteeing survival for the majority of K'iche's, the primary function of land was now to subsidize the economic activity of a community divided along class lines. Wealthy K'iche' tradesmen and merchants, such as Agatón Boj and José María Citalán continued to combine subsistence and commercial agricultural production with their artisan and trade activity. This diversification of production, which was carried out through a mix of household and wage labor, continued to provide these new capitalists with a subsidy for their commercial activity and a refuge from the uncertainties of market production. For poorer K'iche's, the maintenance of household production and lingering access to land assured survival in an economy where wage work was not always guaranteed.

Although they appeared throughout the city, these new class divisions were most prominent between K'iche's in the urban center and their more rural counterparts from the city's hinterlands. Urban K'iche's became artisans, construction contractors, large-scale traders, and shopkeepers, while rural K'iche's tended to swell the ranks of debt and wage labor.[60] In 1884, for example, nearly all the 623 K'iche's who paid the commutation fee to avoid three days of public work came from one of the four central barrios.[61] In contrast, after the state increased its public labor obligation in 1894, nearly all those conscripted were poorer K'iche' farmers or wage workers from the municipio's rural confines.[62]

Increasingly obliged to rely on money to fill basic needs, poorer Indians often had no recourse but to borrow from wealthier Indians, drawing on long-established communal patronage relations.[63] This dependency on money within a more commodified economy transformed indigenous relations of reciprocity into relations of class, a change nowhere better illustrated than in the willingness of Indians to use the recently established Banco de Occidente to finance indigenous borrowing. Increasingly, poorer Indians would put up their remaining land as collateral to borrow money from the bank, while richer Indians would guarantee the loan. For example, in 1884 Silverio Coyoy cosigned a loan from the Banco de Occidente for 300 pesos to José Tucux. When Tucux defaulted, Coyoy paid off the loan and assumed ownership of Tucux's urban property.[64] This dependence on money likewise promoted the division of labor along class lines. In 1896, for example, Agatón Boj assumed the debt of 226 pesos of another K'iche', to be paid back in labor over a set term.[65] The transformation of the class content of debt was furthered by liberal legislation: poorer Indians borrowed money or entered into peonage to avoid work and military obligations, while wealthier K'iche's simply paid the commutation fee.

By the turn of the twentieth century, then, the nature of the relations binding the K'iche' común had changed. Although subsistence household production and reciprocal norms still informed communal identity, the content of that identity had been transformed as the community divided along class lines. Political relations that had governed the común were gradually superseded by economic determinants of a commodified market economy as macehuales became mozos and principales turned into patrones.

Despite the proliferation of commodified exchange relations, caste affiliation was strengthened, in marked contrast to what occurred in many indigenous regions of Mexico.[66] Why? In Guatemala, the unique form taken by liberal development allowed for an intensification of ethnic identity. Without a major export crop, Guatemala's precoffee economy did not integrate Indians, in however exploitative a fashion, into colonial society. In Mexico, a more vibrant economy eroded indigenous communal identity and political autonomy. Thus the 1910 Mexican Revolution, which was fought with massive indigenous participation, manifested no self-conscious "Indian project."[67] In contrast, Indian communities in colonial Guatemala were, for the most part, left alone. Thus, with the advent of coffee, the creation of Guatemala's agrarian proletariat took place along clearly defined ethnic lines. In a less than symbiotic relationship, coffee production parasitically attached itself to indigenous communities, slowly draining pueblos of their subsistence autonomy. Indian towns were obvious sources of labor, and at times whole communities, either through the mandamiento or peonage, became the captive workforce of specific planters. Furthermore, continued access to some degree of subsistence production meshed well with the seasonal cultivation of coffee, allowing growers to maintain a part-time workforce.[68]

Further, caste divisions were strengthened by an intensification of a particular kind of racism among Guatemala's rulers in the latter half of the nineteenth century. According to Steven Palmer, after a brief period of optimism following the takeover of the state, liberal reformers turned bitter, frustrated, and angry at the refusal of the majority of Indians to be constituted as national citizens.[69] This refusal took many forms: a rejection of education and health initiatives, a "tenacious" clinging to communal lands, a refusal to be counted in national surveys. As argued in chapter 3, a racism that purports to promote cultural assimilation can be every bit as vicious as one based on blood ideology. For Ladino intellectuals and reformers, if Indians refused to take advantage of the opportunities afforded them by the new state, their condition was their own doing: "The Indian, firm in his mode of being, tenacious in his primitive methods of life . . . has won out up to now in the struggle to rescue him and has remained . . . resolved to take not a single step forward."[70] This new racism not only justified Guatemala's brutal model of capitalist development but explained its limitations. Guatemalan liberals wanted to be like Europeans, and if they were not, it must be the fault of the Indians. The limitations on development inherent in dependent capitalism were, therefore, easily displaced onto indigenous culture and its perceived obstructionism. Even the most generous liberals, who acknowledged the intrinsic worth of Indians, understood Guatemala's economic development in racial terms. It was the Indian who produced the wealth of the nation, and it was this production that would, in the most charitable versions, transform Indians into citizens.[71]

Liberal ideology regarding race was likewise strengthened by nationalist historiography. From Morelos, to Juárez, to anti-imperialist struggles against the United States and the French, Mexican historians and politicians had to acknowledge and incorporate Indian participation into national history, especially following the Mexican Revolution.[72] In Guatemala, in sharp contrast, nationalists constantly blamed their political failures on indigenous reaction and nearly uniformly wrote Indians out of their narration of national progress and destiny.[73] The fall of Gálvez, the failure of the Estado de Los Altos, the endurance of Carrera's regime were all blamed on Indians. Racism and economic development, therefore, combined with the writing of history to strengthen the importance caste identity played in understanding social relations.

In Quetzaltenango, other factors likewise influenced the deepening of ethnic affiliation. Despite the early and successful transition by many K'iche' peasants and artisans to commercial production, household production and subsistence cultivation endured. Principales still actively participated in the city's cofradía system and continued to bind individuals to them in relations of dependent paternalism. Large K'iche' landholders provided land to poorer Indians to live on and cultivate, in exchange for labor or crops. Others let shepherds graze on their property. Although profit and market concerns came to dominate production decisions, communal norms could still limit accumulation. When Tomás Pac and Pioquinto Guzmán were prevented by indigenous authorities from destroying forest land to plant potatoes, they were repeatedly maligned by the K'iche' municipales as "los ricos."[74]

The survival of community identity and institutions did not signal resistance to capitalism but rather formed the cultural and social matrices through which communal relations articulated with market forces. As we have seen, the accumulation of capital, the accrual of debt, the mobilization of labor, and the commodification of land all took place within the context of communal and family relations. The language of community therefore was a "weapon both of class struggle *and* class transformation."[75] Principales could use relations of reciprocity and patronage to mobilize communal resources; the poor could attempt to use the same relations to hold elites accountable to their needs; and all could use household subsistence production to mediate against the worst effects of the market.

The idiom of community as it stood on the eve of the twentieth century, however, was not sufficient to express the rapid transformations under way in Guatemala. What was needed was a language that wed the economic to the cultural, the local to the national.

Chapter 6
Regenerating the Race: Race, Class, and the Nationalization of Ethnicity

The Ladinos and Indians are two distinct classes; the former march ahead with hope and energy through the paths that have been laid out by progress; the latter, immovable, do not take any part in the political and intellectual life, adhering tenaciously to their old habits and customs.
— *1894 Guatemalan National Census*

If today all we can do is contribute to progress by cultivating the earth and transforming raw material into useful products, then, when the moral atmosphere of the republic permits us to develop our natural faculties, we will be able to cultivate the intelligence of our children and contribute to the social and political revolution of the country. We yearn for the regeneration of the Indians in order to obtain the civil and political equality that is the basis of democracies. — *1894 K'iche' petition*

Guatemalan capitalist development allowed for an intensification of ethnic identity, even as class divisions were forming. While this phenomenon helps outline various possible forms ethnic relations could take under the coffee regime, it does not explain how individuals took advantage of these possibilities to make sense of their world. The next two chapters will explore how Quetzalteco K'iche' elites used the political and cultural resources at their disposal to redefine ethnic identity to fit changing times. Historians and anthropologists have assured us repeatedly that nineteenth-century Indians had only the most distorted and rudimentary understanding of nations, territorial boundaries, governing philosophies, and national visions. Further, scholars often lament that, until fairly recently, Indians left no written record to describe their society and culture. This is not so for Quetzalteco K'iche's. They not only produced a wealth of accounts in their dealings with the local and national state but also erected monuments, constructed buildings, and founded institutions from which their faith in progress and commitment to the Guatemalan nation can be measured. K'iche' elites, in effect, were able to marshal the forces of modernity to develop an identity that was highly modern—that is, historically self-conscious as a subject class in the process of cultural and economic transformation. They were, in the words of Marshall Berman, in a "state of perpetual becoming."[1]

Paradoxically, new liberal ideologies provided K'iche' elites new justifications for their continued caste authority. With the dissolution of the city's agricultural ejidos and Guatemala's transition to coffee capitalism, the authority of principales came to depend on their power to regulate the use of forest and pastureland and on their efforts to become the political representatives not just of Quetzalteco K'iche's but of all the nation's Indians. This chapter will explore how the simultaneous efforts of K'iche' elites to distance themselves from *and* to speak on behalf of poorer, rural Indians produced contradictory interpretations of race, progress, and nation—interpretations that both emerged from and helped shape communal, municipal, and national political relations.

A Positive Antinomy:
The Abolition of the Municipalidad de Indígenas

With the privatization of municipal land came a change in the way Quetzaltenango's ethnic relations were configured. Municipal politics were no longer, primarily, a contest between castes over city resources. As such, K'iche's gradually traded their political autonomy for a role in what became a single municipal body. Yet rather than signaling a loss of political influence, in important ways the political authority of K'iche's grew.

Perhaps chastened by the fate of the preceding generation of municipal authorities, Ladinos did not immediately attempt to abolish the indigenous cabildo after 1871. In fact, K'iche' principales quickly took advantage of the liberal victory to demand that the office of indigenous gobernador be terminated. During the colonial period, as we have seen, gobernadores were generally the most compromised of the K'iche' authorities, using their close ties with Spaniards to enrich themselves and

7. Municipalidad Indígena, 1886. In William Brigham, *Guatemala: Land of the Quetzal.*

Facing page

(*above*) 8. Municipalidad Indígena, 1894.
Photograph by Estudio Piggot y Lesher, courtesy of CIRMA.

(*below*) 9. Combined Ladino, K'iche' municipality, c. 1920
Photograph by Tomás Zanotti, courtesy of CIRMA.

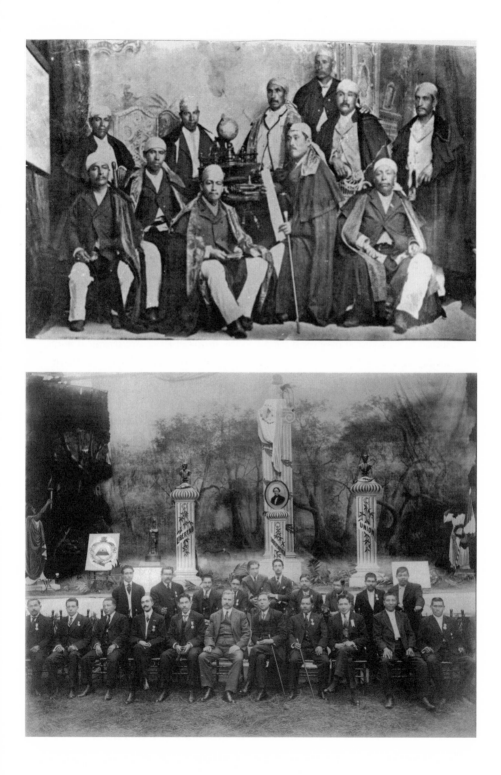

prevent popular unrest. Carrera's restoration of the position, rather than marking a restitution of indigenous autonomy, institutionalized the interdependence of the gobernador and Ladino officials. Immediately following the liberal revolution, principales, acting in the name of the común, complained of abuses committed by the city's two previous gobernadores, José María Paz and Antonio Cajas.[2] The principales demanded that the two be made to account for their handling of community funds. Barrios himself intervened in the dispute and ordered that the office of gobernador be abolished and that its authority devolve to the indigenous alcaldes.[3] In exchange, the principales offered to use the funds misappropriated by Paz and Cajas to buy guns for the new regime. For a brief period, the removal of the gobernador freed principales from the direct control of Ladino elites.

K'iche' authorities did, however, eventually lose their formal political autonomy as Ladinos gradually initiated procedures that would incorporate the indigenous municipal structure into their own. In 1879, the Ladino municipalidad proposed a plan to the minister of government. It was imperative to end the dual system, the Ladinos argued, because there existed a "positive antinomy" between the legislation of the liberal republic and "*monárquica costumbre*" (monarchical practices).[4] Rather than doing away with the K'iche' cabildo "altogether, leaving Indians with nothing," Ladinos proposed that the K'iche's be made to attend Ladino sessions and that a Ladino secretary be appointed to oversee their affairs.[5] In addition, Indians were to assume greater responsibility on city commissions. This, the petition concluded, was the most prudent way of "assimilating the two classes." Throughout the 1880s and 1890s the plan was put into effect. In 1882, the jefe político, Barillas, ordered that a single treasurer be appointed for the two bodies; in the late 1880s, indigenous authorities began to attend Ladino sessions and to serve on municipal commissions; and finally, in 1894, the dual system came to an end with the abolition of the indigenous cabildo.[6]

By this point, however, indigenous political autonomy was little more than a fanciful facade. Carrera's restoration of corporate indigenous protections provided K'iche's with a space in which they could politically and economically regroup, but it could not break the complex social and political relations that bound Quetzalteco Indians and Ladinos to each other. As we have seen, starting deep in the colonial period, Indians had grown to rely on Spaniards and then Ladinos to pursue their interests and maintain their authority. This reliance cut across class and privilege. In 1870, for example, Saturnino Pisquiy, complained to the ministro de gobernación (minister of the interior) that the K'iche' alcaldes were abusing their power by forcing him to serve on cofradías.[7] In 1873, a poor indigenous women, Gregoria Soch, went to the Ladino justice of the peace to seek protection from her abusive K'iche' husband.[8] In 1882, Basilio Tzum, an illiterate indigenous swineherd, signed over power of attorney to a Ladino lawyer in his land struggle with another K'iche'.[9] And in 1895, Tomás Pac, a wealthy K'iche' landowner, complained to the Ladino alcalde that he was being harassed by the indigenous authorities to show title to his land.[10]

The divisions caused by increased political participation—what Rodolfo Pastor has described as the macehualization of indigenous politics—continued throughout the nineteenth century. In 1879, Gregorio Morales was charged with attempting to convene an unauthorized cabildo vote, and in 1881, 88 K'iche's complained that the election for the indigenous municipality, in which 113 voted, was invalid because they had not been informed of the time or place of the balloting.[11] In the 1881 case, both sides complained to the Ladino jefe político that their opponents did not have the political caliber needed to lead the común: "They do not have the character of principales," said the representative of one faction, while a spokesman for the other charged that "disgracefully, there are in our class men who aspire to rule who are good for nothing."[12]

As in other pueblos in this period of liberal state consolidation, social tensions forced competing factions to rely increasingly on the language of community to justify their claims.[13] In 1871, José María Paz, for example, dismissed his detractors as only three Indians "claiming to speak in the name of the pueblo."[14] But in a context of weakening political authority and growing class stratification, indigenous leaders increasingly had to call on the Ladino state to back up their claims. This produced the apparently contradictory effect of deepening community identification while reinforcing the power of the state. The liberal state did not arrive unexpectedly in communities in 1871; it was invited in.

But despite the deepening dependence on Ladino authority, the power of indigenous authorities in some ways increased. The privatization of land removed the common terrain that had bound K'iche's in a field of reciprocal rights and obligations. To be sure, patriarchal relations continued through cofradías, debt, and kinship. K'iche' authorities still, at times, defended their poorer counterparts.[15] Yet relations of deference and obligation gradually weakened as expectations of subsistence rights withered away. The power of principales became much more directly tied to the punitive function of the state. Revenue collection provides an example. In the past, a good part of the community treasury had been raised through the sale of the communal harvest (siembra de la comunidad), the production of which entailed the mobilization of communal labor. Now, in contrast, the majority of K'iche' revenue was collected through fines and fees. In 1876, for example, of the 1,050 pesos taken in, 712 represented fines or money paid to commute prison sentences.[16] The majority of these sentences were for drunk or scandalous behavior. K'iche' authorities also fined more serious infractions such as assault and domestic violence.

As the city grew, Ladinos came to rely to an ever greater extent on indigenous authority. This reliance was explicitly acknowledged when, in 1895, the Ladino alcalde, upon naming a number of K'iche's to act as *jueces* (judges or heads) of municipal committees, admitted "that the commissions of ejidos, roads and forests should be given to various Indian councilmen because they are the ones who can best carry out the functions . . . above all making sure that the forests are not cut down or destroyed."[17] The position of *juez de ejidos* would remain under K'iche' control until the 1960s. That same year, K'iche's were also put in charge of both the electrification and vaccination committees so that they could combat the "general preoccupation among the Indians that their [electricity and vaccines] application is dangerous."[18] Further, although the Municipalidad de Indígenas was abolished in 1894, principales brokered a deal ensuring that the third alcalde and six councilmen in the now single municipality would always be a K'iche'.

K'iche' authorities used their political power to build an extended network of patronage throughout the city and its environs. After 1895, the third alcalde, who also functioned as the third justice of the peace, had at his disposal a large corps of auxiliary alcaldes throughout the municipio. In 1899, for example, he had under his authority forty-nine employees, all K'iche's, including twenty-five alcaldes auxiliaries, twelve forest sentries, and eight night patrollers.[19] By 1910, this number of auxiliaries had increased to 137.[20] Into this century, individuals remained obligated, under penalty of fine or imprisonment, to serve as instructed by the indigenous municipales. In exchange for their services, these auxiliary alcaldes were granted usage rights to land. José María Pac, Serapio García, and José María Orozco were granted twenty-three cuerdas in exchange for acting as forest sentries.[21] Further, the cofradía system continued to be regulated by indigenous authorities. After 1894, the third alcalde was responsible for authorizing and supervising the *entregas* (transferences of cofradía goods and authority) of successive *alcaldes de cofradías*. This authority extended to the poorer cofradías of the rural *aldeas* (hamlets).[22] After Jorge Ubico replaced the position of elected mayors with appointed municipal *intendentes* in 1935, the responsibility for regulating the cofradía system passed to the K'iche' authority in charge of ejidos.

As construction boomed in the region, the power of K'iche' authorities to conscript labor increased. The third alcalde provided weekly work gangs of between thirty and forty indigenous men to maintain the cemetery, build roads, clean the streets, work in the municipal quarry, or attend to other urban needs.[23] The majority of these workers, reflecting the class composition of the city's geography, came from the rural aldeas and cantones. A chronic labor shortage empowered the indigenous alcalde to requisition men from other municipalities, ostensibly outside his jurisdiction, with the authority of the jefe político.[24] By 1912, the third alcalde was communicating with his counterparts in the coffee region and helping to capture escaped colonos.[25]

As private contractors, indigenous elites could use their political connections to secure lucrative deals with the city, which, in turn, helped develop labor relations among K'iche's. Agatón Boj, for example, served in a number of positions in the municipality, becoming the third alcalde in 1900. His son, Enrique, served as regidor in 1903 and 1909. In 1906, Boj won the contract to reconstruct the facade of the municipal theater (see fig. 10), destroyed in the 1902 earthquake, and, in 1907, he was hired to build the pantheon crypt of president Manuel Estrada Cabrera.[26] Estrada Cabrera was a former Quetzalteco mayor with whom Boj undoubtedly had had previous dealings. By 1907, Boj was the largest employer in the city, with over fifty workers, all K'iche', on his payroll. Another K'iche', José María Citalán, who served as regidor in 1899 and alcalde in 1907, signed a four-thousand-peso contract in 1905 to build part of the city's new hospital.[27]

The end of formal K'iche' autonomy, then, brought about new forms of indigenous authority that rested more on the power of the state than on

10. Inauguration of the new façade of Quetzaltenango's municipal theater built by Agatón Boj, 1907. *Photograph by Tomás Zanotti, courtesy of* CIRMA.

communal norms of reciprocity. But while Indians seemingly went along with the political changes, they acted swiftly to retain their cultural authority. To do so, they had to redefine the nature of community.

For the Regeneration of the Race

In January 1894, confronting the abolition of their cabildo, 107 K'iche' principales sent a petition to the municipal council. The petition is so remarkable, so unexpectedly sophisticated, that it could easily be dismissed as a singular yet anomalous instance of the capacity of Indians to say what elites want to hear—except that it was followed by a series of writings and actions that attest that this was no mere subaltern parroting of elite key words. Written by the indigenous alcalde Santiago Coyoy in a clear, sure hand and exact formal Spanish, the petition makes a plea for increased representation in what would become the single municipality:

It pleases us to send petitions to vecinos, who for their rectitude and for their truly liberal principles, and for the fact that they have always shown respect for the special character and needs of aboriginals (*aborígenes*), cannot do less than receive our demand with the attention it deserves.

You desire (*vosotros deseáis*) the political advancement of our race, because you are convinced that we contribute to the realization of the progress of the *patria*. And if today all we can do is contribute to progress by cultivating the earth and transforming raw material into useful products, then, when the moral atmosphere of the republic permits us to develop our natural faculties, we will be able to cultivate the intelligence of our children and contribute to the social and political revolution of the country. We yearn for the regeneration of the Indians in order to obtain the civil and political equality which is the basis of democracies. To beat down, ridicule, scorn the Indian, to remove him from the public realm (*alejarlo de la cosa pública*), to restrict his rights, will not, señores, bring about his advancement. That the Indian knows the interests of the collective; that he defends them; that he learns how to administer them; that justice is heard. This is the desire of this petition.

Señores Concejales: As you well know, Quetzaltenango is, at the very least, composed of two-thirds Indians, all lovers of work, all absolutely respectful of their authorities. But, despite all this, Indians lack real representation in the ayuntamiento. The families of Los Alisos, Pacajá, Chichiguitán, Chicalajá and other municipal hamlets do not possess sufficient Spanish to formulate their demands or defend themselves *in voce* before the justices of the peace, that is to say, where they do not permit the intervention of lawyers. What is the result of this? Some would say that the lack of a judge who speaks the K'iche' dialect would be an incentive for Indians to learn Spanish. It would force them to quickly learn, but at the cost of being unjust. It would be inhuman.

In summary, what we ask for . . . is that the third alcalde, the second syndic, and that six councilmen . . . be, *precisamente*, Indígenas. Also, we ask . . . that there be in this city a judge for Indians and that he always be an Indian.[28]

When the Ladino municipality stonewalled, the K'iche's sent their petition directly to the president, who approved their request.[29]

Led by an emerging class of indigenous urban artisans, Quetzalteco principales fashioned an alternative nationalist discourse in the last half of the nineteenth century. This indigenous nationalism was based on a notion of citizenship predicated on property rights. For perhaps the first time, K'iche' elites did not identify themselves as principales but rather as indigenous property owners, the a priori qualification for any claims made within a liberal political framework. Considering the economic benefits that increased commodification brought to many of the K'iche' artisans, traders, and farmers, this is not surprising. But as Guatemala underwent rapid economic and political transformations, a simple embrace of liberal notions of property would not be enough to ensure and legitimize their complex and contradictory cultural, political, and economic positions. What was needed was an alternative discourse that linked the national to the cultural.

The pressures of agro-export capitalism unraveled the closely knit relations of reciprocity that invested principales with their communal authority. In order to continue to receive the benefits that their role as caste elites brought them, indigenous authorities needed to develop an ethnicity that was intimately connected to the progress of la patria. Unlike Ladinos who tended to view nationalism and Indian ethnicity as mutually exclusive (and to whom the progress of the nation depended on the suppression of the Indian), Indian elites argued that these concepts were mutually dependent, that one could not go forward without the other. In their view, regeneration of the Indian would lead to civil and political equality, which was the basis of a democracy. Their alternative nationalism served a dual purpose. By linking the progress of the nation to cultural renewal, they justified their position of communal authority to the local and national Ladino state; and conversely, linking ethnic advancement to the progress of the nation served to legitimize to other Indians their continued political power. Of course, this ideological maneuver would not be enough to ensure the perpetuation of their political power. They therefore asked for, and received, the institutionalization of their role as cultural and political brokers within the new liberal state. Now, more than ever, it was state sanction rather than communal deference that warranted their authority.

But this emerging identity did more than just provide rhetorical support for principales as they attempted to straddle an increasingly commodified community and an ever expanding nation-state. K'iche' elites shared, at least outwardly, many of the liberal assumptions regarding progress, civilization, education, and economic prosperity. Yet while K'iche's and Ladinos traversed much the same terrain, the moral boundaries of the nation that principales attempted to establish were not co-terminous with those imagined by liberal elites. Where K'iche' elites drew the line, so to speak, was "race." Although they accepted much of the racist, ascriptive features of Ladino nationalism (e.g., that the Indian was corrupted and needed to be regenerated), K'iche's categorically refused to accept the Ladino equation of race and class, which grew increasingly powerful as Guatemala became transformed into a coffee-producing nation.

Under Carrera, in the middle of the nineteenth century, a liberal elite indigenismo had begun to emerge.[30] Like its Mexican counterpart, this new ideology (which was little more than Creole nationalism) had colonial roots.[31] It would reach its nineteenth-century apogee, as it were, under the presidency of José María Reina Barrios (1892–98), and much of the language K'iche's deployed in the above petition, and others like it, freely circulated among Guatemalan intellectuals and politicians during Reina Barrios's tenure. The years 1893 and 1894 were particularly lively for debates regarding the role of Indians in Guatemala's political economy.[32] Intellectuals, politicians, and finqueros engaged in heated discussion, much of it opportunistic, surrounding the effects of the mandamiento on indigenous communities. In October 1893, Reina Barrios announced the official end of the draft beginning 15 March 1894.[33] These debates pulled forth the latent tendency on the part of Ladinos to collapse class with ethnicity and, in keeping with the new role of Indians as semiproletarianized coffee workers, to associate indigenous culture with hard, demeaning labor.[34] The more charitable of these writers would blame the Spaniards: "¡El Indio! Oh, since the first day of the conquest . . . a slave by birth, a beast of burden."[35] With a liberal sleight of hand in which class was eclipsed in the hopeful glare of progress, Indians were "destined to disappear."[36]

There were, of course, variations on this theme. Throughout the 1890s, the economic boom provided by coffee allowed for a somewhat more generous and imaginative vision of Indians' place in the emerging nation than had been previously expressed.[37] Among reformers and intellectuals who seriously thought about the issue there was no consensus about what exactly constituted "progress." *Regeneration*, a word increasingly bandied about, could hold "material, intellectual and moral" content.[38] For the more critical and thoughtful thinkers, such as Antonio Batres Jáuregui, the advanced nature of pre-Columbian civilizations was proof that Indians, although now corrupted and decayed, were redeemable and could participate as active members in "public life." Batres was particularly critical of both the mandamiento and liberal land laws. Yet even Batres, who hoped that some aboriginal "innocent customs" could be retained, believed indigenous culture was ultimately destined to disappear.[39] Exhibiting a decidedly Lamarckian faith in generational improvement through education, technical training, and contact with national society, Ladino reformers believed that Indian ethnicity needed to disappear for the nation to progress:

> We need to give Indians the means to leave their communal system; their common and unchanging dress; their barbaric diet of *totopoxte* (large corn tortilla) and chili; their antediluvian languages; their rural, primitive, and rustic homes. In a word, Indians need to be removed from their manner of being—immutable and oriental. It cannot be doubted, then, that Indians are very able to develop their civilization and promote progress. It will not be the present generation of *aborígenes* . . . but the new generations, young and flexible, will adjust to the demands of the new century. See . . . how pueblos full of Indians now are confused with the rest of the Ladinos. Just a few years ago in Jocotenango, there existed a large number of *aborígenes*, dressed like Indians, speaking their primitive language. Today the children of these Jocotecos are nearly all masons and have left their *condición de indios*, becoming Ladinos, losing their language and dressing like ordinary people.[40]

Although they appropriated much of the rhetoric regarding race and regeneration, K'iche' elites rejected both the equation of indigenous culture with class and the belief that this equation would disappear with progress and civilization.

Previously, indigenous authority and power were predicated on the maintenance of social distance between commoners and elites. This distance, owing to the relative homogeneous nature of the rural highlands, took place for the most part within pueblos. But with Guatemala's transformation to agro-export capitalism, it was no longer sufficient for Quetzalteco principales to establish and reproduce a social distance only within their own community. Wealth from coffee was produced from the labor power of tens of thousands of debt-laden Indians. In the national political discourse, culture was increasingly conflated with class; more and more, to be Indian was to be an impoverished seasonal worker.

But Quetzalteco K'iche' artisans, merchants, and farmers were not coffee pickers. To escape the conflation of class and ethnicity, yet retain their cultural authority, principales needed to do three things. First, as they became increasingly assimilated into what was deemed Hispanic culture—in language, in dress, in occupation, and in urban lifestyle— these city K'iche's had to embrace a racial definition of indigenous culture so as not to lose their ethnic identity. Ironically, they were less equivocal than Ladinos about the racial content of ethnicity: one could adopt as many defined Ladino traits as possible and still remain indigenous.[41] Second, by assuming the role of promoters of "*la raza indígena*," they sought to distance themselves not only from impoverished or common Indians within their community but from all Indians throughout Guatemala. For the K'iche' elite it was a short rhetorical step from claiming the role of defenders of the impoverished, Spanish illiterate K'iche's from their own city's hinterland, as they did in the above 1894 petition, to speaking on behalf of all Guatemalan Indians. In the mid-1890s, they began to use a phrase that would appear repeatedly in their written works: they claimed to speak not just on behalf of "Indians of Quetzaltenango in particular" but for those of the "indigenous class in general."[42]

It is important to note here that the desire of urban K'iche's to distance themselves from more impoverished Indians was not just a question of status or maintenance of privilege. The loss of cultural symbols associated with exploitation—dress, sandals, and the like—was also a matter of survival. At the turn of the century, Quetzaltenango was still a place where poor Indians could be conscripted off the streets without notice and forced to carry freight to the coast, and where a peasant coming in from his field could be nearly beaten to death by city police for openly carrying a machete.[43]

Finally, as a result of their own complicated class position as large landholders and labor contractors, K'iche' elites had to account for economic changes in cultural terms. Thus Santiago Coyoy, who himself owned a large tract of land within the municipal boundaries and had a dozen indigenous peons indebted to him, could thank the president, with little sense of irony, for "the abolition of forced labor that was demanded of Indians by rich Ladinos who have agricultural farms."[44]

The Progress of a Society:
The Establishment of the Sociedad El Adelanto

Indian elites rejected the notion that education, economic progress, and hard work would lead to the *assimilation* of the Indian, as many Ladino elites had advocated. For K'iche' *principales* progress would entail the *regeneration* of the Indian. In 1894, K'iche's institutionalized this hope in the foundation of the Sociedad El Adelanto—an association "composed of Indians to work for the regeneration of the race and the material progress of the city."[45] Modeled on the guilds and mutual aid societies popular throughout Latin America at this time, the sociedad, which exists to this day, primarily promoted education and civic activities during its first decades of existence: it established schools, supported modernization projects, and participated in cultural and political events.[46] One requirement for membership was that each *socio* (member) had to set an example for other Indians and enroll his children until the age of fourteen in school. Indians may have lost a degree of political autonomy with the abolition of their cabildo, but the establishment of the sociedad would ensure the continuation of their cultural and social power. To highlight the continuity between the abolished Municipalidad de Indígenas and El Adelanto, the city's third alcalde, who was always K'iche', was often a recent president of the society.[47]

The society was founded by over sixty "indigenous principales of the city."[48] Although members were drawn from various sectors of the K'iche' population, a majority of the founders shared a number of social characteristics.[49] Nearly all of those about whom information exists lived in the city's center and owned homes in one of the four barrios. With the exception of one who, judging by the one hundred mules he owned, probably made his living as a teamster and four who possessed a large number of sheep and cows, all seemed primarily to be either artisans or merchants who balanced their trade with subsistence and commercial agricultural production. While a few of the founders, such as Santiago Coyoy and Marcos Cojulún, possessed exceptionally large amounts of land, and others, such as Tranquilino Morales, possessed very little, the majority owned medium-sized plots of fifty to two hundred cuerdas on which they grew wheat and corn.

The foundation of El Adelanto echoes the growth of "friendly societies" or trade clubs in early-nineteenth-century England,[50] where legal dissolution of guilds combined with the beginning of the industrial revolution to threaten the status and privileges of skilled artisans. E. P. Thompson writes that closed artisan societies became popular with the skilled tradesman, who was equally "concerned with maintaining his status as against the unskilled man as he was in bringing pressure upon the employers."[51] These efforts to preserve privilege took place within the parameters of an emerging working class. In Guatemala, by contrast, similar efforts occurred within the boundaries of ethnicity. The artisan founders of the Sociedad El Adelanto were not threatened by technological innovation or a rationalization of labor. Industrialization would not come to Guatemala until decades later, and when it did, its effect on artisans was partial and incomplete. What did threaten the K'iche' tradesmen was the national equation of race with proletarianization. They thus founded the sociedad to promote a vision of Indian ethnicity that was not bounded by class. It is noteworthy that few of the exceptionally wealthy K'iche' landowners, such as Silverio Coyoy and Tomás Pac, participated in founding the society; for that matter, they rarely seemed to involve themselves in city politics. The importance of ethnic revival and caste power may have been more urgent for the city's middle indigenous bourgeoisie, whose members, perhaps, had less confidence in the power of the market to ensure their prosperity.

For these K'iche's, the continued ability to mobilize communal resources may still have been an important factor in their successful participation in a commodified economy—hence their interest in cultural revindication. A number of the founders still rotated their community service between cofradía obligations and municipal offices, thus underscoring the permeable line between political and cultural authority.[52] Perhaps not coincidentally, a number of the original founders of the sociedad, such as Agatón Boj, Benito Reyes, and José María Pisquiy, went on to become some of those K'iche's who increased their property holdings (see chap. 5). Further, the membership of the sociedad included both wealthy K'iche' contractors, farmers, workshop owners and merchants, and more humble artisans and wage workers, thereby suggesting that K'iche's used membership in the society itself to maintain patronage relations weakened by commodification.

Although throughout the first half of the twentieth century both wealthy and poor K'iche's joined El Adelanto, since its inception its leadership has always come from the ranks of the former. José Santiago Coyoy López (1861–1906) and Joel Agatón Boj (1848–1915), for example, were two of the most active members in the sociedad and in city politics. As noted before, Boj benefited from the changes brought about by Guatemala's transition to coffee cultivation and not only increased his landholdings in the last years of the nineteenth century but was able to parlay his political influence into becoming the city's most important construction contractor and largest employer. Although Santiago Coyoy was listed in a census as a mason, he made his living mostly as a merchant and wheat and corn farmer. As we have seen, he owned a number of large farms on which upward of a dozen indigenous colonos resided. His economic production was complemented by that of his wife, Micaela Pisquiy de Coyoy, who was a prominent market vendor. Coyoy was the alcalde when the K'iche' cabildo was finally done away with in 1894, and he was instrumental in both brokering the deal that allowed for more indigenous participation in the Ladino municipality and founding El Adelanto, whose first president he became. Prior to 1894, Coyoy served twice as regidor. Following the unification of the municipalities, he went on to be elected two more times as K'iche' alcalde, in 1897 and 1904. Both Coyoy and Boj served as alcaldes of two of the city's most prominent cofradías—Coyoy of the Cofradía Santísimo in 1900 and Boj of the Cofradía Santo Entierro in 1893.

The Meaning of Regeneration

The complicated linkage between the economic, political, and cultural power of the principales is captured in one of the first acts of the sociedad. In 1894, El Adelanto commissioned the construction of a monument honoring Guatemala's president, Reina Barrios, to thank him for abolishing the mandamiento (see fig. 11). Upon hearing of the monument, and apparently for the first time of the sociedad, Quetzaltenango's jefe político sent a letter to the Ladino alcalde, asking him for information:

> I have learned that the señores regidores Indígenas have organized a socie-
> dad. These same Indians have asserted that the monument on the road to
> Almolonga is being raised to celebrate the liberation of the Indians. I want
> you to find out what the real purpose of this sociedad is, because these
> señores still do not know what the *regeneración de la raza Indígena* means.[53]

11. Monument commemorating the "liberation of the Indian,"
1894. *Photograph by Daniel Wilkinson.*

The mayor dispatched the chief of police to the monument site, where he
found four masons commissioned by the "regidores Indígenas . . . who
were made to believe that they were working on a municipal project."[54]
"With this pretext," the chief of police went on, "masons were employed
who should be used on works of true urgency."[55] Despite the jefe político's continued protest, the work was completed, and, by a presidential
decree, the sociedad was established.[56]

K'iche' principales used the political tools available to them—in this case their ability to mobilize labor and funds—to articulate their new, more expansive ethnic identity, as discussed above. That the monument was erected to thank Reina Barrios for ending the mandamiento—a law to which none of the principales (and probably few if any common Quetzaltecos) were subject—emerged from their efforts to assume the role of representative of all Indians, and hence avoid the association of class with ethnicity. That *regeneration* was a contested word likewise reflects the divergence between K'iche' and Ladino visions of the nation's future.

As recent work exploring the cultural processes of state consolidation makes clear, elite unity or cohesion cannot be the starting point for examinations of hegemony.[57] These studies loosen the tight moorings that bound ideas to class position and replace, as Stuart Hall puts it, the "notion of fixed ideological meanings and class-ascribed ideologies with the concepts of ideological terrains of struggle and the task of ideological transformation."[58] These theories likewise have been concerned with delimiting these terrains of struggle so that understandings of ideology do not slip off into an "unsatisfactory discursive notion which implies total free floatingness of all ideological elements and discourse."[59] The battlefield of ideational struggle, therefore, is best described as a "field of force" in which different social groups "read" competing interpretations into *common* social referents.[60] Thus the word *regeneration* had different meanings for the K'iche' elites and the Ladino jefe político, whose job description was literally to "achieve the assimilation of the indigenous class into that of the Ladinos."[61]

Differential access to social power allows political blocs to form and allows those blocs to impose their reading as the dominant interpretation. The ideological and political maneuvers that went into the K'iche' elites' construction of the obelisk are particularly obvious examples of this process.[62] But the crucial point here—which is key to understanding what took place in Quetzaltenango and Guatemala—is that these battlefields contain more than two opposing armies. To understand republican Guatemala as a nation defined *primarily* along ethnic lines is to buy into the racialist assumptions that sought to reduce Guatemala's complex colonial legacy into two competing camps. Struggles within the field of force (that is, history) need instead to be understood as complex alliances of interests and ideologies that are often, but not always, based on class position. It is through these engagements that social identities, ideologically simplified, emerge.

The political tension caused by the interaction of a consolidating state and a regional elite allowed K'iche' principales, as they had in the past, to strategically play non-Indian elites off against each other. Ladino officials, in their efforts to prevent the construction of the monument and the establishment of the sociedad, tried to contain the ability of K'iche's to mobilize political resources for cultural ends. They argued to national authorities that the building of the monument was both a waste of much needed labor and revenue and an abuse of the municipal positions. Santiago Coyoy responded by personally inviting the Ladino municipales to attend the inauguration of the monument. Even though the stone was "not yet polished," the K'iche's rushed to ensure that the monument's unveiling would take place on President Reina Barrios's birthday. Coyoy took the opportunity to remind the Ladinos that the Sociedad El Adelanto had been approved by Reina Barrios himself and to counter charges that he and his fellow K'iche' regidores were abusing their public power for private ends. Coyoy's response captures the combined private and public nature of principal power: "As municipal councilmen, we have nothing to do with" the sociedad.[63] It was as private citizens, however, that these same councilmen just happened also to serve as its officers.

Forests, Pastures, and the Conflicted Terrain of Hegemony

Following the liberal triumph, the extension of cultivation and increased demands for wood and pasture combined with the rapid privatization of municipal property to create new levels of conflict and confusion surrounding land use. These conflicts—which took place among individuals, between the municipality and individuals, and between the city and surrounding pueblos—often had to do with competing types of production. In 1879, the K'iche' Bartolo Ventura and his two mozos were accused by Gregorio Andrade of damaging his corn plot with their sheep.[64] In 1892, the indigenous authorities claimed that Tomás Pac and Pioquinto Guzmán expropriated municipal forest and destroyed trees in order to plant potatoes.[65] And throughout the 1880s and 1890s, the town of San Mateo fought off the expansion of Quetzalteco agriculture onto land it claimed as its forests.[66]

Quetzalteco K'iche' elites attempted to mediate these conflicts, using new national forest regulations to buttress their authority. During this period the liberal state became increasingly concerned with the rapid deforestation under way in the nation's most populated areas. In 1891 a national forest code was enacted, followed a year later by departmental regulations.[67] The new codes, which declared forests to be an "integral part of the wealth of the nation," effectively nationalized municipal woodland, defining all land belonging to the state or municipalities "that are covered with trees for construction, firewood, carbon, and other common uses" as national forests.[68] The codes forbade the cutting of young or green trees and ordered all municipalities to carry out reforestation projects. Seed banks and nurseries were to be established, and individuals were to plant seedlings along property-dividing lines and roads. Pasturing of animals on municipal property was to be limited, and anyone extracting wood from forests was required to plant five seedlings for each tree cut.

The K'iche' authorities vigorously applied these codes, often using the language embedded in the regulations to defend their actions "to protect the general good of the population." Repeatedly, the indigenous municipal officials, through their corps of forest sentries and auxiliaries, prevented what they considered violations of the new regulations. In 1895, they accused Julián Tay of trying to bribe a guardabosque into letting him cut trees and pasture his sheep on municipal land. In 1896, a number of indigenous alcalde auxiliaries confiscated a mule and the cut wood it was carrying from a poor K'iche' "mozo," claiming that he extracted it illegally.[69] And in 1894, the Municipalidad de Indígenas ordered Macaria Cajas to allow vecinos to extract wood for personal use from land that both she and the municipality claimed as their own. Again, these conflicts strengthened the power of the local state, since both sides appealed to the Ladino municipality to support their case. In the land conflict mentioned in chapter 5, Tomás Pac, confronted with a surveying commission headed by Santiago Coyoy (his "enemy," as he put it), went so far as to ask the Ladino authorities to name somebody to the commission "that is not an Indian," arguing that he would never get a fair ruling from the indigenous authorities.[70] The K'iche' municipales responded by stating that as Indians "nobody can have better knowledge of the ejidos than we do."[71]

Aside from whatever political power the enforcement of the forest codes might have garnered K'iche' municipal elites, it was also in their class interest to protect the forests. Access to wood was crucial for the kind of urban production in which many K'iche' political elites were engaged. Masons and carpenters relied on timber for construction, and wood was needed to stoke the fires in the kilns, forges, and furnaces of tanners, smiths, shoemakers, quarrymen, and other artisans. And as only four of the sixty founders of El Adelanto were engaged to a significant extent in animal husbandry and most owned more than enough land for subsistence production, there was little incentive to turn forest land into pasture or agricultural land.

The following incident provides a good example of how K'iche's used the new forest codes not only to maintain their authority over other Indians but also to secure their political power in relation to local Ladinos. On 31 July 1894, Santiago Coyoy petitioned the municipality for a leave of absence from his public responsibilities to travel to the capital to attend to personal business.[72] In Guatemala City, he and the other indigenous regidores, along with a "very respectable number of Indians," met with President Reina Barrios to express their concern about the rapid deforestation of municipal lands.[73] They complained that many individuals, aside from their legitimate personal needs, were showing up with mules and wagons to extract wood illegally for profit, turning the forest into a "*filón* (gold vein, or source of wealth) that is exploited to the detriment of all." They asked the president for help in protecting the woodlands. Manuel Estrada Cabrera, the minister of government who would soon become Guatemala's first twentieth-century dictator, wrote to Quetzaltenango's jefe político, Manuel Solórzano, ordering him to be more vigilant in protecting the city's forests and to build fences and ditches around municipal land.[74] Meanwhile, the jefe político and the alcalde, Mariano Molina, convened a special emergency session to discuss the matter and to "find out the truth and punish those responsible" for the complaint, which, they claimed, was greatly "exaggerated." By going "directly to the government, as if there was no authority here," Molina charged, Coyoy compromised the good name of the municipality.

The exchange between Coyoy and the local Ladino authorities, recorded in script in the municipal minutes, is revealing and warrants extensive presentation. It captures nuances of power that move from the most mundane—that of the common racism of local Ladinos who use their power to silence Indians while at the same time claiming to give them voice—to the highest reaches of national power—that of a consolidating state attempting to check the regional aspirations of local elites.

Molina: I don't understand what reason they had to pass over the municipality and the *jefatura* when here there is full administration of justice. If not, can the indigenous councilmen tell us how many times they came to the municipality or the jefatura with complaints that were not heard and dealt with?

Coyoy: It was not a complaint against the municipality, or the jefatura, that we presented in Guatemala. It was a request that they give us help in conserving the forest, which is for the good of all. It is not a complaint. It is true that when we informed the mayor of some abuses, he gave us orders to correct them; the same happened with the jefe político. It is not a complaint that we made but a request for help in protecting the forests.

Solórzano: I now see that there is a contradiction in what you say and the note sent by the ministro de gobernación.

Daniel Meza [4th regidor]: Tell us who are the ones abusing the forest, because the note from the minister implies that it is a municipal officer. Tell us who are using mules and wagons.

Solórzano: By any chance, does it occur to the Señor concejal [Coyoy] that the wood from the commons are for the fires of all . . . the tailor, the blacksmith, the cook, the machinist, the schools, etc. etc.? It is not just for exclusive use but for everyone. Does it occur to you that there are different kinds of work . . . that some look for their means of subsistence in agriculture, others as artisans, and others as wood sellers? The forest needs to be exploited in the thousand ways that meet the needs of the people; for this there is no other option and today it needs to be accepted.

Coyoy: We do not say that wood should not be used but that only dry wood should be cut. Small trees should not be cut because this damages the forest. We had presented a motion to the municipality, but it was not addressed, maybe because we are Indians (*tal vez por ser indios*).

Alejandro Montes [6th regidor]: The indigenous councilmen presented a motion, but it referred to the prevention of pasturing in the woodland, and not to abuses committed by individuals.

Molina: As Señor Meza well said, the note implied that the municipality is abusing the forests, or that some councilman is, or that the Indians' complaints have not been attended to. As nothing of the sort has happened, it is important to establish the truth in order to demonstrate the injustice of the complaint: How many motions have the concejales Indígenas presented that have not been addressed because they are Indians?

Solórzano: To that I want to add that you (Coyoy) came to inform me that some individual was trying to take a part of the ejidos, and I ordered you to make a deep ditch so as to mark the municipal land. But the note from the minister recommends that I establish markers, surely because you did not tell him that I already gave such orders.

Julián Aguilara [syndic]: There is no truth to the complaint; it is an attack on the municipality and the jefatura, an abuse that should be punished so that it does not happen again. It is clear that the intention of the Indians is that they want to be the only ones to use the forest. They want to be the only ones to sell wood, and because we have not permitted it, they went to complain. I ask that you punish them.

Coyoy: The conservation of the forest is not only for Indians but for all. It is the general good that we want. As I already said, it was not a complaint that we presented. As I am a merchant, I asked for leave to go to the capital. There I met with other merchants and we decided to present the request.

Jefe Político: By what has been said it is clear that you [pointing to Coyoy] asked for permission to go to Guatemala on personal business and there you joined with other merchants and presented a request that the municipality help you in conserving the forests. As there was no lack of support, as you yourself say . . . then there was no reason for the request. It should be declared unjust and improper and a reprimand be issued so that puerile matters are not presented to the government.

Molina: I am in agreement . . . but I insist that Coyoy tell us how many requests or complaints of abuses he made that were not attended to. Until now, he has not given a categorical answer about these abuses or the people committing them.

Montes: The way I see it, the question comes down to two points. First, find out who are the ones abusing the forest so as to prove once and for all the veracity of the complaint. Many times Coyoy has been asked who these people are and he has not answered. Second, establish if the municipality has complied with the forest codes.

Molina: The secretary informs us that the only motion [made by the indigenous regidores] was in reference to the pasturing of livestock in the forests.

José María de León [2nd alcalde]: When the Indígenas reported to me that some were taking wood, I told them to order the forest sentries to make these people replant the trees they had cut.

Coyoy: That order was carried out.

Solórzano: The discussion indicates that the authorities fulfilled their obligation and there is no merit to the complaint.

Antonio Porres [2nd regidor]: I believe that we should vote on a motion of censure so that complaints such as these do not again compromise the good name of the municipality.

The municipality, by majority vote, resolved that the discussion proved that it was living up to its responsibilities, that the complaint was unjust, and that the authors of the complaint be censured. The jefe político closed the proceedings by exhorting the indigenous councilmen to work in harmony with the rest of the municipality, "because all represent the interests of the citizens. There is no justification for the antagonism which has existed between the indigenous and Spanish race, and even less so now under the current regime in which all enjoy the same rights and equality as demonstrated by the fact that *el indio* holds public offices in the same manner as do Ladinos."

Note that we have come a long way from 1826, when the K'iche' authorities were thrown in jail for three days and fined fifty pesos for refusing to cooperate with the Ladinos on land reform. If prison is one of the state's last recourses for those who refuse to submit to its hegemony, then censure, perhaps, is only effective for those who are bound by it. The privatization of land brought with it the dissolution of the colonial compact that supposedly guaranteed access to subsistence production to all. Through this compact, indigenous principales, throughout Guatemala, could defend the community's interest based on the expected entitlement of enough land to survive. In the past, principales defended this land from the advances of other communities and non-Indians or from unsanctioned use by members of their own community. If population growth stretched production thin, they could petition the Crown or state for more land. But with this entitlement removed, K'iche' elites came to rely on new ideologies surrounding land relations—including new forest codes—to regulate land use. In turn, K'iche's used these laws and ideologies to check the power of local Ladinos. They appealed to national elites so as to consolidate their authority as protectors of the municipal forests and to limit the degree of Ladino exploitation of city woodlands. The following year, as noted earlier, K'iche's were put in charge of overseeing the forests. But as K'iche's deftly learned to play within the new rules laid out for them, they, in turn, quickly became bound by them. Municipal forest land was now, K'iche's admitted, for the "common good of all Quetzal-tecos."[75] Hence censure, a weaker measure than jail time but one that actually presupposes greater political power, was the only punishment meted out.

The exchange between Coyoy and the Ladinos cited above suggests how racism structured political relations on a daily level. While Ladino officials felt free to chime in as they wished, the rest of the indigenous authorities—four others attended the session—did not defend Coyoy, perhaps silenced by their inexperience in using Spanish in public debate. Coyoy, well versed in the use of Spanish in political deliberations, after facing a barrage of accusations, was reduced to short affirmative responses. The jefe político's closing cant on the equality of the races and the role of Indians as public officials effectively ended all discussion. And despite Ladino claims to the contrary, the municipality did not take up the motion presented by the indigenous officers until after they received the rebuke from the ministro de gobernación.[76]

Principales repeatedly spoke directly to national elites "as if there was no [local] authority"—a practice that was particularly irksome to the Ladino municipal authorities. This of course was not a new strategy, but it proved particularly effective during the presidency of Reina Barrios, whose policy of strengthening indigenous authority in Quetzaltenango and elsewhere weakened the power of his local rivals.[77] Time after time—most notably with the complaint regarding forest use, the establishment of the sociedad, the construction of the monument, and the demand for greater representation in the municipality—K'iche' elites skillfully played national elites off against local elites.[78] Whereas Carrera had cultivated Indian dissatisfaction to end Guatemala's most successful separatist movement, Reina Barrios, while perhaps not seeking active Indian support, benefited from indigenous indifference in his suppression of what was to be the last serious regional threat to the centralization of state power.

In 1897, highland Ladinos disaffected because of Reina Barrios's economic policies declared themselves in revolt against Guatemala City.[79] The rebellion did not spread throughout the country as the rebels had hoped. After three weeks of laying siege to the insurgent occupied city, the national army entered Quetzaltenango's plaza and the revolution ended.

Again, as during Carrera's time, highland ethnic relations were crucial in the centralization and maintenance of state power. Little information exists regarding the role of the K'iche' elite during the rebels' occupation of the city, but it is clear that surrounding indigenous communities did not support the revolution. A number of key pueblos that provided crucial support to Carrera's 1840 punitive expedition, such as San Sebastián, San Andrés Xecul, and San Cristóbal Totonicapán, immediately declared themselves loyal to Reina Barrios.[80] It was indicative of highland ethnic relations that Ladinos proved incapable of forging sustained military alliances with indigenous communities. Over one hundred Ladino soldiers from San Carlos Sija, for example, arrived in Buenabaj, a hamlet of Momostenango, and killed, looted, and raped members of the community, while in Zunil, Ladino revolutionary leaders arrived, put guns to the chests of the indigenous authorities, and demanded a contribution of 1,500 pesos.[81] Events such as these, opined one rebel leader, were certain to earn indigenous support for government troops.[82] Again, as with Carrera's 1840 incursion, it seems that city Indians hedged their bets and waited for the outcome. Many ran to the woods to wait out events.[83] And while K'iche' municipal officers, including Santiago Coyoy, signed the act in favor of the revolt, those arrested claimed that the first alcalde, once again Mariano Molina, "tricked" and "forced" them to do so.[84]

The ability of Quetzalteco K'iche' elites to play off national and local elites against one another in pursuit of their political and cultural interests strengthened the state and furthered its formation. The historic strategy of appealing to a more distant authority for protection from local elites became nationalized. Moreover, at the same time as they were using the rhetoric of nationalism and liberalism to check local Ladinos, K'iche's were developing an alternative vision of progress and the nation that allowed them to make sense of far-reaching social transformations. In doing so, they helped broker the local creation of the liberal state, limiting regionalist aspirations and translating liberal political economy into ethnic terms.

As Quetzalteco K'iche' principales have demonstrated, subordinate classes and groups can develop alternative conceptions of the nation. Within the process of nation building, these competing visions are in a constant state of contestation and negotiation, a process through which a certain body of ideas becomes linked to an emerging dominant class.

For the K'iche's, their receptivity to new ideological possibilities, as well as their ability to re-articulate them, stemmed from their ambiguous ethnic and class identities and was delimited by their particular historical and political moment. Partha Chatterjee, cited in Mallon, identifies three "moments" within the hegemonic process that are useful in understanding nation building.[85] The first moment—the "moment of departure"—is an open conjuncture where "different possible projects or discourses emerged to compete for influence in the emerging balance of power."[86] It is in this moment that we can best locate alternative indigenous understandings of race and nation. But these alternative visions neither sprung full-blown from K'iche' heads nor suddenly emerged from some buried, autonomous popular tradition. Indian elites drew on their long-standing practice of borrowing from the dominant political discourse to fashion an ideology that could justify their continued cultural authority in the face of rapid and dramatic political and economic changes.

It is in Chatterjee's second moment—a "moment of manoeuvre" when new elites forge a ruling alliance through the "mobilization of the popular elements"—that we can place the K'iche's' attempt to deploy this new ideology in their dealings with Ladinos.[87] Here we can abandon the "simplified" state versus Indian dichotomy that has plagued Guatemalan historiography and move on to a more subtle interpretation. The liberal state, from Barrios to Ubico, was extremely adept at allying itself with certain "popular" sectors to further its aims. In some communities, for example, the promise of liberalism for poorer Indians meant access to municipal land previously deemed off-limits by community elites.[88] In other communities, indigenous principales formed alliances with the new liberal state in order to shore up their authority. In Quetzaltenango, both of these phenomena occurred. These alliances, however, consisted of more than just the dominant emerging class "mobilizing" popular forces for its own ends. In Quetzaltenango, it was the K'iche's who took advantage of local Ladino dependence on them to secure their power in relation to both poorer Indians and local Ladinos.

But at the same time that K'iche's were attempting to articulate this vision, Ladinos, at least partially and superficially, managed to present their project as *the* national project. According to Chatterjee, this is the very nature of hegemony during the third moment—the "moment of arrival": A political discourse emerges that attempts to speak in a "single, consistent, unambiguous voice . . . glossing over all earlier contradictions, divergences and differences."[89] Nonetheless, as we shall see in chapter 7, this dominant discourse never entirely silences alternative voices; rather, it seeks to ignore or reinterpret them.

The question of course remains: Did Coyoy really mean it when he protested to the jefe político that "it is the general good that we want," or was he just playing out an expected performance? Although this is a fair question, it could likewise be asked of the mayor and the jefe político. Did Solórzano, for example, really believe that the new regime had brought about the equality of the races? Did Molina really believe indigenous concerns were addressed with the same attention as those of Ladinos? If Coyoy's options at this point were restrained by fear and power, then the performances of the Ladino officials were similarly conditioned both by their reliance on the indigenous authorities to help administer the city and the restraints imposed by the national state. The initial call to punishment, therefore, devolved into a mild rebuke.

Derek Sayer writes that the rituals that structure hegemony do not entail belief or acceptance but rather the "knowledge of everyone involved that they are living a lie."[90] It is coercion, not acquiescence, that compel individuals to participate. But for Sayer, it is a complex coercion that not only represses but also "powers and enables."[91] With this power, "spaces [are] opened."[92] Whether they believed that liberalism and progress would bring about equality between the races or not, K'iche' elites took advantage of these opened spaces to push forward an alternative vision of the nation and an expanded conception of indigenous identity.

Chapter 7
Time and Space among the Maya: Mayan Modernism and the Transformation of the City

Dazzled by so many and such marvelous inventions, the people of Macondo did not know where their amazement began.
—GABRIEL GARCÍA MÁRQUEZ, *One Hundred Years of Solitude*, 1971

There is a mode of vital experience—experience of space and time, of the self and others, of life's possibilities and perils—that is shared by men and women all over the world today. I will call this body of experience "modernity." To be modern is to find ourselves in an environment that promises us adventure, power, joy, growth, transformation of ourselves and the world—and, at the same time, that threatens to destroy everything we have, everything we know, everything we are. Modern environments and experiences cut across all boundaries of geography and ethnicity, of class and nationality, of religion and ideology: in this sense, modernity can be said to unite all mankind. But it is a paradoxical unity, a unity of disunity: it pours us all into a maelstrom of perpetual disintegration and renewal, of struggle and contradiction, of ambiguity and anguish. To be modern is to be part of a universe in which, as Marx said, "all that is solid melts into air."

People who find themselves in the midst of this maelstrom are apt to feel that they are the first ones, and maybe the only ones, to be going through it; this feeling has engendered numerous nostalgic myths of a pre-modern Paradise Lost. In fact, however, great and ever-increasing numbers of people have been going through it for close to five hundred years. Although most of these people have probably experienced modernity as a radical threat to all their history and traditions, it has, in the course of five centuries, developed a rich history and a plenitude of traditions of its own. —MARSHALL BERMAN, *All That is Solid Melts into Air, 1982*

K'iche's used the forces of modernity to help radically transform the ways in which their city was experienced. Indian elites, who a few decades earlier refused to send their children to school or to participate in health and sanitary reforms, now, among other things, helped to bring the railroad to Quetzaltenango, founded schools, and headed municipal electrification and vaccination commissions. The reason for this turnaround had less to do with the kind of cultural regeneration promoted by Ladinos and K'iche's alike than with class transformation within the indigenous común, as a consolidating group of indigenous contractors, merchants, artisans, and farmers hitched their fortunes to an expanding and more integrated urban and national economy. As K'iche's pushed forward an aggressive program of urban modernization, they reconfigured gender, class, and ethnic relations and ideologies to redefine their sense of community, city, and nation.

Yet like the people of García Márquez's Macondo who had worked to bring the railroad to their town but could not master the destructive forces it helped unleash, Quetzalteco K'iche's were not able to control the consequences of their actions. The idiosyncratic vision of race and progress articulated by K'iche' leaders at the end of the nineteenth century was overwhelmed by the power of a consolidating state and hamstrung by the limits of dependent capitalist development. The state was successful, for the time being, in mobilizing K'iche' nationalism for its own ends. In 1954, the class transformation under way among the K'iche's since the eighteenth century would climax in a bloody conflict that destroyed their dream of an inclusive nation. Nevertheless, despite these challenges, ethnic identity continued to be an important, albeit often politically silenced, medium through which individuals gave meaning to their social relations.

New experiences of time and place were crucial in the development of Guatemalan nationalism, state formation, and capitalist development, and, as with hegemony, the significance of these experiences emerged from social practices.[1] Struggle and conflict resulting from competing social interests gave semantic meaning to new temporal and spatial patterns. The emergence of Guatemalan nationalism entailed much more than the appearance of "homogeneous, empty time"—the ability of individuals, through the development of print media, to conceive of an imagined community engaging in simultaneous action.[2] Multiple conceptions of time and place conflicted as Guatemala was transformed into an agro-industrial nation: When conscripted indigenous peasants fled the regimented railroad work gangs to tend their crops, or when they were punished for not working the number of prescribed hours, two conflicting notions of time—peasant and industrial—revealed themselves. New experiences of time and place could be repressive, as when trains sped troops to different parts of the country to quell dissent and telegraph operators wired orders to local officials to apprehend escaped workers or criminals. They could also be horrific, as when the brakes failed on the train on its first test run into Quetzaltenango, killing three, or when a seventy-three-year-old blind and deaf Indian lost his life crossing the tracks because he could not hear the locomotive's whistle. But they could also be marvelous, as when photographs stopped time, electricity extended daytime into nighttime, and the movies narrated a lifetime in a short time.

Lighting the Long Dark Night

The reconstruction of the city during the golden age of coffee not only symbolized new regional and national identities but also represented the contested social processes that gave these new identities meaning. The region's commercial importance continued with the switch to coffee cultivation. By the end of the nineteenth century, Quetzaltenango had become the largest coffee-producing department in the country. As the region became ever more integrated into a world economy, the importance of the city as the highland's economic, political, and cultural hub increased. In 1881, the Banco de Occidente was established in the city to capitalize coffee production. Many of the coffee elite came from prominent Quetzalteco families; foreign commercial and credit houses, many of them German-owned, set up shop in the city. These houses provided credit to agriculturists and merchants, imported foreign manufactured goods, and exported coffee.[3] A number of these concerns earned substantial profits handling the trade between the surrounding highlands and other regions of Guatemala, Central America, and the world. By the turn of the century, one leading financial newspaper had begun to describe the surrounding region as "tributary departments of the *metrópol Altense.*"[4]

With the coffee boom, foreigners poured into the city: Italian architects, sculptors, and photographers; German merchants, watchmakers, and brewers; and U.S. carpenters and engineers. A literary and cultural scene flourished, and, beginning at the end of the nineteenth century, local poets hyperbolically celebrated the pleasures of a city now affectionately being called by its preconquest name, Xelaju.[5]

Ladinos replaced old wooden and adobe public offices with imposing cut-stone neoclassical structures. Their solidity and form expressed regional and national self-importance and claimed endurance in the midst of revolutionary political and economic change. Throughout the 1880s, the city's plaza was surrounded by scaffolding as K'iche' masons and laborers built the municipal palace, the Banco de Occidente, the departmental penitentiary, the courthouse, and other public and private buildings. It was telling that the penitentiary had been the first building constructed following the liberal triumph, for throughout the next half-century mozos who escaped from plantation labor gangs filled its cells.[6]

The municipality widened boulevards, constructed a theater on a hill just off the city center, turned the central plaza into a landscaped park, and built a market. Indians, however, much to the vexation of municipal officials, continued to ply their goods in the city square.[7] The colonial-style homes with enclosed patios of the wealthy gave way to two-story cut-stone residences with balconies overlooking the street. Ladinos attempted to rename neighborhoods and streets for liberal ideals and heroes. Barrio San Sebastián became Cantón Igualdad (equality) and Calle Cajolá became Calle Morazán. These names however did not stick; saint names remained favored, while Cantón Flores, named after the liberal martyr, gradually became known as Cantón Las Flores.

Electric power represented modernity in its most exhilarating form, and the municipality pushed early on to light the city. However, it generated anxiety among the popular classes, and officials had to rely on K'iche' authorities to calm rumors that its application was dangerous and unnatural.[8] Well into the twentieth century, articles appeared in local

12. Building the second floor of the Banco de Occidente, c. 1910.
Photograph by Tomás Zanotti, courtesy of Museo Girard.

newspapers and magazines that assured readers of its safety, while the
contractors in charge of wiring the city ran ads trying to convince the
population that electricity was cheaper and safer than wood, candles, or
gas.[9] The installation of power lines revealed a public awareness of class
lines. In 1893, over two dozen Quetzaltecos, both K'iche' and Ladinos,
protested that they paid increased taxes "to enjoy the benefit of electric
light . . . and not to pay for fifty or sixty lights on the streets of the rich,
leaving the grand majority of the city's population in the shadows."[10]

As I have argued, this transformation of urban space could not have
taken place without K'iche' support. Indian officials brokered the labor,
Indian contractors supervised the work, and Indian laborers built the
buildings. But as they did so, K'iche' principales used their power to
legitimize their own authority. At the same time that Indian elites were

13. "A Testimony So Eloquent": Procession passing in front of building meant to house the Municipalidad Indígena, next to the city's cathedral, 1994. *Photograph by Daniel Wilkinson.*

raising money for a statue to Agustín Guzmán, Carrera's highland nemesis, they were building their own monument (discussed in chapter 6), to thank the president for ending the mandamiento.[11]

In the 1880s, on land donated by Barrios, K'iche' officials had built their own municipal building, which was strategically located between the cathedral and the Ladino municipality (see fig. 13). The K'iche's, however, never had the chance to move into their new chambers. In 1889, President Barillas ordered the Ladino municipality to install the national telegraph (and later telephone) office in the building, thereby kicking off a struggle over ownership of the building that has lasted to this day.[12] K'iche' officials were relegated to a "miserable" former kitchen in the old colonial government house to conduct their affairs.[13]

The installation of the telegraph office in the K'iche' cabildo had much more than symbolic import. By giving the new state the ability to swiftly communicate orders and dispatch troops, the telegraph and the telephone helped make the difference between the political failure of the first liberal regime and the success of the second.[14]

Principales immediately launched a decades-long struggle to retake possession of their building. In 1895, 376 K'iche' men signed the following petition:

> Fifteen years ago *el pueblo indígena quezalteco*, as one more proof that it loves progress . . . built with its own resources . . . a building that should be in the possession of the authorities of our class. This two-story building, both owing to its architecture and the important place it occupies, embellishes the public plaza of our flourishing city. Our profound love of all that signifies progress and our desire to demonstrate that the indigenous class in general and that of Quetzaltenango in particular is capable of social improvement and should be treated with consideration is proven by the great works of Quetzaltenango. Quetzaltenango, because of its monumental national, municipal and private buildings, is considered by foreigners who come to visit to be one of the most advanced cities in all of the isthmus of Central America. This gives us the honor and the justice to think that if our ancestors have left manifest vestiges that speak to the advanced level of their civilization, then we, despite having crossed the long epoch of colonialism and the dark night of religious fanaticism that the theocratic governments forced us to endure, are able to lift our spirit up and make by means of art, industry and commerce, a testimony so eloquent that it shows that we are not, as many believe, a degenerated and abject race without love for work and without a desire for civilization.
>
> As sincere patriots . . . we have always given our . . . people for the good of the *patria* without refusing any sacrifice. As obedient citizens, we have considered ourselves lucky that, far from the political rebellions, uprisings and insurrections that compromise the tranquillity of other pueblos, we have only been concerned with the development of agriculture and the progress of the craft arts.[15]

If the process of capitalist modernization entails the disruption of traditional practices and the placing of all social relations in a state of perpetual flux, then modernity, or at least one aspect of it, entails the desire to generate new myths and traditions that will lend meaning to that flux.[16] Both by drawing a historical and cultural genealogy between themselves and their precolonial Mayan ancestors and by blaming their inferior social status not simply on Ladinos but on the colonial and postcolonial conser-

14. "Manifest Vestiges": Excavation of Tikal, 1892.
Photograph by Alfred P. Maudslay, courtesy of CIRMA.

vative regimes, Quetzalteco K'iche's not only justified the return of their building but also carved a rhetorical niche for themselves within the formation of the Guatemalan nation. They promoted a nationalism that could imagine a glorious past, account for their current subordinate position, and envision a future that would include social equality while avoiding cultural obsolescence.

When K'iche's made reference to their pre-Columbian heritage to justify their future position in the Guatemalan nation, they were expressing a notion of "explosive time" in which "present and past dissolved into a transcendent future."[17] The K'iche's' contribution in creating a splendid city, unsurpassed throughout the isthmus, affirmed their role in both Guatemala's past and its potential future. This vision built on a budding Ladino indigenista nationalism particularly strong among Los Altos intellectuals, was reinforced by excavations throughout the nineteenth century of pre-Columbian Mayan ruins within Guatemalan national territory (see fig. 14).[18]

Yet while K'iche's shared new senses of historic time with Ladinos, they rejected Ladino efforts to use this history to cast indigenous culture as immutable, backward, and obstructionist. Their municipal building alone (two stories!) was proof of their affinity and capacity for progress. This of course remained in sharp contrast with Ladino nationalism. K'iche' efforts to regain possession of the building was proof enough for local Ladinos that the "obstinate resistance of the indigenous councilmen always stands in the way of progress."[19]

So That They Learn

Although educational changes had been under way since the later years of the Carrera regime, the new liberal state in the 1870s and 1880s issued a series of laws that decreed primary education to be compulsory, free, secular, and practical.[20] Obviously, Guatemala's exploitative model of development limited the ability of these reforms to build a national identity, inculcate civic responsibility, and create productive workers, particularly among the nation's overwhelmingly indigenous and rural population.[21] The political will of the liberal regime went only so far in schooling its populace. The state did not provide enough money to make education accessible to all children, nor was it willing to force finqueros to build schools for their resident colonos, as required by law.

Nevertheless, the educational reforms of the coffee state, if contradictory, incomplete, and self-serving, were consequential, especially in urban centers.[22] Throughout the twentieth century, the growth of an urban public educational system, which included an expanded university system, contributed to the rise of a working and a professional class. By the end of the last century, Quetzaltenango had earned a reputation as an important educational center. By 1896 there were in the city six primary schools for boys, four for girls, and one that was coeducational.[23] These eleven schools had a combined enrollment of 760 boys and 337 girls; 305 students were registered in secondary institutions in preparation for university or a trade. As primary and secondary schools became increasingly militarized and regimented under successive dictators, the public school system came to serve as an important site of social control and discipline.[24]

There were diverse opinions regarding specific pedagogical methods, yet nearly every reformer and politician agreed that education was the best way to transform Indians into productive Guatemalan citizens.[25] Initially it was hoped that a general, noncaste-specific school system would be sufficient to educate the nation's majority indigenous population, but by the late 1870s, a general consensus had been reached that the "special needs" of Indians required schools specifically designed for them. As Rufino Barrios himself put it, only through an educational system "adequate to their character and special circumstances" could Indians, "undoubtedly susceptible to improvement," be removed from the "backward and abject state" forced upon them by the conquest.[26] While some of the more ambitious schemes, such as requiring all teachers to learn an indigenous language, were never seriously considered, the state throughout the 1880s and 1890s founded a number of Institutos Indígenas, designed to teach Indians Spanish, and mathematical, civil, and vocational skills.[27]

In 1880, Barrios ordered that an Instituto Preparatorio de Indígenas be established in Quetzaltenango. By 1890 there were three indigenous primary schools with a total enrollment of 260—79 girls and 181 boys—operating in the city.[28] All of these children lived within the city's four central neighborhoods. In 1892, the Escuela Nacional Elemental de Niños Indígenas had an enrollment of forty-seven K'iche' boys learning a three-grade curriculum that included reading, "practical notions of the nation's language," math, penmanship, drawing, geography and history, morality, urban manners, calisthenics, and military maneuvers.[29]

The founders of the Sociedad El Adelanto took this call to educate Indians seriously. They believed that through education Indians could be regenerated and receive the benefits that the future had to offer. Despite the state's initial enthusiasm for the provision of universal education, by the turn of the century a shortage of revenue and political will led to an increased reliance on private organizations to provide elementary education. The state encouraged mutual aid and workers societies to patronize schools. In Guatemala City in 1878, for example, the Sociedad Central de Artesanos, with Barrios's approval and financial support, founded an adult night school.[30] In Quetzaltenango, during the first decades of this century, the Sociedad de Obreros, the Sociedad Liberal de Artesanos Indígenas, the Sociedad de Albañiles, and the Sociedad El Adelanto founded and supported a number of elementary and vocational schools.[31] Between 1897 and the late 1920s, El Adelanto established and administered seven schools—two primary schools for girls, two for boys (one with evening classes), one coeducational school, a night school for indigenous artisans, and a school of *artes y oficios domésticos* (domestic work and skills) for women (see figs. 15 and 16).[32]

Following the abolition of the Municipalidad de Indígenas in 1894, the Sociedad El Adelanto took up the fight to regain the confiscated municipal building. In 1911, Estrada Cabrera partially yielded to the society's demands and allowed the rent from the building to be used to pay the salaries of its teachers. The executive council of the sociedad wrote to thank him:

> The indigenous people, who want to make something of themselves in this world (*quiere ser algo en el concierto universal*), have not completely lost the notion of their past. In order to achieve success it is as necessary to cultivate intelligence as it is to strengthen the body.
>
> With the school, we will no longer be beasts of burden, poor and lamentable pariahs. We will develop our intelligence and strength; our blood circulates in the national life and with our effort the *Patria de Tecún* [Country of Tecún—the K'iche' warrior who fought Pedro de Alvarado] will be strengthened and advanced.[33]

The provision of education was a natural forum for city K'iche's to fulfill their self-ascribed role as representatives of Guatemala's indigenous population. With a conception of ethnicity based primarily on blood rather than culture, as outlined in chapter 6, these urban K'iche's perhaps felt they had nothing to fear in promoting a curriculum that was designed to integrate Indians into Ladino society. Not only did education allow them to act as spokespeople for Indians, but it also justified their own close adhesion to the Ladino society and economy.

The governing body of El Adelanto had minimal control over the curricula and activities of its schools. Through a number of mechanisms, the state attempted to ensure that education provided by private entities "conformed to the national program."[34] By the 1900s, departmental committees of the national Ministry of Public Education, usually headed by

15. K'iche' apprentice masons and Italian masters in a workshop run by the Sociedad El Adelanto, c. 1935. *Courtesy of Sociedad El Adelanto.*

the department's jefe político, were established "to ensure that education remained practical . . . and to guarantee the hygiene and morality of educational establishments."[35] These local committees were charged with overseeing the administration of public and private schools and had the power to inspect, audit, and administer biannual exams designed by the national ministry.[36] Proposals for new schools had to be approved by the national ministry.[37] The hiring and firing of school staffs—teachers and directors—had to be conducted through the jefe político and the departmental committee rather than through the sociedad. This ensured that teaching would be carried out by Ladinos (it would not be until the 1920s that the committee would approve K'iche's as either directors or teachers). It also limited the authority that the sociedad exercised over its schools. In 1921, for example, after the Ladino staff of one of the boys'

16. "So That They Learn": Schoolchildren of the Sociedad El Adelanto, c. 1920. *Courtesy of Sociedad El Adelanto.*

schools was accused of physical abuse, absenteeism, and drunkenness, El Adelanto had to get permission from the jefe político to reprimand them with the threat of dismissal.[38]

The sociedad's reliance on public funds likewise limited its autonomy. Initially in the late 1890s, the sociedad depended on a municipal subsidy to start and administer its schools.[39] By 1920, a quarter of the sociedad's educational budget was funded by money from the educational ministry, while the rest came from rent on three houses, interest on shares held on the Banco Central in Guatemala City, and the fees and contributions of members.[40] On a number of occasions following a political or economic crisis, these subsidies were held up and teaching stopped for extended periods.[41]

By participating in the liberal regime's efforts at public education, the indigenous leaders of the Sociedad El Adelanto helped integrate the city's population into new cycles of economic and national time.[42] The school day itself was structured to accustom children to an ordered workday, marked by clocks and bells.[43] A dress code attempted to break indigenous sartorial habits—K'iche' girls were to wear white smocks over their huipiles while boys were expected to attend class in pants, a buttoned shirt, and shoes. The school year, which in 1920 ran from February to October, was designed around the demands of coffee planters rather than the needs of subsistence producers and helped discipline Indians into the cycles of agro-industrial production.[44]

The national curriculum likewise conveyed new senses of national pasts and historical destinies. The 1901 essay questions presented to upper-level students—"What should be the role of education for women in the twentieth century?" and "How should children behave when they have received a higher level of education than their parents?"—captured both gender and generational anxiety and conveyed a sense of excitement and expectation as to what the new century would bring.[45] Courses in geography, history, and civic responsibility, taught with textbooks compiled by Guatemalan intellectuals, naturalized the nation's territory and population into a timeless past.[46] Maps of Guatemala, Central America, and the world allowed students to situate their city and their nation within a globalized political economy in which Guatemala was increasingly entrenched.[47] The singing of the national anthem, adopted in 1897, the practicing of military exercises, and the celebrating of annual patriotic holidays in which students from El Adelanto's schools paraded, all combined to create a shared sense of national providence and destiny.[48]

The ability of this new educational regime to condition behavior, however, was seriously limited. Resistance in the form of refusal to enroll children in school and high levels of truancy reveal sharp differences between the values of the urban K'iche's who ran El Adelanto and the poorer K'iche's they sought to represent. Absenteeism chronically plagued the schools. In one school with a total enrollment of 157 students, absentee rates averaged 23 percent a year.[49] El Adelanto created *rondas escolares* (truancy patrols) authorized by the local committee of public education, which went from house to house in search of school-age children.[50] Echoing their ancestors' reaction to vaccination campaigns, Indians hid their children from the inspectors; the difference was that this time the inspectors themselves were K'iche'. In the 1910s, school directors supplied the names of absent students to the jefe político, who in turn would dispatch a truancy officer to their homes. Fines levied against the parents went to the sociedad.

The contrast in the values and perspectives of the founders of the sociedad and poorer Indians still lingers in historical memory. Enrique Tucux, a sociedad member for forty-three years, related what he was told when he entered El Adelanto in 1954:

> Before founding our society, those indígenas did not want to study. They were backward. During those years, 1895 and forward, all the mothers and fathers were campesinos, *verdad*, and parents said during this time, "No, no, we don't want our children to study because schools are only for lazy people, and our boys are going to work in the milpa, in the fields, they are going to gather wood, our girls are going to make tortillas." The founders created the sociedad so that our *niños indígenas* learn. When our rondas went out to look for indigenous boys and girls, the parents said, "No, we want our children to work." But those who did not send their children to school we sent to the tribunal, and if they still did not send their children to school, they had to pay a fine. Many mothers would say, "Here comes those from the ronda—hide the children, hide the children!" They would hide the children in holes in the ground. So that our indigenous children progress through education—that is why the sociedad was formed.[51]

It is true that city K'iche's were more likely than rural Indians to enroll their children in school.[52] Calculating the value of education, however, entailed more than a simple difference in attitude toward the future; there were many reasons for popular recalcitrance. Running throughout key periods of the milpa cycle, the school year ignored the needs of subsistence production. Absenteeism increased dramatically during the months of March and April, when campesinos planted corn, and during July, when families weeded their milpas.[53] Daily chores also needed to be done. For peasant families dependent on household production, the long-term investment in school time was apparently not worth the immediate labor value their children represented. In contrast, urban K'iche' artisans and commercial traders and farmers, more accustomed to monetary relations to meet their daily needs, could afford to invest in educational time. The monthly matriculation fee charged by the sociedad may also have discouraged enrollment.[54] Illness, bad weather, exhaustion after a day's work (particularly for evening students), as well as the monolingualism, racism, and abuse inflicted on indigenous students by Ladino teachers—all undoubtedly contributed to high levels of absenteeism.[55] Further, the fact that the majority of public and private schools were built in the urban center discouraged rural children from attending and deepened the division between campesino and urban K'iche's.[56]

Historically constituted from the conflicts and relations that made up Quetzalteco society, the schools founded by the Sociedad El Adelanto were neither simple ideological state apparatuses nor autonomous popular institutions that held off state penetration.[57] Like other public and private schools of this period, the schools of El Adelanto did indeed promote nationalism and sought to integrate a predominantly peasant population into an agro-industrial regimentation. Yet their ability to do so was limited by the fact that these institutions themselves emerged from and were constrained by the contradictions that formed Quetzalteco and Guatemalan society.

I Hear that Train A' Coming

30 March 1930. In patriotic ecstasy the people of Quetzaltenango awaited the flower-bedecked train that was arriving for the first time over ten years late.[58] Thousands swelled the platform as the parade of societies reached the terminal (see fig. 17). The delegation from the El Adelanto carried a standard bearing an image of a steam locomotive, which had been the symbol used by the society for the last decade. Arbors of electric bulbs powered by a new hydroelectric plant trestled the parade route. Indigenous textile hangings adorned the grand pavilion at the station, where the city's marimba orchestra greeted the marchers. A group of Ladina women sporting bobbed hair and indigenous huipiles mingled with the crowd. Local, national, and foreign dignitaries made speeches. The municipality held a memorial on behalf of the "unknown workers" who had sacrificed their lives to build the line. Municipal authorities also honored the departments of Huehuetenango, San Marcos, Quiché, Sololá, and Totonicapán for their unselfish supply of labor. As the four passenger cars filled with invited guests approached the station, the train's whistle was drowned out by the noise of the crowd, the marimba, and the martial bands.

Powered by electricity supplied by the above-mentioned ambitious hy-

17. Inauguration of the Ferrocarril Nacional de Los Altos, 1930.
Courtesy of Estudio Portillo.

droelectric project, the Ferrocarril Nacional de Los Altos (FNLA) was indeed a remarkable engineering accomplishment. It wove along a treacherous river pass over trestles and through tunnels cut into volcanic folds, and connected Quetzaltenango to the coastal International Railways of Central America (IRCA) at what was then the steepest grade in the world for an electric tram.[59] Plagued by technical problems, a chronic operating deficit, and political hostility, the FNLA operated for a little more than three years. Following a storm that destroyed a bridge, Jorge Ubico, Guatemala's recently invested dictator, refused funds to rebuild the line, eventually ordering that the tracks be pulled up and used for lampposts and girders on public projects throughout the country.[60] Despite its short run, the coming to Quetzaltenango of the train, long coveted as a symbol of modernity, reveals the close connection between economic transformation and the construction of class, ethnic, and national identity.[61]

As early as the late nineteenth century city elites had wanted to build a railway from the coast to the city.[62] The original scheme called for lines to branch out from Quetzaltenango into neighboring departments. The project therefore would not only connect the city to Guatemala City, the Pacific ports, and Mexico, but also open up surrounding highland departments to Quetzalteco commercial houses and make these interior departments even more dependent on the city as a commercial hub.[63] Through the promotion of the "National Railroad of Los Altos," Quetzalteco Ladinos projected their economic and political interests as the general interests of the highlands. Their counterparts from surrounding departments, however, faced with ceaseless demands for labor, often saw the project from a different perspective; in their correspondences they repeatedly referred to the line as "Quetzaltenango's railroad."[64]

After a number of false starts, work on clearing and leveling a rail bed got under way in 1911.[65] Although it was hoped that the project would be completed within a decade, shortage of capital, political instability, and inability to attract a reliable, technically competent workforce and engineering corps led to repeated delays and setbacks. During this first decade, work on the bed often stalled while the managing committee lobbied for more national funds or for permission to contract national and foreign loans. In 1920, local and national elites, on advice from U.S. engineers, decided that the train would be powered by hydroelectricity; and in 1924 the government signed a contract with the German firm Allgemeine Elektrizitäts-Gesellschaft (AEG) to complete the line and build the hydroelectric dike and powerhouse.[66]

The building of the FNLA entailed the creation of an industrial labor force that was stratified by ethnicity. This stratification occurred not just between Ladinos and Indians but also between city K'iche's and Indians from the interior highlands. A key factor in the deepening of class relations among Indians was currency reform. Although uneven and slow throughout the late nineteenth and early twentieth centuries, the issuing of paper currency and efforts to peg its worth to the U.S. dollar commodified time into a standard value. The relative economic worth of a K'iche' master mason in relation to an indigenous peon could now be calibrated with biweekly pay records according to time and money.[67]

For nearly two decades, jefes políticos from the departments of Huehuetenango, Sololá, San Marcos, Totonicapán, and Quiché were each required to conscript and send two hundred mozos a month to work first on the rail bed, and then on the dike and electrical plant.[68] Neither the city nor the department of Quetzaltenango were asked to supply workers. It seems that supervisors were reluctant to use local forced labor on the project. Workers unfamiliar with the region may have been preferable, for when the project did conscript local labor for a brief period in 1919 from nearby Cantel and Olintepeque, incidents of escape from the work camps soared.[69] Nearly all of the skilled workers, on the other hand, were K'iche's from Quetzaltenango. In 1911, for example, the master mason Ramón Sím was contracted to build two bridges at ten pesos a yard, and, in 1921, David Coyoy and Juan Pisquiy were hired to start preliminary work on the dike at wages double those they would have made in the city.[70] The city's indigenous alcalde was responsible for supplying the camps with K'iche' smiths, quarrymen, and carpenters. These workers enjoyed better salaries, living conditions, and respect than did Indian conscripts.[71]

Living and working conditions in the camps ranged from abysmal to dangerous. Conscripted workers slept in open-air shelters and were constantly supervised by armed guards. Jefes políticos from the interior departments often reported that returning workers complained of verbal and physical abuse by the foremen, and they warned that if the complaints were true, they would have trouble supplying men in the future.[72] Foreign technicians, perhaps accustomed to slightly better working conditions in their home country, confirmed the routinely cruel treatment in their reports to the government.[73] Workers were expected to supply their own food. And, at least for a period following the arrest of two indigenous women who tried to enter a camp with a "basket filled with forty-five bottles of liquor hidden under a few roasted chickens," women were banned from the work sites, to prevent drunkenness and prostitution.[74] In the camps nearer to the coast, debilitating and often fatal diseases were a common occurrence.[75] Salaries were low and workers were docked for missing or damaged equipment.[76] Prior to the arrival of AEG when money for the project was short, workers were often given promissory notes in lieu of pay, which meant that they had to return to Quetzaltenango at a later date to receive their salaries.[77]

The work itself was brutal. For nearly fifteen years before the laying of ties and rails, most of the labor entailed the clearing and leveling of the bed and the opening of tunnels. The route climbed an average grade of nine degrees along a steep river pass, thus prohibiting the use of carts to haul the rocks needed to build up the bed. The chief engineer justified delays by citing worker exhaustion: "Nobody has ever built a railroad under conditions such as these."[78]

Despite the fact that some skilled K'iche' workers received significantly better salaries than did their conscripted counterparts, class interests did not automatically determine identity. As municipal authorities, Quezalteco K'iche's paid close attention to the progress of the work. In 1922, the indigenous alcalde requested that the municipality send a commission to the work site in order to be able to quiet the rumors and accusations that circulated in the city as a result of chronic delays.[79] And in 1926, a number of members of the Sociedad El Adelanto inspected the work camps. After receiving a tour of the project by German technicians, the delegation apparently had time to talk with workers about labor conditions in the camps. When the K'iche's returned to Quetzaltenango, they wrote the president regarding their impressions. Affirming that the project was a "sublime step forward not only for the region and the nation, but for all of Central America," the members of El Adelanto asked the president to order AEG to increase the salaries and improve the "bad" working conditions of "the poor Indian workers."[80] The president's response is unknown, but the petition suggests that the realities of capitalist development were beginning to limit the ability of the K'iche's to *both* promote national progress and defend the welfare of Indians.

Work on the line could also be extremely dangerous, and accidents often took life and limb. In 1922, for example, a large explosion caused by improper handling of dynamite wounded a number of workers, sent rocks flying, and destroyed several houses in a nearby town. In 1929, five workers were electrocuted; in that same year, a car derailed, wounding twenty-four.[81]

The value of the lives of conscripted workers while they were living was nil. "If you die, it means little to me," a foreman told a group of unnamed mozos from Sololá; the 1929 accident report merely described the five anonymous electrocuted workers as *"inditos."*[82] Yet dead, their anonymity could be infused with a collective national identity, and capitalism's fatalities could be resurrected as nationalism's martyrs: it was these "unknown fallen workers" whom the municipality honored with a memorial and a wreath on the day of the FNLA's inauguration. Unlike nationalism, capitalism is not particularly concerned with either immortality or endurance.[83]

Worker flight was a constant problem in the construction of the rail line and the hydroelectric dam. In 1923, for example, of the 213 mozos assigned to one work camp, 95 had fled within twenty days.[84] A common strategy of workers was to give one name when they were conscripted, and then a different name when they arrived at the camp.[85] Warrants dispatched for escaped workers would therefore be issued with the wrong name. Conscripted workers also frequently arranged to have their sons sent in their stead. On a number of occasions, the chief engineer asked jefes políticos to stop sending *patojos* (boys) in place of men.[86] Labor shortages were particularly acute during key months of the milpa cycle. Jefes políticos often wrote directly to the president asking for a temporary deferment on their obligation to supply workers until the milpas were planted, cleaned, or harvested. Likewise, labor was scarce during the coffee harvest, as the demands of planters outweighed the needs of an apparently interminable railroad project.[87]

Efforts to discipline a workforce to the dictates of wage labor in an economy where capital was chronically short and wages were dismally low and the population still had partial access to subsistence cultivation inevitably led to repression. This discussion has focused on the construction of the FNLA, but the same holds true for coffee production. Telegraphs and telephones, a fortified militia and military, an expanded bureaucracy and prison system, and revenues from coffee production tipped the balance of power in favor of the state in its ability to create and control a labor force. But a vicious cycle kicked in. Rather than investing money in technological improvement of the means of production, the state and private entrepreneurs invested money in means of repression; rather than promoting technological innovation as a means to accumulation, capitalists came to rely on a coercive state to guarantee their profits.[88]

Yet even Guatemala's exceptionally brutal model of capitalist development could not function through repression alone. As we have seen, alliances with indigenous authorities were crucial in the exercise of social power. This practice continued throughout the twentieth century. More than half the guards in the railroad camps were Indian, and indigenous authorities helped, sometimes zealously, to track down escaped workers. Quetzaltenango's K'iche' mayor regularly collaborated in the capture and incarceration of mozos who fled the camps and fincas.[89] Cantel's indigenous mayor, Emetero Colop, went so far as to hold the wife of an escapee hostage until the worker turned himself in.[90] As described for the colonial period, the maintenance of caste authority benefited not just the K'iche' authorities but Ladino elites as well. With the persistence of some level of indigenous subsistence economy and the inability or unwillingness of Ladinos to establish a straight wage system, Indian elites remain an essential component of agro-export development.

Uneven development is most notable when the rhetoric of nationalism and progress fails to reflect political and economic realities.[91] Quetzaltecos' desire to be modern brought the railroad to the city, but it could not make it successful.

Immediately upon commencement of its operations, diverse sectors of Guatemalan society used the FNLA. In two hours and twenty-five minutes, passengers traveling to the capital could connect with the coastal line of the IRCA. Both the city's commercial houses and individual merchants used the FNLA to ship a variety of products in and out of the city.[92]

Nevertheless, despite this usage, the railroad suffered from a chronic operating deficit and repeatedly had to borrow money to cover costs. Despite a number of reductions in freight charges and special rates for large-scale cargo, the line could not attract enough customers to cover expenses. Technical problems, a shortage of cargo wagons, a tariff dispute with the IRCA that held up transferences of freight from one line to the other, and sabotage by truckers who felt that the line threatened their livelihood caused constant delays and backlogs.[93] Vandalism became such a serious problem that the FNLA's management posted a national decree along the tracks that made it a capital crime to knowingly destroy railroad property (ironically, the decree had been issued by Reina Barrios in response to the 1897 rebellion).[94]

Although trains continued to symbolize modernity and progress for many, 1930 was not 1899. As capitalist relations spread throughout Guatemala, the rate at which goods circulated became a crucial factor in the accruing of profits. Commercial houses grew impatient with the perpetual delays and often switched back to truck transportation, which, owing to the expansion and improvement of the road system under Ubico, rivaled the FNLA in efficiency and speed, if not cost.[95] Further, by the time of the line's destruction in 1933, a new kind of transportation had revolutionized the relation between time and space: "To economize time is to economize money," announced the ad for the newly established Compañía Nacional de Aviación, which ran forty-five-minute daily flights between Quetzalte-nango and the capital.[96]

The promises of economic development are usually understood in cultural terms. From nearly the beginning of its promotion, Ladinos believed that the FNLA would not merely allow for the freer circulation of goods and people but would be also an important step in converting Guatemala into a modern nation. Train transportation would end once and for all the barbaric "blood haulage" (*tracción de sangre*) by which Indians trucked goods on their backs supported by a rope strapped around their foreheads, known as a *mecapal* or tumpline.[97] For reformers, the image of the hunched Indian cargador came to epitomize all that was backward and primitive about Guatemala: "The train is a means of civilization and as such will emancipate the natives from their primitive habit [of using mecapales]."[98]

The preoccupation of reformers with ending this practice is a good illustration of their belief that economic and national progress could be achieved through the alteration of "cultural" habits. Pedagogues at Guatemala's 1894 education conference, for example, singled out the use of tumplines as a particularly pernicious obstacle to efficient production: "Because [the Indians] find themselves unaccustomed to economic ideas, in order to make Indians appreciate the value of time and work, they need to be taught through practical demonstrations [not to use mecapales]."[99]

Records indicate that a number of highland indigenous traders and producers did indeed use the train to transport their goods. In January 1931, for example, Santos Chojolán paid three quetzales and twenty-five cents to ship 1,805 pounds of corn from the coast to the city; Bartolo Coyoy paid fifty-four cents to ship 60 pounds of cigarettes.[100] Surnames indicate that it was not just Quetzalteco Indians who used the train. That same month, Pedro Batz, a K'iche' name common to Totonicapán, shipped 410 pounds of coffee to Quetzaltenango, and J. Machic, a name prevalent in Almolonga, shipped 2,615 pounds of plantains.[101]

Nevertheless, for most Indian traders and producers, time was not quite money; even if it took days, the free use (at least in terms of money) of personal or family labor to transport goods continued to outstrip quicker, but paid for, modes of "modern" transportation. Even though the FNLA lowered the tariff on third-class cargo transport and banned the use of the rail bed for foot transit, most Indians persisted in spurning the railway.[102] Indians certainly did "appreciate the value of time and labor," but in ways that were often more attuned to the realities of the Guatemalan economy than to the hopes of liberal reformers. In the process, many Indians continued to use noncommodified labor to best Ladino producers and merchants in an increasingly commodified society.

The Fetishism of Family and the Secret Thereof

A central theme of this chapter has been to argue that the anxiety of modernity creates the desire for new myths and traditions—beliefs that will bring under control the changes that have undermined all seemingly fixed and stable cultural, political, and economic relations. With their increasing adoption of Ladino lifeways, urban Quetzalteco K'iche's were particularly susceptible to this anxiety. They not only ran the risk of losing their ethnic identity but also the authority that identity afforded them. As social changes became more intense, the cultural identification articulated by Quetzalteco K'iche's became more intensely self-conscious and referential.

The new technology of print media gave to Quetzalteco K'iche's a new way of understanding themselves as a subject class. As we have seen, newspapers, history books, accounts and photographs of archeological digs, and maps provided K'iche' elites with, in the words of Benedict Anderson, an "image of antiquity so central to the subjective idea of the nation."[103] Their uncertain present was now nestled between a magnificent precolonial past and a progressive national future. Furthermore, the issuance and gradual acceptance of standardized currency by Guatemalans likewise allowed K'iche' elites—artisans, contractors, merchants, farmers—to crystallize social labor in paper form, thus validating their status in relation to other indigenous campesinos and workers. Starting in the late nineteenth century, the new art and technology of photographic portraiture gave them yet another tool to get a fix on themselves. Just as money represents a naturalized myth through which the whole world of social production and power gets to be represented, portraits allowed

K'iche' patriarchs a similar opportunity to "commodify"—that is, represent as universal and natural—in a "visual economy" the gender and class contradictions that afforded them power.[104]

Beginning in the late nineteenth century, a number of foreign photographers either visited or set up shop in Quetzaltenango, and K'iche's immediately began experimenting with this new technology. In the 1890s, James Piggot opened a studio; a few years later he was joined by Tomás Zanotti, a Mexican of Italian descent. During the first three decades of this century, thousands of K'iche' families and individuals commissioned the Piggot-Zanotti studio (eventually taken over by Zanotti) to take their portraits.[105] Although Zanotti occasionally photographed K'iche's in poses supposedly characteristic of indigenous culture (see fig. 18), the vast majority of these portraits were classical studio shots (see fig. 19). Unlike the albums of photographs of random "natives" sold throughout Europe and North America either to capture vanishing "races" or to provide the raw material needed by promoters of concocted racial theories, these portraits were solicited and consumed by the K'iche's themselves.[106]

In the face of unrelenting Ladino criticism of indigenous customs, what place would indigenous identity have in the twentieth century? How could these urban K'iche' men help bring about progress, yet retain their identity? In the wake of vast and far-ranging economic changes, what would be the role of community and family, so fundamental to the social power of patriarchs?

As Anne McClintock has noted, collective identities "are frequently figured through the iconography of familial or domestic space."[107] As previously argued, the household was the basic unit of Quetzalteco society: it afforded male patriarchs a competitive advantage in their dealings with Ladinos and provided women with a forum through which they conducted their economic activities and made claims on patriarchal obligations. Yet by the late nineteenth century, the Quetzalteco K'iche' family was an institution in transformation. Reflecting the change from a primarily peasant-subsistence economy to a commodified artisanal-commercial economy, families were shrinking. Although it seems that average family size stayed roughly the same between 1760 and 1813, with an average of 4.8 persons per household, between 1813 and 1896 the household mean decreased from five to four.[108] In addition, the expansion of the regional and national economy undoubtedly allowed women increasing freedom from the patriarchal control inherent in a peasant soci-

18. "Blood Haulage": Studio shot of K'iche' boys using mecapales to carry wood. *Photograph by Tomás Zanotti, courtesy of Museo Girard.*

ety, since there were more opportunities to earn money either for survival or commercial investment, and more opportunities to migrate. Further, aspirations of social mobility could now be represented as generational, as K'iche' children increasingly went to school rather than to the fields or the family workshops.

In the face of this flux, photography allowed K'iche's to reconcile the modern and the traditional in a fixed portrait of stability. In the shots, the women and female children are attired in their finest huipiles and pleated *cortes* (indigenous skirts), and the men are dressed in dark suits and white shirts, occasionally sporting waist belts, an indigenous custom that by the turn of the century was already out of date. At their feet are a combination of studio props—a clay dog or a tiger skin; on their left, an ornately carved table (a constant Ladino refrain was that Indians needed to be taught to use modern furniture); on their right, a staircase, representing the modernity of a two-story house. Under them, rugs cover, partially, bare wood floors. These portraits of K'iche' domesticity could easily have been shot in bourgeois Victorian England—except for the women's dress.

As indigenous ethnicity changed with the dissolution of reciprocal and caste obligations, the *form*, represented better than anywhere in indigenous female dress, became increasingly important in the understanding of Indian identity. Photography helped bring about the reconciliation of modernity and tradition, progress and stability, by presenting an image of the K'iche' family in which men, attired in Western clothes, were the harbingers of progress, and matriarchs, dressed in the huipil and corte, became the standard-bearers of ethnic identity. Further, despite the naturalized assumptions of blood determinism prevalent among Quetzalteco K'iche's, reproduction of the collective took place more through cultural affiliation than endogamous biological reproduction. While there were strong cultural pressures promoting endogamy, intermarriage both with residents of other indigenous towns and with Ladinos continued apace. K'iche' blood ideologies that allowed for assimilation but demanded cultural demarcation, therefore, were aptly captured and reproduced in family portraits.

The importance of family portraiture in representing hierarchy and the aspirations to social mobility is best understood when compared with portraits of individuals.[109] Compare the two individual shots of Agatón Boj and Santiago Coyoy (figs. 1 and 2 on p. 3), both prominent K'iche' businessmen and political leaders, with the two photographs of K'iche'

19. K'iche' woman and child, c. 1930. *Photograph by Tomás Zanotti, courtesy of* CIRMA.

families (figs. 20 and 21 on pp. 188 and 189, respectively). In the individual portraits, the authority of the subjects alone claims the eye of the beholder. In both cases, the social position of the subjects is conveyed in isolation, abstracted from the processes and relations that afforded them power. The averted gaze of both subjects denies a relationship even with viewers of the portraits, while the absence of a backdrop further high-lights the individualism of the bourgeois self.

The family portraits, on the other hand, immediately resituate the patriarch within a context of household power and authority. In both cases, no information is known about the families, and trade tools, so prominent in photographs of Indians in other areas of Latin America, are noticeably absent. In the larger family seen in figure 20, it is not known if the couple seated in the center are the parents of the five other individuals. In any case, it is clear that they are indeed the authorial center of the household. That the son immediately to the left of the father is the only male wearing shoes and a tie suggests that he represents the family's aspirations to social mobility—hence his prominent position at his fa-ther's side. The second family portrait, in figure 21, captures the changing nature of the K'iche' household. Extended patriarchal kinship ties have to this day retained their importance in the K'iche' community, but a shift of emphasis has taken place. As Quetzaltenango was transformed into a more integrated urban economy, the immediate family—represented by a father, a mother, and a reduced number of children—gained in promi-nence. Much more than in the portrait of the larger family, in this photo-graph, the father is the center of authority, as is underscored by both his youthfulness and the absence of older male relations, whether they be grandfathers, uncles, or brothers.

While these family portraits to some degree "demystified" the house-hold relations that afforded K'iche' patriarchs their power, they none-theless presented an image of K'iche' family authority and autonomy abstracted from political and class power. But in the constitution and representation of these relations, photography also played its part. Com-pare the two photographs of municipal authorities (figs. 8 and 9 on p. 133). The first is of the "autonomous" indigenous municipality, taken, I believe, in 1894, the year before it was incorporated into the Ladino municipal body. It is a classical posed studio shot in which the K'iche' municipales are attired in accouterments traditionally associated with indigenous au-thority—scepters, tzute head scarves, and capes. That the alcaldes and regidors are arranged around a globe and a telegraph machine suggests that they were keenly aware of the ever increasing extent to which their social power now revolved around the new spatial and temporal tech-nologies (including photography) of Guatemalan nationalism. In the sec-ond photograph of the now combined K'iche' and Ladino municipality

20. K'iche' family, c. 1915. *Photograph by Tomás Zanotti, courtesy of* CIRMA.

(fig. 9 on p. 133), taken sometime in the 1920s, the backdrop of national paraphernalia, including a statue of Tecún Uman, offers any number of complex readings. What is most striking, however, is the way this photograph captures the ongoing tension between ethnic autonomy and dependence that formed the heart of K'iche' power. By the time the portrait was shot, at least twenty-five years had passed since the K'iche' cabildo had been incorporated into the now single municipal body. Nevertheless, the sitting arrangement—Ladinos on the right of the mayor, K'iche's on his left—suggests that the mutually dependent, yet constantly contested, interethnic alliance described in preceding chapters, which structured city politics, retained a good deal of its vitality well into the twentieth century.

   The ability of K'iche' elites to convert this political authority into class and community power is nowhere better illustrated than in 1886 when the K'iche' alcalde, Florencio Cortez, and three indigenous regidores paid a silver dollar each to U.S. traveler William Brigham for a group portrait (fig. 7 on p. 132).[110] Posed standing in front of a house and dressed in trousers, jackets with wide lapels, and brimmed hats (only one wore a tzute head wrap), the four formed a picture of urbanity and authority that contrasted sharply with contemporary images of "degenerate" Indians.

21. K'iche' family, c. 1930. *Photograph by Tomás Zanotti, courtesy of* CIRMA.

Indeed, to underscore how photography helped commodify communal obligations into class relations, Cortez, in addition to the silver dollar, supplied Brigham with a conscripted mozo to cart his belongings to the next town.

The establishment by the Sociedad El Adelanto of one of Guatemala's first indigenous beauty contests, in 1934, sheds light on how K'iche' elites reconfigured gender relations to situate themselves not only in relation to Ladinos but also in relation to rural peasants. By establishing in the 1920s a school of Artes y Oficios, which taught girls backstrap weaving and embroidering, among other things, El Adelanto had exhibited an awareness of the importance of gender ideologies in maintaining ethnic identity. In 1934, a group of young, educated, and politically active K'iche's proposed to the sociedad that it sponsor an indigenous beauty contest.[111] The point of the contest was not just to elect the Reina Indígena de Xelaju, as the winner would be called, but to use the contest as a means of teaching the city's populace how to participate in democratic elections.

The men decided to sponsor a contest that would be held at the beginning of September, to coincide with the annual independence celebration.[112] The sociedad designed the campaign and electoral procedures to have all the trappings of a political vote. Committees nominated and promoted the virtues of their respective candidates days in advance of the election. Polling was conducted by secret ballot and was open to Ladino and K'iche' men and women over fifteen years of age. There were no literacy requirements; voters were to mark a box on the ballot located under the photo of their preferred candidate. The voting took place at three polling tables located at a park near the headquarters of El Adelanto. Each table was supervised by a member of the press, a representative of each candidate, and a municipal monitor.

The contestants had to be Guatemalan, from Quetzaltenango, between eighteen and twenty-four years of age, and the daughters of indigenous parents. Over the years the candidates usually came from the most prominent and wealthy K'iche' families and demonstrated not only the standard traits extolled by beauty pageants—femininity, innocence, beauty—but also that ineffable balance between tradition and modernity so sought after by urban K'iche's.[113] In fine huipiles, pleated dresses, and a high-backed collar giving way to a long royal train, the winners, coronated with crown and staff, presented an image of matriarchal elegance that drew more from European symbols of nobility than from indigenous traditions.[114] (See figs. 22 and 23. Notice the urban K'iche' audience in the municipal theater in fig. 22.) As with other expressions of Quetzalteco K'iche' identity, the contest emerged from the ambiguous positions of K'iche's as urban Indians. By combining imagined elements of European and indigenous culture, the contest tapped into the indigenista tradition of Ladino nationalism, thereby allowing K'iche's a claim to national authenticity that was unavailable to Ladinos.[115] At the same time, by promoting a highly urbanized, Hispanicized standard of indigenous feminine beauty, Quetzalteco K'iche's were able to set themselves off from rural Indians while at the same time adhering to their ethnic affiliation. (For an example of how rural Indians view urban Quetzalteco K'iche's, see fig. 24.)

El Adelanto touted the contest as a means by which democratic practices could be instilled among the city's population. This allowed K'iche's not only to carry out their roles as political leaders but also to foster a myth of caste, class, and gender equality that belied the realities of Guatemala's political system—a system that denied suffrage to most Indians, women, the illiterate, the propertyless, and the unemployed. The results of the first pageant are telling. Two contestants, Rosa de Paz Chajchalac and Julia Ixcaraguá, vied for the hearts and votes of the populace. After nearly four hours of polling, Ixcaragua emerged victorious with a vote of 895 to 800. The Comité pro-Rosa, however, successfully challenged the results, claiming that Ixcaraguá was underage. Paz was crowned queen. The contest was indeed a clear lesson in the realities of Guatemalan democracy, three years into Ubico's thirteen-year dictatorship: you can vote, but it does not count.

A Republic of Artisans

K'iche' elite nationalism cut two ways. The establishment of new institutions and the innovation of new rituals allowed K'iche's to promote a vision of a biracial nation, but at the same time it afforded the state new mechanisms for control. Especially under Jorge Ubico (1930–44), the state not only continued to use K'iche' and other Mayan elites to procure needed labor and to fill positions in public administration (as we have seen in the case of the FNLA), but it attempted to use indigenous efforts at ethnic maintenance to garner cultural legitimacy. The ability of K'iche's

22. Coronation of Silvia Esperanza Velásquez Xicará, La Reina Indígena, in the municipal theater, 1955. *Courtesy of Silvia Esperanza Velásquez Xicará.*

23. La Reina Indígena, Silvia Esperanza Velásquez Xicará, 1955. *Courtesy of Silvia Esperanza Velásquez Xicará.*

24. Baile de los Convites, Chupol, Chichicastenango, 1999, where Chupol men cross-dress as couples from surrounding indigenous towns. Notice that while the men representing Chichicastenango and Santa Cruz del Quiché are wearing traditional garb, the Quetzalteco man is dressed in a suit and tie. *Photograph and observation courtesy of Carlota McAllister.*

to put forth their idiosyncratic vision of race and nation was severely limited by the pressures of a consolidating state and a changing national economy.

At the end of the last century, as thousands of indigenous peasants were forced to travel to the coast to pick coffee for miserable wages, liberals began to promote the urban artisan as the national archetype. In Guatemala City, Quetzaltenango, and other emerging urban populations, the state and the Liberal Party encouraged the formation of Sociedades de Obreros or Artesanos.[116] For reformers and politicians, these clubs and societies (which they often supported financially) played important roles in promoting national identity, encouraging liberal economic practices, and disciplining plebeian behavior.[117] The associations represented the antithesis of colonial guilds, which liberals disdained for their close affilia-

tion to the Catholic Church and their mercantilist work rules.[118] Workers
societies administered schools, mobilized members to celebrate national
holidays, campaigned for political candidates, and published newspapers
that ran articles promoting work discipline, improved technology, and the
image of Guatemala as a democratic republic of liberal artisans.[119] For
liberals, the ideal national craftsman was stripped of ethnic content and
hence Ladino by default.

In Quetzaltenango, the Sociedad El Adelanto, while continuing to ad-
vocate specifically on behalf of Quetzalteco Indians, increasingly yielded,
at least publicly, to this artisan identity. A number of the K'iche' founders
of El Adelanto were also members of other artisanal and liberal clubs, and
Agatón Boj was also a founding member of the Club Central de Obreros.
Members of El Adelanto often referred to their organization as a worker
or artisan society and marched in the annual May Day parade and on the
occasion of other civil holidays. In 1929, the sociedad commissioned
Enrique Boj, Agatón's son, to build a monument that would honor "the
labor of workers and peons" in the building of the nation.[120] The local
public education committee, on which El Adelanto relied for curriculum
and staff approval, insisted that the first schools the society opened—
despite being named the Escuela de Niñas Indígenas and the Escuela
Mixta de Indígenas—"accept not only Indians . . . but all who desire to
learn," and registration records indicate that indeed a high number of
Ladino children attended the society's schools.[121] Under Estrada Cabrera
and Ubico, the state, represented by the jefe político, increasingly used the
sociedad to effect public administration, ordering its governing body to
collect sundry taxes and ensure that its members attended civil cere-
monies.[122] By 1915, judging from its revised statutes, even the principal
mission of the sociedad had changed. Members were no longer to work
for the "regeneration of the race" but rather for the "diffusion of education among the indigenous class."[123]

Added to this, Ladino indigenismo took a new turn in the 1930s.
Perhaps in response to the world depression that deflated coffee prices,
the state, in search of new revenues, began to promote indigenous culture
as a tourist attraction.[124] Now Quetzalteco K'iche's not only had to contend with a nationalism that sought to assimilate them, but they also had
to deal with a state that intended to turn their ethnicity into national
folklore. Starting in 1934, the municipality of Quetzaltenango set up a
Picturesque Pueblo de Indígenas during its yearly independence festi-

val—a model village at the city's fairgrounds where representatives from each of the department's indigenous communities were expected to perform traditional dances and exhibit their craft and textile specialties.[125]

More than just marginalizing Indian ethnicity, the promotion of Indian "folklore" provided state and military elites with the opportunity to apply local culture to its own ends. The reconfiguration of communal gender ideologies by the K'iche' patriarchs so as to inscribe themselves into national history, for example, allowed state forms to articulate with local culture. In Quetzaltenango, the K'iche' beauty pageant was held to coincide with Guatemala's Independence Day celebration. In the words of one of the contest's founders, Manuel Villagrán Leiva, the Reina Indígena de Xelaju was established with the intent to "represent the origin of the indigenous race in the celebration of our emancipation from Spain."[126] Following her selection as indigenous queen, the winner marched in a city parade and then set up court in her "rancho" (a thatched hut). Throughout the 1930s, Ubico attended these events, and in at least one year he coronated the winner himself. The use of local culture by the state, and increasingly by the military, to promote its authority would continue in later years throughout Guatemala. For example, Carlota McAllister describes how in Cobán the national indigenous pageant was taken over by military dictators in the 1970s.[127]

The situation of El Adelanto grew dire throughout the global depression of the 1930s. Individuals could not pay rent owed or money borrowed from El Adelanto, and many could not keep up with voluntary donations or membership fees.[128] Members did not attend meetings and refused to serve as officers. Ubico militarized schools to a greater extent than did his predecessor Estrada Cabrera and demanded even more servile displays of civil loyalty from societies, clubs, and other private organizations.[129] The hardest blow fell in 1931 when Ubico, in order to "exercise greater control over private education," nationalized the schools of the Sociedad El Adelanto and the Sociedad de Obreros.[130] Furthermore, the municipality, immediately seizing on Ubico's nationalization as a pretext, retook control of the rent from the old indigenous municipal building.

The response to the sociedad's efforts to schedule an audience with Ubico to protest the nationalization indicates the changed nature of the state. Although Ubico had earned a populist reputation in his dealings with indigenous communities—suddenly arriving in highland towns on lightning motorcycle trips to listen and attend to sundry concerns—the accumulated layers of state bureaucracy made it increasingly difficult for Indians to take the initiative and go directly to the president as they had done so many times in the past.[131] When El Adelanto sent a note to Guatemala City asking to see the president, it was told that its request was "*en tramite*" (in process).[132] When the sociedad did send a committee to Guatemala City, it "achieved nothing" except the acquisition of some school supplies from the education ministry.

Despite the growing strength of the state under Ubico, despite the eagerness with which some K'iche's promoted Guatemalan nationalism, and despite the ability of the state to appropriate local rituals to further its cultural legitimacy, the state was unsuccessful in erasing caste affiliation or in convincing K'iche's that equality was enjoyed by one and all. Ethnic resentment would occasionally emerge through the nationalist rhetoric of the K'iche's. This is nowhere clearer than in El Adelanto's reaction to the loss of the rent from its building.

In September 1932, the sociedad convened a series of emergency meetings to discuss the nationalization of the schools and the loss of the municipal building.[133] Speech after speech given by the oldest members of the sociedad, now retired from conducting its daily affairs, reveals a keen awareness of ethnic discrimination and social subordination. Ignacio Sum, identified as a founder, recalled in detail the innumerable sacrifices made by "each and every indio Quetzalteco" to construct the building. Catarino Sum insisted that the loss of the building was proof of the "hatred of the clase indígena" harbored by Ladinos. And David Coyoy, a wealthy construction contractor, insisted that the building belonged to the "indigenous race."

As capitalism and its correlates—commodification, infrastructural development, agro-industrialization, technological innovation, class struggle, migration, militarization, and repression—recast social relations, K'iche's invented new traditions and institutions to control and give meaning to their lives. Through education, architecture, promotion of public works, and engagement with new technologies and art forms, K'iche's developed a very modern, very self-conscious understanding of their cultural identity. As they confronted the ideological challenges presented by both a consolidating Ladino planter state and an increasingly impoverished and proletarianized indigenous population, urban K'iche's incorporated and transformed gender, class, and ethnic norms and relations into new identities that they hoped would reconcile the "traditional" with the "modern."

Throughout the 1930s and 1940s, Quetzalteco K'iche' elites insisted on infusing the national with the cultural, as they continued to promote a unique alternative vision of the nation. Although the distinctive vision of race, class, and nation carved out by the K'iche's was not strong enough to withstand the pressures brought about by years of dictatorship, depression, political repression, and racism, it was able to forestall a complete loss of cultural identification. The dream of an alternative, inclusive nationalism, however, confronted perhaps its greatest challenge from within the K'iche' común, as the class divisions long under way among Indians erupted in the 1950s in a violent political clash. Caste conflict finally gave way to class conflict as poor indigenous campesinos, using new national legislation, struggled with K'iche' elites for control of the city's remaining forest land. It is to this internecine conflict that we finally turn.

Chapter 8
The Blood of Guatemalans: Class Struggle and the Death of K'iche' Nationalism

The sacrifice that I have asked for does not include the blood of
Guatemalans.—JACOBO ARBENZ GUZMÁN, *resignation address,* 1954

Blood on the leaves and blood at the root . . . strange fruit hanging from
the poplar trees.—LEWIS ALLEN (pseudonym for Abel Meeropol),
Strange Fruit, 1937

On an early morning a few days after the fall of Jacobo Arbenz in June
1954, Valentín Coyoy Cruz's family found his body hanging from a tree.
Officially his death was ruled as a suicide.[1] Probably, it was murder.[2] A
K'iche' campesino and political activist from a rural aldea of Quetzaltenango, Coyoy helped organize seven land claims under the famous 1952
agrarian reform: three of them pertained to municipal forest land; five of
them were successful. Although Arbenz may truly have believed that his
resignation would save lives, following the 1954 U.S.-sponsored counterrevolution, hundreds—if not thousands—of peasant leaders like Coyoy
were rounded up and executed.[3] As leaders of the "Liberation" prattled
on about retaining the gains and freedoms of the revolution, campesinos
and political activists crowded the nation's jails and corpses filled its
morgues.[4] There is general consensus today among academics and Guatemalan intellectuals that 1954 signaled the beginning of what would become the most repressive state in the hemisphere—a state responsible for
the torture and murder of two hundred thousand of its citizens.[5]

This chapter will explore how the revolution, specifically the agrarian
reform, played out in Quetzaltenango. Until now, this work has focused
mainly on the actions and aspirations of a small group of urbanized
K'iche' elite men as they tried to situate themselves within a rapidly
changing world. This chapter will shift gears and focus on the political

activity of the people on whose behalf these elites believed they were speaking—K'iche' campesinos from the city's rural confines. We have seen how the involvement of principales with national politics and ideologies furthered the process of state formation. In 1954, the opposite occurred. K'iche' elite opposition to land reform and peasant organizing contributed to the state's unraveling.

The October Revolution

It is difficult to assess the near-mythic importance of the "ten years of spring" (1944–54) for current Guatemalan politics and identity. In 1944, a movement spearheaded by students, teachers, military reformers, and an emerging middle class ousted from power Jorge Ubico and his would-be successor, Federico Ponce.[6] For one decade under two democratically elected presidents—Juan José Arévalo (1945–50) and Jacobo Arbenz Guzmán (1951–54)—Guatemalans enjoyed unprecedented freedom and hope.[7] Social liberals and radicals pushed through an incredibly ambitious series of political and economic reforms intended to make Guatemala an inclusive, modern country.

Strengthened by an urban middle class eager to make good on the promise of democracy and development, three lines of overlapping political thought came together at mid-century to promote the belief that an interventionist state could transform Guatemala into a modern, democratic nation.

First, Guatemala's long tradition of indigenismo had become radicalized by mid-century.[8] As had occurred to a large extent in Mexico, Ladino intellectuals such as David Vela and Miguel Angel Asturias now emphasized social and structural reasons for the failure to assimilate Indians into national life.[9] Critiques of the treatment of Indians meted out by national and foreign landowners became a prevalent theme in indigenista literature. Reformers advocated for increased state intervention (e.g., the foundation of the Instituto Indigenista Nacional, modeled on the Mexican Instituto Nacional Indigenista) that aimed to protect and assimilate the Indian.[10] Encouraged by the perceived successes of Mexican agrarianism, they made land reform a central part of this program. Second, the reforms reflected the mid-century belief among developmental economists, many of them affiliated with the United Nations' Comisión

Económica para América Latina, that economic and political modernization could be achieved through a strong, activist state.[11] Land and labor
reform, which would restrain the power of the "feudal" bourgeoisie,
force investment in productive relations, and create an internal market for
locally produced goods, would be central to this end.[12] Finally, Communists and radical socialists, who came to play a central role in Arbenz's
government, advocated for the reforms as being necessary to complete
the transition to capitalist modernization, a characteristic position for
Latin American Communist Parties during this period.[13]

The most radical of these reforms was, of course, the 1952 congressional decree 900—the agrarian reform. The reform allowed individuals
or peasant organizations to claim the uncultivated land of farms that
were larger than two caballerías, unused municipal property, and national
fincas.[14] There have been many criticisms of the reform: that it was
designed to further capitalist development rather than socialist equality;
that it did not comprehend the complexities of peasant and indigenous
society and created insuperable communal divisions; that it was too cautious and that despite the wave of organizing it unleashed, it was too
deferential to the interests of the planter class; that it was a patronage tool
used to reward allies and tie peasants to the state.[15] Although all these
criticisms are true, to a degree, the reform nevertheless represented a
fundamental shift in the power relations governing Guatemala.

Not only did the agrarian reform present a direct threat to the near-
absolute power wielded by the agro-bourgeoisie since 1871, but for the
first time in Guatemalan history a significant amount of state authority
was used to promote the interests of the nation's disenfranchised masses.
In a little-known essay, Gustavo Porras argues that despite the declared
goals of Arbenz's government—to stimulate capitalist modernization and
strengthen the nonlanded national bourgeoisie—the reforms, in particular the agrarian reform, directly threatened the interests of the landed
ruling class.[16] In Porras's view, the oft-repeated assertion that Arbenz's
national and international opponents did not truly understand what the
agrarian reform was designed to accomplish is simply wrong: they in fact
recognized its threat only too well.

Two aspects of the agrarian reform pushed the legislation well beyond
its stated goal of economic transformation and helped realign political
relations in the countryside. First, the reform weakened the power of the
landed class not only by expropriating unused land but also by declaring

that plantation communities of more than fifteen families now made up their own legal jurisdiction within the national political structure. Considering the degree to which productive relations were based on the control of large numbers of dependent colonos, this measure was a direct threat to the planters' power and authority. Moreover, the new law also declared all roads be opened to public use without any restrictions, thus effectively placing the thoroughfares under the control of the former plantation colonos. This gave the working population of the plantation zones unprecedented freedom of mobility.

Second, the legal mechanisms through which the reform was applied greatly weakened the power of the landed class; as Porras reminds us, "In whatever law, what is important is who applies it." At the local level, the law established Comités Agrarios Locales (CALS)—an "embryo of local power . . . the most democratic institutions that have ever existed in Guatemala." These committees served both as the institutional front line in the struggle waged against the class power of the landed elite and an important arena of political formation. The five-person composition of the CALS ensured that they were always in the control of local campesinos: one committee member was nominated by the governor, one by the respective municipality, and three by the local peasant organization. The CALS were usually indirectly allied with the Communist Party (the Partido Guatemalteco de Trabajo, PGT) through their affiliation with the Confederación Nacional Campesina de Guatemala (CNCG), and by 1954 there were over three thousand of them. They were the linchpin of the agrarian reform's implementation structure, of which the president was the final arbiter, and were completely free from the control of other state structures more easily manipulated by sectors hostile to the land reform. It was to these local committees that land claims were made; moreover, these committees were responsible for inspecting the disputed land, judging the validity of the claims, and then passing the decision on to the Comité Agrario Departmental and the Departamento Agrario Nacional. By the time of Arbenz's overthrow, nearly a million manzanas—17 percent of all private property—"had been expropriated or [were] in the process of being expropriated under the law."[17]

There were many reasons for the failure of Guatemala's brief experiment in democracy. Unlike in Mexico, elites in Guatemala did not eventually coalesce into a ruling coalition party; endemic divisions among political leaders led to endless factional strife. There were plenty of economic nationalists and reformers among the bourgeoisie, but they were not strong enough to withstand the alliance forged between a landed class bent on regaining power and the U.S. Department of State intent on restoring the status quo ante. And although the goals of the Mexican and Guatemalan revolutions were similar, in Mexico, decades of popular violence forced elites to hold to their promises of reform.[18] In Guatemala, on the other hand, without this mobilized violence, some elites resorted to reaction and repression when the governing consensus driving reform broke down. Yet as popular participation, agitation, and demands (although not popular violence) did increase in the years following 1944, reactionary elites effectively used the rhetoric of anticommunism to tap into middle-class anxiety about peasant and Indian rebellion; the state, for its part, was unable to transform increased rural participation into defense of the revolution's gains.

The U.S. Department of State and the Central Intelligence Agency took advantage of this instability and anxiety to promote, plan, and execute the overthrow of Arbenz in 1954. There is debate today as to whether it was anticommunism or the economic interests of the United States Fruit Company that compelled the Eisenhower administration to act against Arbenz.[19] The question is moot: the culture of anticommunism cannot be separated from the political economy of the Cold War. A more interesting but no more resolvable question is now being asked: Would the revolution have endured if the United States had not interfered or would internal contradictions have forced its demise?[20] Although the answer cannot be known, the question shifts the focus to include the role Guatemalans played in the making of their own history. It is important to make this shift not just out of political sympathy but also to understand how larger structures of power articulate with local interests and tensions: if capitalism and imperialism think globally, they need to act locally if they are to succeed.

The Revolution in the City

In the months leading up to the overthrow of the old regime, events in Quetzaltenango kept pace with those taking place in the capital. The city had awakened from decades of liberal dictatorship to a flurry of political activity.[21] Leaders from the Frente Popular Libertador (FPL) and Renovación Nacional (RN), two early revolutionary parties, held regular meet-

25. "A New Guatemala": Juan José Arévalo on the stump, 1944.
Courtesy of CIRMA.

ings in public halls surrounding the central park to campaign for their candidates for the constitutional assembly and for Juan José Arévalo for president. Middle-class reformers and student activists advocated for the rights of workers and peasants; women's organizations pledged their support for Arévalo and demanded the vote; and societies and guilds joined the call for Ponce's resignation.

Tensions mounted, and the national police watched nervously as political opposition grew militant. Activists from the FPL and the RN disrupted meetings of "Ubiquistas" and "Nazistas," jumping up in the middle of speeches to shout *"Vivas"* to Arévalo. On 15 October, during congressional balloting, a truck driver named Ramón Letona was arrested for slapping David Coyoy, a member of a conservative political party, after Coyoy refused to cheer Arévalo. According to police reports, a crowd of 1,300 Arevalistas assembled in the park to demand the release of Letona. The police fired—they claimed into the air, witnesses said into the crowd. One person was killed and six wounded in the ensuing stampede. The municipality condemned the actions of the police; five days later, after military cadets in Guatemala City overthrew Ponce, it declared its allegiance to the new revolutionary junta.

Both in Quetzaltenango and Guatemala City, a middle class—which was often defined as everyone *but* planters, the agro-proletariat, Mayan peasants, and the urban indigent—demanded economic and political reform.[22] Many of the organizers and leaders of new worker and peasant organizations came from the urban middle class. This advocacy may have been an opportunistic ploy to attack the power of the planter class; more often it seemed to have arisen from the enthusiasm of the moment and the promise of national renovation.

Although it is true that Arévalo's labor and social reforms emerged from Guatemala's long tradition of elite paternalism, workers themselves seized the moment to press their interests. In Quetzaltenango, even before the overthrow of Ponce, new unions formed and labor activity was stepped up.[23] In August 1944, wage-earning masons formed the Sindicato de Albañiles. In that same month, all twenty workers walked out of the Capuano é Hijos textile factory in solidarity with a dismissed fellow worker.[24] Before the 1947 labor code made it easier for unions to organize, in 1945 in Quetzaltenango the Federación de Trabajadores del Occidente (FTO) grouped together unions of masons, drivers, carpenters, tailors, metalworkers, cigarette makers, barbers, tanners, carpenters, cantina workers, shoemakers, breadmakers, millers, and distillery workers.[25] In 1945, both the breadmakers and tanners unions demanded raises and better working conditions; in 1947, the shoemakers struck against their workshop owners for higher pay.[26]

The ethnic makeup of the revolution in Quetzaltenango was also complex. Facing increased urban opposition to his rule, Ponce, Ubico's short-lived successor, attempted to cultivate support among rural Indians by encouraging land invasions.[27] Unrest grew in the countryside. Liberal Party activists (supporters of Ubico and Ponce) heightened ethnic fear by organizing demonstrations of machete-wielding indigenous peasants through the streets of Guatemala City. On 21 October, this tactic exploded when a small crowd of Indians in Patzicía, Chimaltenango, killed fourteen Ladinos.[28] In response, squads of Ladinos from surrounding towns arrived in Patzicía and slaughtered hundreds of Indians. Following these killings, newspapers in Quetzaltenango and throughout the country stirred up caste fear by reporting rumors of phantasmal Indian uprisings in various towns—uprisings which never materialized.[29]

In Quetzaltenango, Ubiquistas and Poncistas did try to garner support among Indians. At the end of October, a former municipal officer from

Ostuncalco was accused of "provoking Indios to rise up against Ladinos" and with spreading the rumor that if Arévalo were to win the upcoming election, their children would be sent to state-run barracks.[30]

The class composition of the Quetzalteco K'iche' community, however, was too complex, at least in the city proper, to be easily susceptible to such manipulation. In response to a rumor that the Liberal Party was preparing a demonstration of *machetes y garrotes* (machetes and clubs) of the *indiada* (crowds of Indians) from nearby fincas, K'iche' merchants posted notices in their shop windows urging stores to remain closed during the anticipated march.[31] Likewise, K'iche's who filled the ranks of the budding labor movement supported the revolution. The tanners union, for example, was comprised equally of K'iche's and Ladinos; a K'iche' was the president of the bakers and masons union; and five of the ten members of the executive council of the FTO had K'iche' surnames.

K'iche' elites and intellectuals took various positions. Julio Pérez Cutzal initially supported the revolution, although under the old regime he had served as an *agente confidencial*—one of the many spies who made up Ubico's extensive surveillance network.[32] Although he served in 1953 as a municipal regidor with the Partido Revolucionario de Guatemala (PRG, a revolutionary party), he would play an important role in opposing the land reform. Ismael Coyoy, a member of El Adelanto and former municipal officer, helped found El Frente Obrero (The Workers Front), which was to fight for better working conditions and "the suspension of the institution of the police."[33] On the other hand, David Coyoy, a wealthy contractor and also a member of El Adelanto, sat on the executive committee of a local conservative party that did not support Arévalo's presidential candidacy. Dr. Adrián Chávez, a prominent Mayan intellectual who would later translate the Popul Vuh and standardize a K'iche' alphabet, became the FTO's first secretary of culture.[34] And Licenciado Agusto Sac Racancoj, also a Mayan intellectual, was elected deputy to the national congress as a member of the Partido de Acción Revolucionaria (PAR, another important revolutionary party), although he would go on to criticize the radicalization of the revolution.[35]

The standard interpretation that as the revolution became radicalized it lost middle-class support seems to hold true in the case of Quetzaltenango. The city was home to many planters who viewed the agrarian reform, and the organizing it sparked, as a direct threat to their power and privilege.[36] Furthermore, labor organizing led to increased demands and strikes against small businessmen and undoubtedly led to cooling of whatever support they had given to the revolution in its early years. For example, many members of the Partido de Integración Nacional (PIN), a local party formed in 1949 by Quetzalteco business elites to back Arbenz, turned against the government following the implementation of the agrarian reform.[37] In the first five years alone the unions of millers, masons, breadmakers, tanners, municipal workers, and shoemakers were all involved in labor disputes.[38] Elected municipal officials also often felt threatened, as we shall see below, by the demands placed on them by campesino and municipal unions.

As a result, local chapters of national revolutionary parties were divided in their enthusiasm for reform, with moderates and conservatives eventually taking control.[39] The two main parties, the PAR and the PRG, even included members from the Partido Independiente de Anticomunismo del Occidente (PIACO) on their slates of candidates for municipal office.[40] In addition, three of the city's many newspapers—*El Diario de Quetzaltenango*, *El Correo del Occidente*, and *La Proa*—grew increasingly critical of Arbenz and provided a forum for gathering opposition forces.[41] Anticommunist rhetoric increased, and as early as 1947 unions had to respond to red-baiting.[42]

By 1950, a majority of the voting population within the city of Quetzaltenango had grown disaffected with the revolution. A comparison of the election results of 1944 and 1950 is telling.[43] In 1944 in the municipality of Quetzaltenango, Arévalo beat his opponent, Adrián Recinos, by a staggering vote of 2,581 to 20. Six years later, the results were quite different. Arbenz, the chosen candidate of the revolutionary parties, ran against Miguel Ydígoras Fuentes, a general linked to various coup attempts against Arévalo.[44] As he did throughout the country, Arbenz handily won in the department by a tally of 22,321 to 5,680. Workers in the coffee-producing region overwhelmingly gave him their vote: in the piedmont municipalities of Colomba, Génova, Flores, and Palmar, Arbenz won by a combined count of 7,515 to 832. Yet in the city itself, Arbenz's hometown, the results were much closer—3,391 to 2,139. The numbers were even more sobering when broken down further: in the city proper, according to the tallies of its four voting stations, Arbenz just beat Ydígoras by a count of 1,948 to 1,402. With the addition of ballots cast for other candidates, Arbenz actually received a minority of the total votes: 1,948 to 1,953.

Nearly as many people voted for Arbenz (1,443) in the much less populated rural aldeas and cantones as in the city itself.[45]

By the time of the 1950 election, the revolution in the city and department of Quetzaltenango had crystallized along class lines. Land-hungry peasants and agricultural workers overwhelmingly supported Arbenz, while a majority of voters from the city center spurned their hometown son. The meaning of the referendum was clear to all: Arbenz included a call for land reform in every one of his campaign speeches; planters accused PAR activists of telling campesinos that the next government was going to turn plantations over to them; and Arturo Muller, the German foreman of the finca La Candelaria, told workers that as soon as Ydígoras became president, he would "enjoy treating them like animals again."[46]

Strange Fruit

The valley of Palajunoj stretches sixteen square kilometers southwest from the city center (see fig. 26 and map 2).[47] Ringed by the foothills of the volcanoes Santa María and Cerro Quemado on its south and east, and by the volcanic ridge Siete Orejas on its west, the flat valley basin, with its fertile volcanic soil, good drainage and irrigation from mountain springs, and run-off from the volcanic slopes, consisted of most of the land that had been the town's agricultural common lands, which by mid-century had been converted into individual holdings (see chap. 5). The mountainous land that ringed the valley belonged to the city. In exchange for rent or a fee, peasants could gather wood, pasture animals, and plant corn; however, the municipality strictly regulated and limited these activities in an effort to protect forest cover.

The valley is made up of eight small hamlets, including Llanos de Pinal, Xecaracoj, San José la Viña, and Tierra Colorada. In the 1950s, the population of these aldeas ranged from a few hundred to a little over a thousand. Residents, overwhelmingly K'iche', primarily made their living raising sheep and cultivating small plots of corn and wheat, along with some cabbage, carrots, potatoes, and beans. By the turn of the century the majority of these plots were smaller than forty cuerdas. With municipal approval, men cut trees from city land; women then sold the wood in Quetzaltenango's market. Both a shortage of land and chronic underemployment led to migration. If no work was available in Quetzal-

26. Valley of the Palajunoj from Volcano Santa María. Quetzaltenango is in the background, to the right. *Photograph by author.*

tenango's manufacturing sector, civil bureaucracy, or service industry, men would look for seasonal employment in coffee cultivation, which began just on the far side of Volcán Santa María. In the hamlets of Llanos de Pinal and Pacajá, for example, unemployment and underemployment in the nonagricultural artisan and service sectors ran as high as 60 percent.

The K'iche' women and men who lived in this valley and supplied the city's markets were undoubtedly those the founders of Sociedad El Adelanto had in mind when they advocated for the regeneration of the indigenous race. As one Ladino social worker in 1964 described the people of Palajunoj: they "conserve their anachronistic cultural habits, represented by their houses, food, dress, household and agricultural tools, customs, ideas."[48] Most men by mid-century spoke some Spanish, but the majority of women were monolingual K'iche' speakers; illiteracy reached 75 percent; families lived in one-room adobe dirt-floor thatched houses, which simultaneously served as bedrooms, kitchens, storerooms, and animal pens. Infant mortality was high. Few houses enjoyed piped-in water or electricity, and only two or three street lamps lit the main streets of the aldeas.

Born in 1917 in Llanos de Pinal, Valentín Coyoy Cruz was the son of a peasant shepherd who, according to Coyoy's eldest son, owned a "nice-sized flock."[49] Coyoy apparently did not inherit the flock; instead he made his living sowing the twelve cuerdas of land he owned and another twelve he rented from the municipality. He supplemented his corn production by cutting trees on municipal land, which his wife, Felipa Estacuy, sold in Quetzaltenango's market.[50] Coyoy did not attend school as a child, spoke K'iche' among his family and community, and remained illiterate throughout his life. He was, however, naturally politically astute and, in the early 1940s, he received a degree of training and exposure to the world outside his aldea as a reserve volunteer in Ubico's army, rising to the rank of second sergeant. Even before the October revolution, Coyoy had become active in his community; he organized for the construction of a church, held a number of religious positions, and eventually achieved the esteemed rank of *cofrade principal*.

Following the revolution, Coyoy's natural leadership qualities and ability to speak Spanish, which had perhaps improved during his tenure as sergeant, attracted the attention of PAR activists. His son recalls "he was the sharpest man in the community. He could not read, but he was quick. He had a spark. He knew how to work with Ladinos to get things done." Around 1945, Coyoy worked with these Ladinos to bring the first communal water fountain to Llanos de Pinal; at some point during Arévalo's tenure he helped organize a *comunidad campesina* in the hamlet of Llanos de Pinal.[51] In 1951, Coyoy became a municipal regidor on the PAR ticket; and in 1953, he used his political connections to secure a job with Quetzaltenango's customs agency.[52]

Coyoy's organizing quickly moved to land, the issue that most concerned his fellow campesinos. By the 1940s pressure to exploit the city's forests had reached a boiling point.[53] Rapid deforestation led municipalities and both revolutionary governments to pass laws restricting the use of woodland; moreover, the stepped-up efforts by municipal forest sentries to limit pasture, cultivation, and the felling of trees increasingly resulted in violence. In August 1948, for example, twenty-eight Indians from Llanos de Pinal complained of forest sentries who threatened one vecino with a gun, arrested another, and searched houses to confiscate hatchets and machetes.[54] The sentries in turn sent a letter of resignation to the municipality in which they claimed they had to take refuge in a house after being attacked by thirty Indians.[55] After the crowd surrounded the house, the sentries had to be rescued by the civil police. Still, the municipality refused to let them resign and promised to deploy the military to protect them as they carried out their duties.

It was Coyoy along with his brothers, Encarnación and José Germán, who led much of the organizing, particularly in the aldeas of Llanos de Pinal, Xecaracoj, and Tierra Colorada. In 1945, Coyoy petitioned the municipality for grazing land on behalf of a number of his fellow vecinos;[56] in 1948, he was blamed for helping to organize a demonstration against the municipality in which peasants demanded that more city land be made available for renting.[57] In the conflict described above, the guardabosques complained that the peasants who attacked them "have their general headquarters in Llanos del Pinal; they are led by Valentín Coyoy Cruz, who is now winning adepts in other cantones."[58] As the municipality became increasingly besieged by complaints and demands, Coyoy was singled out as a particularly nettlesome organizer. In 1951, while he was a municipal regidor, his fellow officers voted to censure him because "instead of working with the municipality, capturing those who are destroying the forests, Coyoy acts in their defense."[59] Coyoy, in turn, expanded his political activity beyond agricultural matters, in 1951 accusing the city officer in charge of selling municipal corn of shortchanging market women by selling them nine pounds for the price of ten.[60]

Peasant organizers throughout the municipality of Quetzaltenango immediately took advantage of the June 1952 agrarian reform. Working closely with activists from the Confederación Nacional Campesina de Guatemala, they were undoubtedly well prepped in the mechanisms through which land could be claimed.[61] Throughout 1952, campesino unions and comunidades formed in the aldeas and cantones of Xecaracoj, Tierra Colorada, San José la Viña, Xepaché, Las Tapias, and in the nearby K'iche' municipality of Olintepeque. By the corn planting season of 1953, ten land claims were made. Valentín Coyoy Cruz helped organize at least seven of these claims. Of the ten, seven pertained to private fincas in the coffee piedmont just south of the valley of Palajunoj, where members of the comunidad campesina often found seasonal employment during harvest time. Six of these seven claims were granted by the Departamento Agrario Nacional (DAN), totaling over forty-three caballerías.[62]

The remaining three claims were made on Quetzaltenango's municipal land. On 24 July 1952, just a month after the reform's congressional approval, the Comunidades Campesinas Xecaracoj, Xepaché, and Tierra Colorada petitioned Quetzaltenango's Comité Agrario Local (CAL) for four caballerías of municipal land.[63] Following inspections and recommendations made by the CAL, the DAN approved the claim, and 132 male heads of households were scheduled to divide the grant among them. The second claim was made on 22 January 1953.[64] The Unión Campesina de Llanos del Pinal, with Coyoy as general secretary, denounced a little over two caballerías of land it claimed its members had cultivated without title "from time immemorial."[65]

In response to municipal threats, appeals, and intransigence, the CAL criticized the attitude of city officials and recommended that an even greater quantity of land be expropriated than had originally been petitioned for. The realignment of power relations in the countryside described by Porras above is underscored by the composition of the municipality of Quetzaltenango's CAL. The five-member committee was made up of Valentín Coyoy Cruz and his two brothers, another member of the Unión Campesina de Llanos de Pinal appointed by the departmental governor, and a municipal representative who never attended sessions.[66] In effect, the land claims were initially judged and ruled on by a committee comprised of the leaders of the union making the claim! The DAN ordered the expropriation of twenty caballerías of municipal land, a portion of which would pass to the state as national forest, with the rest to be distributed among the members of the union. The third claim on municipal land was made on 14 May 1953 by the Unión Campesina de San José la Viña; no decision on this case had been reached by the time of Arbenz's overthrow.[67]

By the time a U.S.-supplied plane dropped fliers on the city on 7 June announcing that "the hour of the liberation was at hand," political division within the city had ground the revolution to a standstill.[68] Although the DAN had made its first ruling as early as November 1953, little land was handed over to the campesinos. "Vigilance" and "Anticommunist" committees harassed the beneficiaries and prevented planting; and following Arbenz's overthrow, all the municipal concessions were revoked.

Opposition to land reform and agrarian organizing occurred early on in the revolution and emerged from various sectors of the city's population. As early as 1948, a representative of coffee planters demanded that the municipality do something "in defense of the owners because these outbreaks (labor demands) that are taking place throughout the country are dangerous; unionized campesinos have been and will be tricked; as such, *agricultores* need to respond effectively to these demands."[69] Anticommu-

nist organizing in the city picked up following congressional approval of
the land reform. In December 1952, the Partido Independiente Anticomunista del Occidente won the mayoral elections;[70] and in January the
newly formed Unión Cívica Anticomunista issued a complaint about
what it charged was the bungling on the part of city officials of the claims
on municipal land.[71]

The municipality, already besieged with land and labor demands, strikes
of city workers, and protests from market women, became further divided
as a result of the expropriation of municipal land.[72] Accusations as to who
was responsible for losing the land led to infighting and resignations.[73]
The result was that the base of the revolutionary parties had become
increasingly radicalized, while their party leaders, in control of municipal government and fighting the expropriation, had become increasingly
alienated from the national government and fearful of the course of the
revolution. The censure motion against Coyoy, for example, was made by
a member of the PRG.[74] No matter which of the three major parties had the
majority on the city council, members of all three worked to block the land
concessions by petitioning the president, attending surveying parties, and
filing legal briefs. Despite protests from city officials that they were "not
against the reform, but against its incorrect application," the local CAL declared the municipality "anti-*agrarista*" and an "enemy of the regime."[75]
And although the PAR won back city hall from the anticommunists in 1954,
they continued the efforts of the previous administration to block the
concessions.[76]

However, opposition to the expropriation came from another important
sector: indigenous elites connected to municipal administration. As previously discussed, following the privatization of agricultural ejidos, defense of the city's forest land came to form an important part of the
political authority of the K'iche' elites. Throughout the first half of the
twentieth century, K'iche's remained in charge of the municipal forest
commission. These K'iche' municipal authorities took an active role in
fighting the concession of municipal lands.

Julio Pérez Cutzal, the former Ubico spy, was elected regidor to the
1953 municipal council on the PRG ticket. As the municipal forest commissioner, Pérez was particularly zealous in ensuring that the land concession
not go through. In retaliation for Valentín Coyoy's organizing of the
January 1953 claim, Pérez suggested to his fellow councilmen that they
have Coyoy arrested on the pretext of illegally cutting trees.[77] Pérez

headed a delegation sent to appeal personally to Arbenz, and he, along with a number of other K'iche' municipal officers and concerned vecinos, represented the municipality in the numerous land surveys conducted to determine the validity of the claims.[78]

Coyoy and compañeros presented their claim in January 1953. Within a month, campesinos accused Pérez of mobilizing guardabosques and auxiliary alcaldes in a campaign of intimidation, reportedly threatening beneficiaries that if they got their land, they would be "macheted, tied up, and carried away."[79] In May, the Federación Campesina de Quetzaltenango—the umbrella organization of the municipality's peasant unions and comunidades—demanded Pérez's resignation.[80] In December 1953, as his term as regidor and municipal forest commissioner was ending, Pérez submitted for the municipality's approval the formation of the "Comité de Vecinos para la Vigilancia de los Bosques y Terrenos Comunales," headed by himself and composed of twenty-four K'iche' men.[81] While it was organized by the K'iche' political elite, according to relatives (most of the members of the committee are no longer living) the committee comprised of men from the middle to lower middle sectors of urban Quetzalteco K'iche' society.[82] One woman recalls her grandfather, who was a member of the committee, as being of modest means who "dressed as a campesino." He owned two plots of land on the outskirts of town where he grew subsistence and commercial crops, while his wife worked as a servant. Another relative reports that her uncle, who also served on the committee, was a tailor.

The committee operated until the fall of Arbenz and allowed Pérez to continue fighting the peasant unions after his term of office expired. In the two claims on municipal land that the DAN ruled on, the committee successfully prevented peasants from planting the land granted them.[83]

Despite the middle- to lower-class composition of the committee, surviving members of the peasant unions today remember the committee as being composed primarily of wealthy K'iche's from Quetzaltenango:

The municipality did not want to give us the land, so the *comité anticomunista* would come around and scare people, calling us communists and saying that if we plant, they would kill us. That is how the people became frightened. Jacobo gave us land, but they took it away from us. The committee was made up of people from *la raza* Quetzalteca, *naturales* (popular term for indígenas) from the city who did not want us to have land. They worked with the auxiliaries to take away the land we received. Antonio Juárez, Catarino Coyoy, and Gregorio—I cannot remember his last name—they were bad.[84]

Coyoy's son recalls that "some [Indians from the city] were in favor of the grant, others not. The rich Indians who owned workshops and stores from the city came out against it; the majority were poor and they were in favor."[85] There are perhaps two explanations as to why rural K'iche's identified the committee—which they repeatedly referred to as "anti-communist"—as being composed of wealthy Indians, when in fact it seems as if the majority of its members were from the middle to lower strata of Quetzalteco society. First, it may be that when rural campesinos identify "rich K'iche's" as opposing the land reform, they could in fact be referring to the K'iche' municipal officers who organized the committee, as well as to other K'iche' elites who opposed the revolution, rather than those who actually composed the committee. Second, it may also highlight the cultural content of class identity. Despite the general class correspondence which may have existed between members of the union and members of the "anticommunist" committee, rural K'iche's identified themselves as distinct from city K'iche's. Enrique Sajquim Chávez, a former member of Coyoy's union, recently explained the difference between Indians of the valley and Indians of the city in cultural terms: "Quetzaltecos are embarrassed to speak K'iche'; they go around wearing shoes."[86]

Violence escalated. Coyoy was accused of organizing groups of armed peasants to confront auxiliary alcaldes.[87] On 3 March, members of a campesino union beat and held prisoner an alcalde *auxiliar*;[88] and on 7 April, two auxiliaries were killed while, according to the municipal minutes, "fulfilling their duty."[89] A few months before the fall of Arbenz, Valentín Coyoy and his wife, Felipa Estacuy, were attacked by two K'iche's with a gun and a machete.[90] Estacuy managed to knock the gun from one of the assailants before being cut by the other's machete. They both escaped into the woods.

By June 1954, peasant activists were in retreat, and the leaders of the revolutionary parties—confused, divided, and, some, openly hostile to Arbenz—offered little support or protection. The city's anticommunist forces quickly took advantage of the confusion generated by Arbenz's resignation, on the night of 27 June, to assume power. The municipality

27. Arbencista peasants captured after overthrow of Arbenz, 1954.
Courtesy of CIRMA.

suspended sessions and within a week resigned.[91] The functioning of the
government was handed over to the Comité de Defensa Nacional contra
Comunismo, which appointed Carlos Enrique Guillén as mayor, a former
member of the PIN and now openly anticommunist.[92] Unions dissolved,
individuals hurried to register as anticommunists, and hundreds of PAR
and PRG members filled the city's penitentiary beyond capacity.[93] The
houses of peasants accused of hoarding arms supposedly distributed by
PAR activists were searched and the peasants were imprisoned without
warrant or trial (see fig. 27).[94] Empowered by the new regime, alcaldes
auxiliares harassed beneficiaries of the land reform until the state could
officially revoke the concessions.[95] Whether Coyoy left his house on the
evening of 4 July intending to hang himself or was ambushed by his
enemies is not known, but the revolution he helped bring about had
already perished.

The question remains: Why did some K'iche's so vigorously oppose
the land concessions? Indigenous elites may have had an economic inter-

est in preventing the conversion of forest land into agricultural plots, yet given the commercial and artisanal base of the K'iche' bourgeoisie (Pérez Cutzal, for example, was a weaver who lived in the center of the city), it is doubtful that this was the primary motivation. Nor is it likely that wealthy K'iche's consciously attempted to limit the subsistence capabilities of poorer Indians in the hope of maintaining a dependent and available labor force. It is important to keep in mind that agrarian organizing was taking place within a larger context of political mobilization; if land claims did not directly threaten the economic interest of the K'iche' urban elites, labor demands made by city unions undoubtedly did. For shopkeepers, contractors, and workshop owners, peasant demands undoubtedly went hand in hand with the demands of their own employees. David Coyoy, for instance, was criticized by the PAR for firing a number of mostly indigenous workers from his aqueduct project; and in 1946, five of the eleven owners of tanneries who refused to attend a negotiating meeting with their employees' union were K'iche'.[96] Nonetheless, K'iche' anticommunism cannot be reduced to simple class interests.

In his study on nationalism, Eric Hobsbawm suggests that an anxious European middle class, uncertain of its status and caught somewhere between the "sons and daughters of manual toil and the unquestioned members of the upper and upper middle class," was particularly susceptible to the allure of a conservative state-promoted nationalism and anticommunism.[97] This analysis can be extended to the K'iche' elite, but with an ethnic twist. As this work has argued, much of the ideological formation of the K'iche' elite emerged from its desire to carve out a space situated somewhere between urban Ladinos and rural, increasingly impoverished and proletarianized, Indians. By the mid-twentieth century, the political power and cultural identity of urban K'iche' elites rested on two interrelated pillars: the authority to control and administer the city's forest land and the claim that they represented the interests and hopes of all Indians. The revolution undermined this foundation. Not only were Indian campesinos claiming land administered by the K'iche' elites, but they were doing so on their own behalf. To underscore this shift in the alignment of political forces, when Pérez attempted to speak directly to the president, he was denied an audience.

The ensuing conflict and violence destroyed the lingering conceit that city K'iche's spoke on behalf of "*la raza indígena en general.*" As Catarino Nimatuj, the former secretary of finance of the Comunidad Campesina de

Xecaracoj, put it, "it was la raza Quetzalteca who did not want us to have land."

This ethnic and political anxiety provided fertile ground for the rhetoric of anticommunism. As one former member of the vigilance committee still insists: "They were all communists. Coyoy was a communist. He was tricking the people, getting them all worked up. It was like in the time of Ponce . . . there were too many protests in front of the municipality demanding land. I joined the committee because don Julio asked me to join. We were protecting the city's land. The land belongs to the municipality. It is the patrimony of the city. They were going to plant corn on it."[98]

The equation of the organizing under Arbenz with the "time of Ponce" is instructive. It alludes to a particular moment of racial anxiety, usually associated with Ladinos, when supporters of Ponce attempted to incite rural indigenous anger in an attempt to hold on to power. It indexes a moment when rumors of caste war circulated, when the nation's newspapers reported that masses of Indians bearing machetes and clubs had descended upon the cities to terrorize urban dwellers. But spoken by an urban Indian artisan, the class connotations of this caste panic become more pronounced. For in order to maintain their fragile identity as urban indigenous spokespeople, K'iche' elites had to keep rural Indians out of view, manifest only in political discourse as objects of charity or regeneration. As in the "time of Ponce," the organizing carried out by Coyoy and his compañeros once again threatened to bring rural Indians into the heart of the city, thus exposing the contradiction of Quetzalteco K'iche' nationalism.

Much of the academic writing on the revolution has been concerned with the way the agrarian reform affected indigenous communities.[99] These studies either view the reform as creating bitter political conflicts within the community, thereby weakening or destroying local institutions of communal politics and identification, or else they understand the reform as deepening incipient class divisions. In all of these studies, "conflict" is understood to be antithetical to "community."[100] Yet, as this work has tried to argue, over the course of two centuries, communal institutions and identity emerged from struggle as competing interests vied to project their vision of the community as the dominant vision. An examination of the alliances generated from these interests is indispensable to an understanding of both state formation and popular resistance. For a brief period, the agrarian reform allowed other voices within the community to be heard. This was perhaps what was most threatening to the K'iche' elites.

The agrarian reform, like all other social phenomena, played out in communities along the axes of preexisting divisions, alliances, and interests. Coyoy built upon his position as an elder of his aldea to become one of the most important local leaders in Quetzaltenango: he organized peasant unions not just in the aldeas immediately surrounding his home but also in neighboring municipalities and fincas. Much of Coyoy's local power drew on the same expectations of patriarchal deference and obligations that underwrote the authority of the urban K'iche' elite. When in 1951, for example, Coyoy defended the interests of market women, he was undoubtedly expanding on his local patriarchal obligations. Conversely, Coyoy could use the flip side of these gender ideologies to mobilize his male neighbors, as he did when he taunted Enrique Sajquim Chávez with "not being a man" because Sajquim was not attending union meetings.[101]

Likewise, much of the violence that took place during the reform in Quetzaltenango was activated along lines of local political power, deeply rooted in "communal" structures of authority. At least one K'iche' joined the Comité de Vecinos para la Vigilancia because, as he put it, "don Julio asked me to." More important, K'iche' municipal officers used their authority over alcaldes auxiliares and guardabosques to mobilize opposition to the reform. It was these auxiliaries and sentries, usually from the very aldeas that were receiving land, that harassed and attacked local campesino activists.[102] Rather than creating division, the reform, at least in Quetzaltenango, emerged from preexisting communal relations of conflict and authority.

Whether Valentín Coyoy's ideological formation and motivation drew from democracy, socialism, or perhaps even communism, the political work of this illiterate Mayan peasant born to a K'iche'-speaking swineherd in a remote hamlet of Guatemala's western highlands needs to be understood within its larger historical moment—a moment when citizens in countries throughout the world were organizing and being organized to demand a greater economic and political role in their respective nations.[103] Arbenz once remarked that the agrarian reform was the "most precious fruit of the revolution and the fundamental base of the nation as a new country."[104] To push the metaphor to its obvious conclusion, it was a fruit not allowed to ripen. Guatemala's brief ten-year experience with democracy emerged from the desire of some of its elites to create a more inclusive nation. Was this desire paternalistic? Certainly. Was it rooted in an urban Ladino national vision that did not reflect the ethnic realities of Guatemalan society? Unquestionably. Were some of its proponents biased and even racist? No doubt. But these undeniable facts of the revolution cannot erase the essential truth of the revolution: for a brief moment, a unique alliance of political forces put the power of the state at the service of workers and peasants in order to make a more equitable nation. Peasants, Indians, and workers immediately took advantage of this opening and began a wave of organizing that, for better or worse, altered the course of the revolution.

But the "new country" was not to be. Although throughout the twentieth century some nations continued to respond in varying degrees to the economic and political demands of their citizens, thus strengthening national allegiance, Guatemalan elites clamped down and gave up nothing. Many things ended in June 1954. Along with the repeal of the land reform and the revocation of many social and economic rights, the dream of a more inclusive nationalism advocated by Quetzalteco K'iche' elites was transformed into the nightmare of the Guatemalan terror state. In 1981, the most virulent aspects of Ladino nationalism metastasized into a counterinsurgency that, while it had many causes and purposes, singled out Indians in its rural campaign of repression and murder.[105] Throughout the 1960s and 1970s, Quetzalteco K'iche's, not being involved in the war to the degree other Mayan communities were, turned inward and attended to their trades. It would not be until the late 1970s when they would again begin to discuss, tentatively and quietly, the political relevance of their ethnicity. The twentieth century has indeed borne strange fruit.

Conclusions:
The Limits of Nation, 1954–1999

[The history of the late twentieth century] will inevitably be written as the history of a world which can no longer be contained within the limits of "nations" and "nation-states."—ERIC HOBSBAWM, *Nations and Nationalisms since 1780*, 1992

"Nationalism," remarks an African character in Raymond Williams' novel *Second Generation*, "is like class. To have it, and to feel it, is the only way to end it. If you fail to claim it, or give it up too soon, you will merely be cheated, by other classes and other nations." Nationalism, like class, would thus seem to involve an impossible irony. It is sometimes forgotten that social class, for Karl Marx at least, is itself a form of alienation, canceling out the particularity of an individual life into collective anonymity. Where Marx differs from the commonplace liberal view of such matters is in his belief that to undo this alienation you had to go, not around class, but somehow all the way through it and out the other side. To wish class or nation away, to seek to live sheer irreducible difference *now* in the manner of some contemporary post-structuralist theory, is to play straight into the hands of the oppressor.

—TERRY EAGLETON, *Nationalism: Irony and Commitment*, 1990

Eric Hobsbawm has argued that nationalism, as a historical force intimately linked to the organization of industrial capitalism and the formation of national elites, has run its course; that the cultural movements taking place in countries as diverse as Bosnia, Rwanda, Guatemala, the United States, and Canada will, in this era of globalization and state attrition, never develop a "positive progamme" nor mature into a "genuine" historical project: "It is not implausible to present the history of the Eurocentric nineteenth-century world as that of 'nation-building' . . . as in the title of Eugene Weber's *Peasants into Frenchmen*. Is anyone likely to write the world history of the late twentieth and early twenty-first centuries in such terms? It is most unlikely."[1]

But neither could this book, despite the earlier time period covered, have been titled *Indians into Guatemalans*. In retrospect, at no point in its history could Guatemalan society have developed the criteria Hobsbawm lays out for nationalism. And at no point in Guatemala's emergence as an independent state could its history be contained within, as Hobsbawm puts it, the limits of the nation. Colonialism, regional tensions, coffee export capitalism, and imperialism render such a bounded analysis untenable. After all is said about the particularly racist nature of Guatemala's planter class, it is this economic and political dependency that accounts for the failure of Ladino elites to construct a cohesive national identity and constitute the majority of the population as citizens. A cruel and highly exploitative model of capitalist development could not integrate even a significant minority of Guatemalans into its economic and political structure; the resultant repressive state and elite nationalism could not create among the Guatemalan populace an imagined "nation"—at least to the degree needed to ensure nonrepressive rule.[2] Nevertheless, as this work has argued, ideological struggles surrounding national identity, which involved all sectors of society, were essential components in the political history that made Guatemala what it is today. They continue to be so.

In a beautifully written short pamphlet dealing with the relationship between nationalism and colonialism in Northern Ireland from which the second epigraph above is drawn, Terry Eagleton attempts to reconcile the politics of social liberation with affirmations of national identity—a reconciliation that has proven elusive in much academic writing and political praxis.[3] Less concerned with nationalism's political and economic prerequisites than with its cultural and subjective form, Eagleton reminds us that nationalism, like class, is a form of alienation that cannot be denied:

Are the Irish oppressed as Irish? In one sense surely not: it was never of much interest to British imperialism whether the Irish were Irish or Eskimo, white or black, whether they worshipped tree gods or the trinity. It is not their ethnic peculiarity but their territory and labor power that have entranced the British. The Irish are simply denizens of a convenient neighboring island; as long as they are other than the British they do not . . . require certain specific innate characteristics to be ruled over. In another sense however, it is clearly abstract caviling to maintain that the Irish people has not been oppressed as Irish. However fundamentally indifferent colonialism may be to the nature of the peoples it does down, the fact remains that a particular people is in effect done down *as such*. And it is this fact that the truth of nationalism illuminates.[4]

As in the case of the Irish with regard to the British, the particular nature of the indigenous peoples may not have ultimately mattered much to the Spanish conquerors, bureaucrats, and planters who exploited them. But for the subject populations, after centuries of rule and exploitation, the *specifics* of that caste system mattered greatly.[5]

This is true even to this day. Just because Ladino Left leaders, whether in the 1950s or 1970s and 1980s, had trouble theoretically conceptualizing the subject position of their social base, it does not mean Indians did not participate in successive oppositional movements *as* Indians. Despite the rhetoric of a united universal subject, it was through local relations of communal and patriarchal power that the majority of Indians incorporated themselves into the guerrilla movement.[6] The state's counterinsurgency, likewise, was experienced in racial terms. It is doubtful, given the way the military slaughtered Ladinos in the eastern part of the country during the 1960s, that had the western highlands been populated with Ladino insurgents instead of Mayan rebels, the scorched earth campaign there would have been any less vicious or inhumane.[7] Nonetheless, Indians experienced the repression as Indians. The military's counterinsurgency campaign was intentionally designed to destroy local relations of power and authority—relations that for the majority of Maya in the nation's highlands continue to be the foundation of their identity.[8] The way Indians experienced and resisted this terror campaign, expectedly, emerged from the very same communal relations that the terror sought to eradicate.

Arturo Taracena has suggested that indigenous participation in the revolutionary movement of the 1970s and early 1980s marked a change from past indigenous strategies of dealing with the state.[9] As was the case in Quetzaltenango, throughout the colonial period indigenous communities viewed the state as an arbiter of social relations, capable of mediating pacts, alliances, and conflicts between various social blocs. Following independence, when liberals tried to radically alter this arrangement, Indians, especially Indian elites, allied themselves with Carrera to restore the "colonial compact."[10]

By the late 1970s, however, economic and political changes once again undercut the ability of the state to function as mediator.[11] Between 1950 and 1975, population growth finally closed off subsistence production as an alternative to wage labor for most of the highland population. Many Maya, perhaps a majority of them, sought seasonal employment on coastal plantations to supplement their shrinking milpas, but a significant number of Indians stepped up their nonsubsistence economic activities, such as labor recruitment, commerce, manufacturing, and specialized agricultural production. Studies conducted at this time describe increased social stratification and capital accumulation within communities.[12] Economic divisions within and among communities coincided with a cultural and political rupture. As Ricardo Falla describes it, in San Antonio Ilotenango many of the new merchants embraced Acción Católica because of an expanded worldview and a desire to escape the onerous financial obligations of the cofradía system.[13] The conflicts generated by the arrival of Acción Católica moved quickly from the cultural sphere—for example, debates surrounding religious icons and the right of catechists to participate in cofradía processions—to the economic and political spheres as Acción Católica activists organized cooperatives and ran for local political offices that had long been the domain of principales.

Following the collapse of the Central American Common Market in 1969 and a decline in global agricultural demand in 1973, export production decreased and Guatemala entered a period of economic stagnation. This crisis intensified communal stratification. Many farmers, now tied through debt and reliance on fertilizer to a cash economy, increasingly migrated to the coast as seasonal agricultural laborers. Communities found themselves divided between a newly economically empowered bourgeoisie and an impoverished campesino class.

As I have argued, political and economic divisions had long existed in Guatemalan indigenous communities. But in the context of post–World War II Guatemala—which was marked by a near-complete dissolution of a subsistence economy, a violent breakdown of a governing consensus among Ladino elites, foreign intervention, and escalating state repression—indigenous elites lost the ability to fulfill their historic role as brokers.[14] Many opted to ally themselves with national political parties, while others entered the popular movement, which had grown rapidly in strength throughout the 1970s. Whole extended families and, at times, whole communities, joined their leaders in opposition, thus reflecting the enduring power of patriarchal bonds. Facing increased mobilization and demands for reform, the state and the ruling class, through their police, military, and death squads, responded with untold violence and repression. As a result, large segments of the population, including many Maya who had already been involved in some sort of political work decided to join the armed movement. Taracena argues that rather than negotiate with the government, indigenous communities "confronted the state head on."[15] This participation, in turn, would have a profound effect on Guatemalan national identity.

Much of the ethnic content of the armed struggle found expression in the activity and rhetoric of the Comité de Unidad Campesina (CUC), a peasant federation closely allied with the Ejército Guerrillero de los Pobres (EGP, one of the four armed groups that came to comprise the revolutionary coalition, the Unidad Revolucionaria Nacional Guatemalteca, or URNG). Although a multiethnic organization, the CUC had strong roots in the indigenous communities of Chimaltenango and southern Quiché and greatly reflected the vision and goals of liberation theology.[16] Some analysts, pointing to the class language of the CUC, have drawn a division between its radical leadership and the more conservative indigenous elites who did not support the revolution.[17] A closer look, however, reveals notable similarities. Many of the founders of the organization were from families of principales. Most of them had sufficient land for themselves and their children, and many were engaged in economic activity that would place them squarely within an emerging indigenous bourgeoisie.[18]

A few days following the firebombing of the Spanish embassy in 1980 by the Guatemalan government—an event that left thirty-seven people dead (one of whom was Rigoberta Menchú's father, Vicente)—the CUC called a meeting at the symbolically charged Iximché ruins, the former capital of the Kaqchikel kingdom. Representatives from nearly every important indigenous group attended, including those not allied with the guerrillas. This unprecedented coalition produced a declaration that linked mythical symbols of a pan-Indian past with class-based interests of a brutal present:

To end with all the evils of the invaders' descendants and their government, we must struggle allied with workers, peasants, committed activists, students, settlers, and other democratic and popular sectors and strengthen the unity and solidarity between Indians and poor Ladinos. The solidarity of the popular movement with the indigenous struggle has been sealed with the blood of those who died in the Spanish embassy. Their sacrifice has brought us closer than ever to a new society, to a new indigenous awakening. For a society based upon equality and respect; that our Indian people, as Indians, be able to develop their culture, broken by the criminal invaders. For a just economy in which no one exploits others; that land be communal as it was in the time of our ancestors. For a people without discrimination, that all repression, torture, kidnapping, murder and massacres end; that forced recruitment by the army cease; that we all have the same right to work; that we not continue being utilized as objects of tourism; for the just distribution and utilization of riches as in the times during which our ancestors flourished.[19]

Filtering images of a just and noble society through their daily experiences of cultural and class oppression, CUC leaders were able to create a multiethnic, class strategy in the present and an ethical and egalitarian vision of the future. Thus, while the appeal of the manifesto is obviously twofold, that is, economic and cultural, its strength lies in the interplay between the two: class-based economic demands allowed for a strategically important alliance with Ladinos, while evocations of past traditions and rights justified those demands in the present.[20]

This inclusive vision, however, was not to take hold. The social movement from which this manifesto emerged would be brutally suppressed by the state. The military unleashed a wave of terror that severed alliances, destroyed organizations, and decimated not only the rebels, but nearly all forms of social organization. And although the EGP and another armed group, the Organización Revolucionaria del Pueblo en Armas (ORPA), took important tentative steps in developing a more inclusive revolutionary nationalism, the racial and theoretical premises of the insurgency's Ladino leadership prevented this identity from being fully developed.[21] Following the worst of the repression and decimation of the guerrillas' social base in 1982, first the EGP and then ORPA shut down discussion among their cadre on the "Indian question."

Nevertheless, despite the violence, the ethnic expansion that had begun with the popular movement continued to grow. In the mid-1980s, there emerged new indigenous organizations, many of them linked to the rebels but others independent.[22] By the late 1980s, a growing number of Mayan intellectuals, some of whom were supported and encouraged by foreign academics, formulated in increasingly self-confident terms what it meant to be Mayan. These new leaders found protection in an increasing world-wide interest in indigenous rights. It is as if the defeat of socialism forced sectors of Guatemalan society to find new ways to make their demands known to the state.

At first these demands were defensive; groups associated with the URNG, such as the Coordinadora Nacional de Viudas de Guatemala and the Consejo de Comunidades Etnicas Runujel Junam, and later the Comunidades de Población en Resistencia, deployed the rhetoric of indigenous rights to insist on an end to the repression and the institution of the rule of law. Gradually, other groups emerged that became more proactive. In 1992, for example, a group of indigenous leaders broke from CUC. They formed the Coordinadora Nacional Indígena y Campesina (CONIC), which inherited CUC's role in the fight over land issues but put much greater emphasis on the cultural content of their demands. Indigenous intellectuals and organizations pressed on a range of issues, from the teaching of indigenous languages in primary schools to the congressional adoption of the International Labour Organization's Convention 169, which guaranteed indigenous peoples a wide range of social and cultural rights.

Much of this cultural revival movement took place in the city of Quetzaltenango. Throughout the 1970s, at the same time that the popular and armed movements were forming alliances, study groups and seminars sponsored by the Catholic Church were held in the city in which indigenous activists and professionals came together to discuss the meaning of their ethnicity in a rapidly changing world. The Coordinadora de Grupos Indígenas held annual workshops, one of which took place in Quetzaltenango in 1976. The city was home to Adrián Inés Chávez, one of the first Mayan linguists and founder of the Academia de la Lengua Maya-Kí-ché. (He was also the secretary of culture in the 1940s for Quetzaltenango's Federación del Trabajadores del Occidente.) Around 1992, a younger generation of K'iche's took over the leadership of the Sociedad El Adelanto, and, following a long period of political dormancy, the society once again took a much more proactive role in promoting indigenous culture and education. In 1991, the city hosted the annual meeting of the continental campaign "500 Años de Resistencia Indígena, Negra y Popular," which forced the armed Left to readdress the ethnic question. But unlike the 1980 Declaration of Iximché, neither a class-based vision of Indian ethnicity nor the goal of popular socialism was agreed upon. The presence of Mayan intellectuals and activists mistrustful of the URNG led to divisions over alliances, strategy, and vision.[23] By the time that the Nobel laureate Rigoberta Menchú left the CUC and the EGP in 1993, the debate on the national question had long since escaped the control of the traditional Left.

In 1995, running as a candidate of a local political party, Comité Xel-Jú, Rigoberto Quemé Chay, a Quetzalteco Maya-K'iche', became mayor of Quetzaltenango. It was the first victory in the fourth campaign Xel-Jú had run since 1974, and for many analysts it signaled an important change in the nation's political relations.[24] By cobbling together a coalition comprised of disenfranchised rural Indians from the city's cantons, progressive Ladinos sympathetic to Xel-Jú's call for equal rights, and wealthy Ladinos and K'iche's from the commercial and manufacturing sector concerned with modernizing the city's infrastructure, Quemé was able to mount a campaign that focused on both ethnic pride and improvement in basic municipal services.[25] His victory riled the city's more reactionary elements and revealed (through a nasty graffiti campaign) a racism that in Quetzaltenango usually remains more subdued in comparison with the rest of the country. With his political skills, however, Quemé was able to avoid the divisiveness that marks much of the nation's racial discourse.

It is still too early to say exactly what this victory means, both locally and nationally. On the one hand, the election does seem to suggest a turning point in the nation's second largest city, in which K'iche' and Ladino political elites came together to search for economic and political solutions within the limits set by the neoliberal model of development. Although, as we have seen, Quetzalteco K'iche's have managed to maintain some political power within the municipality throughout the twentieth century (Quemé himself was twice a member of the municipal council), this is the first time that they were able to actually lead a winning coalition. If the political space promised by the peace accords (which ended the war in 1996) materializes, it could be imagined that, in a nation with a majority indigenous population and a sector of the Ladino bourgeoisie intent on economic and political reform, this campaign model might be launched nationally.[26] On the other hand, there exist formidable limitations on this model's possibility of success. Racism is still a powerful ideology in Guatemala, and it manifests itself in multiple ways: social exclusion, political repression, economic exploitation. Confronted with this racism, it is unclear if such a "progressive" alliance would be able to create the same victory nationally that it did locally. Perhaps more seriously restrictive are the contradictions within the alliance itself. Political enfranchisement of the nation's majority indigenous population will, in a country with such gripping poverty, inevitably lead to demands on their political representatives that go beyond political rights, ethnic pride, and infrastructural improvements—demands that the state and the ruling elites may, once more, not be willing or able to satisfy.

Both in Quetzaltenango and throughout the nation, the leadership of the pan-Maya movement emerged from diverse, overlapping sectors.[27] Despite the general association of indigenous culture with rural poverty, in Guatemala there are a number of urban centers where, as in Quetzaltenango, important groups of wealthy, educated, and urban Indians reside. A number of Mayan intellectuals and political leaders emerged from this class. Other activists received their political education in the 1970s from the church or from their participation in organizations linked to the popular or guerrilla movement. And others took advantage of new educational opportunities to become community leaders.

Many of these leaders today "reject what they consider a fatalist vision of the destiny of the indigenous population, relegating it to the eternal condition of poor campesinos."[28] This desire to create an ethnicity not linked to class closely mirrors the discourse used by Quetzalteco K'iche's. Estuardo Zapeta, a Mayan editorialist for a major daily who received his graduate education under the direction of Robert Carmack, worries that "[a]s long as we leave the Maya illiterate, we're condemning them to being peasants. And if that happens their need to acquire farmland will lead us to another civil war." Like the liberal indigenismo espoused by nineteenth-century K'iche's, this insistence on separating ethnic identity from class is reflected in a somewhat naive optimism in the new *maquila* economy; Zapeta goes on to state that "[t]his is a multicultural, multilingual society, and there's room for every one if there's mutual respect and equal opportunities."[29]

If the Left was limited by its own prejudices (as well as by the repression) in articulating a truly liberating popular national identity, the danger faced by many of the current proponents of Mayan nationalism has to do with their trading in the sort of universalisms that will render the creation of an indigenous identity meaningless to the majority of rural, poverty-stricken Maya. We have seen this process play out once, as Quetzalteco K'iche' elites forcefully articulated a discourse of ethnic identity severed from class realities. Quetzalteco K'iche's borrowed from abstract notions of Ladino nationalism and liberalism to promote their interests. The K'iche's developed an alternative nationalism that, as Eagleton puts it, served as a wedge within the "very logic of [the ruling] order's most cherished values in order to unmask the necessary disconnection of this ideal universal realm from the sordidly particularistic appetites it served to mystify. . . . In the manner of Enlightenment radicalism, you can press for the revolutionary extension of universal rights, embarrassing such ideals by reminding them forcibly of the groups and peoples they exclude. . . ."[30] But in doing so, K'iche's developed an equally abstract ideology, which ultimately, in 1954, came into bloody conflict with the community's material particularity.

The more inclusive nationalism advocated by the Quetzalteco K'iche' elites was itself predicated on exclusion—exclusion of peasant Indians and women. When in the 1950s a unique political opening threatened to undermine the brokerage role long held by urban indigenous elites, K'iche' elites responded with violence and opted to ally themselves with anticommunist Ladinos to ensure the continued subordination of the rural majority. K'iche' elites likewise sought to deny women access to political power. As previously noted, in 1815 Quetzalteca commoners made an appeal to imperial authorities to secure the release of their husbands from prison. Without patriarchal sanction and support, and without recourse to the municipal scribe, the petition fell on royal deaf ears, and the women were forced to resort, unsuccessfully, to the rhetoric of paternal charity. When women did make petitions with the approval of male community leaders, as in the 1894 appeal to lower market taxes, they were obliged to do so in ways that highlighted their dependence on men.

Of course, this class and gender exclusion is not only the consequence of male privilege but also its source. The ability of K'iche' patriarchs to combine subsistence production with commercial trade, which allowed them to successfully compete against Creole and Ladino rivals, was based on their ability to mobilize and control family and communal land, labor, and credit. Furthermore, they used their position as caste elites to build economic and political alliances with Creoles and Ladinos, which, in turn, fortified their communal authority. Yet as capitalist relations quickened, the material content of caste authority gave way to much more ideological manifestations of ethnic identity. Women were increasingly subject to patriarchal pressures as they became, at least symbolically, the procreators of the K'iche' collective.

If in the highly contested academic discourse on race there exists any consensus, it is that racial identity is constantly in flux.[31] In her exegesis of Foucault's writings on race, Ann Stoler states that racial ideology is constructed in an "'instrumental space, at once discursive and political' in which each group could infuse a shared vocabulary with different political meanings." Race is a "discourse of vacillations. It operates at different levels and moves not only between different political projects, but seizes upon *different* elements of earlier discourses reworked for new political ends."[32] This is certainly an apt description of what took place, and is still taking place, in Quetzaltenango and indeed throughout Guatemala. Ideologies of blood, culture, the body, sexuality, and social power combine to produce contradictory, ever changing notions of racial identity.[33] Over the course of time, however, a logic emerges between racial identity and political power.

Two very different and yet very similar understandings of race emerged in nineteenth-century Guatemala. Drawing on a neo-Lamarckian scientific discourse prevalent in Latin America, Ladino elites "reworked" colonial racism so as to emphasize the importance of environmental factors to generational "improvement." This accounts for the apparent contradiction, which has long perplexed scholars, of a nationalism that purportedly denies the importance of blood, yet is viciously racist. By promoting racial assimilation while at the same time permitting no middle ground for cultural mestizaje, Ladinos developed a nationalism that deployed culture and class to affirm racial identities. This racism both assuaged the racial anxiety of Ladino elites and allowed them to blame Indians for the failure of Guatemalan development.

K'iche' elites, on the other hand, "seized" on the blood strictures of Spanish colonial racism to formulate an ethnic identity that allowed for cultural assimilation. But of course these blood standards were no less ideological than the cultural and environmental markers of Ladino racism, as they became encoded in women's bodies and dress, as well as represented in the political control indigenous elites exercised over peasants and families. Quetzalteco K'iche' elites took advantage of Carrera's victory to reestablish their political power to decide who was an Indian, while new technologies, institutions, myths, and rituals allowed K'iche's to fix their identity both historically and visually.

Still, it is facile and wrong to set up a dichotomy between cultural Mayan nationalists on the one hand and progressives truly concerned with social change on the other. The recent peace accords, along with other national legislation and international treaties, has created mechanisms for the reestablishment of local forms of power and autonomy. Many indigenous cultural activists are taking advantage of the space offered by these accords to rebuild local political and economic relations destroyed by the war. In some cases, activists are experimenting with new forms of social and economic organizations, supposedly more firmly rooted in communal relations and norms than past developmental schemes.[34]

The rebuilding of local forms of political and economic power is crucial to any effort to reconstruct Guatemalan society, for the only way to understand how the war and violence played out in indigenous communities is to understand how local relations of power functioned prior to the war.[35] Confronted with the social changes discussed above, many indigenous leaders joined the popular movement. However, it was also through these local relations of power that the repression was experienced, as the army perniciously took advantage of divisions within a community.[36] Not all indigenous leaders opted to join the popular or armed movements, and many suffered a loss of power owing to the organizing of Acción Católica, cooperatives, and peasant unions. The military's installation of civil patrols in 1982—which obliged all adult men to serve as armed sentries and placed the onus of keeping a community free of guerrilla influence on the community itself—provided leaders hostile to the guerrillas an opportunity to reestablish a power base within the community.[37]

New legislation regarding indigenous rights have given activists some of the space needed to rebuild local relations. The accord on indigenous rights signed by the URNG and the military, for example, allows some legal infractions to be handled within communal courts, and it stipulates that national tribunals should "take into account the traditional customs which govern communities."[38] Of course, as the conflict leading to the death of Valentín Coyoy Cruz demonstrates, it is sometimes difficult to define which communal traditions and customs should be adhered to. As I have argued, local political and economic relations cannot be isolated from larger structures of social power in which they are embedded. The authority of Quetzalteco K'iche' principales was predicated on access to ideological and social resources that extended well beyond the boundaries of their community. The traditions and customs that create a normative, naturalized community are to a large degree designed to maintain women in their assigned role as procreators (both biologically and ideologically) of the community.[39] Any analysis of local power needs to pay close attention to all forms of political and economic contradictions, not just those between Ladinos and Maya, for these contradictions produce competing notions as to where the boundaries of community lay even among members of the same community.

There is a historical symmetry in the fact that Roberto Gutiérrez, a descendant of Domingo Gutiérrez Marroquín, supported Rigoberto Quemé's bid for the mayor's office. Gutiérrez heads the Quetzaltenango branch of one of Guatemala's wealthiest Ladino families, and it was his distant relative who was involved in the political machinations that led to the impeachment of Manuel Silverio from his position as K'iche' gobernador in 1786. Gutiérrez cited the need for modernization of municipal services in his decision to support Quemé.[40] Yet Gutiérrez's endorsement should not be viewed with surprise. We have seen that beneath the rhetorical veneer of indigenous cultural activism there is a history of multiethnic alliances and political participation. Gutiérrez Marroquín's eighteenth-century Creole and Spanish colleagues joined with K'iche' elites to forestall the demands of the city's popular classes. Nineteenth-century Ladino freemasons and liberals supplied K'iche' principales with the ideological references needed to engage with an emerging Guatemalan nationalism and capitalism. In the 1950s, urban middle-class reformers with their talk of democracy, socialism, and land rights worked with indigenous campesinos to fight for a more inclusive nation. In the 1970s, Mayan organizers seized on the promises of a liberating Catholicism and Marxism offered by Ladinos and foreigners to struggle for a multiethnic and socially just society.

Despite this long history of interethnic alliances, a more inclusive national identity did not emerge. This work has tried to explain why it did not, by examining not just how the pressures of a consolidating state, powerful oligarchy, and highly exploitative economic system led to a strengthening of racism but also by exploring dynamics internal to indigenous society that led to a deepening of ethnic identity. I have argued that for most of Guatemalan history indigenous and Hispanic society articulated through the mediations of their respective elites. In the second half of the twentieth century, however, a radically transformed national and international context undercut the ability of elites to play this role. Faced with an unprecedented challenge to their authority, the state, the military, and the oligarchy, supported by the United States, identified Indians as the collective enemy and launched a wave of repression that the United Nations–administered Truth Commission has characterized as genocide.[41]

This book began with a somewhat bucolic image of a cemetery as an introduction to the complexity of Quetzaltenango history and society. Today in Guatemala, graveyards provide another lesson. The bones, teeth, hair, and shreds of clothing dug up by forensic teams from just a few of the hundreds of clandestine graveyards grimly remind Guatemalans of the brutality of state power and national history. Cemeteries, like the past, tell many stories. These tell of unimaginable terror directed at a majority Indian population: of massacres, of destruction of communities, families, and lives; of flight into the mountains and jungles, of escape into Mexico; of displacement into the city. They tell of an avaricious ruling class unwilling to concede even the smallest of social reforms, and of a grotesque military swollen with economic and technical might, much of it supplied by patron countries such as the United States, Israel, Taiwan, South Africa, and Argentina. But they also tell of a massive popular struggle that for a brief period united Maya and Ladinos in the desire for social justice and in the hope of national redemption. In short, they tell the story of the twentieth century. It is this history that needs to be exhumed.

Epilogue:
The Living among the Dead

Books end; history does not. In August of 1997, Quetzaltecos witnessed an unusual event.[1] A funeral march left the cathedral. Hundreds of urban K'iche's in mourning huiples and dark suits, many from the city's most distinguished families, wound their way around the plaza and headed toward the cemetery. Although a common occurrence, this procession was different. It was led not only by the deceased's mother and brothers but also by demobilized guerrillas carrying blue and white URNG banners. When they arrived at the cemetery, the former insurgents began to chant: "¡Viva la URNG!" and "Gabriel will live forever in our memory!" Sergio Rolando Aguilar Velásquez had come home.

Born in 1959 to a notable Quetzalteco K'iche' family, Sergio Aguilar was a child of the 1954 counterrevolution. One grandfather was a commercial farmer, the other a wealthy merchant, and both participated in the anticommunist politics of the 1950s. Both of his grandmothers were prominent *comerciantes*. Like many other male K'iche's of his generation, Sergio was educated to be a professional. He wanted to be an architect but settled on agronomy since the local university had no such program.

The revolution got in the way. Coming of age in the 1970s, Sergio became involved in politics first at the city's National Boys Institute, then, as a university agronomy student. He left school in 1980, before he could graduate, and moved to Nicaragua to work as a volunteer in the Sandinistas' famous literacy drive. He returned to Guatemala in 1982 and joined Quetzaltenango's urban guerrilla network. As state repression began to pick off his friends, Sergio left for Mexico to receive combat training, returning to Guatemala sometime in the late 1980s and taking the nom de guerre Gabriel. He quickly moved up the ranks, becoming part of the leadership of the Frente Unitario—the front made up of elite members of ORPA, EGP, and the FAR. On 13 September 1992, the military caught the rebels off guard while they rested in the folds of Volcán Agua, killing Sergio and two others. Soldiers bagged and buried the dead in an anonymous grave in Escuintla's general cemetery.

Sergio's family did not learn of his death until December 1996, when the civil war was finally brought to an end. In January 1997, Sergio's mother and two brothers began an exhaustive seven-month search for his body. They spoke with combatants and rebel leaders, traveled from one camp of demobilized guerrillas to another, questioned doctors and firefighters (often responsible for burying casualties of the war), and checked cemetery records. The fate of most of Guatemala's missing has still not been revealed, but the persistence of Sergio's family paid off. In July of 1997, they located his grave. Before proceeding with the exhumation, a K'iche' *sacerdote* (priest), himself a Quetzalteco of Sergio's generation and a former member of ORPA, performed a Maya ritual asking permission to open the earth; Sergio's remains were identified and returned to Quetzaltenango for reburial.

This chronology of Sergio Aguilar's life closely tracks a dominant narrative of recent Guatemalan history: politicization, mobilization, repression, radicalization, death. But what motivated Sergio to pursue a course of life that cost him his life? Family members say he possessed an innate social consciousness—a generosity that was politicized by the heady mix of liberation theology, Marxism, and revolutionary hope that informed Guatemalan politics during the late 1970s. His experience as a literacy worker in Nicaragua, combined with the murder of his friends by the state, led him not only to support the revolution through his work in the city but to become a combatant. He chose this path even though it now seems that by the late 1980s there was no chance of a rebel victory.

What of his ethnicity? He came from a K'iche' family, yet one with a long, close relation to Ladino society. Family members today recall that at one point his maternal grandfather had stopped considering himself indigenous. Yet in the last decade, members of his family have become active in the pan-Maya movement. His brother and sister-in-law remember, however, that it was class exploitation, not cultural rights, that motivated Sergio: "Class was fundamental," they say. Yet, by the time of his death, they suggest that there were signs that his experience in the mountains, leading combatants who were mostly indigenous, had helped Sergio develop a sharpened sense of ethnic identity. In his last conversation with his family, he spoke of the plight of Mayan women, suggesting the close link between ethnicity and gender. Of course, it could be argued that this is a retrospective reading of his life, an attempt to reconcile past commitments and sacrifices with present concerns. But it is just this reconciliation that has proved so elusive in postwar Guatemala.

The coming together of Sergio's comrades and his family and community was not easy. Many Quetzalteco K'iche's stayed out of the war. Some attending the funeral, especially those of Sergio's mother's generation, were suspicious of individuals they identified more as delinquents than as freedom fighters. Others were nervous to be seen walking behind URNG banners. Eight months after the war's end, many were unwilling to believe that political repression might be a thing of the past. And one member of Sergio's family, while sympathetic to the revolution, expressed anger at the leadership of the rebel organizations for its apparent abandonment of rank and file combatants. The wariness that marked Sergio's funeral reflects problems on a national level, for the relationship between the pan-Maya movement and the traditional Left—both heirs to the revolution's legacy—is plagued by anger, mistrust, and mutual accusations.

Despite these difficulties, the procession took place. At the cemetery, in addition to family members, a number of people spoke in remembrance of Sergio. Carlos Coyoy, a conservative K'iche' businessman, praised Sergio's compassion. Two members of the URNG spoke of his valor, skill, and the camaraderie he shared with members of his unit. And Rigoberto Quemé, Quetzaltenango's recently elected K'iche' mayor and close childhood friend of Sergio, recalled what it meant to do political work in the 1970s. Family members say Quemé spoke eloquently and passionately of the exploitation that both provoked the war and compelled Sergio to join the guerrillas. According to Quemé, by the 1980s there remained three possibilities for Quetzaltecos concerned with social change: join the rebels, go into exile, or continue in Quetzaltenango. The last option for many, he said, was a death sentence.

Sergio's mother dedicated his tombstone to the memory of the "New Man," in honor of her son's revolutionary hopes. Yet, in a country with such a history of ethnic and class exploitation, is this hope really so far removed from his ancestors' yearning to regenerate the race and advance the nation? Perhaps there is a lesson to be learned in Sergio's funeral procession; that in claiming the dead, a common path can be found.

Sergio Aguilar's death was not redemptive. There have been too many martyrs in Guatemala. It was his life that had meaning.

Appendix 1: Names and Places

Any study that deals with issues of regional, racial, cultural, and national identity over the course of two centuries will have to confront the fundamental insufficiency of language to fix meaning. Although I hope that throughout the work, context will provide definitions, I also offer the following clarifications.

The city of Quetzaltenango sits on the south side of an extended highland plain just at the edge of where the Sierra Madre drops precipitously to the southern coffee piedmont and the coastal flatlands. In pre-Hispanic times, Xelaju, as the city was then called, was an important commercial and administrative center in the western confines of the Maya-K'iche' kingdom.[1] Immediately surrounding the city, and within its municipal jurisdiction, reside a number of small K'iche' *aldeas* (hamlets). To its northwest lie numerous Maya-Mam *pueblos* (*pueblo* usually refers to the population center of a municipal jurisdiction), which the K'iche's conquered prior to the arrival of the Spaniards. To the city's east communities are to be found that descend from the preconquest K'iche' kingdom. There is a striking difference today between K'iche' towns, some of which are relatively prosperous and economically diverse, and Mam communities, which tend to be more isolated and impoverished. The story of preconquest ethno-political relations throughout the development of Spanish colonialism remains to be written.

Today Quetzaltenango is Guatemala's second largest city. Beginning in the 1700s the town (I use the terms *town* and *village* to indicate any small to medium-sized indigenous community—be it an aldea or a pueblo) expanded rapidly to become an important multiethnic commercial center. At this point, I begin to refer to Quetzaltenango as a city, even though it did not officially achieve this status until the first decades of the nineteenth century. In the nineteenth century, a rising class of Creole and then Ladino elites first pushed for autonomy from Spain, then independence, and then for their own separate nation. For a brief period, from 1838 to 1840, Quetzaltenango was the capital of the sixth Central American state, the Estado de los Altos.[2] In the second half of the nineteenth century, Ladino elites from the region surrounding Quetzaltenango and nearby

San Marcos began to invest in coffee cultivation and led the political and economic revolution that transformed Guatemala into a dependent agro-exporting nation state. Many of these planters were residents of Quetzaltenango, which quickly became an important center of coffee commerce.

This study focuses on the indigenous community of the city of Quetzaltenango. Today, that community is defined by itself and by anthropologists as K'iche', a subgroup with a distinct language—one of over twenty Mayan languages spoken in Guatemala. It is the preferred language in numerous communities in the western highland departments of Quetzaltenango, Totonicapán, and Quiché.

Until around the 1970s, however, the terms *Maya* and *K'iche'* did not have a political meaning.[3] Spanish colonialism attempted to create a caste society based on two political categories: Indios (Indians) and Spaniards. Despite the emergence of other social groups—such as Mestizos and Castas—through the colonial period and continuing after independence, it was chiefly through this political division that rule and exploitation took place.

Wherever there existed large sedentary indigenous populations throughout its American empire, the Spanish Crown attempted to establish a governing system of two "republics": a *república de españoles* and a *república de indios*. Forcibly settled indigenous communities (*pueblos de indios*, in which no non-Indian was legally allowed to reside) were to have existed parallel to administrative and commercial centers populated by Spaniards (*ciudades de españoles*, in which no Indian was to live). Until independence, the community of Quetzaltenango was technically a pueblo de indios, albeit with a steadily growing non-Indian population.[4]

Although it is clear that Indians understood themselves to be members of a larger dominated group, alternatively called *naturales*, indios, and indígenas, during colonial rule and, in some places, well into the twentieth century, the *primary* identity of Guatemala's indigenous population revolved around their local place of residence.[5] Throughout the book, therefore, I use the word *Indian* or *Maya*, unless the context indicates otherwise, to refer to the caste division of Guatemalan society and not to a culturally or politically self-conscious group. In discussing the town of Quetzaltenango, I alternately refer to its indigenous inhabitants as Indians or K'iche's. As the context indicates, at times I also use the word Quetzalteco to refer to all of the city's inhabitants.

Throughout the Spanish Americas during the early colonial period the term *Ladino* referred to baptized or Hispanicized Indians.[6] It also held class connotations, since until relatively recently, non-Indian elites referred to poor non-Indian peasants and urban workers as Ladino. The term continued to connote multiple meanings, but gradually by independence in Guatemala, especially in the highlands around Quetzaltenango, Ladino came to refer, *at least publicly*, to all non-Indians, including Mestizos, Creoles, and Spaniards. Although these multiple meanings are discussed in greater detail in chapter 3, what is important to emphasize here is that Guatemalan *Ladino* is not synonymous with the Mexican or Nicaraguan usage of *Mestizo*. In those countries, the term *Mestizo* came to hold much more self-consciously hybrid (indigenous and Spanish) connotations; in Guatemala, in contrast, the use of Ladino has historically suggested a Hispanicized or European cultural identity. In the first two chapters I use the term Creole — American-born Spaniards — to describe the non-Indian political elites of Quetzaltenango. As the narrative approaches independence in 1821, I increasingly use the word Ladino to describe the city's non-Indian political elite; after independence, I use this description exclusively.

Throughout my discussion of the eighteenth and nineteenth centuries, I use the words *principales* and *indigenous* or *K'iche' elites* interchangeably. By the first decades of the twentieth century, the use of the word *principal* to denote political or hereditary status fell out of use. Therefore, to discuss events from that point on, I employ the terms *indigenous* or *K'iche' elites* to define a group of Quetzalteco Indians who were either politically or economically powerful. This group consisted of agriculturalists and pastoralists whose production involved the accumulation of surplus profit, as well as urbanized K'iche' artisans, construction contractors, merchants, and shopkeepers. I also often refer to this group as patriarchs. The ability of K'iche' elites to mobilize household resources was an essential component in the maintenance of their economic, political, and cultural power.[7] As a fundamental unit of social organization in both colonial and republican Guatemala, material and ideological control of the family, as represented in gender and generational relations, played a key role in the construction of K'iche' nationalism.

I use the terms *caste, culture,* and *ethnicity* interchangeably, to denote a society organized by caste; by caste I mean social divisions culturally and ideological defined and politically enforced. I try to limit my use of the word *race* to when it refers to the perceptions and ideologies Indians and non-Indians had of each other and themselves.[8]

Appendix 2: Glossary

albañil: mason / contractor

alcalde: head of town council; equivalent to mayor

alcalde auxiliar: assistant to municipal authorities usually charged with administering a rural cantón or aldea

aldea: hamlet, located within municipal jurisdiction

Altense(s): highlanders (in this work, usually used to refer to non-Indian elites)

altiplano: highlands

bosque: (common or municipal) forest land

caballería: Scholars identify this measurement as between 104 (George Lovell) and 112 (David McCreery) acres; for Quetzaltenango, it tends toward the higher figure.

cabildo: city council, usually associated with indigenous communities

cantón: rural neighborhood within municipal jurisdiction

cargo: political or religious office

cofradías: cult devoted to worship of its titular saint; often served as mutual aid or burial societies and sources of credit

colono: resident worker

común: indigenous communal corporate identity

corregimiento: administrative unit under colonial and conservative republican regimes roughly equivalent to a department

corrigedor: political administrator of colonial or conservative republican corregimiento; contrasted with liberal jefe político.

corte: indigenous skirt

cuerda: in Quetzaltenango, twenty-five square varas; roughly, 1792 = 1 caballería

ejidos: common land

Estado de Los Altos: Independent highland state (1838–40; 1848), of which Quetzaltenango was the capital

finca: large landholding

gobernador: indigenous political official nominated by corregidor

guardabosques: forest sentries

huipil: female tunic

jefe político /jefatura política: departmental administrator / office associated with liberal administration, in contrast with the corrigedor, associated with colonial or conservative administration

macehual: Nahuatl for peasant or commoner

mandamiento: forced labor draft. Although forced labor existed under colonialism, it is usually associated with its reinstitution in 1877 for coffee production

manzana: 1.7 acres; 66 = 1 caballería

milpa: corn, bean, and squash plot usually associated with indigenous subsistence agriculture

monte: forest or pasture land

mozo (de cargo): common laborer
   (hauler)
padrón: tributary or tax roll
patrón: boss, protector, landlord
principal: indigenous political leader;
   in Quetzaltenango, secondary to
   caciques

protocolos: notary records
regidor: municipal councilmember
ronda: patrol
vecino: resident of a given population, community
Xelaju: precolonial K'iche' name for
   Quetzaltenango

Notes

Introduction: Searching for the Living among the Dead

1. Today, *Ladino* commonly refers to all Guatemalans who are not considered Mayan; K'iche' here refers to the indigenous population of the city of Quetzaltenango. See Appendix 1 for a more detailed discussion of these and other terms and concepts used in this work. Since I use racial/ethnic identity exclusively as a political and social category, I have capitalized all such corresponding terms, such as Ladino, Creole, Mestizo, Casta, and Indian.

2. See John Comaroff and Jean Comaroff, *Ethnography and the Historical Imagination* (Boulder: Westview Press, 1992), p. 11, for a call for an "anthropology of national or international forces and formations."

3. My understanding of this anxiety owes much to Theodor Adorno's *The Jargon of Authenticity*, trans. K. Tarnanski and F. Will (Chicago: Northwestern University Press, 1973).

4. See Ana María Alonso, *Threads of Blood: Colonialism, Revolution, and Gender on Mexico's Northern Frontier* (Tucson: University of Arizona Press, 1995).

5. See Carlota McAllister's essay, "Authenticity and Guatemala's Maya Queen," on the Rabín Ahau, the national indigenous pageant that takes place in Cobán, for an excellent discussion on Mayan "authenticity's" relationship to Guatemalan nationalism, in *Beauty Queens on the Global Stage: Gender, Contests, and Power*, ed. Collen Ballerino Cohen et al. (New York: Routledge, 1996). See Jean Baudrillard, *Simulations*, trans. P. Foss, P. Patton, and P. Beitchman (New York: Semiotext(e), 1983), for the impossibility of authenticity in capitalist culture.

6. See Comisión para el Esclarecimiento Histórico, *Guatemala: Memory of Silence, Conclusions and Recommendations* (Guatemala City: 1999). After a twenty-month investigation, the commission concluded that the state, army, and army-allied paramilitary organizations killed or disappeared over 200,000 people and committed 626 massacres. Ninety-one percent of these violations took place between 1978 and 1984.

7. See Deborah Levenson-Estrada, *Trade Unionists against Terror: Guatemala City, 1954–1985* (Chapel Hill: University of North Carolina Press, 1994), p. 67, for her discussion of what she calls "inverse hegemony"—the phenomenon whereby everything the state does is considered alien or evil. See also David McCreery, *Rural Guatemala, 1760–1940* (Stanford, Calif.: Stanford University Press, 1994), pp. 9–11. See Steven Palmer, "A Liberal Discipline: Inventing Nations in Guatemala and Costa Rica, 1870–1900" (Ph.D. diss., Columbia University, 1990), for a qualified dissenting opinion.

8. Susanne Jonas, *The Battle for Guatemala: Rebels, Death Squads, and U.S. Power* (Boulder: Westview Press, 1991).

9. Comisión para el Esclarecimiento Histórico, *Memory of Silence*, p. 18.

10. See Neil Lazarus, "Transnationalism and the Alleged Death of the Nation State," in *Cultural Readings of Imperialism: Edward Said and the Gravity of History*, ed. Keith Ansell Pearson et al. (New York: St. Martin's Press, 1997).

11. See Eric Hobsbawm's *Nations and Nationalism since 1780: Programme, Myth, Reality* (Cambridge: Cambridge University Press, 1992) for this argument.

12. In Hobsbawm's words: "Nationalism belongs with political theory, ethnicity with sociology or social anthropology"; in "Ethnicity and Nationalism in Europe Today," in *Mapping the Nation*, ed. Gopal Balakrishnan (London: Verso Press, 1996), p. 258.

13. See Brackette Williams, "A Class Act: Anthropology and the Race to Nation across Ethnic Terrain," *Annual Review of Anthropology* 18 (1989): 401–44.

14. See Ranajit Guha, "On Some Aspects of the Historiography of Colonial India," in *Subaltern Studies I: Writings on South Asian History and Society*, ed. Ranajit Guha (Delhi: Oxford University Press, 1986), p. 5, for the "failure of the Indian bourgeoisie to speak for the nation."

15. Thus, rather than viewing Mayan nationalism as "modular," that is, as an aspiration toward some other country's model of what a nation should be, this study will explore the social processes in which it was produced. For modular nationalism, see Benedict Anderson's *Imagined Communities: Reflections on the Origin and Spread of Nationalism* (London: Verso Press, 1991), p. 67.

16. See Charles Hale for a discussion of how the theoretical implications of the "new politics of cultural difference" play out in the Central American context; "Mestizaje, Hybridity and the Cultural Politics of Difference in post-Revolutionary Central America," *Journal of Latin American Anthropology* 2, no. 1 (1996): 37, 39; see also Hale's *Resistance and Contradiction: Miskitu Indians and the Nicaraguan State, 1894–1987* (Stanford, Calif.: Stanford University Press, 1994), chap. 8.

17. An obvious example of this is the tendency of scholars to promote certain Mayan intellectuals and organizations while ignoring those that maintain close alliances with Guatemala's Ladino Left. See the collected essays in Edward F. Fischer and R. McKenna Brown, eds., *Maya Cultural Activism in Guatemala* (Austin: University of Texas Press, 1996).

18. See Ralph Lee Woodward, *Central America: A Nation Divided* (New York: Oxford University Press, 1985); Jim Handy, *Gift of the Devil: A History of Guatemala* (Toronto: Between the Lines Press, 1984); Mario Rodríguez, "The Livingston Codes in the Guatemalan Crisis of 1837–1838," in *Applied Enlightenment: Nineteenth-Century Liberalism, 1830–1839* (New Orleans: Middle American Research Institute, 1955).

19. For Carrera, see Hazel Ingersoll, "The War of the Mountain: A Study in Reactionary Peasant Insurgency in Guatemala, 1837–1873" (Ph.D. diss., George

Washington University, 1972), and Ralph Lee Woodward, *Rafael Carrera and the Emergence of Guatemala, 1821–1871* (Athens: University of Georgia Press, 1993).

20. For a general treatment of indigenous land dispossession and labor exploitation, see Julio C. Cambranes, *Café y campesinos en Guatemala, 1853–1897* (Guatemala City: Editorial Universitaria, 1985). For debt labor and seasonal migration, see David McCreery, "Debt Servitude in Rural Guatemala, 1876–1936," *Hispanic American Historical Review* 63, no. 4 (Nov. 1983): 735–59. And for the most detailed examination of changes in property relations resulting from coffee cultivation to date, see McCreery's *Rural Guatemala*; see also his "An Odious Feudalism: Mandamiento Labor and Commercial Agriculture in Guatemala, 1858–1920," *Latin American Perspectives* 13, no. 1 (winter 1986): 99–118.

21. See David McCreery, "State Power, Indigenous Communities, and Land in Nineteenth-Century Guatemala, 1820–1920," in *Guatemalan Indians and the State 1540–1988*, ed. Carol A. Smith (Austin: University of Texas Press, 1990). See Cambranes, *Café y campesinos*, p. 611, for the Estado Cafetalero.

22. See McCreery, "State Power," pp. 104, 110–11.

23. See, for example, McCreery, "State Power," and Lowell Gudmunson and Hector Lindo-Fuentes, *Central America, 1821–1871: Liberalism before Liberal Reform* (Tuscaloosa: University of Alabama Press, 1995).

24. McCreery, *Rural Guatemala*, pp. 10–11. Despite this, McCreery's work goes far in smoothing out the transition between pre- and postcoffee periods, highlighting continuities as they manifested themselves in interethnic relations.

25. See McCreery, *Rural Guatemala*, pp. 2–3, 333, for a discussion related to Guatemala. See Florencia E. Mallon, *The Defense of Community in Peru's Central Highlands: Peasant Struggle and Capitalist Transition, 1860–1940* (Princeton: Princeton University Press, 1983), for a Peruvian application. See William Roseberry, "Anthropologies, History, and Modes of Production," in *Anthropologies and Histories: Essays in Culture, History, and Political Economy*, ed. William Roseberry (New Brunswick: Rutgers University Press, 1989), and Aidan Foster-Carter, "The Modes of Production Controversy," *New Left Review*, no. 107 (1978): 47–77, for theoretical considerations.

26. See Douglas Brintnal, *Revolt against the Dead: The Modernization of a Mayan Community in the Highlands of Guatemala* (New York: Gordon and Breach, 1979); Waldemar R. Smith, *The Fiesta System and Economic Change* (New York: Columbia University Press, 1977); John M. Watanabe, *Maya Saints and Souls in a Changing World* (Austin: University of Texas Press, 1992); and Kay B. Warren, *The Symbols of Subordination: Indian Identity in a Guatemalan Town* (Austin: University of Texas Press, 1978).

27. This is most explicitly stated in Carol A. Smith's introductory essay to her edited volume, *Guatemalan Indians and the State, 1540–1988* (Austin: University of Texas Press, 1990). Smith writes that the volume's mandate is to "bring a cultural perspective to questions of power," p. 2. For examples of particularly historical-minded anthropologies, see Richard N. Adams, *Crucifixion by Power:*

Essays on Capitalist National Social Structure, 1944–1966 (Austin: University of Texas Press, 1970); Robert M. Carmack, *Rebels of Highland Guatemala: The Quiché-Mayas of Momostenango* (Norman: University of Oklahoma Press, 1995); Watanabe, *Saints and Souls*; and Ricardo Falla, *Quiché rebelde: Estudio de un movimiento de conversión religiosa, rebelde a las creencias tradicionales en San Antonio Ilotenango* (Guatemala City: Editorial Universitaria, 1978).

28. Although many anthropologists working in Guatemala are sensitive to the techniques by which Indians, to the best of their ability, resisted, or adapted institutions of domination, most, by ignoring the ways in which cultural change within and among indigenous communities actively mediated supracommunal power relations, fail to place their work within larger global contexts of state formation. Thus, by default, history transforms culture; culture does not affect history. The work of Richard N. Adams constitutes important exceptions to this. See his collected essays in *Etnias en evolución social: Estudios de Guatemala y Centroamérica* (Mexico: Universidad Autónoma Metropolitana, 1995).

29. The exception to this is in the negative. There has been some interest in how Guatemalan nationalism is based on the real and imagined negation of the Indian. To be Ladino, to be urban, to be a citizen, is to be the antithesis of what it is to be Indian. For this line of inquiry carried to an extreme, see John Hawkins, *Inverse Images: The Meaning of Culture, Ethnicity and Family in Postcolonial Guatemala* (Albuquerque: University of New Mexico Press, 1984). Recently, due to the rapid expansion of Maya ethnicity and the development of the pan-Mayan movement, scholars are beginning to explore the ways in which culture informs supracommunal power relations. See Diane Nelson, *A Finger in the Wound: Body Politics in Quincentennial Guatemala* (Berkeley: University of California Press, 1999).

30. For dependency theory, see Steve J. Stern's critique "Feudalism, Capitalism, and the World-System in the Perspective of Latin America and the Caribbean," in *Confronting Historical Paradigms: Peasants, Labor, and the World System in Africa and Latin America*, ed. Frederick Cooper et al. (Madison: University of Wisconsin Press, 1993). For views that argue for the autonomy of popular classes, see James C. Scott's "Hegemony and the Peasantry," *Politics and Society* 7, no. 3 (1977): 267–96, and *Domination and the Arts of Resistance: Hidden Transcripts* (New Haven: Yale University Press, 1990) as well as some of the early work of Subaltern Studies scholars, such as Ranajit Guha, *Elementary Aspects of Peasant Insurgency in Colonial India* (Delhi: Oxford University Press, 1983).

31. A quick gloss: see, for examples, Jeffrey L. Gould's *To Lead as Equals: Rural Protest and Political Consciousness in Chinandega, Nicaragua, 1912–1979* (Chapel Hill: University of North Carolina Press, 1990), and "Vana Ilusión: The Highland Indians and the Myth of Nicaraguan Mestiza, 1880–1925," *Hispanic American Historical Review* 73, no. 3 (1993): 393–429; Gilbert M. Joseph and Daniel Nugent, eds., *Everyday Forms of State Formation: Revolution and the Negotiation of Rule in Modern Mexico* (Durham: Duke University Press, 1994); Florencia Mallon, *Peasant and Nation: The Making of Postcolonial Mexico and Peru* (Berkeley:

University of California Press, 1995). See also Gilbert M. Joseph, "On the Trail of Latin American Bandits: A Reexamination of Peasant Resistance," *Latin American Research Review* 25, no. 3 (1990): 7–53. The intellectual genealogy of these works is complex and far ranging. See Joseph and Nugent, *Everyday Forms of State Formation*, for an attempt to bring many strands of thought together for an analysis of the Mexican revolution. See especially, in this work, their essay "Popular Culture and State Formation in Revolutionary Mexico."

32. Florencia Mallon, "Nationalist and Antistate Coalitions in the War of the Pacific: Junín and Cajamarca, 1879–1902," in *Resistance, Rebellion, and Consciousness in the Andean Peasant World: 18th to 20th Centuries*, ed. Steve J. Stern (Madison: University of Wisconsin, 1987), p. 234. Mallon is in dialogue with, among others, Hobsbawm's work on nationalism, *Nations and Nationalism*, which has set the debate for Marxist discussions of nationalism. While she accepts Hobsbawm's judgment that nationalism is a form of class struggle, Mallon rejects his notion that it is only an ideology of the bourgeoisie, inextricably linked to industrial organization and state formation.

33. See Partha Chatterjee, *Nationalist Thought and the Colonial World: A Derivative Discourse?* (Delhi: Oxford University Press, 1986), for a discussion on the possibilities and limitations of subject peoples in developing an autonomous nationalist discourse. He writes, pp. 40–42, that by struggling within the terms established by an "entire body of systematic knowledge," postcolonial nationalism produces a "different discourse, yet one that is dominated by another."

34. William Roseberry, "Hegemony and the Language of Contention," in *Everyday Forms of State Formation*, p. 361, and Gould, *To Lead as Equals*.

35. Clifford Geertz, *Negara: The Theatre State in Nineteenth-Century Bali* (Princeton: Princeton University Press, 1980); Michel Foucault, *Discipline and Punish: The Birth of the Prison*, trans. Alan Sheridan (New York: Pantheon Books, 1977). See Scott, *Domination and the Arts of Resistance*, for his argument against an understanding of hegemony as a conscious project on the part of the elites.

36. Roseberry, "Hegemony and the Language of Contention," p. 358. Antonio Gramsci, *Selections from the Prison Notebooks*, trans. Quintin Hoare (New York: International Publishers, 1971).

37. Mallon, *Peasant and Nation*, p. 6.

38. See the collected letters of Subcomandante Marcos in *Shadows of Tender Fury: The Letters and Communiques of Subcomandante Marcos* (New York: Monthly Review Press, 1995).

39. Gould, *To Lead as Equals*, p. 16.

40. The following points will be taken up in greater detail throughout the book. The comparison with Mexico is greatly indebted to Florencia Mallon's important discussion of Mexican, Peruvian, and Bolivian nationalism; Mallon, "Indian Communities, Political Cultures, and the State in Latin America, 1780–1990," *Journal of Latin American Studies* 24 (1992): 35–53.

41. In Mexico, according to Alan Knight, the "progressive breakdown of the

castelike, colonial order and its replacement by a society stratified by class" was a "long, slow" and uneven process by which the balance "gradually tipped from caste to class. . . . Class now counted for more, but caste—ethnic status—was far from irrelevant"; Knight, "Racism, Revolution and Indigenismo: Mexico, 1910–1940," in *The Idea of Race in Latin America, 1870–1940*, ed. Richard Graham (Austin: University of Texas Press, 1994), p. 78. There are important exceptions to this. Aside from the Maya of Chiapas, Zapotec Indians of the southern isthmus of Tehuantepec have maintained a strong ethnic identity. See Howard Campbell, *Zapotec Renaissance: Ethnic Politics and Cultural Revivalism in Southern Mexico* (Albuquerque: University of New Mexico Press, 1994), and Jeffrey W. Rubin, *Decentering the Regime: Ethnicity, Radicalism, and Democracy in Juchitán, Mexico* (Durham: Duke University Press, 1997).

42. In Mexico, indigenous-peasant communities both allied with conservatives and liberals, as circumstances dictated. See John Tutino, *From Insurrection to Revolution in Mexico: Social Bases of Agrarian Violence, 1750–1940* (Princeton: Princeton University Press, 1988); Andres Lira González, *Comunidades indígenas frente a la ciudad de México* (Zamora, Spain: El Colegio de Michoacán, 1983); and Evelyn Hu-dehart, *Yaqui Resistance and Survival: The Struggle for Land and Autonomy, 1821–1910* (Madison: University of Wisconsin Press, 1984), for alliances with conservatives; see Mallon, *Peasant and Nation*, and Peter Guardino, *Peasants, Politics, and the Formation of Mexico's National State: Guerrero, 1800–1957* (Stanford, Calif.: Stanford University Press, 1996), for pacts with liberals.

43. There are many examples of this. For one of them, see Lorenzo Montúfar y Rivera Maestre, *Reseña histórica de Centro América*, 7 vols. (Guatemala City: Tipografía de El Progreso, 1878). An important exception to this is liberal interpretations of the 1820 Tzul uprising in Totonicapán.

44. Although there is debate concerning the degree of indigenous participation, it is clear that large numbers actively supported the rebels not only by taking up arms but also by providing a sympathetic and sustaining medium in which the rebels could operate. Richard N. Adams estimates Indian participation at 500,000; see his "Conclusions: What Can We Know about the Harvest of Violence?" in *The Harvest of Violence: The Maya Indians and the Guatemalan Crisis*, ed. Robert Carmack (Norman: University of Oklahoma Press, 1988). See also the estimates of the U.S. State Department quoted in *The New York Times*, 15 March 1982, which calculates indigenous support in the early months of 1982 at 3,500 armed members, 10,000 members of irregular forces, and 30 to 60,000 others who actively supported the guerrillas.

45. See the dedication in Demetrio Cuxil Cojtí, *El Movimiento Maya (en Guatemala)* (Guatemala City: Cholsamaj, 1997).

46. See the work of Paul Gilroy on British nationalism and racism, in particular his introductory essay to *"There Ain't No Black in the Union Jack": The Cultural Politics of Race and Nation* (Chicago: University of Chicago Press, 1987). Gilroy vigorously argues against perspectives, Marxist and liberal, that view racial iden-

tities and racism as ahistorical. He insists that the "reintroduction of history is crucial in understanding race as more than just an ideological epiphenomena." Many Mayan intellectuals, however, in their efforts to counter the class reductionism found in much Guatemalan academic production, have resorted to a denial of indigenous participation in postconquest Guatemalan history.

47. See William Roseberry and Jay O'Brien, eds., introduction to *Golden Ages, Dark Ages: Imagining the Past in Anthropology and History* (Berkeley: University of California Press, 1991), p. 12.

48. Comisión para el Esclarecimiento Histórico, *Memory of Silence*, p. 22.

49. For two years, from 1821 to 1823, Central America was annexed to independent Mexico.

50. Ingersoll, "The War of the Mountain"; Keith L. Miceli, "Rafael Carrera: Defender and Promoter of Peasant Interests in Guatemala, 1837–1848," *The Americas* 31, no. 1 (1974): 72–95; Rodríguez, "The Livingston Codes"; and Woodward, *Rafael Carrera*.

51. Arturo Taracena Arriola estimates that the population of the territory that would have made up the Estado de los Altos was comprised in 1800 of 71 percent Indians, 28 percent Ladinos, and .02 percent Spanish; Taracena Arriola, *Invención criolla, sueño ladino, pesadilla indígena: Los Altos de Guatemala, de región a Estado, 1740–1850* (Antigua: Centro de Investigaciones Regionales de Mesoamérica, 1997), p. 305.

Prelude: A World Put Right, 31 March 1840

1. The following account is taken from Ingersoll, "The War of the Mountain"; Marcelo Molina y Mata, *Ligeros apuntamientos acerca de los principales sucesos de la carrera literaria y vida pública de Marcelo Molina* (Quetzaltenango: Casa de la Cultura, 1971); Sinforoso Rivera, *Los Manuscritos de un patriota* (Quetzaltenango: La Industria, 1893); and John L. Stephens, *Incidents of Travel in the Central America, Chiapas, and Yucatan*, vol. 2 (New York: Harper & Brothers, 1841). The letter itself is displayed in the Taracena Collection of Quetzaltenango's Museo de Historia.

2. Jorge H. González, "A History of Los Altos, Guatemala: A Study of Regional Conflict and National Integration" (Ph.D. diss., Tulane, 1994).

3. Molina y Mata, *Ligeros apuntamientos*, p. 10; Archivo Histórico de Quetzaltenango (hereafter cited as AHQ), Libro de Actas (hereafter cited as Actas), 29 April and 1 June 1838.

4. Rivera, *Un patriota*, p. 11.

5. Ibid., pp. 26–29.

6. Actually, the government of Guatemala had already reinstituted many colonial protections prior to Carrera's annexation of Los Altos in its Reglamento de Corregidores. See AHQ, Decreto de la Asamblea Constituyente en que señala las

atribuciones del gobernador de los indígenas, 1839. See Archivo de Gobernación de Quetzaltenango (hereafter cited as AGQ), 1840, for the end of the tax.

7. See AGQ, 1840.

8. Ibid.

9. *El Tiempo*, 27 Feb. 1840; Rivera, *Un patriota*, p. 31; AGQ, 1840.

10. Stephens, *Incidents of Travel*, pp. 168–69.

11. Rivera, *Un patriota*, p. 31.

12. See AHQ, Actas. The names of those attending the sessions are listed on the margin of the minutes. Indigenous attendance was spotty, but at least one or two K'iche's usually attended municipal meetings.

13. See AGQ, 1840.

14. See AHQ, Actas, 21 April 1840.

15. See, for example, an 1847 exchange between the Ladinos and the corregidor in which the corregidor refuses a Ladino petition advocating the abolition of the dual municipal system in AHQ, 1847.

16. See AHQ, 1847. This was a notable "invention of tradition," given that the Creole/Ladino municipality was established by Crown decree in 1806.

Chapter 1   The Greatest Indian City in the World:
Caste, Gender, and Politics, 1750–1821

1. What occurred in Quetzaltenango closely resembles what John Chance found in the valley of Oaxaca, where, for indigenous caciques, "the key to Indian noble survival in the late colonial period was the possession of an independent economic base"; Chance, "The Caciques of Tecali: Class and Ethnic Identity in Late Colonial Mexico," *Hispanic American Historical Review* 76, no. 3 (1996): 476–502, p. 478; see also John K. Chance, *Conquest of the Sierra: Spaniards and Indians in Colonial Oaxaca* (Norman: University of Oklahoma Press, 1989). See also James Lockhart, *The Nahuas after the Conquest: A Social and Cultural History of the Indians of Central Mexico, Sixteenth through Eighteenth Centuries* (Stanford, Calif.: Stanford University Press, 1992), pp. 130–40, for social stratification within Nahua society.

2. González, "A History of Los Altos"; Wendy Kramer, *Encomienda Politics in Early Colonial Guatemala, 1524–1544: Dividing the Spoils*, ed. David J. Robinson, Dellplain Latin American Studies, vol. 31 (Boulder: Westview Press, 1994); and Murdo MacLeod, *Spanish Central America: A Socioeconomic History, 1520–1720* (Berkeley: University of California Press, 1973).

3. W. George Lovell, *Conquest and Survival in Guatemala: A Historical Geography of the Cuchumatán Highlands, 1500–1821* (Montreal: McGill-Queen's University Press, 1992), p. 75; Kramer, *Encomienda Politics*, pp. 179–200.

4. Lovell, *Conquest and Survival in Guatemala*, p. 76.

5. The one bright spot in the Altense economic landscape was cacao, which

flourished on the Pacific lowlands during the first two decades of Spanish rule but fell into decline by the beginning of the seventeenth century. See MacLeod, *Spanish Central America*, pp. 68–79.

6. See Greg Grandin, "The Blood of Guatemala: The Making of Race and Nation, 1750–1954" (Ph.D. diss., Yale, 1999), Appendix 1.

7. According to McCreery, *Rural Guatemala*, p. 52, 38.75 caballerías.

8. These ejidos were defined more by local use than by Spanish legalities. Within what communities called their ejido could be the original league, unclaimed land or parcels subsequently purchased by individuals or corporate entities such as *cofradías* kinship clans. In 1700, Indians from Quetzaltenango petitioned for title of the town's ejidos, some 283 caballerías. This included all the land previously claimed by K'iche's and Spaniards and smaller plots and ranches worked by Indians and Ladinos, as well as common pasture and woodland. Eventually, as municipal borders in the region became standardized, the limits of these 283 caballerías became coterminous with Quetzaltenango's municipal boundaries. See Grandin, "Blood," Appendix 1.

9. For an 1817 description of land use, see Archivo General de Centro América, Sección de Tierras (hereafter cited as AGCA-ST): 1 17. All references, unless otherwise noted, are for the department of Quetzaltenango; first number indicates *paquete* (packet); second number indicates *expediente* (file).

10. See AGQ, Libro de matrículas de terrenos del Departamento, 1874, as well as the four volumes of *protocolos* in Archivo de Protocolos de la Corte Suprema (hereafter cited as APCS) covering the years 1800–1865. Property was obviously alienable among Quetzalteco K'iche's, yet it is not known what moral constraints governed land relations. Robert Carmack writes that in Momostenango, despite the appearance of a commodified land market, property relations were strictly governed through membership in *parcialidades* (extended kin group) which determined both access to land and norms surrounding its use; Carmack, *Rebels*, pp. 79–81. See also Robert Hill and John Monaghan, *Continuities in Highland Mayan Social Organization: Ethnohistory in Sacapulas, Guatemala* (Philadelphia: University of Pennsylvania Press, 1987), for Sacapulas. In Quetzaltenango, while extended relations of gender and kinship bound men and women to K'iche' patriarchs, these kin groups were not as structured or continuous as they were in the eastern K'iche' towns of Momostenango, Totonicapán, or Sacapulas. Quetzaltenango was divided into four neighborhoods—San Antonio, San Nicolás, San Bartolomé, and San Sebastián—and early in the colonial period occasional allusions were made to the "heads of the four parcialidades." Likewise, in the century following the conquest, certain principales did claim precolonial noble pedigrees. But by the middle of the eighteenth century, mention of political divisions within the town disappeared, perhaps now dissolved under the combined pressure of population growth and colonial restructuring. For references to parcialidades, see AHQ, Libro de pago de tributos de los indígenas al Rey, 1681–1713. Early lineage groups or parcialidades may have disappeared under colonial pressures, as oc-

curred in the Zapoteca communities by 1730; cf. Chance, *Conquest of the Sierra*, pp. 130–31.

11. The size of a cuerda varies according to local custom. In Quetzaltenango, a cuerda measured 25 squared varas, a vara being .836 meters or 2.8 feet.

12. Archivo General de Centro América (hereafter cited as AGCA). In citations "A" indicates colonial holdings and "B" indicates postindependence holdings; the first number corresponds to *signatura* (category), the second to *legajo* (packet), the third to *expediente* (file), and the fourth to *folio* (page); A 1.24 1583 10227 266.

13. Joseph Hidalgo, "Memoria para hacer una descripción del Reino de Guatemala," *Anales de la Sociedad de Geografía e Historia de Guatemala* 26, nos. 3–4 (1952): 381–413.

14. González, "A History of Los Altos," chap. 3; Severo Martínez Peláez, *La patria del criollo: Ensayo de interpretación de la realidad colonial guatemalteca*, 4th ed. (Guatemala City: Editorial Universitaria, 1976), p. 74; Francis Gall, *Cerro Quemado: Volcán de Quetzaltenango (Estudio de Geografía histórica regional)* (Guatemala City: Editorial José de Pineda Ibarra, 1966), p. 26; and Domingo Juarros, *Compendio de la historia del reino de Guatemala* (Guatemala City: Tipografía Nacional, 1936), p. 42.

15. Taracena Arriola, *Invención criolla*.

16. For wheat, see AGCA, A1 195 3947 folios 20–25; AGCA, A3.5 321 6783; and Juarros, *Compendio*, pp. 48–50; for textiles, see Hidalgo, "Memoria," p. 392. For more on Quetzalteco colonial textile production, see Manuel Rubio Sánchez, "Historia del ganado caprino y ovino en Guatemala," *Anales de Academia de Geografía e Historia de Guatemala* 61 (enero–dec. 1987): 121–22; and Antonio José de Iribarri, *El cristiano errante: Novela que tiene mucho de historia*, vol. 2 (Guatemala City: Editorial del Ministerio de Educación Pública, 1960), p. 172.

17. See Grandin, "Blood," Appendix 2.

18. AGCA, A1 390 8117.

19. The following description of highland trade is from AGCA, A3.5 321 6783; A1 390 8117; A1 390 8119; A1 390 8132; and AGCA-ST, 1 17; as well as from numerous incidental references from documents in the AGQ and AHQ. For the Cuchumatanes, see Lovell, *Conquest and Survival in Guatemala*.

20. See Juarros, *Compendio*, p. 42, for a more detailed description of the plaza at the turn of the nineteenth century. See de Iribarri, *El cristiano errante*, for another effusive description.

21. Increasingly, research is revealing that in many important regions of Spanish America, the absence of coercive colonial labor institutions seems to have been the rule rather than the exception. For central Mexico, see Eric Van Young, *Hacienda and Market in Eighteenth-Century Mexico* (Berkeley: University of California Press, 1981), and Tutino, *From Insurrection to Revolution*.

22. In the eighteenth century, when Spaniards from the city of Quetzaltenango did petition for repartimiento labor, the request was invariably for Indians from communities other than Quetzaltenango. See AGCA, A2.12 2775 40104, A3 2776

40112, and AI 192 3926 folios 1–18. For a 1793 ban of repartimento, see Miles Wortman, *Government and Society in Central America 1680–1840* (New York: Columbia University Press, 1982), p. 180.

23. See AGCA, AI 391 8143.

24. See AGCA, A3.16 2891 42641.

25. See AGCA, A3 240 4768.

26. In 1892, of the twenty-eight flocks comprising fifty to ninety-nine sheep, twenty-two were owned by men with K'iche' surnames; of the twenty-one flocks of a hundred sheep or more, sixteen were owned by men with K'iche' surnames; AHQ, Censo de ganados de la República de Guatemala, Quetzaltenango, 1892.

27. Juarros, *Compendio*, p. 42.

28. See APCS, tomo 1–4.

29. See AGCA, AI 192 3926. See also AGCA, A3 223 3985, for another complaint from wealthy Creole merchants that Quetzalteco K'iche''s were demanding and receiving wages above levels established by the Audiencia and setting bad examples for other communities.

30. Tutino, *From Insurrection*, p. 59.

31. Aside from the complaints already mentioned, see AGCA, A2.12 2775 40104, A3 2776 40112, AI 192 3926 folios 1–18, and AGCA AI 390 8117, for the quote.

32. See AGQ, 1835.

33. The K'iche' *gobernador*, Anizeto López, for example, borrowed in advance of his corn harvest 1,300 pesos from Prudencio de Cozar, Quetzaltenango's corregidor. See APCS, tomo 1. See Grandin, "Blood," Appendix 4, for other, similar transactions.

34. Compared, for example, with the agricultural and textile trade that developed in the sixteenth and seventeenth centuries around Mexico City. See Leslie Lewis, "In Mexico's Shadow: Aspects of Economic Activity and Social Processes in Texcoco, 1570–1620," in *Provinces of Early Mexico: Variants of Spanish American Regional Evolution*, ed. Ida Altman and James Lockhart (Los Angeles: Latin American Center Publications, University of California, 1976).

35. Taracena Arriola, *Invención criolla*, pp. 31–37.

36. de Iribarri, *El cristiano errante*, p. 172.

37. See Grandin, "Blood," Appendix 5 for a breakdown of city debt during the years 1801–5.

38. For instances of bartered debt, see the wills of the Spaniard doña Antonia Barreto de Arco y Pompa and the K'iche' principal Lucas Cajas in APCS, tomo 1.

39. See AGCA, AI 2168 15607 and 15613.

40. The corregidor often complained he could not audit K'iche' spending because Indians, perhaps engaged in a bit of bureaucratic resistance, did not keep written records. See AGCA, A 396 3973, and AGCA, AI 2165 1506.

41. See AGCA, A 1578 10222.

42. See AGCA, AI 2165 15597, and AGCA, AI 390 8110.

43. See AGCA, A 390 8120.

44. See, for example, AGCA, AI 390 8122.

45. Archivo Histórico Arqidiocesano "Francisco de Paula García Peláez" (hereafter cited as AHA), Visita de Cortés y Larraz, tomo 24. While the large number of indigenous cofradías prevented the development of a tightly intertwined civil-religious hierarchy such as was found in other Mesoamerican indigenous communities, principales were always associated with one or another of the more prestigious and wealthy fellowships.

46. See AHA, Visita de García Peláez, tomo 47, folio 335–80, for the comparison with Ladino cofradías. See AHQ, Estado de las cofradías y hermandades de Quetzaltenango, 1810, for cofradía capital.

47. See Adriaan C. Van Oss, *Catholic Colonialism: A Parish History of Guatemala, 1524–1821*, Cambridge Latin American Studies, vol. 57, ed. Simon Collier (Cambridge: Cambridge University Press, 1986); John K. Chance and William B. Taylor, "Cofradías and Cargos: An Historical Perspective on the Mesoamerican Civil-Religious Hierarchy," *American Ethnologist* 12 (1985): 1–26, for fees; and numerous wills in APCS, tomo 1, for examples of wax, and AHA, Visita de García Peláez, tomo 47, folios 335–80, for icons.

48. For how this functioned in Guatemala as a whole, see McCreery, *Rural Guatemala*, pp. 25–26.

49. See AHQ, Estado de las cofradías y hermandades del Quetzaltenango, 1810.

50. See APCS, tomo 1. That same year, Patricio Estacuy paid to the church an annual rent of two pesos on a chantry of an unspecified amount of land, and José de Mara paid to the church six pesos a year to farm 170 cuerdas; see APCS, tomo 1.

51. See AGCA, A1 199 4045.

52. See AGCA, A1 290 8122.

53. See AGCA, A1 199 4045.

54. See AHQ, Actas, 20 Nov. 1810.

55. See also AGCA, A1 290 8122, for another example of emergency relief. As late as 1904, the municipality, working to alleviate the effects of a bad harvest, received permission from the national government to import tax-free corn and wheat for distribution at cost to "la gente proletaria"; see AHQ, caja 1904. Individuals also requested aid from the municipality; for example, Juan Xicará, an indigenous mason who lost an eye on a public works project in 1895, asked and received of the municipality forty pesos to cover medical expenses; see AHQ, caja 1895.

56. See AGCA, A3 2430 35677.

57. For example, one K'iche' merchant family transported on a bimonthly basis one to three 75-pound crates of textiles to Guatemala City; AGCA, A3 2430 35677.

58. See detailed discussion in chap. 4.

59. See AGCA, A3.13 2841 41362.

60. See AGQ, 1831.

61. See APCS, tomo 1; see, for another example, the will of Anizeto López, which records that he is the "tutor" of Matías Sacor, son of the deceased Francisco Sacor; AGCA, Libros de Protocolos (hereafter cited as AGCA-LP), Domingo Estrada, leg. 3043.

62. The following information comes from AHA, legajo 1; no. 10.

63. See AGCA, A3.13 2841 41362.

64. See AGCA-LP, Domingo Estrada, legajo 3043.

65. For another case of debt, see AGCA, A3.4 49 930.

66. Evidence for this comes from a number of archival documents describing the city's agricultural production; AGQ, 1834 and 1835.

67. See, for example, AGQ, 1869, and AHQ, Las vendedoras del mercado sobre que se les rebaje lo que pagan por el puesto de venta, 1893.

68. See AGCA, AI 391 8143.

69. See Grandin, "Blood," Appendix 5, for a breakdown of Quetzalteco debt.

70. See, for example, the will of Marta Galindo, "indígena," who left all her estate to cofradías; APCS, tomo 1.

71. The following discussion is greatly indebted to Florencia Mallon, "Patriarchy in the Transition to Capitalism: Central Peru, 1830–1950," *Feminist Studies* 13, no. 2 (1987): 379–407.

72. See AGCA, A3 2776 40112, and AGCA, B 28537 42.

73. See Grandin, "Blood," Appendix 2 and Appendix 3.

74. See APCS, tomo 1.

75. See AGCA-LP, J. Domingo Andrade, 24 June 1876.

76. See Grandin, "Blood," Appendix 5. See also APCS, tomo 1.

77. Evidence confirms Mallon's contention, in "Patriarchy," that gender is the missing relation needed to resolve the debate on the role of peasant production in the transformation to agrarian capitalism. Only an analysis of patriarchal control of productive resources can explain the cycles of capital accumulation and dissolution that mark peasant society.

78. Lowell Gudmunson (personal communication) points out that my claim that widows of wealthy K'iche's often fell into poverty or difficult circumstances is perhaps peculiar to indigenous social relations and is not typical of general Hispanic patterns, especially in southeastern Central America.

79. See APCS, tomo 1.

80. See APCS, tomo 1. This phenomenon of women selling property to men because they could cultivate land or pay for the property's upkeep continued throughout the nineteenth century. See AGCA-LP, Sinforoso Aguilar, for a number of gendered transactions.

81. See APCS, tomo 1.

82. See APCS, tomo 3.

83. See Rodolfo Pastor, *Campesinos y reformas: La Mixteca, 1700–1856* (Mexico: Colegio de México, 1987), pp. 323–35. For the quote, see Steve J. Stern, "The Struggle for Solidarity: Class, Culture, and Community in Highland Indian America," *Radical History Review*, no. 27 (1983): 31.

84. See APCS, tomo 1.

85. Ibid.

86. Ibid.

87. See his will in AGCA-LP, Domingo Estrada, leg. 3043.

88. See AGCA-LP, Domingo Estrada, leg. 3043.

89. See APCS, tomo 1.

90. See APCS, tomo 1, and AHQ, Estado de las cofradías y hermandades de Quetzaltenango, 1810. López likewise made a profit when, in 1803, he sold two caballerías of farm and grazing land for 1,340 pesos, 200 pesos of which went to satisfy a church chantry, with the balance going to López to pay for 600 cuerdas of milpa, 718 sheep, and other improvements he made to the land; APCS, tomo 1.

91. See AGCA, A1.15 5496 47283.

92. See AGCA, A1.52 6052 53494.

93. See AGCA-LP, Domingo Estrada, leg. 3043.

94. See APCS, tomo 1, and AGCA-LP, Domingo Estrada, leg. 3043.

95. See AGCA-LP, Domingo Estrada, leg. 3043.

96. See Jean-Christophe Agnew, "History and Anthropology: Scenes from a Marriage," *The Yale Journal of Criticism* 3, no. 2 (1990): 29–50, and William Roseberry, "Balinese Cockfights and the Seduction of History," in *Anthropologies and Histories*, for efforts to infuse Geertzian cultural anthropology with an analysis of history and power.

97. The administrative complexity found in the studies by Robert Haskett did not exist. See Haskett, *Indigenous Rulers: An Ethnohistory of Town Government in Colonial Cuernavaca* (Albuquerque: University of New Mexico Press, 1991), and Lockhart, *Nahuas*.

98. See, for comparison, Haskett, *Indigenous Rulers*, chap. 4, and Chance, *Conquest of the Sierra*, chap. 5.

99. Compare the 1712 nomination of don Joseph Gómez Tih, in AGCA, A1.24 1579 10223, with the 1780 nomination of Manuel Silverio, in AGCA, A1 195 3960.

100. See AGCA, A1 195 3960.

101. Pastor, *Campesinos*, pp. 323–44.

102. No slaves or dependent serfs existed, and, as we have seen, only four K'iche' households employed servants. For comparisons with Oaxaca, see Chance, *Conquest of the Sierra*, pp. 125–32. For comparisons with the social complexity of central Mexico, see Lockhart, *Nahuas*, especially chap. 4, and Pastor, *Campesinos*, pp. 281–358.

103. See AGCA, A1.24 1581 10225.

104. The Libros de defunciones, matrimonios, and bautismos located in the Archivo Eclesiástico de Quetzaltenango (hereafter cited as AEQ) do not provide the social status of the people mentioned in the entries.

105. See AGCA, A1 11.15 5797 48859.

106. See, for example, the wills of María Ygnacia Coyoy, APCS, tomo 1, and Anizeto López, AGCA, Protocolos, Domingo Estrada, leg. 3043; see also AHA, tomo 47, Visita de García Peláez, folios 335–80.

107. See AEQ, Libros de defunciones.

108. In 1804, for instance, nearly one hundred years after Sebastián Tzunún's death, masses were still being said for his soul; APCS, tomo 1. See also AHQ, Copia del estado de cofradía y hermandades del Quetzaltenango, 1910, for large indigenous chantries of long duration.

109. Olga Arriola de Geng, *Los tejedores en Guatemala y la influencia española en el traje indígena* (Guatemala City: Litografías Modernas, 1991).

110. In Quetzaltenango, the most notable fusion of indigenous and Hispanic traits in residential structures continues to be the combination of a courtyard, which marked Spanish-style colonial homes, with a large compound, which was characteristic of indigenous residences.

111. The requests are to be found in AHQ, 1825–60.

112. See AGCA, A1.1 29 845, for a particularly doleful lament regarding the habits of the poorer classes.

113. See AHQ, Libro de pago de tributos de los indígenas al Rey, 1681–1713, for the quote. To underscore the importance of the ability of K'iche' principales to communicate in Spanish, I should add that I have found only two documents from the community of Quetzaltenango written in K'iche'. See AGCA, A3.15 2788 40336, and A1.57 5967 522381. For an example of an early K'iche' petition informed by Spanish legalisms and rhetoric, see Sebastián Tzunún's early eighteenth-century reproduction of a supposed sixteenth-century *titulo*; Francis Gall, *Título del Ajpop Huitzitzil Tzunún: Probanza de méritos de los De León y Cardona* (Guatemala City: Editorial José de Pineda Ibarra, 1963). See also APCS, tomos 1–4, for the large number of legal transactions by Indians.

114. See AGCA, A1 5502 47451.

115. Ibid. The prisoners were finally released in 1817; see AGCA, A1 5502 47460.

116. See AHQ, Las vendedoras del mercado sobre que se les rebaje lo que pagan por el puesto de venta, 1893.

117. See, for example, AGCA, B 2866 373.

118. See, for example, AGCA, A1 192 3926.

119. See Stephens, *Incidents of Travel*, and William Tufts Brigham, *Guatemala: The Land of the Quetzal* (New York: C. Scribner's Sons, 1887), for various examples of this phenomenon in Guatemala. See Brigham, pp. 147–49, for the K'iche' alcalde, Florencio Cortez, who conscripted a fifteen-year-old mozo in return for having his photograph taken.

120. Stephens, *Incidents of Travel*, pp. 219–21.

121. No documentation exists for the colonial period outlining the scope of this authority. The following description comes from later nineteenth-century sources, when principales, as will be discussed, institutionalized their power under Carrera and the second liberal regime. See especially, AHQ, Libro de sentencias ordenarias, 1863, which gives the barest information regarding cases judged by K'iche' authorities.

122. See AGCA, B 2826 373.

123. Ibid.

124. See Pastor, *Campesinos*, p.325, for this phenomenon in indigenous communities in the Mixteca region of Mexico.

125. For fights with other indigenous communities over land borders, see AHQ, cajas 1840 and 1853 (for a struggle with Cantel), and AHQ, caja 1889 (for a conflict with San Mateo).

126. The following incident is in AGCA, A1 195 3968.

127. See AGCA, A1 195 3968.

128. Ibid.

129. Enrique Tandeter, et al., "Indians in Late Colonial Markets: Sources and Numbers," in *Ethnicity, Markets, and Migration in the Andes: At the Crossroads of History and Anthropology*, ed. Brooke Larson, Olivia Harris, and Enrique Tandeter (Durham: Duke University Press, 1995), p. 199.

Chapter 2   Defending the Pueblo:
Popular Protests and Elite Politics, 1786–1826

1. See David Frye, *Indians into Mexicans: History and Identity in a Mexican Town* (Austin: University of Texas Press, 1996), pp. 75–76, for a similar process in Mexquitic, Mexico. Frye writes that indigenous "elites did not always present a unified front; frequently the elite of a town . . . was internally divided, and each side took to the colonial justice system with claims of truly representing the neglected 'sons of the pueblo.' "

2. See Pastor, *Campesinos*, pp. 324–28, and Stern, "Struggle for Solidarity," for examination of the ties binding indigenous elites to commoners.

3. Christopher H. Lutz, "Evolución demográfica de la población no indígena, 1524–1700," in *Historia General de Guatemala*, ed. Jorge Luján Muñoz (Guatemala City: Fundación Cultura y Desarrollo, 1993).

4. See AGCA, A3.16 2891 42641. See also A1 210 5009, the 1741 relación geográfica, for more evidence of high rates of exogamy, both in Quetzaltenango and surrounding K'iche' towns.

5. See AGCA, A1 210 5009.

6. Complaints from Crown officials were numerous. See for example, AGCA, A1 5485 47193. See also AGCA, A1 199 4046, regarding an 1819 attempt to collect taxes from former Ladino *milicianos*, who, even though their militia unit had been abolished in 1814, continued to insist that they were covered by the military *fuero* (exception). This phenomenon would continue after independence as K'iche' authorities collected more revenue under the contribución directa than did their Ladino counterparts, even though the city's indigenous population was at that point a minority. This will be discussed in greater detail in chap. 3.

7. See AGCA, A3.13 2841 41362. See also AGCA, A1.24 1562 10206, and AGCA,

A1.24 1570 10214, for a 1658 and 1698 appeal for Mestizo status so as to avoid tribute payment.

8. See AGCA, A3.13 2841 41362.

9. Ibid.

10. See AGCA, A3.16 2891 42641.

11. For a discussion of how the colonial ambition of living as close to the plaza as possible had both Iberian and indigenous roots, see Haskett, *Indigenous Rulers*, pp. 168–69.

12. AGCA, A1 2807 24687.

13. See AGCA, A1.21 5485 47194, for an expediente containing accusations against sixteen accused bootleggers during the nine months that Rodríguez controlled the asiento.

14. See AGCA, A1.21 5485 47194.

15. Ibid.

16. Ibid. For an example of patterns of alcohol production, trade, and consumption in nearby Totonicapán, see AGCA, A 6111 56090, and AGCA, A1.34 60 1188.

17. Of the seventeen arrested in the sixteen cases above, only one was identified as an Indian. This does not mean that K'iche's were not involved in the liquor economy, for other evidence, particularly for the postindependence period, reveals they were. Rather, it suggests that Rodríguez was careful not to provoke indigenous anger. He released the one jailed Indian into the custody of the indigenous alcaldes after they intervened on his behalf, so as to, in his words, "prudently avoid" problems; see AGCA, A1.21 5485 47194, Contra Antonio Alvarado.

18. See AGCA, A1 5485 47193.

19. See AGCA, A1 5487 47198, and AGCA, 5488 47202.

20. See AGCA, A1 5485 47193.

21. Ibid.

22. Ibid.

23. See Frye, *Indians into Mexicans*, chap. 4, and John Tutino, "Provincial Spaniards, Indian Towns, and Haciendas: Interrelated Agrarian Sectors in the Valleys of Mexico and Toluca, 1750–1810," in *Provinces of Early Mexico: Variants of Spanish American Regional Evolution*, ed. Ida Altman and James Lockhart (Los Angeles: Latin American Center Publications, University of California, 1976), pp. 185–86, for similar political divisions in indigenous towns in Mexico.

24. González, "A History of Los Altos," chap. 4.

25. See AGCA, A1 5488 47202.

26. See AGCA, A1 5485 47193, and AGCA, A1 5488 47207.

27. See AGCA, A1 49 929.

28. Ibid.

29. See AGCA, A1 5485 47193.

30. Ibid.

31. See AGCA, A1.21 5485 47194.

32. See AGCA, A3.9 49 930, for the suit and for Corona's charge that the three asentistas were behind the grievance.

33. See AGCA, A1 195 3968.

34. Ibid.

35. See AGCA, A1 5485 47193.

36. Ibid.

37. See AGCA, A1 5485 47194.

38. As one witness put it: "Fue terrible así por estar comprendido en la mayor parte de los milicianos" (It was terrible because the majority [of the rioters] were militia members); AGCA, A1 5485 47193.

39. The Crown eventually commuted all the death sentences to prison terms of various lengths followed by exile from Quetzaltenango.

40. The dual nature of the importance of militia is manifest in the following example from 1819. Following Napoleon's defeat, former milicianos continued to wear their uniforms and enjoy their military privileges and tax exemptions. When the corregidor attempted to revoke this privilege, a former officer protested that "entre tantos pueblos numerosos de Indios . . . que rodean esta cabeza, no hay más tropa que ésta, y según larga experiencia con frecuencia, aún se necesita usar de ella para contenerla" (among the numerous pueblos de indios . . . that surround this city, there are no more troops [than in the city of Quetzaltenango] and, based on long and frequent experience, they are still needed to control [the Indians]). The Audiencia allowed them to retain their fuero and dress; AGCA, A1 199 4046.

41. The following quotations are from AGCA, A1 5488 47202.

42. See AGCA, A1 5487 47198.

43. These claims, however, should be regarded with some skepticism. The cabildo did indeed calm the first day's riot by spreading, "in their tongue," the corregidor's order to expel the three asentistas. But the principales's attempt to distance themselves from the actions of the crowd can be attributable to fear of reprisals. Likewise, the corregidor's testimony that he did not see any blue capes may have been given to protect his allies. Witnesses hostile to Corona testified to the participation of principales during the first day, but it was limited. No principal activity had been reported during the second day of disturbances, when the crowd was described as primarily indigenous.

44. See AGCA, A1 5488 47202.

45. The following analysis draws from Stern, "The Struggle for Solidarity"; Karen Spalding, "Social Climbers: Changing Patterns of Mobility among the Indians of Colonial Peru," *Hispanic American Historical Review* 50, no. 4 (1970): 645–64; Chance, *Conquest of the Sierra*; William B. Taylor, *Landlord and Peasant in Colonial Oaxaca* (Stanford, Calif.: Stanford University Press, 1972); and Terry Rugeley, *Yucatán's Maya Peasantry and the Origins of the Caste War* (Austin: University of Texas Press, 1996). See also Gavin Smith, "The Production of Culture in Local Rebellion," in *Golden Ages, Dark Ages: Imagining the Past in*

Anthropology and History, ed. William Roseberry and Jay O'Brien (Berkeley: University of California Press, 1991).

46. Following the riot, López maintained his alliance with the faction represented by the asentistas. In 1804, he was advanced money on his corn harvest by María Encarnación Güelle, Gutiérrez's wife. See Grandin, "Blood," Appendix 5.

47. See AGCA, A3.4 49 930.

48. Stern, "The Struggle for Solidarity," p. 37. Rugeley, in *Yucatán's Maya Peasantry*, p. 60, writes of the Yucatec Mayan elite: "Their hopes for mobility were greater than those of the Maya masses, but they had also learned something about insecurity. As long as certain colonial status quo persisted, as long as taxation and church patronage continued, there would still be room for middlemen. But if that old status quo were to vanish, then individuals who had prospered as middlemen would risk alienation and downward mobility."

49. The immediate consequences of the riot are ambiguous. The death sentences of the militia members were commuted. Indians and Ladinos were collectively pardoned as a class for their role in the riot, as was Corona, who, after being removed from office, was reinstated. The three asentistas never received compensation for their damage claims. Gutiérrez and Rodríguez temporarily moved out of Quetzaltenango, and the Audiencia ordered Rodríguez to pay to the royal treasury 399 pesos for the nine months he held an asiento. AGCA, A3.4 49 938.

50. See Campbell, *Zapotec Renaissance*, for pacts between Zapotec elites and royal officials to quell indigenous resistance.

51. See AGCA, A1.15 5496 47283.

52. Ibid.

53. See Taracena Arriola, *Invención criolla*, chap. 2, and González, "A History of Los Altos," chap. 4, for a discussion of the emergence of this group.

54. Wortman, *Government and Society*, pp. 204–97.

55. See González, "A History of Los Altos," chap. 5, for the increasing Altense demands.

56. See, for example, AGCA, A1 199 1809.

57. These dates, of course, represent the Túpac Amaru rebellion, the French Revolution, the Haitian Revolution, and the Hidalgo revolt—all frightening (to a certain class) manifestations of popular vengeance. Local riots took place in Cobán in 1803, Sololá in 1813, San Martín Jilotepeque in 1815, and Quetzaltenango in 1786 and 1815.

58. See, for examples, AHQ, Actas, 11 March, 9 August, 27 September, 19 and 22 November 1811, and 6 December 1811.

59. See AHQ, Actas, 19, 22, and 26 November, and 6 December 1811, for example.

60. See AHQ, Actas, 11 March, 9 August, 27 September, and 6 December 1811. See also AGCA, A1 199 4046. The president of the Audiencia likewise cautioned the ayuntamiento to prevent "the poisonous seed [of sedition] from being planted among the lower classes"; AHQ, Actas, 6 December 1811.

61. See AHQ, Actas, 6 December 1811. According to González, "A History of Los Altos," chap. 5, printed matter relating Salvadoran events was censored.

62. See AHQ, Actas, 6 December 1811.

63. See AHQ, Actas, 26, 27, and 29 April 1813.

64. Lira González, *Comunidades indígenas*, p. 202–6, and Pastor, *Campesinos*, 421–22, for examples of how the establishment of municipalities allowed local Hispanic elites access to indigenous resources. But see Guardino, *Peasants*, pp. 88–98, for more emphasis on struggle and contestation between Hispanic and indigenous elites.

65. See AGCA, AI 198 40002, and AHQ, Actas, 3 January 1806. See González, "A History of Los Altos," chap. 4; AGCA, A1.21 197 3993; and AGCA, A1.21.9 197 3994, for the disputes between city and Crown officials.

66. In fact, years prior to the establishment of the ayuntamiento, the corregidor increasingly levied new local taxes to pay for projects outside the purview of the principales; see AGCA, AI 2165 15600; AGCA, AI 2167 15616; and AGCA, AI 391 8150.

67. See AGCA, AI 390 8112.

68. See AGCA, AI 390 8119.

69. See AGCA, AI 390 8116; AGCA, AI 390 8117; AGCA, AI 391 8144; and AGCA, AI 199.

70. See "El síndico del ayuntamiento de Quetzaltenango, pidió la aceptación de las instrucciones," *Boletín de Archivo General de Guatemala* 3, no. 1 (1937): 500–503.

71. See AGCA, AI 390 8117.

72. See Mario Rodríguez, *The Cádiz Experiment in Latin America, 1808–1826* (Berkeley: University of California Press, 1978), pp. 53–86, for a detailed discussion of how these reforms came about.

73. For comparisons with the way events surrounding independence in Mexico affected indigenous communities, see Guardino, *Peasants*; Rugeley, *Yucatán's Maya Peasantry*; and Lira González, *Comunidades indígenas*. In the Yucatán, as in Quetzaltenango, indigenous cabildos were not abolished during the first Spanish constitutional period (1812–14).

74. This is what happened in Quetzaltenango, as we shall see below. See AGCA, 1.21 199 4040.

75. See AGCA, 1.21 199 4040.

76. Ibid. Arguing to the Audiencia that he was left no choice, owing to the intransigence of the principales, the corregidor acceded to the demands and left the tribute in place.

77. See AGCA, AI 5502 47451 and 47460; see also AGCA, 261 5801.

78. For the 1820 tribute uprising in Totonicapán, which raised up an "Indian King," see J. Daniel Contreras, *Una rebelión indígena en el partido de Totonicapán* (Guatemala: Universidad de San Carlos, 1968), and David McCreery, "Atanasio Tzul, Lucas Aguilar, and the Indian Kingdom of Totonicapán," in *The Human*

Tradition in Latin America: The Nineteenth Century, ed. Judith Ewell and William H. Beezley (Wilmington, Del.: Scholarly Resources, 1989).

79. McCreery, "Atanasio Tzul," p. 50.

80. That the corregidor outlawed meetings of K'iche's and Ladinos suggests that, as in 1786, there was fear of cross-ethnic participation.

81. As suggested by McCreery; "Atanasio Tzul," p. 55.

82. McCreery, "Atanasio Tzul," p. 51.

83. Rugeley, *Yucatán's Maya Peasantry*, p. 44.

84. See Lovell, *Conquest and Survival in Guatemala*, pp. 140–72, especially tables 16 to 22. See also Noble David Cook and W. George Lovell, eds., *Secret Judgments of God: Old World Disease in Colonial Spanish America* (Norman: University of Oklahoma Press, 1992).

85. See Lovell, *Conquest and Survival in Guatemala*. This phenomenon continued well into the nineteenth century. In 1884, in Cantel, for example, although hundreds of indigenous children died of whooping cough, no mention of this was made in the local papers or in the departmental archives. See Municipalidad de Cantel, Libro de defunciones, 1884.

86. Catherine J. Kudlick, *Cholera in Post-Revolutionary Paris: A Cultural History* (Berkeley: University of California Press, 1996), pp. 34–36.

87. See Lovell, *Conquest and Survival in Guatemala*, pp. 160–61, for the Crown's more activist stance against an outbreak of smallpox in 1802. See AHQ, tomo 2, Instrucción sobre el modo de practicar la inoculación de las viruelas, y método para curar esta enfermedad acomodado a la naturaleza, y modo de vivir de los indios, del reyno de Guatemala, 1794, for the shift to cure and prevention. See Kudlick, *Cholera*, pp. 34–36, for the birth of the concept of "public health" in Paris. The earliest mention I found in Quetzaltenango of *salud pública* was in a municipal memo that refers to an outbreak of smallpox in 1815; AHQ, 1815. See also AHQ, Actas, 28 July 1826, for "public health" in reference to the moving of the cemetery away from the population.

88. See Ramón Salazar, *Historia del desenvolvimiento intelectual de Guatemala* (Guatemala City: Tipografía Nacional, 1897), chap. 8, and Lovell, *Conquest and Survival in Guatemala*, p. 162, for the mission.

89. Lovell, *Conquest and Survival in Guatemala*, p. 162.

90. See AGCA, AI 119 4029 and 4039, and AHQ, 1815.

91. See AGCA, A1.47 261 5726.

92. Ibid.

93. Ibid.

94. In Comitancillo, for example, the priest from Tejutla reported that since the indigenous authorities were not cooperating and the houses were dispersed, hardly anybody had been vaccinated; AGCA, A1.47 261 5726.

95. See AGCA, A1.47 261 5726.

96. Ibid.

97. See AGCA, A1.47 261 5805.

98. Ibid.

99. See AGCA, A1.47 261 5801.

100. See AGCA, A1 5502 47450.

101. See AHQ, Actas, 4 April 1826, and 12 and 21 May 1826.

102. Cemetery reforms will be discussed in greater detail in chap. 3.

103. See AHQ, Actas, 28 July 1826.

104. See AHQ, Actas, 28 July, and 1 and 2 August 1826.

105. For a discussion of political rivalries in Quetzaltenango that might have led to Flores's death, see Taracena Arriola, *Invención criolla*, pp. 115–19. See also González, "A History of Los Altos," chap. 7; cf. Julio César de la Roca, *Biografía de un pueblo: Síntesis monográfica de Quetzaltenango, interpretación de su destino* (Guatemala City: Editorial José de Pineda Ibarra, 1966), pp. 269–301, for a collection of primary documents related to the attack.

106. See Alejandro Marure, *Bosquejo histórico de las revoluciones de Centro-America: Desde 1811 hasta 1834* (Guatemala, 1877).

107. Rugeley, *Yucatán's Maya Peasantry*, pp. 44–52.

108. See AGCA, A1 391 8153.

109. Ibid.

110. In 1826, for example, during the outbreak of smallpox, they attended municipal sessions and were placed on the vaccination committee and the *junta de sanidad*; AHQ, Actas, 18 June 1824, and 14 July 1826.

111. Guatemala, *Recopilación de leyes agrarias* (Guatemala: Tipográfico La Unión, 1890), pp. 52–59.

112. Ibid.; see articles 22 to 24, p. 55.

113. See ibid., pp. 59–73, for the laws; see McCreery, *Rural Guatemala*, pp. 55–58, for a discussion of the subject.

114. See Ingersoll, "The War of the Mountain," pp. 45–76; McCreery, *Rural Guatemala*, p. 56; and Miceli, "Rafael Carrera." See also Michael Forrest Fry, "Agrarian Society in the Guatemalan Montaña, 1700–1840" (Ph.D., diss., Tulane, 1988), pp. 222–27, for eastern Guatemala.

115. McCreery, *Rural Guatemala*, p. 56.

116. Valerio Ignacio Rivas, *Vindicación que hace Valerio Ignacio Rivas sobre la impostura que el C. Macario Rodas le suscitó en el Departamento de Quetzaltenango: Infracciones cometidas por el juez de primera instancia de aquella ciudad, y avances de poder cometidos en su persona e intereses por el que se dice gobierno provisorio de Los Altos* (Guatemala: Imprenta del Gobierno, 1838); see also AGCA, B100.1 1418 33196 and 33221, for documents related to Rivas's accusations. Guzmán would later lead Los Altos's defending force that was defeated by Carrera's invading army.

117. Guatemala, *Recopilación de leyes agrarias*, p. 58, article 25.

118. Ibid., p. 53, article 5.

119. See AHQ, Actas, 21 July 1826.

120. Ibid., 14 October 1825.

121. Ibid., 1 August 1826.

122. Ibid., 1 and 4 August 1826.

123. See AHQ, caja 1826.

124. Ibid.

125. It was not until 1835 that Ladinos again raised the land issue. This time it was in response to the 1832 land tax, which assessed a half peso on each caballería of land. Principales once more claimed that the city's land documents were lost. Accusing them of lying, the head of the commission charged with surveying claimed that these same indigenous authorities had only recently presented their titles during a land conflict with a neighboring pueblo. "These documents," the surveyor admonished, "should always be kept in a public archive," thus nicely capturing the tension that ensues when a bureaucratizing state confronts popular custom and subaltern resistance; see AHQ, caja 1835.

126. See AHQ, Actas, 8 August 1826.

Chapter 3   A Pestilent Nationalism: The 1837 Cholera Epidemic Reconsidered

1. For a brilliant discussion of how the complex, contradictory, permutations of blood, bodies, and culture play out across class, ethnic, and gender lines in Guatemala, see Diane Nelson, *A Finger in the Wound*.

2. See chap. 6.

3. See Ingersoll, "The War of the Mountain," p. 45; Fry, "Agrarian Society," pp. 226–30; McCreery, *Rural Guatemala*, pp. 23, 56; and Miceli, "Rafael Carrera." For the nineteenth-century liberal polemics, see Montúfar y Rivera Maestre, *Reseña histórica*, vol. 1, pp. x–xi; vol. 2, pp. v–vii.

4. See Taracena's conclusion in *Invención criolla*.

5. See Christopher H. Lutz, *Santiago de Guatemala, 1541–1773* (Norman: University of Oklahoma Press, 1994).

6. See AGCA-ST, I 17.

7. See Nelson, *A Finger in the Wound*, especially chap. 6, "Bodies That Splatter."

8. Marta Casaus Arzú, *Guatemala: Linaje y racismo* (Guatemala City: Facultad Latinoamericana de Ciencias Sociales, 1995), pp. 119–26. See also Carol A. Smith, "Origins of the National Question in Guatemala: A Hypothesis," in Smith, ed., *Guatemalan Indians and the State*, pp. 86–87.

9. Publicly describing all non-Indians as Ladinos started in the colonial period. Since Quetzaltenango was a pueblo de indios, the church maintained only one set of baptism, marriage, and death books until the mid-eighteenth century. At that point it started a separate series of Ladino records that included all non-Indians: marriage books start in 1740, deaths in 1796, and baptisms in the 1780s (the first volume is missing; the second starts in 1789). For example, fourteen-year-old don Manuel, born in Galicia, Spain (4 September 1804), an anonymous forastero (outsider) found dead on the road into town (13 October 1796), a

woman with a distinct K'iche' surname, Luiza Antonia Coyoy (9 June 1799), and don Nicolás Franco (16 December 1807), an important city politician and merchant, could all be recorded in the first *libro de ladinos difuntos*. See also the city's *padrones*, which in 1813 broke the city's population into four categories— españoles, mestizos, ladinos, and indios—yet in 1826 used only the categories indígenas and ladinos. See AHA 1 10, 1813, and AHQ, caja 1826. Also following independence, the Spanish ayuntamiento was referred to as the Municipalidad de Ladinos.

10. There was little effort on the part of Crown officials to apply blood standards unless they were forced to, as in the impeachment proceedings against Manuel Silverio.

11. Casaus Arzú, *Guatemala: Linaje y racismo*, pp. 119–23. Lorenzo Montúfar had no doubts as to the genetic makeup of Guatemalan elites: "Mientras más antiguas sean las familias centro-americanas, más clara es su procedencia indígena" (The older the Central American family, the clearer is their indigenous provenance); Montúfar, *Reseña histórica*, vol. 1, p. xi.

12. For colonial examples, see the discussions of Altense petitions presented to the Cortes de Cádiz in chap. 2 and, more fully, in Grandin, "Blood," chap. 2.

13. See Kudlick, *Cholera*, pp. 31–64, for a similar process in Paris.

14. For France, see Louis Chevalier, *Laboring Classes and Dangerous Classes in Paris during the First Half of the Nineteenth Century*, trans. Frank Jellinek (Princeton: Princeton University Press, 1973); François Delaporte, *Disease and Civilization: The Cholera in Paris, 1832*, trans. Arthur Goldhammer (Cambridge: MIT Press, 1986); and Kudlick, *Cholera*; for the United States, see Charles Rosenberg, *The Cholera Years: The United States in 1832, 1849, and 1866* (Chicago: University of Chicago Press, 1987); and for Italy, see Frank Snowden, "Cholera in Barletta, 1910," *Past and Present* 132 (Aug. 1991): 67–103.

15. The equation of indigenous culture with disease would continue to resonate throughout the twentieth century. This is nowhere more obvious than in the *indigenista* fiction of the 1930s and 1940s, of which the epigraph at the beginning of this chapter is an example. See, for example, Mario Monteforte Toledo, *Entre la piedra y la cruz* (Guatemala City: Editorial El Libro de Guatemala, 1948).

16. David Arnold, *Colonizing the Body: State Medicine and Epidemic Disease in Nineteenth-Century India* (Berkeley: University of California Press, 1993), p. 162.

17. R. J. Evans, "Epidemics and Revolutions: Cholera in Nineteenth-Century Europe," *Past and Present* 120 (Aug. 1988): 123–45. See Kudlick, *Cholera*, pp. 53–63, for the disease's association with poverty; see Rosenberg, *The Cholera Years*, pp. 55–64, for its connection with African-Americans, the Irish, and poverty in U.S. cities; and for its association with colonialism and race in India, see Arnold, *Colonizing the Body*, pp. 159–99. See also Pedro Molina, *Instrucción, preservativa, y curativa de cólera morbus* (Guatemala City: Imprenta Nueva, 1832), for an 1832 guide to cholera based on information received from Paris and written by a Guatemalan physician.

18. See AGQ, 1834, 1835, and 1836.

19. See AHQ, Actas, 4 April 1837, for the supplies; see Horacio Figueroa Marro-quín, *Biografía del Doctor José Luna Arbizú* (Guatemala City: Tipografía Nacio-nal, 1983), p. 35, for the 1835 scare.

20. Kudlick, *Cholera*, pp. 75–81; for the debate in the United States, see Rosen-berg, *The Cholera Years*, pp. 73–81.

21. The Parisian medical community during this time was increasingly influ-enced by the emerging Lamarckian belief that changes brought about in a species from the environment would be passed down to future generations. While there is debate as to just how influential Lamarck's ideas were when they were first presented at the beginning of the nineteenth century, it is clear that they were part of an intellectual milieu that increasingly focused on environmental regulation as a means of promoting generational improvement. See Pietro Corsi, *The Age of Lamarck: Evolutionary Theories in France, 1790–1830*, trans. Jonathan Mendel-baum (Berkeley: University of California Press, 1988), and Nancy Leys Stepan, *"The Hour of Eugenics": Race, Gender, and Nation in Latin America* (Ithaca, N.Y.: Cornell University Press, 1991), pp. 64–76.

22. Kudlick, *Cholera*, p. 77.

23. Rosenberg, *The Cholera Years*, pp. 78–79.

24. Kudlick, *Cholera*, pp. 77–78.

25. Charles Rosenberg, *The Cholera Years*, pp. 79–81.

26. In Latin America, French was usually the second language of elites, medical professionals went to France to receive their training, and many of the scientific works from Europe made their way to Latin American nations in French transla-tion. See Stepan, *"The Hour of Eugenics,"* pp. 72–73.

27. Figueroa Marroquín, *Biografía del Doctor José Luna Arbizú*, p. 29.

28. The opinion is in AGCA, B 1102 24410; a copy of it is in AGQ, 1834. The French works cited in the opinion are F. J. V. Broussais, *Le choléra-morbus épidé-mique observé et traité selon la méthode physiologique* (Paris, 1832), and Alexandre Moreau de Jonnès, *Rapport au conseil supérieur de santé sur le choléra-morbus pestilentiel* (Paris, 1832). See also Molina, *Instrucción*; Mariano Padilla, *Método de precaver, conocer, y curar el cólera mórbus* (Guatemala City: Academia de Ciencias, 1837); and Pedro Vázquez, *Método curativo del cólera-morbo* (Guatemala City: Academia de Ciencias, 1837).

29. See AGCA, B 1102 24410.

30. Padilla, *Método de precaver*, p. 9.

31. Molina, *Instrucción*, and Padilla, *Método de precaver*.

32. Padilla, *Método de precaver*, p. 8.

33. Ibid., pp. 5–6.

34. See AGCA, B 2521 56993, and AGCA, B 2521 56997.

35. See AGCA, B 1103 24445 and 24471. For death tolls in the east, see Ingersoll, "The War of the Mountain," p. 99.

36. See the Acuerdos of 23 September 1836 and 18, 19, 29, and 31 March 1837, in

Manuel Pineda de Mont, ed., *Recopilación de las leyes de Guatemala, compuesta y arreglada por don Manuel Pineda de Mont, à virtud de orden especial del gobierno supremo de la república*, vol. 1 (Guatemala City: Imprenta de la Paz, 1869–72), pp. 704–10.

37. Ingersoll, "The War of the Mountain," p. 97.

38. Ibid.

39. Ibid.

40. See AGCA, B 82.3 1094 24006 for instructions in 1826 to prevent the spread of measles, which foreshadowed some of the earlier anticholera initiatives.

41. Figueroa Marroquín, *Biografía del Doctor José Luna Arbizú*, p. 20, and Kudlick, *Cholera*, pp. 187–88.

42. See AGCA, B 1102 24446, folio 1.

43. See AGCA, B 1103 24471, and AGCA, B 1102 24446, folio 55. See Rosenberg, *The Cholera Years*, p. 30, for a prohibition against raw fruit and vegetables in New York. See AGCA, B 1102 24410, for the French opinion that cherries caused cholera.

44. See AGCA, B 1102 24446, folio 55.

45. Ibid.; see also AGCA, B 3588 82118.

46. See AGCA, B 1104 24560.

47. See AGCA, B 2521 56993.

48. See AGCA, B 1105 24560, folio 51.

49. See AGCA, B 1104 24545, folio 49.

50. *Boletín Extraordinario*, 21 April 1837, located in AHQ.

51. See AGCA, B 1106 24572, folio 216, and AGCA, B 1105 24560, folio 51.

52. See AGCA, B 1104 24538.

53. See AGCA, B 1105 24560, folio 32.

54. Ibid., folio 106.

55. See Ingersoll, "The War of the Mountain," pp. 99–113.

56. See AGCA, B 1104 24558, and AGCA, B 3588 82091.

57. See AGCA, B 1105 24570.

58. See AGCA, B 1102 24345, folio 10. These suspicions were not unique to Guatemala's rural population. In 1832, in Paris, rumors spread that cholera was in fact a plot by elements of the bourgeoisie to rid the city of the lower classes. See Kudlick, *Cholera*, pp. 183–92.

59. See AGCA, B 3588 82114, and AGCA, B 1104 24545, folio 12.

60. Louis Chevalier, ed. *Le Choléra: La Premiere Épidémie du dix-neuvième siècle* (La Roche-sur-Yon: Centrale de L'Ouest, 1958), p. 13. Quoted in Kudlick, *Cholera*, p. 3. For the growing sense of panic among Guatemala City's political elites, see the series of letters between Gálvez and José Barrundia published by the newpaper *La Oposición*, which can be located in the Colección Valenzuela. The panic among state agents may be judged from the government's order that all public employees remain at their post and refrain from leaving their towns; *Boletín Extraordinario*, 21 April 1837.

61. The *Boletines de Cólera* were obviously modeled after the *Bulletins du Choléra*, a newsletter distributed in Paris during the 1832 epidemic; they most likely reflect the influence of Dr. José Luna Arbizú. See Kudlick, *Cholera*, pp. 123–32.

62. *Boletín de Cólera Morbo*, 21 April 1837.

63. Ibid.

64. See AGCA, Actas, 13 April 1837.

65. See, for example, the numerous documents related to the epidemic in AHQ, caja 1837, and AGQ, 1837. See also AHQ, Actas, 24 April, 30 June, and 5 July 1837.

66. By 14 June, cholera was in nearly every indigenous pueblo of the department of Sololá; AGCA, B 3588 82116. In that department's capital, of the 56 deaths that occurred, 52 were Indians. In Panajachel, a pueblo de indios, there were over 100 deaths. See González, "A History of Los Altos," chap. 8. In Chichicastenango, another pueblo de indios, by 31 July there were 154 deaths reported; AGCA, B 1106 24576.

67. See AHQ, Actas, 5 July 1837.

68. For the broadsheets, see AHQ, Actas, 25 April 1837; for the *juntas de caridad*, see AHQ, Actas, 13 July 1837; for the commissions, see AHQ, Actas, 24 April and 5 July 1837.

69. For the cordon, see AHQ, Actas, 29 April 1837; for the quarantine, see AHQ, Actas, 16 June 1837.

70. See AHQ, Actas, 26 June 1837.

71. See AHQ, Actas, 29 April 1837.

72. See AHQ, Actas, 19 April 1837.

73. See AHQ, Actas, 13 April 1837.

74. Ibid.

75. See discussion in González, "A History of Los Altos," chap. 8.

76. See AHQ, Actas, 12 May, 8 June, and 16 June 1837.

77. See AHQ, Actas, 8 June 1837. See also AHQ, Actas, 12 July 1837. The smallpox attack of 1826 led municipal authorities to try to borrow money from cofradías as well; AHQ, Actas, 18 July 1826. Similarly, the municipality used cofradía money for the water project, a "work of true urgency"; see AGQ, Informes . . . relativos . . . a la . . . obra de la introducción de la agua, 1834.

78. See AHQ, Actas, 13 July 1837. Some money was collected, however, as Indians took advantage of an 1848 visit by Guatemala's archbishop to complain that the municipality had never paid back the one thousand pesos it appropriated from a cofradía. See AHA, tomo 47, Visita de García Peláez.

79. See AHQ, Actas, 23 May 1837.

80. See AHQ, Actas, 6 and 12 May 1837; also AHQ, Actas, 13 July 1837.

81. See AHQ, Actas, 26 June 1837, and 13 and 18 July 1837.

82. Taracena Arriola, *Invención criolla*, p. 308.

83. See AHQ, Actas, 25 June 1837.

84. See *El Editor*, 31 August 1837.

85. See González, "A History of Los Altos," chap. 8, for the lifting of the tax; Ingersoll, "The War of the Mountain," pp. 132–33, for the judicial reforms; and McCreery, *Rural Guatemala*, p. 56, for the suspension of the land laws.

86. See AHQ, Actas, 26 June 1837.

87. MacLeod, *Spanish Central America*, pp. 98–100, lists over thirty highland epidemics between 1519 and 1746; Lovell, *Conquest and Survival in Guatemala*, p. 149, counts twenty-two for the Cuchumatanes alone.

88. See AHQ, Actas, 6 April 1824, and 28 July 1826.

89. Regarding Indians' refusal to present themselves, one doctor complained that he "had not cured one Indian, because not one has called on my services"; AHQ, caja 1837.

90. See AHQ, Actas, 20 July 1837.

91. See AHQ, padrón, 1830.

92. See AHQ, caja 1837.

93. See AGQ, 1837.

94. Stephens, *Incidents of Travel*, pp. 371–72.

95. Douglass Creed Sullivan-González, *Piety, Power, and Politics: Religion and Nation Formation in Guatemala, 1821–1871* (Pittsburgh: University of Pittsburgh Press, 1998).

96. Sullivan-González, *Piety, Power, and Politics*, chap. 3.

97. See AEQ, Libro de defunción de indígenas, no. 8.

98. On 19 May 1804, for example, the widow María Tzó was entombed in the cathedral, in the chapel of the cofradía Nuestra Señora del Rosario, and on 5 July, don Anizeto López was buried in the cathedral; see AEQ, Libro de defunción de indígenas, no. 8. For church burials into the 1820s, see, for examples, AEQ, Libro de defunción de indígenas; no. 10, 22 April 1825; 14 and 26 January 1826; and 6 February 1826.

99. See AHQ, Actas, 28 July 1826.

100. See AHQ, caja 1837.

101. See AEQ. For the Libro defunción de indígenas, no. 10, there are no entries between 1 July and 20 October; for the Libro de ladinos, no. 3, there are no entries between 30 June and 9 October; and for the Libro de párvulos, no. 6, there are none between 29 June and 12 November.

102. See AHQ, Actas, 30 June 1837.

103. Ibid.

104. See AHQ, Actas, 23 June and 5 July 1837.

105. See AHQ, Actas, 18 July 1837.

106. See AHQ, Actas, 5 July 1837, and AGQ, 1837.

107. Cambranes, *Café y campesinos*, p. 71. But see Steven Palmer's comparison between Costa Rican and Guatemalan nationalism. Palmer argues against common conceptions that the second liberal state was being influenced by the biolog-

ical component of Herbert Spencer's social Darwinism. Rather, for prominent liberal thinkers, it was culture and history that formed race. See Steven Palmer's "A Liberal Discipline," chap. 7, especially pp. 174–81, and "Racismo intelectual en Costa Rica y Guatemala, 1870–1920," *Mesoamérica* 31 (1996): 99–121. Palmer, however, misses the ways Guatemalan reformers understood culture, environment, and history within a Lamarckian framework of racial transformation.

108. Alan Knight, in his essay on Mexican indigenismo, makes the following point regarding nationalism based on culture and environment rather than blood: "To equate ethnicity and race, and to suppose that they determine significant ascribed characteristics of such strength and staying power that they are, in practical terms, immutable, is to fall prey to racism, even if those characteristics are not alleged to be biologically determined. In other words, if Mexican Indians are what they are because of environmental pressures—and what they are scarcely admits of change, since it is part of their very being—then the question of whether biological, environmental, or historical factors determined this being is secondary. It is the inescapable ascription that counts"; Knight, "Racism, Revolution and Indigenismo," p. 93.

109. Stepan, *"The Hour of Eugenics,"* pp. 67–76.

110. Ibid., p. 84.

111. Ibid., p. 85.

112. See AHQ, Actas, 13 April 1837.

113. For a more detailed analysis of the long, slow rise and quick fall (1838–40) of the Estado de Los Altos than that which will be offered here, see Taracena Arriola, *Invención criolla*. The inability of the Ladinos to establish cultural or political legitimacy among the majority of the population resulted in an increased reliance on force to maintain order. In the years prior to the separation of the Estado de los Altos, fear of both conservative efforts to retake power and indigenous unrest had led the national government to fortify Los Altos's defenses; Taracena Arriola, *Invención criolla*, chap. 6, pp. 149–62. See also González, "A History of Los Altos," chap. 8. As the region grew in military importance, Altenses developed not only a deeper sense of regional identity but the strength to pursue their long-sought independence. If during the last decades of Spanish colonialism, the Altenses' fear of popular rebellion forced them to remain loyal to the Crown, now an expanded army gave them the nerve to go it alone. In the years leading up to and following their separation from Guatemala, indigenous communities became increasingly disaffected with Ladino designs, and Altenses would repeatedly need to dispatch troops to repress riots and uprisings in nearby towns. See González, "A History of Los Altos," chaps. 9 and 10. Indeed, although support for Carrera remained fragmented and contained in the highlands, the first major uprising against Gálvez's reforms took place a short distance from Quetzaltenango, in San Juan Ostuncalco on 6 March 1837. See González, "A History of Los Altos," chap. 8.

Chapter 4   A House with Two Masters:
Carrera and the Restored Republic of Indians

1. The following description of Good Friday, 1840, is drawn from Stephens, *Incidents of Travel*, pp. 212–13.

2. For a more detailed examination of these reforms than will be offered here, see Rodríguez, *The Cádiz Experiment*, chap. 9, and Ralph Lee Woodward, "The Aftermath of Independence, 1821–c.1870," in *Central America since Independence*, ed. Leslie Bethell (Cambridge: Cambridge University Press, 1991), pp. 7–20.

3. See Rodríguez, "The Livingston Codes."

4. Taracena Arriola, *Invención criolla*, p. 309.

5. Jorge Skinner-Klée, ed. *Legislación indigenista de Guatemala*, 2d ed. (Mexico: Instituto Indigenista Interamericano, 1995), p. 20. See p. 17 for the quote.

6. Skinner-Klée, ed., *Legislación indigenista*, p. 17.

7. See AHQ, Actas, 15 September 1826.

8. Ibid., 18 June 1824.

9. See AHQ, Libro en que se asienta las certificaciones y recibos de las cantidades que se enteran en la administración de rentas del departamento respecto a la contribución directa, 1833–36. Despite the liberals' fetishism of individuals, city K'iche's, when it suited Ladinos' interests, were still treated as a corporate class. In an aborted attempt to collect the tax in 1830, an assessment was made of how much the city's population was expected to pay. K'iche' authorities were summoned, and after a "long discussion" it was decided that the parcialidad de indígenas was to pay collectively 1,500 pesos. For Ladinos, a census was conducted and individuals were assessed varying amounts. See AHQ, Padrón de contribuyentes de esta ciudad, 1830. See David McCreery, *Desarrollo Económico y política nacional: El Ministerio de Fomento de Guatemala, 1871–1885*, trans. Stephen Webre (Antigua: Centro de Investigaciones Regionales de Mesoamérica, 1981), pp. 138–42, for other examples of Indians who continued to be treated collectively.

10. See Jean Piel, *Sajcabaja: Muerte y resurección de un pueblo de Guatemala, 1500–1970* (Mexico: CEMCA/Seminario de Integración Social de Guatemala, 1989), pp. 284–85, for this strategy that was used during the 1820 Tzul uprising; see Taracena Arriola, *Invención criolla*, 315–19, for its deployment during the Estado de Los Altos; and Greg Grandin, "The Strange Case of 'La Mancha Negra': Maya-State Relations in Nineteenth-Century Guatemala," *Hispanic American Historical Review* 77, no. 2 (1997): 211–43, for a discussion on how its effectiveness evolved throughout the nineteenth century.

11. Taracena Arriola, *Invención criolla*, p. 312. Many of these letters are reprinted in Montúfar y Rivera Maestre, *Reseña histórica*, vol. 3, pp. 152–55.

12. Taracena Arriola, *Invención criolla*, p. 312.

13. Ibid. See also AHQ, Sobre reclamo de los vecinos de esta ciudad para que sean abolidos los impuestos municipales, 1831. Indians from surrounding towns

accused the toll collectors of using "violent and offensive means" to collect the taxes. Municipal authorities complained that the city has become the "hated target of all the surrounding towns." Traders now circumvented the town to avoid—as the Ladinos say the Indians put it—the "thieving Quetzaltecos."

14. Taracena Arriola, *Invención criolla*, p. 314. See also Ingersoll, "The War of the Mountain."

15. Carrera evoked fears of caste war to forestall the development of any possible oppositional alliance between Los Altos and the Oriente, and he used his ability to call on militant indigenous support to check both liberal and conservative elites. For how evocations of a caste war played out in the city of Quetzaltenango during Carrera's first two forays into Los Altos, see Taracena Arriola, *Invención criolla*, pp. 319–21. For references to events in Yucatán in 1848 and 1849, see ibid., pp. 373–74, and AGCA, B 28547 203 and 28549 7.

16. See Skinner-Klée, ed., *Legislación indigenista*, pp. 22–33. See especially decrees 17 August 1839, 26 November 1839, 29 March 1845, 3 October 1851, and 8 November 1851. See also Pineda de Mont, ed., *Recopilación de las leyes*, pp. 847–48.

17. Taracena Arriola, *Invención criolla*, p. 325. See also Grandin, "La Mancha Negra," for the case of Cantel.

18. See Woodward, *Rafael Carrera*, p. 423, for a suggestion that cochineal production provided respite from demands placed on indigenous communities.

19. See McCreery, *Rural Guatemala*, p. 114, and Robert Williams, *States and Social Evolution: Coffee and the Rise of National Governments in Central America* (Chapel Hill: University of North Carolina Press, 1994), pp. 24–31.

20. See González, "A History of Los Altos;" Ingersoll, "The War of the Mountain"; Miceli, "Rafael Carrera"; Taracena Arriola, *Invención criolla*; and Woodward, *Rafael Carrera*.

21. See Rugeley, *Yucatán's Maya Peasantry*, p. 49, for the importance of corporal punishment in maintaining order in indigenous communities.

22. Skinner-Klée, ed., *Legislación indigenista*, pp. 30–31.

23. Ibid., p. 30.

24. See AHQ, caja 1853.

25. Many recent investigations have focused on the continuities between the first liberal government, the Carrera period, and the liberal restoration of 1871. For an excellent treatment of the ongoing secularization of the state, see Sullivan-González, *Piety, Power, and Politics*, particularly his conclusion. For the foundation laid of the second liberal state during the Carrera period, see Gudmunson and Lindo-Fuentes, *Central America*. See Woodward, *Rafael Carrera*, pp. 422–27, for Carrera's policy toward Indians.

26. Skinner-Klée, ed., *Legislación indigenista*, p. 23.

27. Decreto de la Asamblea Constituyente, de 26 de noviembre de 1839, declarando a quién corresponde el nombramiento de los Gobernadores de Indígenas, y las atribuciones de éstos, in Skinner-Klée, *Legislación indigenista*, p. 24. A copy can also be found in AHQ, caja 1840.

28. A later modification (1851) demanded that gobernadores, in order to prevent abuses, needed to be "of the same class" as Indians; Skinner-Klée, *Legislación indigenista*, p. 31. But this imprecise qualification is a far cry from the blood restrictions that allowed for the divestment of Manuel Silverio in 1785.

29. See AGCA, B 2826 373.

30. Skinner-Klée, ed., *Legislación indigenista*, p. 31.

31. See AGCA, B 28537 42.

32. "José María Paz has conducted himself very well in the position of gobernador. It is difficult to find another Indian who works as well with Ladinos and who maintains the tranquillity of the naturales"; AGCA, B 28537 42.

33. For the Ladino protest and the corregidor's decision, see the numerous letters related to the conflict in AHQ, caja 1840. The ley de municipalidades was passed by the Asamblea on 2 October 1839; see Pineda de Mont, ed., *Recopilación de las leyes*, tomo 1, pp. 504–11.

34. The following petition can be found in AHQ, caja 1846. Carrera was a master at playing liberals and conservatives off against each other. In 1844, he officially gained the presidency for the first time, aided by liberal support. In September 1845, the national congress, influenced by this brief liberal comeback, repealed some of the protections afforded to Indians. The Quetzaltenango municipality undoubtedly tried to take advantage of this change in the political current with their 1846 petition. Despite the 1845 law, in 1846, the *ministro de relaciones del gobierno* wrote the corregidor that "having seen how the 1845 congressional decree regarding municipal elections has caused a commotion in indigenous pueblos and is dangerous to the public order, the president orders that no change be made from past laws and old customs." Uprisings in the east and liberal opposition forced Carrera into a brief exile in 1847. Following his return to power in 1848, Carrera ruled Guatemala until his death in 1865 in a close, but mutually suspicious, alliance with the church and conservatives. This conservative alliance accounts for the flurry of new indigenista legislation in 1851. For a concise discussion of these political switchbacks, see Woodward, "The Aftermath of Independence," pp. 20–21. For the 1845 law, see Pineda de Mont, ed., *Recopilación de las leyes*, tomo 1, pp. 572–74.

35. See AGQ, 1846.

36. The minister's ruling is quoted in a letter from the corregidor informing the Ladino municipality of the decision; see AHQ, caja 1847.

37. See AHQ, caja 1847.

38. See AHQ, caja 1845.

39. Ibid.

40. See AHQ, caja 1830. See AHA 1 10, for an 1813 padrón supervised by the priest. See Pineda de Mont, ed., *Recopilación de las leyes*, tomo 1, p. 855, for instructions in 1831 that placed the municipality in charge of conducting population counts.

41. In 1847, for example, the corregidor sent a census form to the Ladino

municipality to conduct a tally of the Ladino population. "With respect to the Indians," the corregidor went on, "I have sent their authorities instructions on how to conduct their census"; AHQ, caja 1847.

42. See AHQ, caja 1840.

43. The conservative government made significant efforts to encourage capitalist development, providing tariff exemptions for new crops and encouraging communities to rent unused land. See, especially, Gudmunson and Lindo-Fuentes, *Central America*; For land rental, see McCreery, *Rural Guatemala*, pp. 122, 163–64.

44. Woodward, "The Aftermath of Independence," pp. 32–36.

45. See Williams, *States and Social Evolution*, pp. 24–31, and Wortman, *Government and Society*, pp. 219, 241–45, 248–59.

Chapter 5 Principales to Patrones, Macehuales to Mozos:
Land, Labor, and the Commodification of Community

1. For the nature of the liberal state, see Cambranes, *Café y campesinos*; McCreery, *Rural Guatemala*; and Carol A. Smith, "Local History in a Global Context: Social and Economic Transitions in Western Guatemala," *Comparative Studies in Society and History* 26, no. 2 (1984): 193–228.

2. See González, "A History of Los Altos," and Taracena Arriola, *Invención criolla*.

3. For one such Highland family, the Sánchezes, see Nora Thompson, *Delfino Sanchez: A Guatemalan Statesman, 1840–1885* (Ardmore, Pa.: Nora Thompson, 1977), pp. 25–94.

4. See González, "A History of Los Altos," chaps. 12 and 13, for the Altense elites' transformation into coffee finqueros. At the turn of the twentieth century, a little less than half of all the coffee finqueros in the coffee piedmont south of the city lived in Quetzaltenango; AHQ, Censo de fincas de café, 1907.

5. As previously indicated, historians have recently attempted to stress continuities extending from the colonial period through the second liberal period in the state's relationship with its majority Indian population. McCreery's *Rural Guatemala* is the most important effort in this direction so far. Nevertheless, it needs to be stressed that coffee cultivation *was* different. Never before in Guatemala's history — not with cacao, not with tribute payment, not with indigo, and not with cochineal — was so much land and labor required for production. For all its abuse, exploitation, and destructiveness to communal relations, Guatemala's colonial labor drafts, in the end, pale in comparison to their coffee counterparts. See David McCreery, "Coffee and Class: The Structure of Development in Liberal Guatemala," *Hispanic American Historical Review* 56, no. 3 (1976): 438–60, p. 456.

6. Part of the liberal state's strategy of highland control, especially under Barrios, entailed giving large tracts of land to Ladino towns, which in turn sup-

plied men for regional militia units. In 1883, Barrios expropriated ten caballerías from Cajolá, a Mam town, and gave it to San Carlos Sija, a nearby Ladino municipality. Also in that year, he gave ten caballerías of land belonging to Cantel, a K'iche' pueblo, to Salcajá, another Ladino municipality. See Grandin, "La Mancha Negra." In Quetzaltenango, however, Barrios was careful not to anger the town's indigenous population, as will be seen below.

7. See Guatemala, *Recopilación de leyes agrarias*; McCreery, "State Power"; and Julio César Méndez Montenegro, *444 años de legislación agraria, 1513–1957* (Guatemala City: Imprenta Universitaria, 1961).

8. See, McCreery, "State Power," pp. 106–7. In fact, the ability to dispense or take away large tracts of municipal land was key in Barrios's caudillo management style. See Grandin, "La Mancha Negra."

9. K'iche' authorities facilitated the privatization process. The Municipalidad de Indígenas, which Ladino officers did not attempt to abolish until much later in the century, was responsible for distributing the land, and, later, it advocated on behalf of the beneficiaries who sought titles to their concessions. See AHQ, Yndice del libro de concesiones del Llano del Pinal, 1889; AHQ, Sobre repartir el terreno de Chichiquitán, 1892; and AHQ, La Municipalidad Indígena pide se mande otorgar certificaciones de propiedad a los agraciados con el terreno "Xechiguitán," 1895.

10. Prior to the establishment of a national property registry in 1879, in Quetzaltenango individuals were required to register their land in Libros de Matrículas, which ran from 1874 to 1879.

11. See AGQ, Libro Quinto de Matrículas de Terrenos, 1875–79, 1879. For other examples, see Cresencio Sáenz's registration of 2 caballerías and Roberto Nimatuj's registration of 166 cuerdas of corn and wheat land, both in AGQ, Libro de anotaciones de los matriculantes de terrenos, 1876. There exists in the AHQ over three hundred requests for *títulos supletorios*, mostly from the years 1879 (this is the year the national registry was established; title was needed to register) and 1884, primarily from K'iche' medium-size landholders. See, for example, Bernardino Coyoy's request for titles for five lots of property, ranging from thirty to seventy cuerdas, which he claims to have come into the possession of through a combination of inheritance and purchase. See also AGCA, index for Quetzaltenango's Segundo Juzgado de Primera Instancia, Civil, which lists twenty-nine *legajos* of títulos supletorios from the years 1898 to 1945.

12. See AGQ, Libro Quinto de Matrículas de Terrenos, 1875–79.

13. This mostly occurred in the area east of the city known as La Ciénaga. In 1877, fifteen manzanas of rented land were converted into the private property of seven Ladinos. Individuals also used the 1877 decree to purchase stores they rented on the plaza. See AHQ, Denuncias de algunos particulares hechas en virtud de la ley de redención de censos, 1877. For a discussion of the law, see McCreery, "State Power," pp. 106–7.

14. See AHQ, Yndice del libro de concesiones del Llano del Pinal, 1889.

15. See AHQ, caja 1876.

16. See AGQ, 1887.

17. See AHQ, caja 1892. In this distribution, 1,418 cuerdas were apportioned among 387 male K'iche's.

18. What is considered unsuitable corresponds of course to need. In 1744, principales claimed that only 117 caballerías within the municipal limits were farmable; in 1882, 150 were considered arable; see AGCA-ST, 30 1 and AHQ, caja 1882. It is doubtful that this extension was accompanied by an intensification of production. Data indicate that between the 1880s and the early 1900s, yields per cuerda remained the same. One hundred cuerdas of land produced roughly forty-five fanegas of corn or thirty fanegas of wheat; see AHQ, caja 1882, and the 1901 *Ministerio de Fomento* survey.

19. See chap. 6.

20. See AHQ, Libro de ejidos, 1879.

21. See AHQ, Tomás Pac quejándose de la comisión que fue a medir su terreno, caja 1892, and Tomás Pac y Pioquinto Guzmán presentan sus títulos, 1895; see also AGQ, José María Citalán, mayor de edad y de este vecindario, 1910.

22. According to the 1950 agricultural census, the most reliable and thorough to date, the total number of farms of all sizes within the municipality had diminished to 1,970; Dirección General de Estadística, *Censo agropecuario: Agricultura*, vol. 1 (Guatemala City: Dirección General de Estadística, 1950), p. 29.

23. See AGCA-LP, J. Domingo Andrade, 5 November 1870; Sinforoso Aguilar, 19 February 1896; and SRP tomo 76, folio 66, no. 12218. See also the examples of Francisca Hernández, Desideria Chávez, and María Cotom, all widows who sold recently bequeathed property, in, respectively, AGCA-LP, J. Domingo Andrade, 26 July 1876, and Sinforoso Aguilar, 28 April 1896 and 29 July 1897.

24. See AGCA-LP, J. Domingo Andrade, 29 January 1875.

25. Ibid., 24 June 1876. See also Mariana Chubac's sale of a bequeathed house to her cousin; AGCA-LP, J. Domingo Andrade, 7 February 1875.

26. See AGCA, Sinforoso Aguilar, 27 March 1897, and the Segundo Registro de Propiedad (hereafter cited as SRP), located in Quetzaltenango, tomo 29, folio 276, no. 3397.

27. Friedrich Katz's study of the way the rise of a peasant middle class furthered the process of land privatization and state formation in Mexico is helpful in understanding how these processes occurred in Quetzaltenango; "The Liberal Republic and the Porfiriato, 1867–1910," in *Mexico since Independence*, ed. Leslie Bethell (Cambridge: Cambridge University Press, 1991), especially, p. 97. See also Grandin, "La Mancha Negra," for an attempt to apply Katz's observations to another area of Guatemala.

28. See AGQ, 1884.

29. See AGQ, 1891.

30. See AGCA-ST, 21 9; see also discussion in Grandin, "La Mancha Negra," p. 230.

31. Although the mandamiento was officially abolished in 1894, the state, through a series of debt and vagrancy laws, continued to use its political power to assure a captive labor force. Despite its official abolition, forced conscription of work gangs continued into the 1920s.

32. For the mandamiento and debt labor, see McCreery's "Debt Servitude" and *Rural Guatemala*, pp. 266–81.

33. There were numerous protests by alcaldes, who claimed that they could not find the requested number of workers, for they were all working voluntarily on the coast. The mayor of Cajolá in 1892, for example, complained to the jefe político that although there exist 615 "able-bodied men," he could not fulfill a mandamiento order, since they were all already working on coastal *fincas* of their own volition; AGQ, 1892.

34. The contribución de caminos was based on a long-standing practice in which communities annually provided workers for a few days, usually after the rainy season, to repair roads, bridges, drainage, and other public projects.

35. The laws governing military service changed over time, as did the requirements for exemption. See AHQ, Reglamento sobre servicio militar, 1887. See also the number of peon rolls listing those colonos exempted from military service because of debt; AGQ, 1894.

36. See AGQ, peon rolls, 1894. Mam towns also supplied a disproportionately high number of men for work on infrastructure projects, such as the southern coast railroad. See AGQ, 1883, related documents.

37. See AGQ, 1884.

38. See AGQ, 1886.

39. See AGQ, 1894. See also Sol Tax, *Penny Capitalism*, Publications in Social Anthropology, no. 15 (Washington D.C.: Smithsonian Institution, 1953), p. 15, for another discussion on how intracommunal labor relations in the twentieth century provided an alternative to debt migration.

40. The insistence of Alan Knight and John Tutino, among others, on examining the incentives (i.e., political coercion versus market forces) that drove workers into debt so as to differentiate the variety of forms capitalism took in Latin American countries is obviously important in understanding Guatemalan economic development. Knight describes Guatemala as a classic case of "servile peonage," where money had to be invested in repression and policing, rather than productive technology, thereby explaining the origins of Guatemala's repressive state. While Knight's assessment generally holds true, the case of Quetzaltenango suggests that even within classic models of coercive development, variation existed; see Alan Knight, "Debt Bondage in Latin America," in *Slavery and Other Forms of Unfree Labour*, ed. Leonie Archer (New York: Routledge, 1989), and Tutino, *From Insurrection*, p. 59. See also John Swetnam, "What Else Did Indians Have to Do with Their Time? Alternatives to Labor Migration in Prerevolutionary Guatemala," *Economic Development and Cultural Change* 38, no. 1 (1989), for

a discussion of how coercive labor relations limited the development of an internal market.

41. See AHQ, caja 1894. This source does not specifically indicate ethnicity.

42. See AGQ, Encuesta de Ministerio de Fomento, 1901. This source does indicate ethnicity.

43. As of 1899, seven colonos resided on one of Coyoy's fincas—one for seven years, two for three years, and another two for two years; AGQ, Lista de los mozos colonos de la finca denominado "Los Molinos," 1899.

44. See AGQ, José María Citalán, mayor de edad y de este vecindario, 1910.

45. See AGCA, B 28572 72.

46. For an example of this gendered commerce in 1936, see Felix Webster McBryde, *Geografía Cultural e Histórica del Suroeste de Guatemala*, trans. Francis Gall, vol. 2 (Guatemala City: Editorial José de Pineda Ibarra, 1969), which provides a map of Quetzaltenango's market by product, gender, and origin of vender.

47. A census of city masons demonstrates that the trade was often conducted by all the males within a household; AHQ, Censo general del nombre de los albañiles, 1894.

48. See AHQ, caja 1839.

49. According to a city survey, nearly all the masons listed in the 1894 census were K'iche'; AHQ, Censo general del nombre de los albañiles, 1894.

50. See AHQ, caja 1853.

51. Ibid. While occasionally the number of workers increased, the work crew remained more or less the same throughout the project and was comprised of individuals who all had indigenous surnames. In other projects as well, the names of the workers were overwhelmingly K'iche'.

52. See AHQ, cajas 1860 and 1894. Taking into account inflation, which in the early 1890s was just beginning to inch up, this is still a considerable increase.

53. See, for example, AHQ, Planilla de operarios que trabajaron en el Palacio Municipal de catorce al diez y nueve de julio de 1884. Put in perspective, in 1884, sixteen acres of good corn land in the region surrounding the city could be purchased for two to three pesos. See the numerous petitions for titles in AHQ, caja 1884. For another example, see AHQ, Planilla de los mozos que trabajaron en el tanque del 14–19 de julio de 1884, which is made up of sixty-five K'iche' names, including nine albañiles who earned between three and seven reales a day and fifty-six mozos who earned one and a half reales a day on a job that lasted four months.

54. See AHQ, Planilla de operarios que trabajaron en el Palacio Municipal de catorce al diez y nueve de julio de 1884.

55. See AHQ, Cuadro que manifiesta el número de la sociedad ó compañías y de los individuos . . . en el departamento de Quetzaltenango, 1907.

56. See AHQ, Contrato con los albañiles Felix y Esteban Sum, 1894.

57. See AHQ, Esteban Tum, sobre que se aumente al valor del contrato es-

tipulado para la construcción del un puente, 1900. See also AHQ, Contrato cele-
brado entre el concejal de aguas, don Carlos Villagrán y Manuel Coyoy para
construir una pila en Los Chocoyos, 1902.

58. See AHQ, Cuadro que manifiesta el número de la sociedad ó compañías y de
los individuos . . . en el departamento de Quetzaltenango, 1907.

59. See AGQ, 1907.

60. The large number of K'iche' shepherds who tended to reside in the city's
rural cantones constituted an exception to this classification.

61. See AHQ, Contribución de caminos, 1884.

62. In 1894, when the state officially ended the mandamiento, it put in its place
an intensified public works program. Squads of *zapadores* (sappers), modeled on
military battalions, were now conscripted for extended work on public projects.

63. Tom Brass's critique of Knight and other revisionists of debt labor is useful
in understanding the development of a regional labor force in and around the city
of Quetzaltenango. When Brass accuses the revisionists of not looking at the class
content of debt—that is, what the borrowing was being used for—he touches on
something that he does not fully develop, namely the existence of class tensions
within the peasantry that may have contributed to the creation of a workforce;
Tom Brass, "The Latin American Enganche System: Some Revisionist Interpretations Revisited," *Slavery and Abolition* 11, no. 1 (1990): 74–103.

64. See SRP, 4 August 1884, tomo 2, folio 205, no. 385; see also AHQ, caja 1889,
when Miguel Menchú guaranteed a loan of forty-five pesos for Miguel Son.

65. See AHQ, caja 1897.

66. For Mexico, see the discussion in Knight, "Racism, Revolution and Indigenismo," p. 78. There are important exceptions to Knight's general conclusions,
however. Aside from the Maya of Chiapas, Zapotec Indians of the southern
isthmus of Tehuantepec have maintained a strong ethnic identity. See Howard
Campbell, *Zapotec Renaissance*, and Jeffrey W. Rubin, *Decentering the Regime:
Ethnicity, Radicalism, and Democracy in Juchitán, Mexico* (Durham: Duke University Press, 1997).

67. Knight, "Racism, Revolution and Indigenismo," p. 76.

68. See Swetnam's "What Else Did Indians Have to Do with Their Time?" for a
discussion of how seasonal coffee labor articulated, at times, with community
production.

69. Palmer, "A Liberal Discipline," p. 187.

70. "La civilización de los indios," *Diario de Centro-América*, 10 December 1880,
quoted in Palmer, "A Liberal Discipline," p. 188.

71. See discussion in chap. 6.

72. See Knight, "Racism, Revolution, and Indigenismo."

73. See chap. 6.

74. See AGQ, 1894.

75. Mallon, *The Defense of Community*, p. 341.

Chapter 6   Regenerating the Race: Race, Class,
and the Nationalization of Ethnicity

1. Marshall Berman, *All That Is Solid Melts into Air: The Experience of Modernity* (New York: Penguin, 1982), p. 16.

2. See AGQ, El común de indígenas de esta ciudad sobre que los ex-gobernadores rindan cuentas, 1871.

3. In 1882, during a conflict between the Municipalidad de Indígenas and a city priest over who was to keep the fees charged to ring church bells for the dead, Barrios again sided with the K'iche' authorities. He ordered the priest to turn over the funds. See AGCA, B 28691 439.

4. See AGCA, B 28670 299.

5. See AGCA, B 28670 292.

6. For the single treasurer, see AHQ, caja 1882. For the municipal sessions and commissions, see AHQ, Actas, 1886–94. Although Barillas, now president, officially abolished the K'iche' cabildo in 1887, it continued to function until 1894. For ignored decrees abolishing the indigenous municipalidad, see AGCA, B 28710 1489, and AHQ, caja 1887; for the real end of the municipality, see AHQ, caja 1894, and below.

7. See AGCA, B 2826 373.

8. See AGQ, 1873.

9. See AGCA-LP, J. Domingo Andrade, 12 June 1882.

10. See AHQ, Tomás Pac y Pioquinto Guzmán presentan sus títulos, 1895.

11. See AGQ, Denuncia de la Municipalidad de Indígenas contra Gregorio Morales, 1879, and AHQ, Elección verificada el 11 de diciembre de 1881, 1881.

12. Ibid.

13. See Grandin, "La Mancha Negra," for this situation in nearby Cantel.

14. See AGQ, El común de indígenas de esta ciudad sobre que los ex-gobernadores rindan cuentas, 1871.

15. As they did, for example, in 1879, when then protested a new market tax on "la más pobre y mas infeliz." See AHQ, caja 1879.

16. See AHQ, Estado de ingresos y egresos, 1875 and 1876.

17. See AHQ, Actas, 2 January 1895

18. Ibid.

19. See AHQ, caja 1899.

20. See AHQ, caja 1910.

21. See AHQ, José María Pac, Serapio García, y José María Orozco, guardabosques . . . declaran no tener ningún derecho de propiedad en los terrenos que la municipalidad les ha permitido sembrar, 1903.

22. See AHQ, Libro de entregas y de inventarios de las cofradías de esta ciudad, 1928, and Libro de inventarios, 1928–49.

23. In 1895, for example, repair of the road to the coast was done by a work

gang of two hundred men, all from the rural cantones of Xecaracoj, Pie de Volcán, Chicalajá, and Pacajá, and all recruited by the K'iche' alcalde; see AHQ, caja 1895.

24. Throughout the 1890s, public work gangs were brought in from the nearby Mam towns to work on city projects; see, for example, AHQ, correspondencia, 1896.

25. See AHQ, partes de tercer alcalde, 1912.

26. See AHQ, Escritura publica en que don Agatón y don Enrique Boj y don Felix del mismo apellido, se comprometen a construir la nueva fachada del teatro municipal, 1906; Agatón Boj encargado de la construcción de la fachada del teatro, 1907; and AHQ, Agatón Boj pide en nombre de Manuel Estrada Cabrera se le venda veinticinco varas cuadradas de terreno en el cementerio, 1907.

27. See AHQ, Actas, 24 November 1905. There was also the case of the construction contractor David Coyoy, who in the twentieth century was a prominent member of Sociedad El Adelanto (see below) and held a number of municipal offices, including third alcalde in 1924. He won a number of lucrative city and national contracts, including work on the Ferrocarril Nacional de los Altos in the 1920s and the construction of an underground aqueduct in 1950. See *El Correo de Occidente*, 4 July 1950. See *El Correo de Occidente*, 22 November 1950, for protests of his firing of a number of the project's workers.

28. See AHQ, Los regidores indígenas sobre que se críen varios funcionarios de su clase, 1894.

29. See AGCA, B 28868 1009. From 1895, a fixed number of K'iche' councilmen served in the city government. This endurance of Indian power was not unique to Quetzaltenango. In other "pueblos de indios" that also contained large numbers of non-Indians, such as Chichicastenango, Totonicapán, and Sololá, various working arrangements allowed for differing levels of indigenous autonomy. Likewise, Reina Barrios issued a number of decrees that guaranteed indigenous representation in selected municipalities. See Skinner-Klée, ed. *Legislación indigenista*, pp. 46–68.

30. Starting in the middle decades of the last century, national historians increasingly began accounts of Guatemala's long march toward the present with a description of preconquest society and history, and the 1820 uprising in Totonicapán was heralded as a precursor to independence. See, for example, Antonio Batres Jáuregui's *Los indios: Su historia y su civilización* (Guatemala City: Tipográfico La Unión, 1894), and *La América Central ante la historia*, vols. 1 and 2 (Guatemala City: Marroquín Hermanos "Casa Colorada," 1915); Jesús Carranza, *Un pueblo de los altos: Apuntamientos para su historia, Totonicapán* (Quetzaltenango: Tipografía Popular, 1897); Francisco de Paula García Peláez, *Memorias para la historia del antiguo Reyno de Guatemala*, vol. 1 (Guatemala City: Tipográfico de L. Luna, 1951); and Juan Gavarrete Escobar, *Anales para la historia de Guatemala: 1491–1811* (Guatemala City: Editorial José de Pineda Ibarra, 1980). One of José María Reina Barrios's first acts as president in 1892 was to sponsor a

national essay contest whose topic was the best system to "civilize Indians"; Batres Jáuregui's essay, subsequently published as *Los indios*, was the winner. During his six years as president Reina Barrios founded and funded a number of Escuelas de Indígenas in various parts of the country and passed numerous pieces of legislation that were supposed to protect the rights of Indians qua Indians. This liberal indigenista nationalism would continue into the twentieth century in the works of Adrián Recinos, *Memorial de Solola, Anales de los Cakchiqueles* (Mexico: Fondo de Cultura Económica, 1950); Virgilio Rodríguez Beteta, *Ideologías de la Independencia* (Paris: Editorial París-America, 1926); José Antonio Villacorta Calderón, *Memorial de Tecpán-Atitlán* (Guatemala City: Tipografía Nacional, 1934), and *Prehistoria e historia antigua de Guatemala* (Guatemala City: Tipografía Nacional, 1938).

31. See, for example, Francisco Antonio Fuentes y Guzmán, *Recordación florida* (Guatemala: Ministerio de Educación Pública, 1951).

32. There is little scholarship on Reina Barrios's very important transitional period of Guatemalan liberalism. Palmer, "A Liberal Discipline," pp. 189–97, offers the best discussion to date.

33. As McCreery points out, the end of the mandamiento did not necessarily mean the end of the mandamiento. The same decree that abolished the corveé expanded forced public work obligations. And under Reina Barrios and his successor, Manuel Estrada Cabrera, the state repeatedly made exceptions and allowed for labor drafts. Further, the state, until 1944, vigorously enforced peonage and vagrancy laws. See McCreery, *Rural Guatemala*, pp. 189–94.

34. See, for examples, the debate in *Diario de Centro América*, 10 and 14 April, and 5 October 1893, and *La Nueva Era*, 14 and 21 April 1893.

35. Batres Jáuregui, *La América Central*, p. 448.

36. Ibid. It must be said, however, that Batres was less sanguine about the possibilities the future offered. For other examples of the liberal belief in the disappearance of the Indians, see Rodríguez Beteta, *Ideologías de la Independencia*, and Villacorta Calderón's *Memorial de Tecpán-Atitlán* and *Prehistoria e historia antigua de Guatemala*, especially p. 180.

37. A good example of this diversity of opinion could be found at the First Central American Pedagogical Congress, which took place in Guatemala in 1893. One delegate called for the creation of indigenous protected areas where instruction would be provided in native languages so as to gradually incorporate Indians into the national life; see Juan Fernández Ferraz, *Estudio acerca las nueve tesis del programa del primer congreso pedagógico Centroamericano* (San José, Costa Rica: Tipografía Nacional, 1893), pp. 9–14. See also Nicolás Aguilar, *Discurso pronunciado por el Doctor D. Nicolás Aguilar, delegado de El Salvador . . .* (Guatemala City: Tipografía La Unión, 1893), and José María Vela Irisarri, Angel María Bocanegra, and Lucas T. Cojulún, *Informe presentado al primer congreso pedagógico Centro-América sobre el tema VIII* (Guatemala City: Sánchez y De Guise, 1893), for the conference. See Francisco Lainfiesta, *A vista de pájaros (cuento fantástico)*

(Guatemala: El Progreso, 1879) for a particularly upbeat view of the Indian in the future nation; then see Francisco Lainfiesta, "La esclavitud del indio," *La República*, 27 June 1893, written after his optimism turned sour; also see Palmer, "A Liberal Discipline," pp. 194–195. The logic of Guatemala's political economy was of course often at odds with these more imaginative programs; see David McCreery, "Coffee and Class: The Structure of Development in Liberal Guatemala," *Hispanic American Historical Review* 56, no. 3 (1976): 452.

38. Batres Jáuregui, *Los indios*. Later, during the Mexican Revolution, *Regeneración* would be the name of the Magón brothers' influential anarchist newspaper.

39. See Batres Jáuregui's *La América Central*, p. 448, and *Los indios*, pt. 3 and chaps. 3 and 4. Batres, the archetypal indigenista nationalist, wrote scores of books on *lo Americana*, which, aside from his work on history and indigenous culture, include topics on creole colloquialisms and literature.

40. Batres Jáuregui, *Los indios*, pp. 177–78. These views were not new to the later part of the nineteenth century, although they did become more pronounced. See José Luis Reyes M., *Apuntes para una monografía de la Sociedad Económica de Amigos del País* (Guatemala City: Editorial José de Pineda Ibarra, 1964), and Manuel Rubio Sánchez, *Historia de la Sociedad Económica de Amigos del País* (Guatemala City: Editorial Académica Centroamericana, 1981), for the work of the Sociedad Económica, which Batres served as president for a period.

41. From a series of interviews I conducted in July 1997 with older members of the Sociedad El Adelanto (which will be discussed below), it is clear that this antiassimilationist, racialist view of indigenous ethnicity still resonates among Quetzalteco K'iche's. For these men, ethnicity was defined by blood rather than cultural or class traits. "We have the blood of Tecún, they [the Ladinos] have the blood of Pedro de Alvarado," replied one interviewee to the question: "What is the difference between Indians and Ladinos?" Genovevo Bautista Coyoy, interview by author, Quetzaltenango, 9 July 1997.

42. See AHQ, caja 1892.

43. See "Pobre Raza," in *La Lechuza*, 11 October 1896, and *El Comercio*, 5 October 1899.

44. See AHQ, caja 1894.

45. Sociedad El Adelanto, *Estatuto de la Sociedad El Adelanto* (Quetzaltenango: Tipográfico "La Unión Liberal," 1894), found in AHQ, Sobre la fundación de la sociedad "El Adelanto," 1894.

46. Another intriguing aspect of the establishment of the Sociedad El Adelanto is its apparent connection with the Masonic movement in Quetzaltenango. Although no member today can explain why, El Adelanto's first standard bore the Masonic symbol of a compass and ruler. Late-nineteenth-century Guatemalan liberals were strongly influenced by Freemasonry and its promotion of enlightened rationalism. By 1901, there existed fifteen thousand masons and twenty-one lodges in Central America. Quetzaltenango's lodge was under the jurisdiction of Mexican masons. See Unknown (H. P. F.), *Resumen de las conferencias dadas en la*

resp. log. Alianza no. 24 (Guatemala City: Tipografía de Síguere y Cía, 1903). With its use of artisan symbols and rhetoric, there was perhaps a natural affiliation with the workers societies being established throughout Guatemala. See also the newspaper *El Fénix*, published in 1895 by Quetzaltenango's Masonic lodge, and *El Ron-Ron*, an early promoter of Freemasonry in Quetzaltenango.

47. The society's president told me in 1994 that "El Adelanto was founded one hundred years ago; before that we were the Municipalidad de Indígenas."

48. Sociedad El Adelanto, *Estatuto*, lists fifty-nine founding members, while Sociedad El Adelanto, *100 años de vida social y educativa, 1894–1994* (Quetzaltenango: Sociedad El Adelanto, 1994), only lists thirty. Not all the names on the two lists correspond. The names in Grandin, "Blood," Appendix 8, are taken from the former, with the exception of Lorenzo Aguilar.

49. See Grandin, "Blood," Appendix 8.

50. E. P. Thompson, *The Making of the English Working Class* (New York: Vintage, 1963), chap. 8. In Quetzaltenango, in the decades that followed the establishment of the Sociedad El Adelanto, artisans and Indians founded a number of similar societies and guilds, which provided important welfare services. See chap. 7.

51. Thompson, *The Making of the English Working Class*, p. 244.

52. The information on cofradía charges is incomplete, covering only a few years. The information also only lists those who filled the two most important positions—that of alcalde and mayordomo—and ignores those who occupied lesser positions. For this reason, it is difficult to assess the relevance of the city's cofradía system at any given point. See Grandin, "Blood," Appendix 8.

53. See AHQ, Sobre la fundación de la sociedad "El Adelanto," 1894.

54. Ibid.

55. Ibid.

56. For the president's approval, see AGCA, Libro de Acuerdos y Decretos de Gobernación, folio 125, 1894.

57. See Joseph and Nugent, eds., *Everyday Forms of State Formation*.

58. Stuart Hall, "The Problem of Ideology: Marxism without Guarantees," in *Stuart Hall: Critical Dialogues in Cultural Studies*, ed. David Morley and Kuan-Hsing Chen (New York: Routledge, 1996), p. 41.

59. Hall, "The Problem of Ideology," p. 41.

60. For "field of force," a metaphor first used by E. P. Thompson, see Roseberry, "Hegemony and the Language of Contention," and Hall, "The Problem of Ideology," pp. 41–42. For how the concept of "liberalism" came to hold diverse meanings for competing groups in prerevolutionary Nicaragua, see Gould, *To Lead as Equals*.

61. See AGCA, Libro de acuerdos de gobernación, B 32880.

62. The linking of hegemony to political formation owes much to a return to Gramsci's original work on the concept; see Hall, "The Problem of Ideology," and Roseberry, "Hegemony and the Language of Contention."

63. See AHQ, La sociedad "El Adelanto" compuesta de indígenas de esta cabecera, 1894.

64. See AHQ, caja 1879.

65. See AHQ, Tomás Pac quejándose de la comisión que fue a medir su terreno, 1892, and Tomás Pac y Pioquinto Guzmán presentan sus títulos, 1895.

66. See AGQ, La Municipalidad de San Mateo solicita del Supremo Gobierno les conceda el terreno denominado "Las Barrancas," 1887.

67. Both are in AHQ, cajas 1891 and 1892.

68. See AHQ, caja 1891.

69. See AHQ, cajas 1895 and 1896.

70. See AHQ, Tomás Pac y Pioquinto Guzmán piden que en la comisión que debe informar sobre la remedida de sus terrenos asiste un miembro imparcial, 1896.

71. Ibid.

72. See AHQ, caja 1894.

73. The account of the following encounter is taken from AHQ, Actas, 25 August 1894.

74. A copy of the letter is in AHQ, caja 1894.

75. See AGQ, Letter from the K'iche' juez de ejidos to jefe político, 1897.

76. The K'iche's presented the motion in May, and by July it had still not been addressed. On 10 July 1894, three weeks before Coyoy requested his leave, he once again urged the municipality to attend to the issue, claiming that a good part of the forest was being destroyed by sheep; AHQ, La Municipalidad de Indígenas de esta ciudad con el más profundo respeto pasamos a exponer que hace más de dos meses que presentamos una moción, 1894.

77. In 1892, Reina Barrios also institutionalized the power of indigenous authorities in nearby Totonicapán when he ordered that the municipality's third mayor, second syndic, and six of thirteen regidores be indigenous. In 1893, he ordered that separate elections be held for Indians and Ladinos, and in 1894, he decreed that two more indigenous regidores be added to the municipal corporation, from the "parcialidad de principales." See Skinner-Klée, ed. Legislación indigenista, pp. 48, 50–51, and 68.

78. An example of a more mundane petition is the request by Lorenzo Aguilar, an original founder of El Adelanto, that President Manuel Estrada Cabrera compensate him for land he lost owing to an expansion of the city's graveyard. Estrada Cabrera personally ordered that Aguilar be given land in another part of town. See AGCA, Libro de Acuerdos, 32916, 12 February 1910.

79. For the causes of this revolt, see Todd Little-Siebold, "Guatemala y el anhelo de modernización: Estrada Cabrera y el desarrollo del estado, 1898–1920," Anuario de Estudios Centroamericanos 20, no. 1 (1994): 25–41; J. Lizardo Díaz O, De la democracia a la dictadura (Guatemala City: Imprenta Hispana, 1946); Un Patriota, La verdad de los hechos (Guatemala City: 1899), located in

Biblioteca César Brañas, call no. 18697; Dolores de Aparicio, *Acusación contra el coronel y diputado Roque Morales presentada a la Asamblea Legislativa* (Guatemala City: Tipografía A. Síguere & Cía, 1898). See also Salvador Meza, *Manuel M. Reyna, justas aclaraciones* (Cobán: Tipografía El Porvenir, 1898); the opposition paper started in Quetzaltenango in early 1897, *El Sufragio*, which opposed Reina Barrios; *La Guillotina*, which supported him; and *Los Ecos de la Revolución*.

80. Díaz O, *De la democracia*, pp. 24–25.

81. See AGQ, Letter from Manuel de León to Prospero Morales, 1897; see also AGQ, La Municipalidad de Zunil solicita exhonerarse de 1,500 pesos que hurtaron los reveldes, 1897.

82. See AGQ, Letter from Manuel de León to Prospero Morales, 1897, and *Los Ecos de la Revolución*, 30 September 1897.

83. *Los Ecos de la Revolución*, 17 September 1897.

84. Díaz O, *De la democracia*, pp. 84–88. There is circumstantial evidence suggesting that some indigenous authorities may have aided the revolutionaries. Sinforoso Aguilar, a prominent liberal and mason who actively supported and perhaps influenced the Sociedad El Adelanto's educational initiatives, was one of the opposition leaders killed by government officials. Personal allegiances may have led some of the indigenous authorities to support the rebellion.

85. See Partha Chatterjee, *Nationalist Thought and the Colonial World: A Derivative Discourse?* (Delhi: Oxford University Press, 1986), pp. 50–52, for the following "moments."

86. Cited in Mallon, *Peasant and Nation*, p. 13.

87. Chatterjee, *Nationalist Thought*, p. 51.

88. This is what happened in nearby Cantel, where poor Indians allied themselves with the state to push through privatization. See Grandin, "La Mancha Negra."

89. Chatterjee, *Nationalist Thought*, p. 52.

90. Derek Sayer, "Everyday Forms of State Formation: Some Dissident Remarks on 'Hegemony,'" in Joseph and Nugent, eds., *Everyday Forms of State Formation*, p. 374.

91. Sayer, "Some Dissident Remarks," p. 376.

92. Ibid.

Chapter 7   Time and Space among the Maya: Mayan Modernism
and the Transformation of the City

1. See for discussion Pierre Bourdieu, *Outline of a Theory of Practice* (Cambridge: Cambridge University Press, 1977), p. 163, and David Harvey, *The Condition of Postmodernity: An Inquiry into the Origins of Cultural Change* (Cambridge: Blackwell, 1989), chaps. 13 and 14.

2. See Benedict Anderson's discussion of the concept's relation to the development of nationalism, originally drawn from Walter Benjamin; Benedict Anderson, *Imagined Communities*, pp. 22–36, and Walter Benjamin, *Illuminations: Essays and Reflections*, edited by Hannah Arendt (New York: Schocken Books, 1968), p. 265.

3. In Quetzaltenango, for example: E. Ascoli y Cía, Maegli y Gaegauf, A. Zadik, G. Meyer, Groebli y Hurter, and Koch Hnos.

4. *El Comercio*, 24 August 1899.

5. See Roberto Bran Azmitia, ed. *Parnaso quezalteco: De todos los tiempos* (Guatemala City: Editorial José de Pineda Ibarra, 1982).

6. See various *partes de penitenciaria*, AHQ, during the last decades of the nineteenth century.

7. See AHQ, *Informe de mercado*, 1902.

8. Starting in 1895, K'iche's often headed the municipal electrification committee.

9. *El Comercio*, 24 August and 3 September 1899; *La Vida*, July 1922.

10. See AHQ, Varios vecinos de esta ciudad que han visto con alarma que esta corporación haya permitido que funcione únicamente el alumbrado de particulares, 1893.

11. See AHQ, Subscripción levantada entre los indígenas de esta Ciudad para el monumento del General Guzmán, 1892. Thirty-four principales contributed a total of 32.50 pesos. See Taracena Arriola, *Invención criolla*, chaps. 6, 7, and 11, for the confrontations between Guzmán and Carrera.

12. See various letters related to the affair in AHQ, caja 1889.

13. See AHQ, La clase indígena de Quetzaltenango pide al Presidente de la República que ordene se les ponga en posesión de su edificio municipal, 1895.

14. The state installed the first telegraph line in 1873. The number of governmental messages sent by wire jumped from one thousand a month in the early 1870s to fifteen thousand by 1898. This new technology gave the government and planters unprecedented social control over territory and workforce, as the state now could quickly respond to reports of rebellions and invasions, circulate capture orders for escaped workers, and coordinate large-scale public works projects, such as rail and road construction. See McCreery, *Rural Guatemala*, pp. 179–80. For comparative and theoretical discussions, see John Foster, *Class Struggle in the Industrial Revolution: Early Industrial Capitalism in Three English Towns* (London: St. Martin's Press, 1975), and Harvey, *The Condition of Postmodernity*.

15. See AHQ, La clase indígena de Quetzaltenango pide al Presidente de la República que ordene se les ponga en posesión de su edificio municipal, 1895.

16. Harvey, *The Condition of Postmodernity*, p. 216, and Berman, *All That Is Solid Melts into Air*, pp. 15–16.

17. Harvey, *The Condition of Postmodernity*, p. 225.

18. As early as the formation of the Estado de los Altos, Altenses promoted the pre-Colombian K'iche' civilization to counter the dominance of Guatemala City;

see Taracena Arriola, *Invención criolla*, chap. 9. In the first decades of this century a cult developed among Quetzalteco Ladino intellectuals of Tecún Umán, the K'iche' warrior who battled Pedro de Alvarado on the plains of Quetzaltenango. See the series of articles published in July 1933 in the Quetzalteco magazine *Ideas y Noticias* under the title "La Sociedad de Geografía e Historia emitió su jucio sobre Tecún Umán"; see also the poem "La Glorificación a Tecún Umán," in *Ideas y Noticias*, 23 August 1933. See Gabriel Angel Casteñeda, *Monumento a Tecún Umán* (Guatemala City: Tipografía Nacional, 1965), for how this cult was appropriated and militarized by the central government and the army. For other examples of Altense cultural and political indigenismo in this century, see Jesús Castillo, *La música maya-quiché* (Quetzaltenango: n.p., 1941), and the poetry and essays of Carlos Wyld Ospina: for example, see Mario Gilberto González R., *Pequeña reseña bio-bibliográfica de Carlos Wyld Ospina* (Guatemala City: Editorial del Ministerio de Educación Pública, 1957), and Carlos Wyld Ospina, *El autó-crata: Ensayo politico-social* (Guatemala City: Editorial José de Pineda Ibarra, 1967). For the unearthing of ruins in the nineteenth century, see AGCA, B 95.1, 1398; AGCA, B 8.50 887 21584; and Lindesay Brine, *Travels Amongst American Indians, Their Ancient Earthworks and Temples; Including a Journey in Guatemala, Mexico and Yucatan . . .* (London: Sampson Low, Marston & Company, 1894), pp. 180–220. Alfred Percival Maudslay's and Teobert Maler's photographs of Tikal circulated in Guatemala in the 1880s and 1890s; see William R. Coe, *Tikal: A Handbook of the Ancient Maya Ruins* (Philadelphia: University of Pennsylvania Press, 1967), pp. 12–17, for a history of Tikal's nineteenth-century excavation.

19. See AHQ, La clase indígena de Quetzaltenango pide al Presidente de la República que ordene se les ponga en posesión de su edificio municipal, 1895.

20. For the educational reforms attempted by the first liberal state, see Miriam Williford, "The Educational Reforms of Dr. Mariano Gálvez," *Journal of Inter-American Studies* 10, no. 3 (1968): 461–73; for education under Carrera, see Woodward, *Rafael Carrera*, chap. 21; for post–1871 educational legislation, see Carlos González Orellana, *Historia de la educación en Guatemala* (Guatemala City: Editorial José de Pineda Ibarra, 1970), pp. 269–79.

21. See Palmer, "A Liberal Discipline," pp. 107–12, for liberal educational philosophy and its application. Many of these limitations continue to the present day; see Oscar H. Horst and Avril McLelland, "The Development of an Educational System in a Rural Guatemalan Community," *Journal of Inter-American Studies* 10, no. 3 (1968): 474–97.

22. In the department of Quetzaltenango, from 1876 to 1886, the number of primary boys' schools increased from twenty-three to forty and the number of primary girls' schools increased from eight to fourteen, while the total number of students rose from 823 to 2,697; González Orellana, *Historia de la educación*, p. 280, and AHQ, Estadística de instrucción pública del Departamento de Quetzaltenango, 1886. The national state paid for the majority of the funding for this

expansion of education. Of a total operating budget of 19,848 pesos, the municipality contributed only 780 pesos; see AHQ, Estadística de Instrucción Pública del
Departamento de Quetzaltenango, 1886.

23. See AHQ, Estadística de instrucción pública del Departamento de Quetzaltenango, 1886.

24. For the militarization of education under Estrada Cabrera and Ubico, see
González Orellana, *Historia de la educación*, pp. 332–62.

25. See Palmer, "A Liberal Discipline," pp. 107–12. See also the discussion in the
previous chapter on indigenista pedagogy.

26. A trademark of nineteenth-century elite liberal indigenismo was, of course,
forced assimilation. This was nowhere better illustrated than in Barrios's famous
1879 decree that abolished the municipality of the indigenous pueblo of Jocote-
nango, placed its population under the jurisdiction of the capital, and sold its
communal land to establish a *colegio de Indígenas*. It is from this decree that the
quotations are taken; see Skinner-Klée, ed. *Legislación indigenista*, pp. 42–43.

27. See Fernández Ferraz, *Estudio acerca las nueve tesis*, for a call to teachers to
learn indigenous languages. See González Orellana, *Historia de la educación*,
p. 312, for the foundation of the Escuela Especial para Indígenas under Justo
Rufino Barrios and the foundation of the Instituto Agrícola Para Indígenas under
José María Reina Barrios. See also Skinner-Klée, ed. *Legislación indigenista*, pp.
42–44, 47, 48, 51, and 52–68, for the establishment of schools for Indians during
the presidencies of Barrios and Reina Barrios. Discussions surrounding the best
way to educate Indians were closely tied to debates surrounding the end of the
mandamiento.

28. Skinner-Klée, ed., *Legislación indigenista*, p. 43; AGQ, 1890.

29. See AHQ, Estado que manifiesta el número de alumnos que asisten a la
Escuela Nacional Elemental de Niños Indígenas de Quetzaltenango, 1892.

30. See González Orellana, *Historia de la educación*, pp. 320–31.

31. In the 1920s, for instance, the Sociedad Liberal de Artesanos founded the
Escuela Nocturna Particular de Arquitectura, and the Sociedad de Albañiles
established an Escuela de Arquitectura.

32. See the Archivo de la Sociedad El Adelanto (hereafter cited as ASA), Libro
de Actas no. 1, 1897; Libro de Actas no. 2, 1911–12; Matricula de la Escuela de
Primaria de Niñas, 1926; and Inscripción de Niños en Edad Escolar Correspondiente a la Escuela Diurna de Liceo de Varones, 1926.

33. Manifestación que la sociedad "El Adelanto" de indígenas de Quetzaltenango . . . hacen al señor presidente, found in Quetzaltenango's Museo de
Historia.

34. See ASA, miscellaneous, Letter to the Ministry of Public Education, 3 April
1920.

35. See ASA, correspondencias, 1911. But this state control needs to be qualified
in that often K'iche' elites, including members of El Adelanto, sat on the education committee, as did, for example, Ismael Coyoy in 1923.

36. See ASA, Actas de Liceo de Varones "El Adelanto," 1911–19.

37. See ASA, miscellaneous, Letter to Ministry of Public Education, 9 September 1915. See, for examples, ASA, miscellaneous, 23 May 1923, when the jefe político ordered the director of the school to show him the speech that was to be read for Arbor Day. See ASA, Actas de la escuela "El Adelanto" de Niñas no. 2, 19 and 23 August 1919, for inspections by the Junta Local de Educación Pública. The attempt of the local and national Ladino state to effect control of the schools of El Adelanto was evident early on. During the inauguration of two schools in 1897, Ladino municipal officials in attendance reiterated that "the education [of the school] will completely conform with the official program"; see ASA, Libro de Actas no. 1, 1 May 1897.

38. See ASA, miscellaneous, Letter to jefe político, 16 May 1921.

39. In 1897, El Adelanto received 140 pesos a month to pay the salaries of a director (100) and a teacher (40); see AHQ, caja 1897.

40. See a 1920 budget in ASA, miscellaneous; see also, for other examples of funding: ASA, miscellaneous, Letter to Junta Local de Educación Pública, 21 March 1920, in which El Adelanto asked that the state pay the salary of the foreign director of a new school; see also ASA, miscellaneous, Prospecto de la Escuela Nocturna para Artesanos, 1938.

41. This is what happened after the 1897 revolution and during the depression of the 1930s. For the former, see the various petitions in AHQ, caja 1898, asking for the resumption of the municipal subsidy. For the latter, see the editorial in the *Liberal Progresista*, 16 May 1933, criticizing the sociedad for not paying its Ladino teachers.

42. For theory and comparisons of educational systems, see Horst and McLelland, "The Development of an Educational System"; Deborah Reed-Danahay, "Farm Children at School: Educational Strategies in Rural France," *Anthropological Quarterly* 60, no. 2 (1987): 83–89; Elsie Rockwell, "Schools of the Revolution: Enacting and Contesting State Forms in Tlaxcala, 1910–1930," in Joseph and Nugent, eds., *Everyday Forms of State Formation*; E. P. Thompson, "Time, Work-Discipline, and Industrial Capitalism," *Past and Present* 38 (1967): 55–97; Philip Wexler, Tony Whitson, and Emily J. Moskowitz, "Deschooling by Default: The Changing Social Functions of Public Schooling," *Interchange* 12, nos. 2–3 (1981): 2–3; and Paul Willis, *Learning to Labour: How Working-Class Kids Get Working-Class Jobs* (London: Gowet, 1977).

43. See ASA, Actas del Liceò de Varones, 9 March and 3 October 1911.

44. The high point of the coffee harvest extends from October to January.

45. See ASA, miscellaneous, 1901.

46. See Grandin, "Blood," chap. 7, for the books listed in a 1911 inventory of the Escuela de Varones "El Adelanto."

47. See ASA, miscellaneous and Inventario, Liceo de Varones, 1911.

48. See, for comparisons with Mexico, Josefina Z. Vásquez, *Nacionalismo y educación en México* (Mexico City: El Colegio de México, 1970), and Mary Kay

Vaughan, "The Construction of Patriotic Festival in Central Mexico: Puebla (1900–1946)," in *Rituals of Rule, Rituals of Resistance: Public Celebrations and Popular Culture in Mexico*, ed. William H. Beezly, Cheryl E. Martin, and William E. French (Wilmington, Del.: Scholarly Resources, 1994). See Sarah Radcliffe and Sallie Westwood, *Remaking the Nation: Place, Identity and Politics in Latin America* (London: Routledge, 1996), pp. 51–62, for the role of education in Ecuador in crafting a national identity. In 1915, a school inspector from the local public education committee noted that all the boys in one El Adelanto school "practiced military exercises and sang the hymn with impressive zeal"; see ASA, Actas, 15 October 1914.

49. This figure was arrived at by taking the total number of school days missed and dividing it by the total number of possible class days; ASA, Lista General de Los Alumnos Inscritos en el Liceo de Varones "El Adelanto" tanto de la Escuela Diurna como de la Nocturna Anexa, 1924.

50. See ASA, miscellaneous, 1909, and author's interview with Pablo Enrique Tucux Pac, 15 July 1997.

51. Pablo Enrique Tucux Pac, interview by author, Quetzaltenango, 15 July 1997.

52. Nearly all of the children enrolled in schools supported by the sociedad lived in the city center. See ASA, Inscripción de Niños en Edad Escolar Correspondiente a la Escuela Diurna de Liceo de Varones, 1926, and Matricula de la Escuela de Primaria de Niñas, 1926. See Carmack, *Rebels*, pp. 201–2, for a discussion of indigenous reaction to forced educational requirements in nearby Momostenango.

53. For the year 1924, while the average absenteeism rate of a primary boys' school was 23 percent, during the months of March and April it rose to 26 percent and in the month of July increased to 34 percent. In contrast, in February, the first month of the school year, absenteeism was only 9 percent; ASA, Lista General de Los Alumnos Inscritos en el Liceo de Varones "El Adelanto" tanto de la Escuela Diurna como de la Nocturna Anexa, 1924.

54. In 1910, the fee was one peso a month.

55. See Horst and McLelland, "The Development of an Educational System," pp. 488–90, for reasons for absenteeism in this century. In 1911, the exam juror sent by the Junta Local de Educación Pública to administer exams in the Escuela de Varones blamed the high failure and absenteeism rate on the inability of teachers to speak K'iche'; see ASA, Actas de Escuela de Varones, 3 October 1911.

56. Even when rural Indians did want to send their children to school, a number of obstacles stood in their way. In 1892, forty-three indigenous fathers from the rural aldea of Xecaracoj twice petitioned the municipality for their own "modern" school. They complained that the closest one was over a league away and during the rainy season floods deepened the ravines separating their aldea from the school, thus preventing their children from attending classes; AHQ, caja 1892.

57. See Rockwell, "Schools of the Revolution," p. 174. See also Mary Kay Vaughan, "Primary Education and Literacy in Mexico in the Nineteenth Century:

Research Trends, 1968–1988," *Latin American Research Review* 24, no. 3 (1990): 33–66, for a review of the literature and debate on liberal and revolutionary Mexican educational reform.

58. See Gabriel García Márquez, *One Hundred Years of Solitude*, trans. Gregory Rabassa (New York: Avon, 1971), p. 210, for the (paraphrased) first sentence of this paragraph. The following description of the inauguration of the Ferrocarril Nacional de Los Altos comes from the Museo del Ferrocarril Nacional de Los Altos (hereafter cited as MFNLA), in Quetzaltenango; Roberto Calderón Gordillo, *Semblanza histórica del Ferrocarril Nacional de Los Altos* (Quetzaltenango: Taller "El Estudiante," 1987), pp. 13–17; and *"Preciosas Telas Indígenas,"* in *Ideas y Noticias*, 30 August 1933.

59. By this point, all of Guatemala's other rail lines were administered by the U.S.-controlled International Railways of Central America.

60. The refusal of Ubico to use national funds to rebuild the line still raises regionalist hackles. It is cited by local historians as evidence of Ubico's hatred for the freedom-loving Quetzaltecos. See Francisco José Cajas Ovando, *Reseña histórica de Ferrocarril de Los Altos* (Quetzaltenango: Taller "El Estudiante," 1995), and Calderón Gordillo, *Semblanza histórica*. Ubico's refusal to support the restoration is indeed indicative of regional-national tensions, some of which have been laid out previously in this work. See also Municipalidad de Quetzaltenango, *Sesiquicentario* (Quetzaltenango: Serviprensa, 1975) for Ubico's hostility toward the city. But there are other reasons for the failure of the FNLA. The line operated on a chronic deficit and had trouble convincing both wealthier commercial houses and poorer Indian traders to use its services. In 1932, on advice from its manager, the budget was reduced twice in an effort to make ends meet; see MFNLA, correspondencia, 1932. The global depression likewise limited the local and national funds that were available for repairs. As such, despite much hyperbole following the storm, there was insufficient political or economic will to reconstruct the line. Local commercial houses continued to use trucks, on roads built by Ubico, to transport their merchandise. Further, other departments did not answer Quetzaltenango's "patriotic call" to supply men and money for repairs; see *Ideas y Noticias*, 18 November 1933.

61. In Guatemala as early as 1879 the possibility of electric trains symbolized modernity and progress; see Lainfiesta, *A vista de pájaros*, p. 174–75.

62. See *El Comercio*, a Quetzalteco weekly, which was an ardent promoter of the project; also see the series of editorials and stories it ran on 1 June, 13 July, and 24 August 1899.

63. *El Comercio*, 13 July and 24 August 1899.

64. See MFNLA, correspondencia, 1923 and 1924.

65. See MFNLA, Oficios de la Inspección general y dirección técnica, 1911. President Manuel Estrada Cabrera lent the Comité de Ferrocarril de Los Altos tools and machinery from the recently completed Ferrocarril del Norte.

66. Cajas Ovando, *Reseña histórica*, p. 5.

67. In 1926, the quetzal became the standard currency, equivalent to the U.S. dollar until the early 1980s. The transition to agrarian capitalism, until relatively recently, did not entail adoption of a straight wage salary. A mix of compensation, including food, medical attention, access to land, credit, relief from military service and past debt—all backed up by state force—were key components of the labor relations that supported the expansion of agricultural capitalism. Thus, the use of straight wage compensation in the building of the FNLA is somewhat anomalous and perhaps serves to explain the high degree of worker flight discussed below. McCreery writes that a straight wage system, "which threatened to leave them at the mercy of unstable grain prices," was not very attractive to Indians; McCreery, *Rural Guatemala*, p. 329.

68. See, for example, MFNLA, legajo 3, 1911; Oficios del cuarto campamento, 1912; Informe de trabajos, 1919; Planilla, 1922.

69. See MFNLA, Informe de trabajo, 1919.

70. See MFNLA, correspondencia de jefatura técnica, 1922.

71. Because of the fluctuation in the value of the peso and its replacement by the quetzal as national currency in 1926, it is hard to fix the relative worth of salary differentials. Throughout the project, skilled workers, unless hired by fixed contract, tended to make from double to triple what conscript laborers made. In 1911, for example, forced mozos were earning eighteen pesos a day, while a squad of seven Quetzalteco K'iche' masons made thirty-three pesos; the master mason, Víctor Coyoy, earned thirty-nine pesos. See MFNLA, Nómina de los zapadores que fueron licenciados, 1911.

72. See MFNLA, legajo 3, 1911, and correspondencia de jefatura técnica, 1922, for example.

73. See MFNLA, correspondencia de jefatura técnica, 1922

74. See MFNLA, legajo 3, 1911.

75. See, for example, MFNLA, correspondencia de jefatura técnica, 1923, for an unidentified fever epidemic that killed thirteen workers.

76. See MFNLA, jefatura técnica, 1922.

77. See MFNLA, Nómina de los zapadores, 1911.

78. See MFNLA, jefatura técnica, 1922.

79. See AHQ, Actas, 28 July 1922.

80. See ASA, miscellaneous, 30 August 1926.

81. See MFNLA, Informe de accidentes, 1929.

82. See MFNLA, correspondencia, 1920, and Informe de accidentes, 1929.

83. See Anderson's discussion of tombs of unknown soldiers in *Imagined Communities*, pp. 9–10.

84. See MFNLA, jefatura técnica, 1923. Complaints of worker flight are to be found in nearly every bundle of documents in the MFNLA.

85. See MFNLA, jefatura técnica, 1923.

86. See, for example, MFNLA, jefatura técnica, 1926 and 1927.

87. See MFNLA, correspondencia de los jefe políticos, 1923 and 1927.

88. One of McCreery's most important insights is an elaboration of how the failure of early Guatemalan capitalism to develop a free wage labor market contributed to this cycle: "The whole structure of Guatemala's export production rested on the assumed availability of state-coerced 'cheap' labor. This made the planters very dependent on the state and on state agents not only to obtain labor directly from drafts and to enforce the debt peonage system, but also to quickly and effectively stifle resistance and to guarantee the repression necessary to socialize losses when the economy turned down. This dependence on the state accentuated the trend toward large-scale production, for small growers typically lacked the political access necessary to guarantee themselves labor or protect their lands"; *Rural Guatemala*, pp. 334–35.

89. See, for examples, AHQ, correspondencia del tercer alcalde, 1913.

90. See MFNLA, miscellaneous, 1920.

91. See Palmer, "A Liberal Discipline," chap. 5, for a marvelous examination of the relationship between the railroad and the promise of progress in Costa Rica and Guatemala.

92. These included oil, gas, grains, wine, office supplies, clothing, sugar and panela, machinery, tobacco, salt, coffee, and so on. See MFNLA, Estadística de fletes. Data were kept on a monthly basis from April 1930 to September 1933.

93. See MFNLA, Informe de accidentes, 1931.

94. Ibid.

95. See MFNLA, correspondencia, 1932.

96. *La Época*, 20 October 1933.

97. *El Comercio*, 7 September 1899.

98. *Ideas y Noticias*, 14 October 1933.

99. Guatemala, *Primer Congreso Pedagógico Centroamericano y Primera Exposición Escolar Nacional* (Guatemala City: Tipografía Nacional, 1894), p. 286. See also the 1879 *ley para las municipalidades*, which charged municipal authorities with ending the practice of "carrying goods on the head and the back," in Guatemala, *Recopilación de las leyes emitidas por el gobierno democrático de la República de Guatemala*, 2 vols. (Guatemala: Tipografía El Progreso, 1881), vol. 2, pp. 283–93.

100. See MFNLA, Registro de carga recibida, estación de Quetzaltenango, 1931.

101. Ibid.

102. See MFNLA, miscellaneous, 1932. See also *Ideas y Noticias*, 14 October 1933, for an article calling for an even greater tariff reduction as a way to save the enterprise.

103. Anderson, *Imagined Communities*, p. 44.

104. The writing on the social and cultural importance of monetization is vast, and all of it is indebted to Marx's insights on commodity fetishization. See Karl Marx, *Capital: A Critical Analysis of Capitalist Production*, ed. Frederick Engels, trans. Samuel Moore and Edward Aveling (New York: International Publishers, 1987), pp. 67–144. See also Harvey, *The Condition of Postmodernity*, pp. 99–105.

The following discussion on Quetzalteco photography is greatly indebted to Deborah Poole's *Vision, Race, and Modernity: A Visual Economy of the Andean Image World* (Princeton: Princeton University Press, 1997), chap. 5, where she discusses photographic portraiture as a kind of global currency.

105. At first, in the 1890s, only a few curious K'iche's paid to have their portraits taken; the majority of the studio's clients were upper-class Ladinos and Germans. By the 1930s, however, Zanotti's clients were overwhelmingly indigenous. Compare Piggot's 1897 libro de cuentas with Zanotti's 1937–40 libro de cuentas; see the Zanotti collection, located at the photograph archive of Centro de Investigaciones Regionales de Mesoamérica (CIRMA). In 1897, on average, prices ranged from four pesos for a set of six miniatures to twelve pesos for six double imperials.

106. Poole, *Vision, Race, and Modernity*, p. 203. Zanotti's portraits differ from those of other photographers and anthropologists, in the Americas and throughout the world, who used the new technology as an ethnographic tool to record physical or cultural traits of other "races." In Guatemala, the German photographer Emilio Herbruger, who worked in the 1860s, provides such an example; see his collection in CIRMA. Some of these photographers, such as Edward Curtis, went so far as to touch out traces of modernity; clocks, cars, and umbrellas were erased from the negatives. There is much written on the colonial photographic "gaze" but relatively little on how the subjects themselves appropriated this new technology. See Cristraud M. Geary, *Images from Bamumi: German Colonial Photography at the Court of King Njoya, Cameroon, West Africa, 1902–1915* (Washington, D.C.: Smithsonian Institution Press, 1988); Catherine A. Lutz and Jane Collins, *Reading National Geographic* (Chicago: University of Chicago Press, 1993); and Christopher Lyman, *The Vanishing Race and Other Illusions: Photographs of Edward S. Curtis* (New York: Pantheon Books, 1982).

107. Anne McClintock, "Family Feuds: Gender, Nationalism, and the Family," *Feminist Review* 44 (1993): 62–63.

108. The 1813 census likewise indicates that K'iche' families who lived closer to the center of town tended to be smaller than those residing on the city's rural limits. See Grandin, "Blood," Appendix 11, for the source of the 1760 average. For the 1813 average and mean, see AHA 1 10; the 1896 mean was taken from a partial census of Barrio San Nicolás in AHQ, caja 1896.

109. See Poole, *Vision, Race, and Modernity*, p. 203.

110. Brigham, *Guatemala*, p. 147.

111. See ASA, Libro de sesiones no. 7, 1928–41, 3 September 1934. The following discussion is greatly indebted to a talk given by Susan Besse at the Yale Council on Latin American Studies lecture series, 25 October 1996, "Defining a 'National Type': Brazilian Beauty Contests in the 1920s." See also Colleen Balerino Cohen, Richard Wilk, and Beverly Stoeltje, eds., *Beauty Queens on the Global Stage: Gender, Contests, and Power* (New York: Routledge, 1996).

112. Information on the foundation and inaugural event of the contest comes from ASA, Libro de sesiones no. 7, 1928–41, 5 September 1934, and Gloria

Virginia Tzunún M. and Olegario Obispo Nimatuj J., *1934–1984: Historial del certamen de la belleza indígena de Quetzaltenango* (Quetzaltenango: Casa Publicitaria "GOF," 1985), unless otherwise noted. The contest continues to be held to this day. In 1979, the name of the pageant was changed to the "Um'ial Tinimit Re Xelajuj No'j," which may be translated as Daughter of the People of Xelaju.

113. See Tzunún and Nimatuj, *Historial del certamen*, for brief biographies of all the winners from 1934 to 1984.

114. In recent years these European symbols have given way to images perceived to be more indigenous. Aside from the name change mentioned in n. 112, the crown and long train and collar were replaced by a head wrap and ceremonial huipil. See Tzunún and Nimatuj, *Historial del certamen*.

115. See McAllister, "Authenticity," on the ways this quest for the "really real" plays out on a national level.

116. See the discussion in chap. 6 of the foundation of the Sociedad El Adelanto. See also the number of newspapers published by these societies in the late nineteenth and early twentieth centuries: in Guatemala City, *El Obrero* and *El Eco del Trabajo*; in Quetzaltenango, *El Obrero Altense* and *La Voz del Obrero*. See AGCA, B 119.4 2559 60072, for an attempt to establish a Sociedad de Artesanos during the first liberal period in 1830; AGCA, B 78.49 1513 36265, for the 1877 inauguration of the Sociedad de Artesanos; and AGCA, B 85.1 3601 82952, for the 1874 establishment of the Sociedad de Carpinteros.

117. Justo Rufino Barrios himself patronized Guatemala City's Sociedad Central de Artesanos. Sinforoso Aguilar, a prominent Quetzalteco liberal politician, worked closely with the founders of the Sociedad El Adelanto and procured a monthly stipend from the municipality with which to pay teachers' salaries. Hugo Fleishmann, a wealthy German living in Quetzaltenango, was a "*socio honorario*" of the Sociedad de Artesanos de Quetzaltenango.

118. See Lorenzo Montúfar's speech at the inauguration of the Sociedad Central de Artesanos in Sociedad El Porvenir de Los Obreros, *Medio siglo de vida, 1892–1942* (Guatemala City: Tipografía Nacional, 1942), p. 21. For colonial guilds and societies, see Héctor Humberto Samayoa Guervara, *Los gremios de artesanos de la Ciudad de Guatemala, 1542–1821* (Guatemala: Editorial Piedra Santa, 1978). See also AGCA, drawer 5–21 of its card catalog, for guilds from the colonial period to the late nineteenth century.

119. See, for example, "Mandamientos del trabajo," in *El Obrero*, 18 January 1891, which exhorted apprentices and workers to obey their masters and treat customers fairly; "La clase obrera," in *El Eco del Trabajo*, 1 March 1891, which promoted the ideal of Guatemala as a republic of artisans; "Lorenzo Montúfar, candidato de la clase obrera para presidente," in *El Eco del Trabajo*, 4 July 1891; the "Sección de conocimientos útiles," in *El Obrero Altense*, which ran descriptions of new trade techniques for various crafts; "Cómo se forman los capitales" and "El ahorro," in *El Obrero Altense*, 25 February and 1 March 1901, which encouraged "modern" economic habits; and "El 2 de Abril," in *El Obrero Altense*,

2 April 1901, which commemorated Barrios's death. Obviously, as with schools, these institutions constituted more than a means of enforcing ideological state control; they went on to become important oppositional organizations, playing a key role in the overthrow of Estrada Cabrera and in the emergence of workers unions. See Carlos Figueroa Ibarra, "Contenido de clase y participación obrera en el movimiento antidictatorial de 1920," *Política y Sociedad* 4 (1974): 5–51; Arturo Taracena Arriola, "La confederación obrera de Centro América (COCA): 1921–1928," *Anuario de Estudios Centroamericanos* 10 (1984): 81–94; and Renate Witzel, ed., *Más de 100 años del movimiento obrero urbano en Guatemala: Artesanos y obreros en el período liberal, 1877–1944*, vol. 1 (Guatemala City: Asociación de Investigación y Estudios Sociales Guatemala, 1991).

120. See ASA, correspondencia, 1929. There are numerous other examples of how El Adelanto promoted Guatemalan nationalism. For instance, the annual election of the governing body of El Adelanto took place on 2 April and commemorated Barrios's death; members of El Adelanto often gave speeches during independence celebrations, so as to teach other Indians "what 15 September means" (see the magazine *Quetzaltenango: Feria de Septiembre*, vol. 2, no. 2, 1931); and in 1936, the sociedad organized a "united front of all workers societies" to celebrate independence (see ASA, correspondencia, 1936). See, for other examples, *La Voz de los Obreros*, 1 January 1905; ASA, correspondencia, 1923; ASA, miscellaneous, 1930.

121. See ASA, Libro de Actas no. 1, 2 April 1898; ASA, Matricula de la Escuela primaria de niñas and Inscripción de niños en edad escolar, 1926.

122. See *Prensa Nueva*, 2 October 1934, for the jefe político's order that El Adelanto collect road and city taxes from its members.

123. Sociedad El Adelanto, *Estatutos de la Sociedad El Adelanto* (Quetzaltenango: Tipografía La Industria, 1915), p. 5.

124. See "Preciosas Telas Indígenas," in *Ideas y Noticias*, 30 August 1933.

125. See AHQ, Memoria de los trabajos . . . de la municipalidad, 1934, and Memoria de los trabajos efectuados por la Junta Municipal de . . . Quetzaltenango durante el año 1935, 1935.

126. See ASA, miscellaneous, 1962.

127. McAllister, "Authenticity," pp. 112–13. To this day, there is an important, but unresearched, relationship between the military and elite indigenous rituals. Benedicto Lucas, for example, who as head of the military initiated the scorched earth campaign in 1981, patronizes indigenous cofradías in Cobán and attends the annual fiesta of a prestigious Quetzaltenango K'iche' cofradía. For an example of a debate within the Guatemalan military on the possibility of using indigenous culture for counterinsurgency goals in the Ixil region, see Captain Juan Fernando Cifuentes, "Apreciación de Asuntos Civiles (G-5) para el área Ixil," in *Revista Militar* (Dec. 1982): 25–73.

128. See ASA, miscellaneous, 1933–36, for various examples of financial crisis.

129. For the general drift toward liberal caudillismo and repression under

Estrada Cabrera and Ubico, see Palmer, "A Liberal Discipline," chap. 9; for the militarization of schools and public holidays, and increased state control of public education, see González Orellana, *Historia de la educación*, pp. 332, 359–64; for workers societies under Ubico, see Witzel, ed. *Más de 100 años del movimiento obrero*, pp. 255–322.

130. See ASA, correspondencia, 18 September 1931

131. Federico Hernández de León, *Viajes presidenciales: Breves relatos de algunas expediciones administrativas del general d. Jorge Ubico, presidente de la república*, 2 vols. (Guatemala City: Tipografía Nacional, 1940).

132. See ASA, miscellaneous, 18 November 1932.

133. See ASA, Libro de sesiones no. 7, 1928–41, 3 September and 13 October 1932.

Chapter 8   The Blood of Guatemalans: Class Struggle
and the Death of K'iche' Nationalism

1. Registro Civil de Quetzaltenango (hereafter cited as RCQ), tomo 43, no. 325, 5 July 1954.

2. According to his son, the events surrounding his death are uncertain: "The truth is we do not know what happened. It was night and he left the house and never came back. He was not drunk. The next day we found him"; a member of one of the campesino unions Coyoy helped organize, claims that the "anti-communist committee was going to kill [Coyoy]; that is why he hung himself"; interviews by author, Quetzaltenango, 19 July and 23 July 1997. In Quetzaltenango, according to the civil registry, in the days following Arbenz's resignation, a number of young men died under suspicious, violent circumstances. See RCQ, tomo 43, no. 307, 28 June; no. 310, 28 June; no. 311, 28 June; no. 319, 30 June; no. 321 1 July; and no. 331, 10 July. One elderly man from the outskirts of Quetzaltenango recalls that in the days following the fall of Arbenz, "many were killed"; eighty-year-old campesino from Xecaracoj, interview by author, Quetzaltenango, 19 August 1997.

3. Jim Handy, *Revolution in the Countryside: Community, Land, and Reform in Guatemala* (Chapel Hill: University of North Carolina Press, 1994), pp. 194–95. For the clearest admission of U.S. responsibility in the overthrow of Arbenz, see a recently declassified report written by a historian who was granted access to classified CIA documents, Nicholas Cullather, "Operation PBSUCCESS: The United States and Guatemala, 1952–1954" (Washington D.C.: Center for the Study of Intelligence, Central Intelligence Agency, 1994), a copy of which can be located in the National Security Archive, Gelman Library, Suite 701, George Washington University. See also Piero Gleijeses, *Shattered Hope: The Guatemalan Revolution and the United States, 1944–1954* (Princeton: Princeton University Press, 1991), and Stephen C. Schlesinger and Stephen Kinzer, *Bitter Fruit: The Untold Story of the American Coup in Guatemala* (New York: Doubleday, 1982).

4. According to one report in an anti-Arbenz Quetzalteco newspaper, by 6 July, 2,200 "communists" were behind bars; see *El Diario de Quetzaltenango*, 6 July 1954. See Jim Handy, *Revolution in the Countryside*, chap. 8, for a discussion of the politics of the "Liberation," and the book by Guillermo Toriello, Arbenz's minister of foreign relations, that contains a "partial list" of 217 assassinated workers and peasants, most of whom were from the southern and Atlantic coasts. The list was compiled by the Confederación General de Trabajadores de Guatemala; Guillermo Toriello, *La batalla de Guatemala* (Mexico City: Cuadernos Americanos, 1955), pp. 331–33. Richard N. Adams, in a personal communication, reports that Guatemala City jails held three thousand prisoners arrested following Castillo Armas's victory. Cindy Forster, in an unpublished manuscript based on interviews she conducted on the south coast, estimates that one thousand agricultural workers were killed by members of Castillo Armas's army in the Finca Jocatán, in Tiquisate, Escuintla.

5. In addition to the Comisión para el Esclarecimiento Histórico's report, *Guatemala: Memory of Silence*, see the Oficina de Derechos Humanos del Arzobispado de Guatemala, *Guatemala: Nunca más* (Guatemala City: Oficina de Derechos Humanos del Arzobispado de Guatemala, 1998).

6. See Oscar de León Aragón, *Caída de un Régimen: Jorge Ubico-Federico Ponce, 20 de Octubre 1944* (Guatemala City: Facultad Latinoamericana de Ciencias Sociales, 1995).

7. Luis Cardoza y Aragón, *La revolución guatemalteca* (Montevideo, Uruguay: Ediciones Pueblos Unidos, 1956), pp. 47–102.

8. See Knight, "Racism, Revolution and Indigenismo," and Francois Chevalier, "Official 'Indigenism' in Peru in 1920: Origins, Significance, and Socioeconomic Scope," in *Race and Class in Latin America*, ed. Magnus Mörner, 1970, for similar processes in Mexico and Peru.

9. See Miguel Angel Asturias's infamous university thesis, published as *El problema social del indio y otros textos* (Paris: Centre de Recherches de l'Institut d'Etudes Hispaniques, 1971), in which he argues for miscegenation. In *El Señor Presidente*, although Asturias still depicts Indians as anonymous victims trapped by their own psychological pathologies, he brings the debate on the "Indian problem" to the level of national politics through an examination of the impact of decades of corruption and dictatorship; *El señor presidente*, trans. Frances Partridge (New York: Atheneum, 1983). In Asturias's famous "banana trilogy," he moves the discussion into the economic realm; see *Viento fuerte* (Buenos Aires: Editorial Losada, 1950); *El Papa verde* (Buenos Aires: Editorial Losada, 1954); and *Los ojos de los enterrados* (Buenos Aires: Editorial Losada, 1960). See also Monteforte Toledo, *Entre la piedra y la cruz*, and Flavio Herrera, *El tigre* (Guatemala City: Editorial Universitaria, 1989), for two novels that explore, somewhat luridly, the impact of migration and plantation labor on Indians.

10. See Dennis Floyd Casey, "Indigenismo: The Guatemalan Experience" (Ph.D. diss., University of Kansas, 1979), chap. 6.

11. See Stern, "Feudalism, Capitalism, and the World-System," pp. 26–27, for a more extensive discussion. See Eric Hobsbawm, *The Age of Extremes: A History of the World, 1914–1991* (New York: Vintage Books, 1994), pp. 175–77, for this subject in the context of post–World War II politics and optimism.

12. See Jim Handy, *Revolution in the Countryside*, pp. 82–83, for the influence of international economic agencies in promoting support in Guatemala for land reform.

13. It was activists and intellectuals of the PGT (Partido Guatemalteco de Trabajo, or Communist Party) who both crafted and played a key role in implementing the legislation. See Gleijeses, *Shattered Hope*, and Gustavo Porras, "Análisis estructural y recomposición clasista de la sociedad guatemalteca de 1954–1980," in *Seminario Estado, Clases Sociales y Cuestión Etnico-Nacional*, ed. Centro de Estudios Integrados de Desarrollo Comunal (Mexico City: Editorial Praxis, 1992).

14. For a more extensive discussion of the reform, see Handy, *Gift of the Devil*, 1984, chap. 4.

15. See the prologue in Cardoza y Aragón, *La revolución guatemalteca*; Handy, *Gift of the Devil*; and Robert Wasserstrom, "Revolution in Guatemala: Peasants and Politics under the Arbenz Government," *Comparative Studies in Society and History* 17 (October 1975): 443–78. See also Jim Handy, "National Policy, Agrarian reform, and the Corporate Community during the Guatemalan Revolution, 1944–1954," *Comparative Studies in Society and History* 30 (1988): 698–724, for a discussion of some of these positions. See Luis Cardoza y Aragón's interview "The Revolution of '44–'54—A Reappraisal," in *Guatemala*, ed. Susanne Jonas and David Tobis (New York: North American Congress on Latin America, 1974), p. 55, where he states that "none of the laws, including the agrarian reform, were more than moderate."

16. Porras, "Análisis estructural y recomposición clasista"; see pp. 87–94, 89, and 88 for the quotations that follow. See Gleijeses, *Shattered Hope*, chap. 8, and Handy, *Revolution in the Countryside*, chap. 4, for more detailed discussions on how the reform was implemented. See Guillermo Paz Cárcamo, *Guatemala: Reforma Agraria*, 3d ed. (Guatemala City: Facultad Latinoamericana de Ciencias Sociales, 1997), for a description of how the reform was designed to force investment in productive relations by strengthening the power of the peasantry. A close examination of the connection between the rural peasant organization of the 1950s and the Guatemalan insurgency of the 1960s and 1970s has not yet been undertaken. Based on research conducted by Daniel Wilkinson, it appears that much of the initial base of the Organización Revolucionaria del Pueblo en Armas in the San Marcos region were political activists during the Arbenz period.

17. Handy, *Gift of the Devil*, p. 94.

18. See Tutino, *From Insurrection*, pp. 343–47, where he discusses agrarian violence, including the Cristero revolt of west central Mexico. Tutino writes: "The extent, endurance, and intensity of the Cristero revolt forced the rulers of

revolutionary Mexico to understand that partial and politicized land redistribution would not pacify the countryside and allow the consolidation of state power. . . . The Cristero revolt left Mexican leaders to choose between halting or completing the agrarian reform. The depression opened up the possibility of completing it"; pp. 346–47.

19. See Gleijeses, *Shattered Hope*, for the former argument and Schlesinger and Kinzer, *Bitter Fruit*, for the latter.

20. Handy's *Revolution in the Countryside* makes an important contribution to this discussion.

21. The following description is drawn from weekly informes de la Policía Nacional, located in the AGQ, which give detailed accounts of daily political activity.

22. Alfonso Bauer Paiz defines the revolution as being led by the national petite-bourgeoisie: "The revolution . . . was anti-feudal and anti-imperialist. Its vanguard was a combination of social forces made up of university and secondary education students, teachers, low-level military officials and professionals, mostly young, and a minority of the national bourgeoisie. The real social base of the revolution was constituted from these sectors of the national petite-bourgeoisie in alliance with workers and peasants, but always led by the petite-bourgeoisie"; see Alfonso Bauer Paiz's "La revolución guatemalteca del '20 de octubre de 1944,'" and "Acotaciones y comentarios de Alfonso Bauer Paiz al libro de Luis Cardoza y Aragón, 'la revolución guatemalteca,'" in his *Antología de ensayos* (Guatemala City: Consejo de Instituciones de Desarrollo de Guatemala, 1995); see p. 44 for the quote.

23. See Handy, *Revolution in the Countryside*, pp. 27–30, and Levenson-Estrada, *Trade Unionists*, for a more detailed examination of the emergence of organized labor during this period.

24. See AGQ, jefatura política, 1944.

25. *El Popular*, 25 January 1947.

26. See AGQ, jefatura política, 1945 and 1947.

27. See Richard N. Adams, "Ethnic Images and Strategies in 1944," in *Guatemalan Indians and the State, 1540–1988*, ed. Carol A. Smith (Austin: University of Texas Press, 1990), pp. 142–43, and Handy, *Revolution in the Countryside*, p. 54.

28. Richard N. Adams, "Las matanzas de Patzicía en 1944: Una reflexión," in *Etnias en evolución social: Estudios de Guatemala y Centroamérica* (Mexico: Universidad Autónoma Metropolitana, 1995).

29. Adams, "Ethnic Images and Strategies in 1944," pp. 144–45.

30. See AGQ, 1944.

31. See AGQ, Informe de Policía Nacional, 1944.

32. Evidence of this is found in a certificate issued by the National Police in Guatemala City, dated 5 May 1944 and found in the AGQ. It reads: "Se hace constar que el portador, Julio Pérez Cutzal es Agente Confidencial de este cuerpo, por lo que se suplica guardarle las consideraciones del caso como tal y prestarle el auxilio que requiera para el legal cumplimiento de su deber."

33. See AGQ, partes de la policía, October 1944.

34. *El Popular*, 25 January 1947.

35. See *El Popular*, 21 March and 16 May 1947.

36. See Jim Handy, *Revolution in the Countryside*, pp. 83–84, 88, for opposition to the reform from the Asociación General de Agricultores; see p. 68 for its demand for government protection from peasant unrest.

37. Gleijeses, *Shattered Hope*, p. 73; and Bauer Paiz, "La revolución guatemalteca, p. 44.

38. For Coyoy, see *El Correo del Occidente*, 22 November 1950; for the tanners, see AGQ, partes del jefe político, 1946.

39. See *El Correo del Occidente*, 27 November 1952 and 23 July 1953; and *El Popular*, 9 October 1948, for divisions over political positioning within the revolutionary parties. See *El Diario del Occidente*, 7 June 1954, for a committee from the Quetzalteco chapter of the PAR that went to ask Arbenz to control campesinos and communists.

40. *El Correo del Occidente*, 8 December 1952.

41. See, for example, the editorial in *El Correo del Occidente*, 14 December 1953, entitled "Habrá que poner un límite, Presidente," which criticized Arbenz for letting the agrarian situation get out of hand; also see *La Proa*, 21 February 1953, which criticized the agrarian reform as a political tool to reward supporters, and the editorial written a few days after Arbenz's resignation by Carlos Enrique Guillén, a former mayor affiliated with the PIN, in *El Diario de Quetzaltenango*, 1 July 1954.

42. Interview by author, Quetzaltenango, 9 July 1997. One retired K'iche' shoemaker recalls that during the 1947 shoemakers' strike, shop owners, some of them K'iche', accused the leaders of being communists. See also *El Correo del Occidente*, 8 and 11 July 1950, for charges that the Sindicato de Albañiles was Marxist.

43. The following voting data for 1944 and 1950 come from the AGQ.

44. Handy, *Revolution in the Countryside*, p. 37.

45. See Cindy Forster, "Reforging National Revolution: Campesino Labor Struggles in Guatemala, 1944–1954," in *Identity and Struggle at the Margins of the Nation-State: The Laboring Peoples of Central America and the Hispanic Caribbean*, ed. Aviva Chomsky and Aldo Lauria-Santiago (Durham: Duke University Press, 1998), for a further discussion of radicalized rural and coastal workers.

46. Jim Handy, *Revolution in the Countryside*, pp. 37–38, for Arbenz's speeches; see AGQ, jefatura política, 1950 for the complaint and threat.

47. The following description of the valley comes from Catalina Izás Ferriño, *Problemas socio-económicos de Pacajóa y Llano del Pinal: Comunidades del Valle de Palajunoj, Quetzaltenango* (Quetzaltenango: Universidad de San Carlos, Escuela de Servicio Social Rural, 1966).

48. Izás Ferriño, *Problemas socio-económicos*, p. 28.

49. Information on Valentín Coyoy Cruz, unless otherwise cited, comes from

two interviews conducted by the author with his older son, Quetzaltenango, on 23 and 25 August 1997.

50. See AGQ, Formulario de Solicitud de Explotación Forestal, Valentín Coyoy Cruz, 1948.

51. In 1946, the Arévalo government legally recognized the existence of comunidades indígenas or comunidades campesinas. The establishment of these separate political organizations within municipalities provided activists from revolutionary parties and unions a ready-made base from which to organize. Many of the conflicts that erupted in municipalities during the Arbenz years took place between these comunidades and the municipality. Handy, *Revolution in the Countryside*, pp. 149–57.

52. According to a surviving member of the Unión Campesina de Llanos de Pinal, five of the key campesino organizers from the valley used their PAR connections to obtain employment in the customs agency. Interview by author, Quetzaltenango, 3 September 1997.

53. See, for example, AHQ, Memoria de la Municipalidad, 1931, for the report on illegal cultivation and pasture in city forests.

54. *El Popular*, 7 August 1948.

55. See AHQ, Actas, 14 October 1948; see also Actas, 26 February and 10 September 1952 for other conflicts surrounding municipal forests.

56. See AHQ, Vecinos de los Cantones Xecaracoj and Xepach solicitan se les permita pastar, 1945.

57. See AHQ, Actas, 27 September 1948; see also Actas, 1 February 1949, for peasant demand that the municipality make more land available for rental; see AGQ, Jefatura política, 1949, for the complaint that Coyoy organized the demand.

58. See AHQ, Actas, 14 October 1948.

59. Ibid., 17 January 1951.

60. Ibid., 16 June 1951.

61. For the specifics on how the reform functioned, see Handy, *Revolution in the Countryside*, pp. 86–100.

62. See Instituto Nacional de Transformación Agraria (hereafter cited as INTA), Private Fincas: San José Patzulin; El Faro; Buena Vista o Monte Cristo; Palajunoj; La Providencia; San Rafael; El Silencio; La Libertad.

63. See INTA, Municipal Lands, Quetzaltenango: Terrenos Comunales.

64. See INTA, Municipal Lands, Quetzaltenango: Cerro Chiquito y Cerro Quemado.

65. A surviving member of the union claims the land had been granted them by Ubico in the 1930s; in the late 1940s, the municipality began to charge rent for the land.

66. See INTA, Municipal Lands, Quetzaltenango: Cerro Chiquito y Cerro Quemado. The municipal representative to the CAL in 1952 was the K'iche' Juez de Ejidos Julio Pisquiy. See AHQ, Actas, 29 October 1952.

67. See INTA, Municipal Lands, Quetzaltenango: Pié de Tigre.

68. *El Diario de Quetzaltenango*, 8 June 1954. For U.S.-supplied planes and the preinvasion propaganda campaign, see Cullather, "Operation PBSUCCESS," pp. 46–51.

69. See AHQ, Actas, 27 September 1948.

70. *El Correo del Occidente*, 8 December 1952; see also 20 August 1952 for rumors spread by anticommunists that the city was about to be attacked by communists supplied with weapons from Eastern Europe.

71. See AHQ, Actas, 11 January 1953.

72. See AHQ, Actas, 5 April 1954, for protest by market women.

73. See *El Correo del Occidente*, 27 November and 9 December 1952; AHQ, Actas, 11 February 1953.

74. For other examples of divisions within the revolutionary parties, see *El Correo del Occidente*, 9 and 27 November 1952; and see 8 December 1953, for the PRG allying with the PIACO in an effort to have the municipal elections (which the PAR won) nullified.

75. See INTA, Municipal Lands, Quetzaltenango: Cerro Chiquito y Cerro Quemado; AHQ, Actas, 5 July 1954.

76. See AHQ, Actas, 20 January 1954.

77. Ibid., 30 March 1953.

78. Ibid., 22 October 1953, and INTA, Municipal Lands, Quetzaltenango: Cerro Chiquito y Cerro Quemado. Pérez's zealous defense of city lands notwithstanding, racism still infused whatever alliance existed among K'iche' and Ladino elites. In March 1953, Pérez asked his fellow council members if he could represent the municipality's interests to the department's agrarian commission. His Ladino colleagues declined his help and ruled that somebody better versed in law and politics be appointed. See AHQ, Actas, 4 March 1953.

79. See INTA, Municipal Lands, Quetzaltenango: Cerro Chiquito y Cerro Quemado.

80. See AHQ, Actas, 17 May 1953.

81. Ibid., 28 December 1953.

82. Despite the middle- to lower-class composition of the committee, it is clear from interviews that there was general dissatisfaction with both Arbenz and the land reform among many K'iche' elites. In a personal communication, Irma Nimatuy reports that one wealthy Quetzalteco K'iche' was friends with a founder of the *Movimiento de Liberación Nacional*—a right-wing political party infamous for organizing Guatemala's first death squad—and that following Arbenz's overthrow he helped organize at least one meeting of the party among urban K'iche's. Furthermore, there seems to have been concern among the general urban K'iche' population regarding the political activity that was taking place during Arbenz's tenure. According to interviews conducted by Nimatuy, at one point during Arbenz's rule, a group of K'iche's arrived at the house of a neighboring K'iche' "communist" and demanded that he stop his organizing work.

83. See INTA, Municipal Lands, Quetzaltenango: Terrenos Comunales; INTA, Municipal Lands, Quetzaltenango: Cerro Chiquito y Cerro Quemado.

84. Interview by author, Quetzaltenango, 19 July 1997. Antonio Juárez, Catarino Coyoy, and Gregorio Macario Jocol were active in the committee formed by Pérez. See AHQ, Actas, 28 December 1953, and INTA, Municipal Lands, Quetzaltenango: Terrenos Comunales; INTA, Municipal Lands, Quetzaltenango: Cerro Chiquito y Cerro Quemado.

85. Interview by author, Quetzaltenango, 23 July 1997.

86. Interview by author, Quetzaltenango, 29 July 1997.

87. See *El Diario de Quetzaltenango*, 28 February 1953.

88. See AHQ, Actas, 3 March 1954.

89. Ibid., 7 April 1954.

90. Interview, 25 August 1997.

91. See AHQ, Actas, 5 July 1997.

92. See AGQ, 1954; *El Diario de Quetzaltenango*, 1 and 6 July 1954.

93. Ibid., 14 July 1954.

94. Interview by author, Quetzaltenango. Informant was a member of the Unión Campesina de Llanos del Pinal and in the month following Arbenz's resignation was arrested twice for organizing opposition to the counterrevolution.

95. Interview by author, Quetzaltenango, 3 August 1997. See INTA, Municipal Lands, Quetzaltenango, for the revocations.

96. For Coyoy, see *El Correo del Occidente*, 22 November 1950; for the tanners, see AGQ, partes del jefe político, 1946.

97. Hobsbawm, *Nations and Nationalism*, p. 120.

98. During the Arbenz years informant worked as a tailor in his own shop, which employed two K'iche's. Interview by author, Quetzaltenango, 25 July 1997.

99. For example, see Ralph Beals, "Acculturation," in *Social Anthropology*, ed. Manning Nash (Austin: University of Texas Press, 1967); Handy, "National Policy"; Wasserstrom, "Revolution in Guatemala."

100. In Wasserstrom's "Revolution in Guatemala," which emphasizes class conflict within the community, "class" is juxtaposed to "community." Jim Handy has recently presented the most detailed and diverse analysis of the complex ways the reform played out in a number communities, and he concludes that "[t]hroughout rural Guatemala, vecinos of municipalities used the agrarian reform Law, despite its intentions, as a weapon in age-old conflicts specific to their communities." Nevertheless, Handy remains hesitant to analyze how these conflicts create the very idea of "community," arguing that "much of the unrest that exploded in rural Guatemala during the revolution was a function of the continuing strength of community identification"; see Handy, *Revolution in the Countryside*, pp. 166, 139.

101. Interview by author, Quetzaltenango, 29 July 1997.

102. According to Coyoy's son, the two alcaldes auxiliaries who attacked his mother and father with a gun were from Pacajá, a neighboring aldea. Another informant also confirms that most of the violence was conducted by local auxiliaries and guardabosques by order of Julio Pérez Cutzal.

103. Hobsbawm, *The Age of Extremes*, pp. 175–77.

104. Quoted in Handy, *Revolution in the Countryside*, p. 78.

105. The state's counterinsurgency campaign was directed at a powerful, threatening, leftist insurgency. Many of the Indians who were killed, tortured, and otherwise persecuted, as well as many of the indigenous communities that were destroyed, were singled out by the military because they in fact supported the guerrillas and not because they were Indians. Nevertheless, the campaign did have a strong ethnic dimension. The equation of communism with rural indigenous society, as this work has demonstrated, has deep roots and cannot be abstracted from general caste anxiety.

Conclusions: The Limits of Nation, 1954–1999

1. Hobsbawm, *Nations and Nationalism*, p. 191.

2. This assertion needs to be qualified socially and geographically, for significant portions of the urban middle and upper class clearly can imagine a nation, as is demonstrated by the ongoing resentment caused by the loss of Belize (the "dismemberment of the nation" as it is sometimes described); see *Prensa Libre* 9 November 1997.

3. Nationalism immediately posed a theoretical challenge to nineteenth- and early-twentieth-century Marxist political activists. For a summary of the early debates within Marxism on the "national question," see James M. Blaut, *The National Question: Decolonizing the Theory of Nationalism* (London: Zed, 1987). Far from resolving themselves, these debates have ongoing relevance in a range of political arenas—from struggles involving "third world" movements for national liberation and the relationship of these movements to indigenous populations within their national borders to what Cornel West has called the "new politics of cultural identity" in developed countries. See the discussion in Hale, "Mestizaje, Hybridity and the Cultural Politics of Difference," especially pp. 37–38. These debates are too complex and far-ranging to go into here, but they all share a foundational dilemma: On what social position and identity should resistance and political strategy be based? Throughout the twentieth century in Latin America, orthodox Communist Parties have managed, at various points, to champion the creation of national capitalism and fight for national liberation, while simultaneously dismissing ethnic identity as a false, or reactionary, consciousness. This contradiction was made possible by a linking of nationalism and state formation to the national organization of international capitalism; thus

nationalism was afforded a position of epistemological privilege not granted to other equally subjective identities such as ethnicity and gender. See the Lenin-Luxembourg debate summarized in Blaut, *The National Question*.

4. Terry Eagleton, "Nationalism: Irony and Commitment" in *Nationalism, Colonialism and Literature*, ed. Terry Eagleton, Fredric Jameson, and Edward Said (Minneapolis: University of Minnesota Press, 1990). Of course, by equating nationalism with class, Eagleton stresses the subjective nature of both and removes the "objective" vantage point from which judgments regarding political strategies can be made. My own understanding, succinctly, is informed by the work of Philip Corrigan and Derek Sayer: capitalism produces multiple identities, class consciousness being one of them. This is not to say that strategies and analysis can use equally any one of these subjectivities as a starting point; both analysis and tactics need to be rooted in the material processes that produce these identities. See the essays collected in Philip Corrigan, ed., *Capitalism, State Formation, and Marxist Theory* (London: Quartet Books, 1980). This view differs from the work of E. P. Thompson in that although Thompson stresses the cultural production of class identity, that identity is always inherent in the material processes. No other identity could have emerged. See Thompson, *The Making of the English Working Class*. Also see Stuart Hall on this question in "Race Articulation and Societies Structured in Dominance," in *Sociological Theories: Race and Colonialism*, ed. UNESCO (Paris: UNESCO, 1980), wherein Hall writes: "Race is the modality through which class is lived." See also Ernesto Laclau and Chantal Mouffe, *Hegemony and Socialist Strategy* (London: Verso Press, 1985).

5. See Hale, "Mestizaje, Hybridity and the Cultural Politics of Difference," for efforts currently under way by Ladinos to define a more Mestizo, or hybrid, national identity.

6. Carol A. Smith argues that the Left "subjected [Indians] to an intense barrage of revolutionary rhetoric designed to break down the parochial bases for their grievances against the state and unite them (with lower-class Ladino cadres) into a national-liberation movement against the state in which they would be unified by the grievances of all oppressed . . . and end the divided, exploited, and assumed marginal existence of Maya communities." Carol A. Smith, "Race-Class-Gender Ideology in Guatemala: Modern and Anti-Modern Forms," in *Women Out of Place: The Gender of Agency and the Race of Nationality*, ed. Brackette F. Williams (New York: Routledge, 1996), p. 67. In my opinion, this view confuses revolutionary rhetoric with the revolutionary experience. Notwithstanding the rhetoric of Left leaders, Indians—especially in the EGP area—joined the revolution in some cases as whole communities and in other cases as extended families. This perspective also does not take into account the role of the CUC leadership (which was overwhelmingly Indian) in defining revolutionary experiences and goals. Rather than break them down, the strength of the CUC derived from its ability to *articulate* local grievances with a larger national liberation movement. See Grandin, "To End with All These Evils: Ethnic Transforma-

tion and Community Mobilization in Guatemala's Western Highlands, 1954–1980," *Latin American Perspectives* 24, no. 2 (1997): 7–33, for a discussion of how local power relations (including communal divisions) came to articulate with the goals of the popular and armed movements.

7. Generally speaking, Guatemala has experienced two broad periods of insurgency and counterinsurgency. The first period took place in the Ladino east between 1962 and 1970. In order to defeat a couple of hundred rebels, the counterinsurgency there left about ten thousand dead. The second period of insurgency occurred in various areas of the country, including the indigenous western highlands. Although massacres and other forms of political repression have been common throughout the last thirty years, when people talk of the scorched earth campaign, they are usually referring to a contained, intensified period of counterinsurgency, under the regimes of Lucas García and Ríos Montt between the months of September 1981 and October 1982, in which hundreds of massacres of indigenous communities took place throughout the highlands. For descriptions of the logic of the terror in 1981–82, see Ricardo Falla, *Masacres de la selva: Ixcán, Guatemala 1975–1982* (Guatemala City: Editorial Universitaria, 1993).

8. See Asociación para el Avance de las Ciencias Sociales en Guatemala (AVANCSO), *¿Dónde está el futuro? Procesos de reintegración en comunidades de retornados* (Guatemala City: AVANCSO, 1992).

9. Víctor Gálvez Borrell et al., *¿Qué sociedad queremos? Una mirada desde el movimiento y las organizaciones mayas* (Guatemala City: Facultad Latinoamericana de Ciencias Sociales, 1997), pp. 63–65.

10. See McCreery, *Rural Guatemala*, p. 334, for the "colonial compact."

11. A number of factors contributed to this. See Shelton Davis, "Introduction: Sowing the Seeds of Violence," in *The Harvest of Violence: The Maya Indians and the Guatemalan Crisis*, ed. Robert Carmack (Norman: University of Oklahoma Press, 1998). This analysis conforms with the findings of the Comisión para el Esclarecimiento Histórico (the Guatemalan Truth Commission). See *Memory of Silence*, p. 18.

12. See Brintnall, *Revolt against the Dead*; Falla, *Quiché Rebelde*; W. Smith, *The Fiesta System*; Davis, "Introduction"; and Lester Schmid, *Papel de la mano de obra migratoria en el desarrollo económico de Guatemala* (Guatemala City: Universidad de San Carlos, 1973).

13. Falla, *Quiché Rebelde*. See also Warren, *Symbols of Subordination*, for a discussion of Acción Católica.

14. John Tutino (personal communication) points out that "prior to 1954, Guatemalan history was fundamentally negotiated among internal forces. Since 1954, [national] elites have been able to derive power from outside [i.e., the United States]; thus they have found little need to negotiate as much with local elites and popular groups. That would make that key year of U.S. intervention the point of watershed in a history long marked by internal negotiations; now increasingly marked by imposed brutality."

15. Gálvez et al, *¿Qué sociedad queremos?*, p. 63.

16. See Rigoberta Menchú and Comité de Unidad Campesina, *Trenzando el futuro: Luchas campesinas en la historia reciente de Guatemala* (Madrid: Tercera Prensa-Hirugarren Prentsa, S.L., 1992); José Manuel Fernández Fernández, *El Comité de Unidad Campesina: Origen y desarrollo* (Guatemala City: Centro de Estudios Rurales Centroamericanos, 1988); and Grandin, "To End with All These Evils."

17. See Arturio Arias, "Changing Indian Identity: Guatemala's Violent Transition to Modernity," in *Guatemalan Indians and the State, 1540–1988*, ed. Carol A. Smith (Austin: University of Texas Press, 1990).

18. These observations are drawn from a series of interviews I conducted with CUC members. The results were published in Grandin, "To End With All These Evils."

19. See Diócesis de Quiché, *El Quiché: El pueblo y su iglesia* (Santa Cruz Quiché: Diócesis del Quiché, 1994), for the Spanish text of the Declaration of Iximché, pp. 265–73.

20. This rhetoric was backed up by social power. A few weeks after Iximché, the CUC would lead the largest strike in Guatemala's history. In the economically important agro-export zone of the southern coast, the strike—which was formed from an unprecedented coalition of seventy-five thousand Ladinos and Indians, including both seasonal migratory workers from the highlands and permanent unionized coastal workers—shut down sugar and cotton production.

21. Despite serious limitations, the EGP and ORPA were by far the most sensitive to indigenous concerns of the four rebel groups. See Organización Revolucionaria del Pueblo en Armas, *La verdadera magnitud del racismo (Racismo II)*, 1978, and Centro de Estudios Integrados de Desarrollo Comunal, *Guatemala: Seminario sobre la realidad étnica*, vol. 2 (Mexico City: Centro de Estudios Integrados de Desarrollo Comunal, 1990), which contains the positions on ethnicity, racism, and national identity of the EGP, ORPA, and the two other groups in the URNG (the Fuerzas Armadas Rebeldes and the Partido Guatemalteco de Trabajo). The EGP's position was anonymously written up by Mario Payeras, and it has since been published posthumously in Mario Payeras, *Los pueblos indígenas y la revolución guatemalteca* (Guatemala City: Luna y Sol, 1997). In this work Payeras defines Guatemala as a "multi-*national* country" (emphasis mine; observation by Marcie Mersky).

22. For a more detailed discussion of the emergence and program of these groups, see Santiago Bastos's and Manuela Camus's *Quebrando el silencio: Organizaciones del pueblo maya y sus demandas* (Guatemala City: Facultad Latinoamericana de Ciencias Sociales, 1992) and *Abriendo caminos: Las organizaciones mayas desde el Nobel hasta el Acuerdo de Derechos Indígenas* (Guatemala City: Facultad Latinoamericana de Ciencias Sociales, 1995), as well as Gálvez et al., *¿Qué sociedad queremos?*

23. See Bastos's and Camus's *Quebrando el silencio* and *Abriendo caminos*, pp. 169–74.

24. For a brief history of Comité Xel-Jú, see Gálvez et al., *¿Qué sociedad queremos?*, pp. 58–60.

25. Tim Johnson, "Maya Mayor Triumphs over Entrenched Racism," *Miami Herald*, 15 January 1996. The case of Quetzaltenango begs for comparison with that of Juchitán, Mexico, a Zapotec town of about one hundred thousand residents, where since the beginning of the 1980s, the Coalición Obrera Campesina Estudiantil del Istmo (COCEI), has been the primary political power. Two recent books, Rubin's *Decentering the Regime* and Campbell's *Zapotec Renaissance*, detail the historic development of ethnic, class, and national relations in terms similar to those I have described as taking place in Quetzaltenango. In Juchitán, in marked contrast, intracommunal struggles to define the community resulted in a powerful, class-based ethnic ideology: "Until the 1970s Juchiteco politicians used Zapotec ethnicity and claims to cultural authenticity primarily as weapons against political [outside] opponents. . . . As class differentiation divided the Juchiteco community . . . poorer, politically marginalized . . . elements [which make up COCEI] within Juchitán also began to use ethnicity as weapon against members of the old [pro-Institutional Revolutionary Party] Juchiteco elite"; Campbell, p. 243.

26. It was this "progressive" sector of the bourgeoisie, as represented by the Partido de Avanzada Nacional, which was in power when the peace treaty was finally signed in 1996. On this point, see Jeffrey M. Paige's analysis of the rise of the nonagricultural bourgeoisie in Central America, in *Coffee and Power: Revolution and the Rise of Democracy in Central America* (Cambridge: Harvard University Press, 1997).

27. See Gálvez et al., *¿Qué sociedad queremos?*, pp. 49–69, for a more in-depth discussion of some of the points raised here.

28. Gálvez et al., *¿Qué sociedad queremos?*, p. 52.

29. Colin Woodward, "After the Long Civil War, Academics in Guatemala Remain Cautious," *Chronicle of Higher Education*, 11 July 1997, A35. In another parallel, this one to events in 1953–54, Zapeta repeatedly criticizes indigenous organizations such as CONIC for their lack of respect for private property, calling on the state to forcibly evict Indians and campesinos involved in land struggles. See his editorial, "Luz de Mackenney, Madre Angustiada," in *Siglo Veintiuno*, 28 August 1997, p. 15. By citing Zapeta, I do not suggest that he is representative of pan-Mayan activists. His confrontational language and close ties to the right have caused many Mayan activists in fact to distance themselves from him, and a few who have read this manuscript have questioned why I chose to cite him. My reason is that despite Zapeta's marginalization in the pan-Mayan movement, he is the most vocal person in articulating an ethnic identity separate from class position, a position shared by many Mayan cultural activists.

30. Eagleton, "Nationalism," p. 31.

31. Paul Gilroy, for example, talks of the "cultural mutation and restless (dis)continuity that exceed racial discourse and avoid capture by its agents"; Gilroy, *The Black Atlantic: Modernity and Double Consciousness* (Cambridge: Harvard University Press, 1993), p. 2.

32. Ann Laura Stoler, *Race and the Education of Desire: Foucault's History of Sexuality and the Colonial Order of Things* (Durham: Duke University Press, 1995), p. 72.

33. See Nelson, *A Finger in the Wound*, for an astute discussion of these identities in contemporary Guatemala.

34. See, for example, the work of the Asociación de Cooperación para el Desarrollo Rural de Occidente (CDRO), which is discussed in Morna Macleod, *Poder Local: Reflexiones sobre Guatemala* (Oxford: Oxfam, 1997), chap. 5. The research currently being conducted by Monica Dehart promises to shed much light on the potential and limitations of these forms of ethnic-based development projects. Throughout the developing world, the term *local power* trips off the lips of representatives of international development agencies like a mantra. The concept, with its implication of decentralization and reduced state obligations, and its emphasis steered away from macroeconomic power relations, conveniently dovetails with many of the designs of neoliberal restructuring. Nevertheless in Guatemala, the term should not so readily be dismissed, as discussed below.

35. I am greatly indebted to Liz Oglesby and Marcie Mersky for my understanding of this point.

36. For the strategic hamlets, see Centro de Estudios Integrados de Desarrollo Comunal, *Guatemala, polos de desarrollo*; for the civil patrols, see Joel A. Solomon, *Violencia Institucional: Las Patrullas de Autodefensa Civil en Guatemala, 1993–1994*, trans. P. O. Coj (Washington D.C.: Robert F. Kennedy Memorial Center for Human Rights, 1994); for the displaced, see AVANCSO's *Política institucional hacia el desplazado interno en Guatemala* (Guatemala City: AVANCSO, 1988), *Vonós a la capital: Estudio sobre la emigración rural reciente en Guatemala* (Guatemala City: AVANCSO, 1990) and *¿Dónde está el futuro?*

37. David Stoll is correct when he identifies local conflicts, rather than ideological persuasion, as the reason many Indians joined the guerrillas. He is wrong, however, in the conclusion he draws. Because local grievances rather than ethnic or class resentment fueled the initial stages of the insurgency, Stoll thinly argues that the violence did not have "social roots." See his theoretical framework in *Between Two Armies in the Ixil Towns of Guatemala* (New York: Columbia University Press, 1993), pp. 14–20. A more thorough engagement with the scholarship on Mexican agrarian violence would be a salubrious corrective to the anemic analyses so far brought to bear on the Guatemalan revolution. See especially John Tutino's important work, *From Insurrection to Revolution*.

38. See the accord, which is in Skinner-Klée, ed. *Legislación indigenista*.

39. See Ayelet Shachar, "Group Identity and Women's Rights in Family Law: The Perils of Multicultural Accommodation," *The Journal of Political Philosophy* 6, no. 3 (1998): 285–305, for a general discussion of legal contradictions between gender and cultural rights. See also Catharine MacKinnon, "Whose Culture? A Case Note of Martínez v. Santa Clara Pueblo," in her *Feminism Unmodified* (Cambridge: Harvard University Press, 1987), for a discussion of this contradiction within a historical context of racial, class, and gender power. In this work, MacKinnon concludes: "Cultural survival is as contingent upon equality between women and men as it is upon equality among people"; p. 68.

40. See the paid advertisement in the *Nuevo Quetzalteco* supplement of *Prensa Libre*, 4 November 1995, p. 17.

41. Comisión para el Esclarecimiento Histórico, *Memory of Silence*, pp. 40–41. The exceptions that prove the case for genocide also support my arguments concerning alliances and negotiations. Despite the fact that the army did direct the majority of its repression at indigenous communities, it was more than willing to work with indigenous elites and indigenous communities considered hostile to the guerrillas. And even the communities deemed subversive were considered to be "recoverable" once the ties with the insurgency were violently severed.

Epilogue: The Living among the Dead

1. I thank Jorge Aguilar and Irma Velásquez for sharing memories of their brother with me.

Appendix 1: Names and Places

1. Xelaju was the name of the precolonial K'iche' settlement where Quetzaltenango, the Náhuatl name given to the resettled colonial pueblo de indios, now stands. Today, Xela (short for Xelaju) is the preferred name for the city among K'iche''s and Ladinos alike. See Robert Carmack, *The Quiché Mayas of Utatlán: The Evolution of a Highland Guatemala Kingdom* (Norman: University of Oklahoma Press, 1981), for a discussion of preconquest history. See Francis Gall, *Diccionario geográfico de Guatemala*, 3 vols. (Guatemala City: Instituto Geográfico Nacional, 1980), pp. 3:18–36, for a brief description of the city and its namesake department. According to Gall, the Mam name for Quetzaltenango is Culahá.

2. For the most comprehensive history to date of the Estado de los Altos's long rise and quick fall, see Taracena, *Invención criolla*; see also J. H. González, "A History of Los Altos."

3. See Bastos's and Camus's *Quebrando el silencio* and *Abriendo caminos,* as well as Gálvez et al.'s *¿Qué sociedad queremos?,* for the pan-Mayan movement and efforts to invest the terms *K'iche'* and *Maya* with political and cultural meaning and

cohesiveness. Within the pan-Mayan movement there are numerous divisions, some of which run along geographical and linguistic lines. Along with Kaqchikels, a linguistic group from the region northwest of Guatemala City, and Q'eqchi's from the area surrounding Cobán, K'iche's from the departments of Quetzaltenango, Totonicapán, and Quiché dominate the organizations of both the leftist popular and the pan-Mayan movements (there is much overlap between the two "movements").

4. In 1806, the Crown granted Creoles permission to form their own municipal government parallel to that of the K'iche' cabildo, and in 1825, the national government declared Quetzaltenango a city. See Asamblea Nacional Constituyente del Estado de Guatemala, *Título de Ciudad a Quetzaltenango* (Guatemala City: Editorial José de Pineda Ibarra, 1978 [1825]).

5. See Sol Tax, "The Municipios of the Midwestern Highlands of Guatemala," *American Anthropologist* 39, no. 3 (1937): 423–44.

6. The term has a long and complicated history. See Lutz, *Santiago de Guatemala,* and Jeffrey L. Gould, "Gender, Politics, and the Triumph of Mestizaje in Early Twentieth-Century Nicaragua," *Journal of Latin American Anthropology* 2, no. 1 (1996): 4–33.

7. For a discussion of the nature of patriarchy, see Steve J. Stern, *The Secret History of Gender: Women, Men and Power in Late Colonial Mexico* (Chapel Hill: University of North Carolina Press, 1995), and Susan K. Besse, *Restructuring Patriarchy: The Modernization of Gender Inequality in Brazil, 1914–1940* (Chapel Hill: University of North Carolina Press, 1996). See also Heidi Tinsman's review of these two works, "Reviving Patriarchy," *Radical History Review* 71, (1988): 182–95.

8. I use no biological definition of "race" but rather try to understand the political significance of the changing definitions of the term. As Alan Knight has pointed out, although race is often used as incorrect shorthand for ethnicity, it still holds cultural and political relevance for the people using it; see Knight, "Racism, Revolution and Indigenismo," p. 72. A definition advanced by Richard N. Adams is helpful. According to Adams, an "ethnic group" is a "[s]elf-reproducing social collectivity identified by myths of a common provenance and by identifying markers." This collective identity could either be "externally identified" by an outside group or "self-identified by individuals who thereby constitute such a group. . . . The sociological salience of an ethnic group emerges most importantly, however, when it is both self-identified and externally identified, when its existence is significant both to members and to outsiders"; see Richard N. Adams, "Ethnic Images and Strategies in 1944," p. 152. See also Paul Brass, *Ethnicity and Nationalism: Theory and Comparison* (New York: Sage, 1991); the latter views ethnicity as a "modern" political construction intimately linked to the "activities of a centralizing state."

Works Cited

Archives

Quetzaltenango

Archivo de Gobernación de Quetzaltenango (AGQ)
Archivo Eclesiástico de Quetzaltenango (AEQ)
Archivo Histórico de Quetzaltenango (AHQ)
Holdings of the Sociedad El Adelanto, which I have called the Archivo de la
    Sociedad El Adelanto (ASA)
Municipalidad de Cantel, Libro de defunciones
Museo de Historia de la Casa de la Cultura
Museo del Ferrocarril Nacional de Los Altos (MFNLA)
Registro Civil de Quetzaltenango (RCQ)
Segundo Registro de Propiedad (SRP)
    (Neither the AGQ nor the AHQ are ordered in any way except by year. Docu-
ments from the AHQ are kept in boxes (*caja*) by year, and that is how I have
identified their location, unless another reference was available. I have cited
material used from the AGQ by year only. For these two collections, where
possible I also noted the type or title of document.)

Guatemala City

Archivo de Protocolos de la Corte Suprema (APCS)
Archivo General de Centro América (AGCA)
Archivo Histórico Arquidiocesano "Francisco de Paula García Peláez" (AHA)
Instituto Nacional de Transformación Agraria, which holds the records of the
    Departamento Agrario Nacional (INTA)

Antigua

Centro de Investigaciones Regionales de Mesoamérica's photograph archive
    (CIRMA)

Newspapers and Magazines

Guatemala City

Boletín de Cólera Morbo   *Diario de Centro-América*
Boletín Extraordinario   *El Eco del Trabajo*

El Editor	*La Lechuza*
El Obrero	*La Nueva Era*
El Popular	*La República*
El Sufragio	*La Voz del Obrero*
El Tiempo	*Liberal Progresista*
Ideas y Noticias	*Prensa Libre*
La Clase Obrera	*Siglo Veintiuno*
La Época	

Quetzaltenango

El Bien Público	*La Oposición*
El Comercio	*La Proa*
El Correo de Occidente	*La Voz del Obrero*
El Diario de Occidente	*Los Ecos de la Revolución*
El Diario de Quetzaltenango	*Prensa Nueva*
El Fénix	*Quetzaltenango: Feria de Septiembre,*
El Obrero Altense	*1931*
El Ron-Ron	*Sesiquicentario*, Municipalidad de
La Guillotina	Quetzaltenango, 1975

Published Primary Sources

Aguilar, Nicolás. *Discurso pronunciado por el Doctor D. Nicolás Aguilar, delegado de El Salvador. . . .* Guatemala City: Tipográfico La Unión, 1893.

Archivo General de Gobierno. "El síndico del ayuntamiento de Quetzaltenango, pidió la aceptación de las instrucciones . . . ." *Boletín de Archivo General de Guatemala* 3, no. 1 (1937): 500–503.

Asamblea Nacional Constituyente del Estado de Guatemala. *Título de Ciudad a Quetzaltenango*. Guatemala City: Editorial José de Pineda Ibarra, 1978 [1825].

Broussais, F. J. V. *Le Choléra-morbus épidémique observé et traité selon la méthode physiologique*. Paris, 1832.

Cortés y Larraz, Pedro. *Descripción geográfico-moral de la diócesis de Goathemala*. 2 vols. Guatemala City: Biblioteca "Goathemala" de la Sociedad de Geografía e Historia de Guatemala, 1958 (1769–70).

de Aparicio, Dolores. *Acusación contra el coronel y diputado Roque Morales presentada a la Asamblea Legislativa*. Guatemala City: Tipografía A. Síguere & Cía, 1898.

Dirección General de Estadística. *Censo general de la república de Guatemala*. Guatemala City: Tipografía Nacional, 1894.

———. *Censo agropecuario: Agricultura*. Vol. 1. Guatemala City: Dirección General de Estadística, 1950.

Fuentes y Guzmán, Francisco Antonio. *Recordación florida*. Guatemala City: Ministerio de Educación Pública, 1951.

Gall, Francis. *Título del Ajpop Huitziṭil Tẓunún: Probanza de méritos de los De León y Cardona*. Guatemala City: Editorial José de Pineda Ibarra, 1963.

García Peláez, Francisco de Paula. *Memorias para la historia del antiguo Reyno de Guatemala*. Vol. 1. Guatemala City: Tipográfico de L. Luna, 1951.

Gavarrete Escobar, Juan. *Anales para la historia de Guatemala: 1491–1811*. Guatemala City: Editorial José de Pineda Ibarra, 1980.

Guatemala. *Primer Congreso Pedagógico Centroamericano y Primera Exposición Escolar Nacional*. Guatemala City: Tipografía Nacional, 1894.

Hidalgo, Joseph. "Memoria para hacer una descripción del Reino de Guatemala." *Anales de la Sociedad de Geografía e Historia de Guatemala* 26, nos. 3–4 (1952): 381–413.

Juarros, Domingo. *Compendio de la historia del reino de Guatemala*. Guatemala City: Tipografía Nacional, 1936.

Meza, Salvador. *Manuel M. Reyna, justas aclaraciones*. Cobán: Tipografía El Porvenir, 1898.

Molina, Pedro. *Instrucción, preservativa, y curativa de cólera morbus*. Guatemala City: Imprenta Nueva, 1832.

Molina y Mata, Marcelo. *Ligeros apuntamientos acerca de los principales sucesos de la carrera literaria y vida pública de Marcelo Molina*. Quetzaltenango: Casa de la Cultura, 1971.

Moreau de Jonnès, Alexandre. *Rapport au conseil supérieur de santé sur le choléra-morbus pestilentiel*. Paris, 1832.

Padilla, Mariano. *Método de precaver, conocer, y curar el cólera mórbus*. Guatemala City: Academia de Ciencias, 1837.

Rivas, Valerio Ignacio. *Vindicación que hace Valerio Ignacio Rivas sobre la impostura que el C. Macario Rodas le suscitó en el Departamento de Quetzaltenango: Infracciones cometidas por el juez de primera instancia de aquella ciudad, y avances de poder cometidos en su persona e intereses por el que se dice gobierno provisorio de Los Altos*. Guatemala: Imprenta del Gobierno, 1838.

Rivera, Sinforoso. *Los manuscritos de un patriota*. Quetzaltenango: La Industria, 1893.

Rubio Sánchez, Manuel. "Historia del ganado caprino y ovino en Guatemala." *Anales de Academia de Geografía e Historia de Guatemala* 61 (enero–dec. 1987): 121–23.

Sociedad El Adelanto. *Estatuto de la Sociedad El Adelanto*. Quetzaltenango: Tipografico "La Unión Liberal," 1894.

——. *Estatutos de la Sociedad El Adelanto*. Quetzaltenango: Tipografía "La Industria," 1915.

——. *100 años de vida social y educativa, 1894–1994*. Quetzaltenango: Sociedad El Adelanto, 1994.

Sociedad El Porvenir de Los Obreros. *Medio siglo de vida, 1892–1942.* Guatemala City: Tipografía Nacional, 1942.

Tzunun M., Gloria Virginia, and Olegario Obispo Nimatuj J. *1934–1984: Historial del certamen de la belleza indígena de Quetzaltenango.* Quetzaltenango: Casa Publicitaria "GOF," 1985.

Unknown (H. P. F.). *Resumen de las conferencias dadas en la resp. log. Alianza no. 24.* Guatemala City: Tipografía de Síguere y Cía, 1903.

Un Patriota. *La verdad de los hechos.* Guatemala City, 1899.

Vázquez, Pedro. *Método curativo del cólera-morbo.* Guatemala City: Academia de Ciencias, 1837.

Vela Irisarri, José María, Angel María Bocanegra, and Lucas T. Cojulún. *Informe presentado al primer congreso pedagógico Centro-América sobre el tema VIII.* Guatemala: Sánchez y De Guise, 1893.

Published Legislation

Guatemala. *Recopilación de las leyes emitidas por el gobierno democrático de la República de Guatemala.* 2 vols. Guatemala City: Tipografía El Progreso, 1881.

——. *Recopilación de leyes agrarias.* Guatemala City: Tipográfico La Unión, 1890.

Méndez Montenegro, Julio César. *444 años de legislación agraria, 1520–1957.* Guatemala City: Imprenta Universitaria, 1961.

Pineda de Mont, Manuel, ed. *Recopilación de las leyes de Guatemala, compuesta y arreglada por don Manuel Pineda de Mont, á virtud de orden especial del gobierno supremo de la república.* Vol. 1. Guatemala City: Imprenta de la Paz, 1869–72.

Skinner-Klée, Jorge, ed. *Legislación indigenista de Guatemala.* 2d ed. Mexico: Instituto Indigenista Interamericano, 1995.

Guatemalan Nationalist and Indigenista Writing
(History, Economics, Literature, and Pedagogy)

Asturias, Miguel Angel. *Viento fuerte.* Buenos Aires: Editorial Losada, 1950.

——. *El Papa verde.* Buenos Aires: Editorial Losada, 1954.

——. *Los ojos de los enterrados.* Buenos Aires: Editorial Losada, 1960.

——. *El problema social del indio y otros textos.* Paris: Centre de Recherches de l'Institut d'Etudes Hispaniques, 1971.

——. *El señor presidente.* Translated by Frances Partridge. New York: Atheneum, 1983.

Batres Jáuregui, Antonio. *Los indios: Su historia y su civilización.* Guatemala City: Tipográfico La Unión, 1894.

——. *La América Central ante la historia.* Vols. 1 and 2. Guatemala City: Casa Colorada, 1915.

Bran Azmitia, Roberto, ed. *Parnaso quezalteco: De todos los tiempos*. Guatemala City: Editorial José de Pineda Ibarra, 1982.

Carranza, Jesús. *Un pueblo de los altos: Apuntamientos para su historia, Totonicapán*. Quetzaltenango: Tipografía Popular, 1897.

Castañeda, Gabriel Angel. *Monumento a Tecún Umán*. Guatemala City: Tipografía Nacional, 1965.

Castillo, Jesús. *La música maya-quiché*. Quetzaltenango: n.p., 1941.

Centro de Estudios Integrados de Desarollo Comunal. *Guatemala: Seminario sobre la realidad étnica*. Vol. 2. Mexico City: Centro de Estudios de Desarollo Comunal, 1991.

Cifuentes, Juan Fernando. "Apreciación de Asuntos Civiles (G-5) para el área Ixil." In *Revista Militar* (Dec. 1982): 25–73.

de Iribarri, Antonio José. *El cristiano errante: novela que tiene mucho de historia*. Vol. 2. Guatemala: Editorial del Ministerio de Educación Pública, 1960.

de la Roca, Julio César. *Biografía de un pueblo: Síntesis monográfica de Quetzaltenango, interpretación de su destino*. Guatemala City: Editorial José de Pineda Ibarra, 1966.

Fernández Ferraz, Juan. *Estudio acerca las nueve tesis del programa del primer congreso pedagógico Centroamericano*. San José, Costa Rica: Tipografía Nacional, 1893.

González R., Marío Gilberto. *Pequeña reseña bio-bibliográfica de Carlos Wyld Ospina*. Guatemala City: Editorial del Ministerio de Educación Pública, 1957.

Herrera, Flavio. *El tigre*. Guatemala City: Editorial Universitaria, 1989.

Lainfiesta, Francisco. *A vista de pájaros (cuento fantástico)*. Guatemala: Imprenta El Progreso, 1879.

Marure, Alejandro. *Bosquejo histórico de las revoluciones de Centro-America: Desde 1811 hasta 1834*. Guatemala City, 1877.

Monteforte Toledo, Mario. *Entre la piedra y la cruz*. Guatemala City: Editorial El Libro de Guatemala, 1948.

Montúfar y Rivera Maestre, Lorenzo. *Reseña histórica de Centro América*. 7 vols. Guatemala City: Tipografía de El Progreso, 1878.

Organización Revolucionaria del Pueblo en Armas. *La verdadera magnitud del racismo (Racismo II)*. N.p., 1978.

Payeras, Mario. *Los pueblos indígenas y la revolución guatemalteca*. Guatemala City: Luna y Sol, 1997.

Racancoj A., Victor M. *Socioeconomía Maya precolonial*. Guatemala City: Cholsamaj, 1994.

Recinos, Adrián. *Memorial de Sololá, Anales de los Cakchiqueles*. Mexico: Fondo de Cultura Económica, 1950.

Reyes M., José Luis. *Apuntes para una monografía de la Sociedad Económica de Amigos del País*. Guatemala City: Editorial José de Pineda Ibarra, 1964.

Rodríguez Beteta, Virgilio. *Ideologías de la Independencia*. Paris: Editorial París-America, 1926.

Rubio Sánchez, Manuel. *Historia de la Sociedad Económica de Amigos del País.* Guatemala City: Editorial Académica Centroamericana, 1981.

Salazar, Ramon. *Historia del desenvolvimiento intelectual de Guatemala.* Guatemala City: Tipografía Nacional, 1897.

Salvatierra, Sofonías. *Contribución a la historia de Centro América.* Vol. 2. Managua: n.p., 1939.

Sociedad de Geografía e Historia de Guatemala. *La Sociedad de Geografía e Historia de Guatemala: Breve recuento de sus labores al cumplir sus bodas de plata.* Guatemala City: Sociedad de Geografía e Historia de Guatemala City, 1948.

Villacorta Calderón, José Antonio. *Memorial de Tecpán-Atitlán.* Guatemala City: Tipografía Nacional, 1934.

——. *Prehistoria e historia antigua de Guatemala.* Guatemala City: Tipografía Nacional, 1938.

Wyld Ospina, Carlos. *El autócrata: Ensayo politico-social.* Guatemala City: Editorial José de Pineda Ibarra, 1967.

Travel Narratives

Brigham, William Tufts. *Guatemala: The Land of the Quetzal.* New York: C. Scribner's Sons, 1887.

Brine, Lindesay. *Travels Amongst American Indians, Their Ancient Earthworks and Temples; Including a Journey in Guatemala, Mexico and Yucatan. . . .* London: Sampson Low, Marston & Company, 1894.

Stephens, John L. *Incidents of Travel in the Central America, Chiapas, and Yucatan.* Vol. 2. New York: Harper & Brothers, 1841.

Unpublished Manuscripts and Dissertations

Bogenschild, Thomas E. "The Roots of Fundamentalism in Liberal Guatemala: Missionary Ideologies and Local Responses, 1882–1944." Ph.D. diss., University of California at Berkeley, 1992.

Casey, Dennis Floyd. "Indigenismo: The Guatemalan Experience." Ph.D. diss., University of Kansas, Lawrence, 1979.

Cullather, Nicholas. "Operation PBSUCCESS: The United States and Guatemala, 1952–1954." Washington D.C.: Center for the Study of Intelligence, Central Intelligence Agency, 1994.

Fry, Michael Forrest. "Agrarian Society in the Guatemalan Montaña, 1700–1840." Ph.D. diss., Tulane, 1988.

González, Jorge H. "A History of Los Altos, Guatemala: A Study of Regional Conflict and National Integration." Ph.D. diss., Tulane, 1994.

Grandin, Greg. "The Blood of Guatemala: The Making of Race and Nation, 1750–1954." Ph.D. diss., Yale, 1999.

Ingersoll, Hazel. "The War of the Mountain: A Study in Reactionary Peasant Insurgency in Guatemala, 1837–1873." Ph.D. diss., George Washington University, Washington, D.C., 1972.

Palmer, Steven. "A Liberal Discipline: Inventing Nations in Guatemala and Costa Rica, 1870–1900." Ph.D. diss., Columbia University, 1990.

Secondary Sources

Adams, Richard N. *Crucifixion by Power: Essays on Capitalist National Social Structure, 1944–1966*. Austin: University of Texas Press, 1970.

——. "Conclusions: What Can We Know about the Harvest of Violence?" In *The Harvest of Violence: The Maya Indians and the Guatemalan Crisis*. Edited by Robert Carmack. Norman: University of Oklahoma Press, 1988.

——. "Ethnic Images and Strategies in 1944." In *Guatemalan Indians and the State, 1540–1988*. Edited by Carol A. Smith. Austin: University of Texas Press, 1990.

——. *Etnias en evolución social: Estudios de Guatemala y Centroamérica*. Mexico: Universidad Autónoma Metropolitana, 1995.

——. "Las matanzas de Patzicía en 1944: Una reflexión." In *Etnias en evolución social: Estudios de Guatemala y Centroamérica*. Mexico: Universidad Autónoma Metropolitana, 1995.

Adorno, Theodor. *The Jargon of Authenticity*. Translated by K. Tarnanski and F. Will. Chicago: Northwestern University Press, 1973.

Agnew, Jean-Christophe. "History and Anthropology: Scenes from a Marriage." *The Yale Journal of Criticism* 3, no. 2 (1990): 29–50.

Alonso, Ana María. *Threads of Blood: Colonialism, Revolution, and Gender on Mexico's Northern Frontier*. Tucson: University of Arizona Press, 1995.

Anderson, Benedict. *Imagined Communities: Reflections on the Origin and Spread of Nationalism*. London: Verso Press, 1991.

Arias, Arturo. "Changing Indian Ethnicity: Guatemala's Violent Transition to Modernity." In *Guatemalan Indians and the State, 1540–1988*. Edited by Carol A. Smith. Austin: University of Texas Press, 1990.

Arnold, David. *Colonizing the Body: State Medicine and Epidemic Disease in Nineteenth-Century India*. Berkeley: University of California Press, 1993.

Arriola de Geng, Olga. *Los tejedores en Guatemala y la influencia española en el traje indígena*. Guatemala City: Litografías Modernas, 1991.

Asociación para el Avance de las Ciencias Sociales en Guatemala. *Política institucional hacia el desplazado interno en Guatemala*. Guatemala City: Asociación para el Avance de las Ciencias Sociales en Guatemala, 1988.

——. *Vonós a la capital: Estudio sobre la emigración rural reciente en Guatemala*.

Guatemala City: Asociación para el Avance de las Ciencias Sociales en Guatemala, 1990.

———. *¿Dónde está el futuro? Procesos de reintegración en comunidades de retornados.* Guatemala City: Asociación para el Avance de las Ciencias Sociales en Guatemala, 1992.

Balerino Cohen, Colleen, Richard Wilk, and Beverly Stoeltje, eds. *Beauty Queens on the Global Stage: Gender, Contests, and Power.* New York: Routledge, 1996.

Bastos, Santiago, and Manuel Camus. *Quebrando el silencio: Organizaciones del pueblo maya y sus demandas.* Guatemala City: Facultad Latinoamerica de Ciencas Sociales, 1992.

———. *Abriendo caminos: Las organizaciones mayas desde el Nobel hasta el Acuerdo de Derechos Indígenas.* Guatemala City: Facultad Latinoamericana de Ciencias Sociales, 1995.

Baudrillard, Jean. *Simulations.* Translated by P. Foss, P. Patton, and P. Beitchman. New York: Semiotext(e), 1983.

Bauer Paiz, Alfonso. "Acotaciones y comentarios de Alfonso Bauer Paiz al libro de Luis Cardoza y Aragón, 'la revolución guatemalteca.'" In *Antología de ensayos.* Guatemala City: Consejo de Instituciones de Desarrollo de Guatemala, 1995.

———. "La revolución guatemalteca del '20 de octubre de 1944.'" In *Antología de ensayos.* Guatemala City: Consejo de Instituciones de Desarrollo de Guatemala, 1995.

Beals, Ralph. "Acculturation." In *Social Anthropology.* Edited by Manning Nash. Austin: University of Texas Press, 1967.

Benjamin, Walter. *Illuminations: Essays and Reflections.* Edited by Hannah Arendt. New York: Schocken Books, 1968.

Berman, Marshall. *All That Is Solid Melts into Air: The Experience of Modernity.* New York: Penguin, 1982.

Besse, Susan K. *Restructuring Patriarchy: The Modernization of Gender Inequality in Brazil, 1914–1940.* Chapel Hill: University of North Carolina Press, 1996.

Bethell, Leslie, ed. *Mexico since Independence.* Cambridge: Cambridge University Press, 1991.

Black, George. *Garrison Guatemala.* New York: Monthly Review Press, 1984.

Blaut, James M. *The National Question: Decolonizing the Theory of Nationalism.* London: Zed, 1987.

Bourdieu, Pierre. *Outline of a Theory of Practice.* Cambridge: Cambridge University Press, 1977.

Brass, Paul. *Ethnicity and Nationalism: Theory and Comparison.* New York: Sage, 1991.

Brass, Tom. "The Latin American Enganche System: Some Revisionist Interpretations Revisited." *Slavery and Abolition* 11, no. 1 (1990): 74–103.

Brintnal, Douglas. *Revolt against the Dead: The Modernization of a Mayan Community in the Highlands of Guatemala.* New York: Gordon and Breach, 1979.

Cajas Ovando, Francisco José. *Reseña histórica de Ferrocarril de Los Altos*. Quetzaltenango: Taller "El Estudiante," 1995.

Calderón Gordillo, Roberto. *Semblanza histórica del Ferrocarril Nacional de Los Altos*. Quetzaltenango: Taller "El Estudiante," 1987.

Cambranes, Julio C. *Café y campesinos en Guatemala, 1853–1897*. Guatemala City: Editorial Universitaria, 1985.

Campbell, Howard. *Zapotec Renaissance: Ethnic Politics and Cultural Revivalism in Southern Mexico*. Albuquerque: University of New Mexico Press, 1994.

Cardoza y Aragón, Luis. *La revolución guatemalteca*. Montevideo, Uruguay: Ediciones Pueblos Unidos, 1956.

———. "The Revolution of '44–'54—A Reappraisal." In *Guatemala*. Edited by Susanne Jonas and David Tobis. New York: North American Congress on Latin America, 1974.

Carmack, Robert M. *The Quiché Mayas of Utatlán: The Evolution of a Highland Guatemala Kingdom*. Norman: University of Oklahoma Press, 1981.

———. "Social and Demographic Patterns in an Eighteenth-Century Census From Tecpanaco, Guatemala." In *Historical Demography of Highland Guatemala*. Edited by Robert Carmack, John D. Early, and Christopher Lutz. Albany: State University of New York, 1982.

———. *Rebels of Highland Guatemala: The Quiché-Mayas of Momostenango*. Norman: University of Oklahoma Press, 1995.

Casaus Arzú, Marta. *Guatemala: Linaje y racismo*. Guatemala City: Facultad Latinoamerica de Ciencias Sociales, 1995.

Centro de Estudios Integrados de Desarrollo Comunal. *Guatemala, polos de desarrollo: El caso de la desestructuración de las comunidades indígenas*. Vol. 2. Mexico City: Centro de Estudios Integrados de Desarrollo Comunal, 1990.

Chance, John K. *Conquest of the Sierra: Spaniards and Indians in Colonial Oaxaca*. Norman: University of Oklahoma Press, 1989.

———. "The Caciques of Tecali: Class and Ethnic Identity in Late Colonial Mexico." *Hispanic American Historical Review* 76, no. 3 (1996): 476–502.

Chance, John K., and William B. Taylor. "Cofradías and Cargos: An Historical Perspective on the Mesoamerican Civil-Religious Hierarchy." *American Ethnologist* 12 (1985): 1–26.

Chatterjee, Partha. *Nationalist Thought and the Colonial World: A Derivative Discourse?* Delhi: Oxford University Press, 1986.

Chevalier, Francois. "Official 'Indigenism' in Peru in 1920: Origins, Significance, and Socioeconomic Scope." *In Race and Class in Latin America*. Edited by Magnus Mörner. New York: Columbia University Press, 1970.

Chevalier, Louis. *Laboring Classes and Dangerous Classes in Paris during the First Half of the Nineteenth Century*. Translated by Frank Jellinek. Princeton: Princeton University Press, 1973.

Chevalier, Louis, ed. *Le Choléra: La Premiere Épidémie du dix-neuvième siècle*. La Roche-sur-Yon: Centrale de L'Ouest, 1958.

Coe, William R. *Tikal: A Handbook of the Ancient Maya Ruins*. Philadelphia: University of Pennsylvania, 1967.

Cojtí, Demetrio Cuxil. *El Movimiento Maya (en Guatemala)*. Guatemala City: Editorial Cholsamaj, 1997.

Comaroff, John, and Jean Comaroff. *Ethnography and the Historical Imagination*. Boulder: Westview Press, 1992.

Comisión para el Esclarecimiento Histórico. *Guatemala: Memory of Silence, Conclusions and Recommendations*. Guatemala City, 1999.

Contreras, J. Daniel. *Una rebelión indígena en el partido de Totonicapán*. Guatemala City: Universidad de San Carlos, 1968.

Cook, Noble David, and W. George Lovell, eds. *Secret Judgments of God: Old World Disease in Colonial Spanish America*. Norman: University of Oklahoma Press, 1992.

Cooper, Frederick. "Africa and the World Economy." In *Confronting Historical Paradigms: Peasants, Labor, and the World System in Africa and Latin America*. Edited by Frederick Cooper et al. Madison: University of Wisconsin Press, 1993.

Cope, R. Douglas. *The Limits of Racial Domination: Plebeian Society in Colonial Mexico City, 1660–1720*. Madison: University of Wisconsin Press, 1994.

Corrigan, Philip, ed. *Capitalism, State Formation, and Marxist Theory*. London: Quartet Books, 1980.

Corsi, Pietro. *The Age of Lamarck: Evolutionary Theories in France, 1790–1830*. Translated by Jonathan Mendelbaum. Berkeley: University of California Press, 1988.

Davis, Shelton. "Introduction: Sowing the Seeds of Violence." In *The Harvest of Violence: The Maya Indians and the Guatemalan Crisis*. Edited by Robert Carmack. Norman: University of Oklahoma Press, 1988.

Delaporte, François. *Disease and Civilization: The Cholera in Paris, 1832*. Translated by Arthur Goldhammer. Cambridge: MIT Press, 1986.

de León Aragón, Oscar. *Caída de un Régimen: Jorge Ubico-Federico Ponce, 20 de Octubre 1944*. Guatemala City: Facultad Latinoamericana de Ciencias Sociales, 1995.

Díaz O, J. Lizardo. *De la democracia a la dictadura*. Guatemala City: Imprenta Hispana, 1946.

Diócesis de Quiché. *El Quiché: El pueblo y su iglesia*. Santa Cruz Quiché: Diócesis del Quiché, 1994.

Dunkerley, James. "Guatemala since 1930." In *Central America since Independence*. Edited by Leslie Bethell. Cambridge: Cambridge University Press, 1991.

Eagleton, Terry. "Nationalism: Irony and Commitment." In *Nationalism, Colonialism and Literature*. Edited by Terry Eagleton, Fredric Jameson, and Edward Said. Minneapolis: University of Minnesota Press, 1990.

Evans, R. J. "Epidemics and Revolutions: Cholera in Nineteenth-Century Europe." *Past and Present* 120 (Aug. 1988): 123–45.

Falla, Ricardo. *Quiché Rebelde: Estudio de un movimiento de conversión religiosa, rebelde a las creencias tradicionales en San Antonio Ilotenango.* Guatemala City: Editorial Universitaria, 1978.

——. *Masacres de la selva: Ixcán, Guatemala 1975–1982.* Guatemala City: Editorial Universitaria, 1993.

Fernández Fernández, José Manuel. *El Comité de Unidad Campesina: Origen y desarrollo.* Guatemala: Centro de Estudios Rurales Centroamericanos, 1988.

Figueroa Ibarra, Carlos. "Contenido de clase y participación obrera en el movimiento antidictatorial de 1920." *Política y Sociedad* 4 (1974): 5–51.

Figueroa Marroquín, Horacio. *Biografía del Doctor José Luna Arbizú.* Guatemala City: Tipografía Nacional, 1983.

Fischer, Edward F., and R. McKenna Brown, eds. *Maya Cultural Activism in Guatemala.* Austin: University of Texas Press, 1996.

Forster, Cindy. "Reforging National Revolution: Campesino Labor Struggles in Guatemala, 1944–1954." In *Identity and Struggle at the Margins of the Nation-State: The Laboring Peoples of Central America and the Hispanic Caribbean.* Edited by Aviva Chomsky and Aldo Lauria-Santiago. Durham: Duke University Press, 1998.

Foster-Carter, Aidan. "The Modes of Production Controversy." *New Left Review* no. 107 (1978): 47–77.

Foster, John. *Class Struggle in the Industrial Revolution: Early Industrial Capitalism in Three English Towns.* London: St. Martin's Press, 1975.

Foucault, Michel. *Discipline and Punish: The Birth of the Prison.* Translated by Alan Sheridan. New York: Pantheon Books, 1977.

Frye, David. *Indians into Mexicans: History and Identity in a Mexican Town.* Austin: University of Texas Press, 1996.

Gall, Francis. *Cerro Quemado: Volcán de Quetzaltenango (Estudio de geografía histórica regional).* Guatemala City: Editorial José de Pineda Ibarra, 1966.

——. *Diccionario geográfico de Guatemala.* Vol. 3. Guatemala City: Instituto Geográfico Nacional, 1980.

Gálvez Borrell, Víctor, Claudia Dary Fuentes, Edgar Esquit Choy, and Isabel Rodas. *¿Qué sociedad queremos? Una mirada desde el movimiento y las organizaciones mayas.* Guatemala City: Facultad Latinoamericana de Ciencias Sociales, 1997.

García Márquez, Gabriel. *One Hundred Years of Solitude.* Translated by Gregory Rabassa. New York: Avon, 1971.

Geary, Cristraud M. *Images from Bamumi: German Colonial Photography at the Court of King Njoya, Cameroon, West Africa, 1902–1915.* Washington, D.C.: Smithsonian Institution Press, 1988.

Geertz, Clifford. *Negara: The Theatre State in Nineteenth-Century Bali.* Princeton: Princeton University Press, 1980.

Gilroy, Paul. *"There Ain't No Black in the Union Jack": The Cultural Politics of Race and Nation.* Chicago: University of Chicago Press, 1987.

———. *The Black Atlantic: Modernity and Double Consciousness*. Cambridge: Harvard University Press, 1993.

Gleijeses, Piero. *Shattered Hope: The Guatemalan Revolution and the United States, 1944–1954*. Princeton: Princeton University Press, 1991.

González Orellana, Carlos. *Historia de la educación en Guatemala*. Guatemala City: Editorial José de Pineda Ibarra, 1970.

Gould, Jeffrey L. *To Lead as Equals: Rural Protest and Political Consciousness in Chinandega, Nicaragua, 1912–1979*. Chapel Hill: University of North Carolina Press, 1990.

———. "Vana Ilusión: The Highland Indians and the Myth of Nicaraguan Mestiza, 1880–1925." *Hispanic American Historical Review* 73, no. 3 (1993): 393–429.

———. "Gender, Politics, and the Triumph of Mestizaje in Early Twentieth-Century Nicaragua." *Journal of Latin American Anthropology* 2, no. 1 (1996): 4–33.

Gramsci, Antonio. *Selections from the Prison Notebooks*. Translated by Quintin Hoare. New York: International Publishers, 1971.

Grandin, Greg. "The Strange Case of 'La Mancha Negra': Maya-State Relations in Nineteenth-Century Guatemala." *Hispanic American Historical Review* 77, no. 2 (1997): 211–43.

———. "To End with All These Evils: Ethnic Transformation and Community Mobilization in Guatemala's Western Highlands, 1954–1980." *Latin American Perspectives* 24, no. 2 (1997): 7–33.

Guardino, Peter. *Peasants, Politics, and the Formation of Mexico's National State: Guerrero, 1800–1957*. Stanford, Calif.: Stanford University Press, 1996.

Gudmunson, Lowell, and Hector Lindo-Fuentes. *Central America, 1821–1871: Liberalism before Liberal Reform*. Tuscaloosa: University of Alabama Press, 1995.

Guha, Ranajit. *Elementary Aspects of Peasant Insurgency in Colonial India*. Delhi: Oxford University Press, 1983.

———. "On Some Aspects of the Historiography of Colonial India." In *Subaltern Studies I: Writings on South Asian History and Society*. Edited by Ranajit Guha. Delhi: Oxford University Press, 1986.

Hale, Charles. *Resistance and Contradiction: Miskitu Indians and the Nicaraguan State, 1894–1987*. Stanford, Calif.: Stanford University Press, 1994.

———. "Mestizaje, Hybridity and the Cultural Politics of Difference in post-Revolutionary Central America." *Journal of Latin American Anthropology* 2, no. 1 (1996): 34–61.

Hall, Stuart. "Race Articulation and Societies Structured in Dominance." In *Sociological Theories: Race and Colonialism*. Edited by UNESCO. Paris: UNESCO, 1980.

———. "The Problem of Ideology: Marxism without Guarantees." In *Stuart Hall: Critical Dialogues in Cultural Studies*. Edited by David Morley and Kuan-Hsing Chen. New York: Routledge, 1996.

Handy, Jim. *Gift of the Devil: A History of Guatemala.* Toronto: Between the Lines Press, 1984.

———. "National Policy, Agrarian Reform, and the Corporate Community during the Guatemalan Revolution, 1944–1954." *Comparative Studies in Society and History* 30 (1988): 698–724.

———. *Revolution in the Countryside: Community, Land, and Reform in Guatemala.* Chapel Hill: University of North Carolina Press, 1994.

Harvey, David. *The Condition of Postmodernity: An Inquiry into the Origins of Cultural Change.* Cambridge: Blackwell, 1989.

Haskett, Robert. *Indigenous Rulers: An Ethnohistory of Town Government in Colonial Cuernavaca.* Albuquerque: University of New Mexico Press, 1991.

Hawkins, John. *Inverse Images: The Meaning of Culture, Ethnicity and Family in Postcolonial Guatemala.* Albuquerque: University of New Mexico Press, 1984.

Hernández de León, Federico. *Viajes presidenciales: Breves relatos de algunas expediciones administrativas del general d. Jorge Ubico, presidente de la república.* 2 vols. Guatemala City: Tipografía Nacional, 1940.

Hill, Robert, and John Monaghan. *Continuities in Highland Mayan Social Organization: Ethnohistory in Sacapulas, Guatemala.* Philadelphia: University of Pennsylvania Press, 1987.

Hobsbawm, Eric. *Nations and Nationalism since 1780: Programme, Myth, Reality.* Cambridge: Cambridge University Press, 1992.

———. *The Age of Extremes: A History of the World, 1914–1991.* New York: Vintage Books, 1994.

———. "Ethnicity and Nationalism in Europe Today." In *Mapping the Nation.* Edited by Gopal Balakrishnan. London: Verso Press, 1996.

Horst, Oscar H., and Avril McLelland. "The Development of an Educational System in a Rural Guatemalan Community." *Journal of Inter-American Studies* 10, no. 3 (1968): 474–97.

Hu-dehart, Evelyn. *Yaqui Resistance and Survival: The Struggle for Land and Autonomy, 1821–1910.* Madison: University of Wisconsin Press, 1984.

Izás Ferriño, Catalina. *Problemas socio-económicos de Pacajóa y Llano del Pinal: Comunidades del Valle de Palajunoj, Quetzaltenango.* Quetzaltenango: Universidad de San Carlos, Escuela de Servicio Social Rural, 1966.

Jackson, Jean. "Culture, Genuine and Spurious: The Politics of Indianness in the Vaupes, Columbia." *American Ethnologist* 22, no. 1 (1995): 3–27.

Jonas, Susanne. *The Battle for Guatemala: Rebels, Death Squads, and U.S. Power.* Boulder: Westview Press, 1991.

Joseph, Gilbert M. "On the Trail of Latin American Bandits: A Reexamination of Peasant Resistance." *Latin American Research Review* 25, no. 3 (1990): 7–53.

Joseph, Gilbert M., and Daniel Nugent. "Popular Culture and State Formation in Revolutionary Mexico." In *Everyday Forms of State Formation: Revolution and the Negotiation of Rule in Modern Mexico.* Edited by Joseph and Nugent. Durham: Duke University Press, 1994.

Joseph, Gilbert M., and Daniel Nugent, eds. *Everyday Forms of State Formation: Revolution and the Negotiation of Rule in Modern Mexico*. Durham: Duke University Press, 1994.

Katz, Freidrich. "The Liberal Republic and the Porfiriato, 1867–1910." In *Mexico Since Independence*. Edited by Leslie Bethell. Cambridge: Cambridge University Press, 1991.

Knight, Alan. "Debt Bondage in Latin America." In *Slavery and Other Forms of Unfree Labour*. Edited by Leonie Archer. New York: Routledge, 1989.

——. "Racism, Revolution and Indigenismo: Mexico, 1910–1940." In *The Idea of Race in Latin America, 1870–1940*. Edited by Richard Graham. Austin: University of Texas Press, 1994).

Kramer, Wendy. *Encomienda Politics in Early Colonial Guatemala, 1524–1544: Dividing the Spoils*. Dellplain Latin American Studies, vol. 31. Boulder: Westview Press, 1994.

Kudlick, Catherine J. *Cholera in Post-Revolutionary Paris: A Cultural History*. Berkeley: University of California Press, 1996.

Laclau, Ernesto, and Chantal Mouffe. *Hegemony and Socialist Strategy*. London: Verso Press, 1985.

Lainfiesta, Francisco. "La esclavitud del indio." *La República*, 27 June 1893.

Larson, Brooke, Olivia Harris, and Enrique Tandeter, eds. *Ethnicity, Markets, and Migration in the Andes: At the Crossroads of History and Anthropology*. Durham: Duke University Press, 1995.

Lazarus, Neil. "Transnationalism and the Alleged Death of the Nation State." In *Cultural Readings of Imperialism: Edward Said and the Gravity of History*. Edited by Keith Ansell Pearson et al. New York: St. Martin's Press, 1997.

Levenson-Estrada, Deborah. *Trade Unionists against Terror: Guatemala City, 1954–1985*. Chapel Hill: University of North Carolina Press, 1994.

Lewis, Leslie. "In Mexico's Shadow: Aspects of Economic Activity and Social Processes in Texcoco, 1570–1620." In *Provinces of Early Mexico: Variants of Spanish American Regional Evolution*. Edited by Ida Altman and James Lockhart. Los Angeles: Latin American Center Publications, University of California, 1976.

Lira González, Andres. *Comunidades indígenas frente a la ciudad de México*. Zamora, Spain: El Colegio de Michoacán, 1983.

Little-Siebold, Todd. "Guatemala y el anhelo de modernización: Estrada Cabrera y el desarrollo del estado, 1898–1920." *Anuario de Estudios Centroamericanos* 20, no. 1 (1994): 25–41.

Lockhart, James. *The Nahuas after the Conquest: A Social and Cultural History of the Indians of Central Mexico, Sixteenth through Eighteenth Centuries*. Stanford, Calif.: Stanford University Press, 1992.

Lovell, W. George. *Conquest and Survival in Guatemala: A Historical Geography of the Cuchumatán Highlands, 1500–1821*. Montreal: McGill-Queen's University Press, 1992.

Lutz, Catherine A., and Jane Collins. *Reading National Geographic*. Chicago: University of Chicago Press, 1993.

Lutz, Christopher H. "Evolución demográfica de la población no indígena." In *Historia General de Guatemala*. Edited by Jorge Luján Muñoz. Guatemala City: Fundación Cultura y Desarrollo, 1993.

——. *Santiago de Guatemala, 1541–1773*. Norman: University of Oklahoma Press, 1994.

Lyman, Christopher. *The Vanishing Race and Other Illusions: Photographs of Edward S. Curtis*. New York: Pantheon Books, 1982.

MacKinnon, Catharine. "Whose Culture? A Case Note of Martínez v. Santa Clara Pueblo." In MacKinnon, Catharine, *Feminism Unmodified*. Cambridge: Harvard University Press, 1987.

Macleod, Morna. *Poder Local: Reflexiones sobre Guatemala*. Oxford: Oxfam, 1997.

MacLeod, Murdo. *Spanish Central America: A Socioeconomic History, 1520–1720* Berkeley: University of California Press, 1973.

Mallon, Florencia E. *The Defense of Community in Peru's Central Highlands: Peasant Struggle and Capitalist Transition, 1860–1940*. Princeton: Princeton University Press, 1983.

——. "Nationalist and Antistate Coalitions in the War of the Pacific: Junín and Cajamarca, 1879–1902." In *Resistance, Rebellion, and Consciousness in the Andean Peasant World: 18th to 20th Centuries*. Edited by Steve J. Stern. Madison: University of Wisconsin Press, 1987.

——. "Patriarchy in the Transition to Capitalism: Central Peru, 1830–1950." *Feminist Studies* 13, no. 2 (1987): 379–407.

——. "Indian Communities, Political Cultures, and the State in Latin America, 1780–1990." *Journal of Latin American Studies* 24 (1992): 35–53.

——. *Peasant and Nation: The Making of Postcolonial Mexico and Peru*. Berkeley: University of California Press, 1995.

Marcos, Subcomandante. *Shadows of Tender Fury: The Letters and Communiques of Subcomandante Marcos*. New York: Monthly Review Press, 1995.

Martínez Peláez, Severo. *La patria del criollo: Ensayo de interpretación de la realidad colonial guatemalteca*. 4th ed. Guatemala City: Editorial Universitaria, 1976.

Marx, Karl. *Capital: A Critical Analysis of Capitalist Production*. Edited by Frederick Engels and translated by Samuel Moore and Edward Aveling. New York: International Publishers, 1987.

McAllister, Carlota. "Authenticity and Guatemala's Maya Queen." In *Beauty Queens on the Global Stage: Gender, Contests, and Power*. Edited by Collen Ballerino Cohen et al. New York: Routledge, 1996.

McBryde, Felix Webster. *Geografía Cultural e Histórica del Suroeste de Guatemala*. Translated by Francis Gall. Vol. 2. Guatemala City: Editorial José de Pineda Ibarra, 1969.

McClintock, Anne. "Family Feuds: Gender, Nationalism, and the Family." *Feminist Review* 44 (1993): 61–78.

McCreery, David. "Coffee and Class: The Structure of Development in Liberal Guatemala." *Hispanic American Historical Review* 56, no. 3 (1976): 438–60.

———. *Desarrollo Económico y política nacional: El Ministerio de Fomento de Guatemala, 1871–1885.* Translated by Stephen Webre. Antigua: Centro de Investigaciones Regionales de Mesoamérica, 1981.

———. "Debt Servitude in Rural Guatemala, 1876–1936." *Hispanic American Historical Review* 63, no. 4 (Nov. 1983): 735–59.

———. "An Odious Feudalism: Mandamiento Labor and Commercial Agriculture in Guatemala, 1858–1920." *Latin American Perspectives* 13, no. 1 (winter 1986): 99–118.

———. "Atanasio Tzul, Lucas Aguilar, and the Indian Kingdom of Totonicapán." In *The Human Tradition in Latin America: The Nineteenth Century.* Edited by Judith Ewell and William H. Beezley. Wilmington, Del.: Scholarly Resources, 1989.

———. "State Power, Indigenous Communities, and Land in Nineteenth-Century Guatemala, 1820–1920." In *Guatemalan Indians and the State, 1540–1988.* Edited by Carol A. Smith. Austin: University of Texas Press, 1990.

———. *Rural Guatemala, 1760–1940.* Stanford, Calif.: Stanford University Press, 1994.

Menchú, Rigoberta, and Comité de Unidad Campesina. *Trenzando el futuro: Luchas campesinas en la historia reciente de Guatemala.* Madrid: Tercera Prensa-Hirugarren Prentsa, S.L, 1992.

Miceli, Keith L. "Rafael Carrera: Defender and Promoter of Peasant Interests in Guatemala, 1837–1848." *The Americas* 31, no. 1 (1974): 72–95.

Municipalidad de Quetzaltenango. *Sesiquicentario.* Quetzaltenango: Serviprensa, 1975.

Nelson, Diane. *A Finger in the Wound: Body Politics in Quincentennial Guatemala.* Berkeley: University of California Press, 1999.

Oficina de Derechos Humanos del Arzobispado de Guatemala. *Guatemala: Nunca más.* Guatemala City: Oficina de Derechos Humanos del Arzobispado de Guatemala, 1998.

Paige, Jeffery M. *Coffee and Power: Revolution and the Rise of Democracy in Central America.* Cambridge: Harvard University Press, 1997.

Palmer, Steven. "Racismo intellectual en Costa Rica y Guatemala, 1870–1920." *Mesoamérica* 31 (1996): 99–121.

Pastor, Rodolfo. *Campesinos y reformas: La Mixteca, 1700–1856.* Mexico: Colegio de México, 1987.

Paz Cárcamo, Guillermo. *Guatemala: Reforma Agraria.* 3d. ed. Guatemala City: Facultad Latinoamerica de Ciencas Sociales, 1997.

Piel, Jean. *Sajcabaja: Muerte y resurección de un pueblo de Guatemala, 1500–1970.* Mexico: CEMCA / Seminario de Integración Social de Guatemala, 1989.

Poole, Deborah. *Vision, Race, and Modernity: A Visual Economy of the Andean Image World*. Princeton: Princeton University Press, 1997.

Porras, Gustavo. "Análisis estructural y recomposición clasista de la sociedad guatemalteca de 1954–1980." In *Seminario Estado, Clases Sociales y Cuestión Etnico-Nacional*. Edited by Centro de Estudios Integrados de Desarrollo Comunal. Mexico City: Editorial Praxis, 1992.

Radcliffe, Sarah, and Sallie Westwood. *Remaking the Nation: Place, Identity and Politics in Latin America*. London: Routledge, 1996.

Reed-Danahay, Deborah. "Farm Children at School: Educational Strategies in Rural France." *Anthropological Quarterly* 60, no. 2 (1987): 83–89.

Rockwell, Elsie. "Schools of the Revolution: Enacting and Contesting State Forms in Tlaxcala, 1910–1930." In *Everyday Forms of State Formation: Revolution and the Negotiation of Rule in Modern Mexico*. Edited by Gilbert M. Joseph and Daniel Nugent. Durham: Duke University Press, 1994.

Rodríguez, Mario. "The Livingston Codes in the Guatemalan Crisis of 1837–1838." In *Applied Enlightenment: Nineteenth Century Liberalism, 1830–1839*. New Orleans: Middle American Research Institute, 1955.

——. *The Cádiz Experiment in Latin America, 1808–1826*. Berkeley: University of California Press, 1978.

Roseberry, William. "Anthropologies, History, and Modes of Production." In *Anthropologies and Histories: Essays in Culture, History, and Political Economy*. Edited by William Roseberry. New Brunswick: Rutgers University Press, 1989.

——. "Balinese Cockfights and the Seduction of History." In *Anthropologies and Histories: Essays in Culture, History, and Political Economy*. Edited by William Roseberry. New Brunswick: Rutgers University Press, 1989.

——. "Hegemony and the Language of Contention." In *Everyday Forms of State Formation: Revolution and the Negotiation of Rule in Modern Mexico*. Edited by Gilbert M. Joseph and Daniel Nugent. Durham: Duke University Press, 1994.

Roseberry, William, ed. *Anthropologies and Histories: Essays in Culture, History, and Political Economy*. New Brunswick: Rutgers University Press, 1989.

Roseberry, William, and Jay O'Brien, eds. Introduction to *Golden Ages, Dark Ages: Imagining the Past in Anthropology and History*. Edited by William Roseberry and Jay O'Brien. Berkeley: University of California Press, 1991.

Rosenberg, Charles. *The Cholera Years: The United States in 1832, 1849, and 1866*. Chicago: University of Chicago Press, 1987.

Rubin, Jeffrey W. *Decentering the Regime: Ethnicity, Radicalism, and Democracy in Juchitán, Mexico*. Durham: Duke University Press, 1997.

Rugeley, Terry. *Yucatán's Maya Peasantry and the Origins of the Caste War*. Austin: University of Texas Press, 1966.

Samayoa Guervara, Héctor Humberto. *Los gremios de artesanos de la Ciudad de Guatemala, 1542–1821*. Guatemala City: Editorial Piedra Santa, 1978.

Sayer, Derek. "Everyday Forms of State Formation: Some Dissident Remarks on 'Hegemony.'" In *Everyday Forms of State Formation: Revolution and the Negotiation of Rule in Modern Mexico.* Edited by Gilbert M. Joseph and Daniel Nugent. Durham: Duke University Press, 1994.

Schlesinger, Stephen C., and Stephen Kinzer. *Bitter Fruit: The Untold Story of the American Coup in Guatemala.* New York: Doubleday, 1982.

Schmid, Lester. *Papel de la mano de obra migratoria en el desarrollo económico de Guatemala.* Guatemala City: Universidad de San Carlos, 1973.

Scott, James C. "Hegemony and the Peasantry." *Politics and Society* 7, no. 3 (1977): 267–96.

———. *Domination and the Arts of Resistance: Hidden Transcripts.* New Haven: Yale University Press, 1990.

Shachar, Ayelet. "Group Identity and Women's Rights in Family Law: The Perils of Multicultural Accomodation." *The Journal of Political Philosophy* 6, no. 3 (1998): 285–305.

Smith, Carol A. "Local History in a Global Context: Social and Economic Transitions in Western Guatemala." *Comparative Studies in Society and History* 26, no. 2 (1984): 193–228.

———. "Origins of the National Question in Guatemala: A Hypothesis." In *Guatemalan Indians and the State: 1540–1988.* Edited by Carol A. Smith. Austin: University of Texas Press, 1990.

———. "Race-Class-Gender Ideology in Guatemala: Modern and Anti-Modern Forms." In *Women Out of Place: The Gender of Agency and the Race of Nationality.* Edited by Brackette F. Williams. New York: Routledge, 1996.

Smith, Carol A., ed. *Guatemalan Indians and the State, 1540–1988.* Austin: University of Texas Press, 1990.

Smith, Gavin. "The Production of Culture in Local Rebellion." In *Golden Ages, Dark Ages: Imagining the Past in Anthropology and History.* Edited by William Roseberry and Jay O'Brien. Berkeley: University of California Press, 1991.

Smith, Waldemar R. *The Fiesta System and Economic Change.* New York: Columbia University Press, 1977.

Snowden, Frank. "Cholera in Barletta, 1910." *Past and Present* 132 (Aug. 1991): 67–103.

Solomon, Joel A. *Violencia Institucional: Las Patrullas de Autodefensa Civil en Guatemala, 1993–1994.* Translated by P. O. Coj. Washington D.C.: Robert F. Kennedy Memorial Center for Human Rights, 1994.

Solórzano Fonseca, Juan Carlos. "Haciendas, ladinos y explotación colonial: Guatemala, El Salvador y Chiapas en el siglo XVIII." *Anuario de Estudios Centroamericanos* 10 (1984): 95–123.

Spalding, Karen. "Social Climbers: Changing Patterns of Mobility among the Indians of Colonial Peru." *Hispanic American Historical Review* 50, no. 4 (1970): 645–64.

Stepan, Nancy Leys. *"The Hour of Eugenics": Race, Gender, and Nation in Latin America*. Ithaca, N.Y.: Cornell University Press, 1991.

Stern, Steve. *Peru's Indian Peoples and the Challenge of Spanish Conquest, Huamanga to 1640*. Madison: University of Wisconsin Press, 1982.

——. "The Struggle for Solidarity: Class, Culture, and Community in Highland Indian America." *Radical History Review*, 27 (1983): 21–48.

——. "Feudalism, Capitalism, and the World-System in the Perspective of Latin America and the Caribbean." In *Confronting Historical Paradigms: Peasants, Labor, and the World System in Africa and Latin America*. Edited by Frederick Cooper et al. Madison: University of Wisconsin Press, 1993.

——. *The Secret History of Gender: Women, Men and Power in Late Colonial Mexico*. Chapel Hill: University of North Carolina Press, 1995.

Stoler, Ann Laura. *Race and the Education of Desire: Foucault's History of Sexuality and the Colonial Order of Things*. Durham: Duke University Press, 1995.

Stoll, David. *Between Two Armies in the Ixil Towns of Guatemala*. New York: Columbia University Press, 1993.

Sullivan-González, Douglass Creed. *Piety, Power, and Politics: Religion and Nation Formation in Guatemala, 1821–1871*. Pittsburgh: University of Pittsburgh Press, 1998.

Swetnam, John. "What Else Did Indians Have to Do with Their Time? Alternatives to Labor Migration in Prerevolutionary Guatemala." *Economic Development and Cultural Change* 38, no. 1 (1989): 89–112.

Tandeter, Enrique, Vilma Milletich, María Matilde Ollier, and Beatríz Ruibal. "Indians in Late Colonial Markets: Sources and Numbers." In *Ethnicity, Markets, and Migration in the Andes: At the Crossroads of History and Anthropology*. Edited by Brooke Larson and Olivia Harris. Durham: Duke University Press, 1995.

Taracena Arriola, Arturo. "La confederación obrera de Centro América (COCA): 1921–1928." *Anuario de Estudios Centroamericanos* 10 (1984): 81–94.

——. *Invención criolla, sueño ladino, pesadilla indígena: Los Altos de Guatemala, de región a Estado, 1740–1850*. Antigua: Centro de Investigaciones Regionales de Mesoamérica, 1997.

Tax, Sol. "The Municipios of the Midwestern Highlands of Guatemala." *American Anthropologist* 39, no. 3 (1937): 423–44.

——. *Penny Capitalism*. Publications in Social Anthropology, no. 15. Washington D.C.: Smithsonian Institution, 1953.

Taylor, William B. *Landlord and Peasant in Colonial Oaxaca*. Stanford, Calif.: Stanford University Press, 1972.

——. *Drinking, Homicide and Rebellion in Colonial Mexican Villages*. Stanford, Calif.: Stanford University Press, 1979.

Thompson, E. P. *The Making of the English Working Class*. New York: Vintage, 1963.

——. "Time, Work-Discipline, and Industrial Capitalism." *Past and Present* 38 (1967): 55–97.

Thompson, Nora. *Delfino Sanchez: A Guatemalan Statesman, 1840–1885*. Ardmore, Pa.: Nora Thompson, 1977.

Tinsman, Heidi. "Reviving Patriarchy." *Radical History Review* 71 (1988): 182–95.

Toriello, Guillermo. *La batalla de Guatemala*. Mexico City: Cuadernos Americanos, 1955.

Tovar Gómez, Marcela. *Perfil de los pueblos indígenas de Guatemala: Situación y perspectivas de los pueblos indígenas de Guatemala, en el marco del nuevo milenio*. Guatemala: World Bank, 1997.

Tutino, John. "Provincial Spaniards, Indian Towns, and Haciendas: Interrelated Agrarian Sectors in the Valleys of Mexico and Toluca, 1750–1810." In *Provinces of Early Mexico: Variants of Spanish American Regional Evolution*. Edited by Ida Altman and James Lockhart. Los Angeles: Latin American Center Publications, University of California, 1976.

——. "Power, Class, and Family: Men and Women in the Mexican Elite, 1750–1810." *The Americas* 39, no. 3 (1983): 359–81.

——. *From Insurrection to Revolution in Mexico: Social Bases of Agrarian Violence, 1750–1940*. Princeton: Princeton University Press 1988.

Tzunún, M., Gloria Virginia, and Olegario Obispo Nimatuj J. *1934–1984: Historial del certamen de la belleza indígena de Quetzaltenango*. Quetzaltenango: Casa Publicitaria "GOF," 1985.

Van Oss, Adriaan C. *Catholic Colonialism: A Parish History of Guatemala, 1524–1821*. Cambridge Latin American Studies, vol. 57. Edited by Simon Collier. Cambridge: Cambridge University Press, 1986.

Van Young, Eric. *Hacienda and Market in Eighteenth-Century Mexico*. Berkeley: University of California Press, 1981.

Vásquez, Josefina Z. *Nacionalismo y educación en México*. Mexico City: El Colegio de México, 1970.

Vaughan, Mary Kay. "Primary Education and Literacy in Mexico in the Nineteenth Century: Research Trends, 1968–1988." *Latin American Research Review* 24, no. 3 (1990): 33–66.

——. "The Construction of Patriotic Festival in Central Mexico: Puebla (1900–1946)." In *Rituals of Rule, Rituals of Resistance: Public Celebrations and Popular Culture in Mexico*. Edited by William H. Beezly, Cheryl E. Martin, and William E. French. Wilmington, Del.: Scholarly Resources, 1994.

Warren, Kay B. *The Symbols of Subordination: Indian Identity in a Guatemalan Town*. Austin: University of Texas Press, 1978.

Wasserstrom, Robert. "Revolution in Guatemala: Peasants and Politics under the Arbenz Government." *Comparative Studies in Society and History* 17 (October 1975): 443–78.

Watanabe, John M. *Maya Saints and Souls in a Changing World*. Austin: University of Texas Press, 1992.

Wexler, Philip, Tony Whitson, and Emily J. Moskowitz. "Deschooling by Default: The Changing Social Functions of Public Schooling." *Interchange* 12, nos. 2–3 (1981): 2–3.

Williams, Brackette. "A Class Act: Anthropology and the Race to Nation across Ethnic Terrain." *Annual Review of Anthropology* 18 (1989): 401–44.

Williams, Robert. *States and Social Evolution: Coffee and the Rise of National Governments in Central America*. Chapel Hill: University of North Carolina Press, 1994.

Williford, Miriam. "The Educational Reforms of Dr. Mariano Gálvez." *Journal of Inter-American Studies* 10, no. 3 (1968): 461–73.

Willis, Paul. *Learning to Labour: How Working-Class Kids Get Working-Class Jobs*. London: Gowet, 1977.

Witzel, Renate, ed. *Más de 100 años del movimiento obrero urbano en Guatemala: Artesanos y obreros en el período liberal, 1877–1944*. Vol. 1. Guatemala City: Asociación de Investigación y Estudios Sociales Guatemala, 1991.

Woodward, Colin. "After the Long Civil War, Academics in Guatemala Remain Cautious." *Chronicle of Higher Education*, 11 July 1997, A35.

Woodward, Ralph Lee. *Central America: A Nation Divided*. New York: Oxford University Press, 1985.

——. "The Aftermath of Independence, 1821–c.1870." In *Central America since Independence*. Edited by Leslie Bethell. Cambridge: Cambridge University Press, 1991.

——. *Rafael Carrera and the Emergence of Guatemala, 1821–1871*. Athens: University of Georgia Press, 1993.

Wortman, Miles. *Government and Society in Central America, 1680–1840*. New York: Columbia University Press, 1982.

Index

Greg Grandin is an Assistant Professor of History
at Duke University.

Library of Congress Cataloging-in-Publication Data

Grandin, Greg.
The blood of Guatemala : a history of race and nation / Greg Grandin.
p. cm. — (Latin America otherwise)
Includes bibliographical references and index.
ISBN 0-8223-2458-X (cl. : alk. paper). —
ISBN 0-8223-2495-4 (pa. : alk. paper)
1. Quichâ Indians—Politics and government.   2. Guatemala—Politics and
government.   3. Guatemala—Race relations.   4. Mayas—Guatemala—Social
conditions.   I. Title.   II. Series.
F1465.2.Q5   G73   2000
972.81004'974152—dc21   99-045640